Regional Worlds

A key concern in the debate and empirical research on the geography of regions is the evolution of the conceptualizations and practical uses of the idea of 'region'. This idea prioritizes both the intellectual and the practical development of regional studies. This book drives the discussion further. It stresses the complex forms of agency/advocacy involved in the production and reproduction of regional spaces and space of regionalism as well as the importance of geohistory and context. The book moves beyond the territorial/relational divide that has characterized debates on regions and regional borders since the 1990s.

The contributors answer key questions from different conceptual and concrete-contextual angles and motivate readers to reflect on the perpetual significance of regional concepts and how they are mobilized by various actors to maintain or transform the contested spatialities of societal power relations.

This book is based on a special issue of *Regional Studies*, with an additional panel discussion involving leading international scholars.

Martin Jones is Professor of Urban and Regional Political Economy and Director of the White Rose Social Science DTC at the University of Sheffield, UK. Martin is an interdisciplinary researcher, interested in the geographies of state and government intervention through economic and social policy in cities and regions, and subnational political economies therein.

Anssi Paasi is a Professor at the Department of Geography at the University of Oulu. Anssi's research fields are social construction of regions and territorial identities; theories of region, place and regionalism; the links between territories, boundaries and individual/social consciousness; the rhetoric of globalization and geopolitical imagination; the Europe of regions/regional planning and development.

Regions and Cities

Series Editor in Chief
Susan M. Christopherson, *Cornell University, USA*

Editors
Maryann Feldman, *University of Georgia, USA*
Gernot Grabher, *HafenCity University Hamburg, Germany*
Ron Martin, *University of Cambridge, UK*
Martin Perry, *Massey University, New Zealand*

In today's globalised, knowledge-driven and networked world, regions and cities have assumed heightened significance as the interconnected nodes of economic, social and cultural production, and as sites of new modes of economic and territorial governance and policy experimentation. This book series brings together incisive and critically engaged international and interdisciplinary research on this resurgence of regions and cities, and should be of interest to geographers, economists, sociologists, political scientists and cultural scholars, as well as to policy-makers involved in regional and urban development. For more information on the Regional Studies Association visit www.regionalstudies.org

85. Soft Spaces in Europe
Re-negotiating governance, boundaries and borders
Edited by Philip Allmendinger, Graham Haughton, Jörg Knieling and Frank Othengrafen

84. Regional Worlds: Advancing the Geography of Regions
Edited by Martin Jones and Anssi Paasi

83. Place-making and Urban Development
New challenges for contemporary planning and design
Pier Carlo Palermo and Davide Ponzini

82. Knowledge, Networks and Policy
Regional studies in postwar Britain and beyond
James A. Hopkins

81. Dynamics of Economic Spaces in the Global Knowledge-based Economy
Theory and East Asian cases
Sam Ock Park

80. Urban Competitiveness
Theory and practice
Daniele Letri and Peter Kresl

79. Smart Specialisation
Opportunities and challenges for regional innovation policy
Dominique Foray

78. The Age of Intelligent Cities
Smart environments and innovation-for-all strategies
Nicos Komninos

77. Space and Place in Central and Eastern Europe
Historical trends and perspectives
Gyula Horváth

76. Territorial Cohesion in Rural Europe
The relational turn in rural development
Edited by Andrew Copus and Philomena de Lima

75. The Global Competitiveness of Regions
Robert Huggins, Hiro Izushi, Daniel Prokop and Piers Thompson

74. The Social Dynamics of Innovation Networks
Edited by Roel Rutten, Paul Benneworth, Dessy Irawati and Frans Boekema

73. **The European Territory**
From historical roots to global challenges
Jacques Robert

72. **Urban Innovation Systems**
What makes them tick?
Willem van Winden, Erik Braun, Alexander Otgaar and Jan-Jelle Witte

71. **Shrinking Cities**
A global perspective
Edited by Harry W. Richardson and Chang Woon Nam

70. **Cities, State and Globalization**
City-regional governance
Tassilo Herrschel

69. **The Creative Class Goes Global**
Edited by Charlotta Mellander, Richard Florida, Bjørn Asheim and Meric Gertler

68. **Entrepreneurial Knowledge, Technology and the Transformation of Regions**
Edited by Charlie Karlsson, Börje Johansson and Roger Stough

67. **The Economic Geography of the IT Industry in the Asia Pacific Region**
Edited by Philip Cooke, Glen Searle and Kevin O'Connor

66. **Working Regions**
Reconnecting innovation and production in the knowledge economy
Jennifer Clark

65. **Europe's Changing Geography**
The impact of inter-regional networks
Edited by Nicola Bellini and Ulrich Hilpert

64. **The Value of Arts and Culture for Regional Development**
A Scandinavian perspective
Edited by Lisbeth Lindeborg and Lars Lindkvist

63. **The University and the City**
John Goddard and Paul Vallance

62. **Re-framing Regional Development**
Evolution, innovation and transition
Edited by Philip Cooke

61. **Networking Regionalised Innovative Labour Markets**
Edited by Ulrich Hilpert and Helen Lawton Smith

60. **Leadership and Change in Sustainable Regional Development**
Edited by Markku Sotarauta, Ina Horlings and Joyce Liddle

59. **Regional Development Agencies: The Next Generation?**
Networking, knowledge and regional policies
Edited by Nicola Bellini, Mike Danson and Henrik Halkier

58. **Community-based Entrepreneurship and Rural Development**
Creating favourable conditions for small businesses in Central Europe
Matthias Fink, Stephan Loidl and Richard Lang

57. **Creative Industries and Innovation in Europe**
Concepts, measures and comparative case studies
Edited by Luciana Lazzeretti

56. **Innovation Governance in an Open Economy**
Shaping regional nodes in a globalized world
Edited by Annika Rickne, Staffan Laestadius and Henry Etzkowitz

55. **Complex Adaptive Innovation Systems**
Relatedness and transversality in the evolving region
Philip Cooke

54. **Creating Knowledge Locations in Cities**
Innovation and integration challenges
Willem van Winden, Luis de Carvalho, Erwin van Tujil, Jeroen van Haaren and Leo van den Berg

53. **Regional Development in Northern Europe**
Peripherality, marginality and border issues
Edited by Mike Danson and Peter De Souza

52. **Promoting Silicon Valleys in Latin America**
Luciano Ciravegna

51. **Industrial Policy Beyond the Crisis**
Regional, national and international perspectives
Edited by David Bailey, Helena Lenihan and Josep-Maria Arauzo-Carod

50. **Just Growth**
Inclusion and prosperity in America's metropolitan regions
Chris Benner and Manuel Pastor

49. **Cultural Political Economy of Small Cities**
Edited by Anne Lorentzen and Bas van Heur

48. **The Recession and Beyond**
Local and regional responses to the downturn
Edited by David Bailey and Caroline Chapain

47. **Beyond Territory**
Edited by Harald Bathelt, Maryann Feldman and Dieter F. Kogler

46. **Leadership and Place**
Edited by Chris Collinge, John Gibney and Chris Mabey

45. **Migration in the 21st Century**
Rights, outcomes, and policy
Kim Korinek and Thomas Maloney

44. **The Futures of the City Region**
Edited by Michael Neuman and Angela Hull

43. **The Impacts of Automotive Plant Closures**
A tale of two cities
Edited by Andrew Beer and Holli Evans

42. Manufacturing in the New Urban Economy
Willem van Winden, Leo van den Berg, Luis de Carvalho and Erwin van Tuijl

41. Globalizing Regional Development in East Asia
Production networks, clusters, and entrepreneurship
Edited by Henry Wai-chung Yeung

40. China and Europe
The implications of the rise of China as a global economic power for Europe
Edited by Klaus Kunzmann, Willy A Schmid and Martina Koll-Schretzenmayr

39. Business Networks in Clusters and Industrial Districts
The governance of the global value chain
Edited by Fiorenza Belussi and Alessia Sammarra

38. Whither Regional Studies?
Edited by Andy Pike

37. Intelligent Cities and Globalisation of Innovation Networks
Nicos Komninos

36. Devolution, Regionalism and Regional Development
The UK experience
Edited by Jonathan Bradbury

35. Creative Regions
Technology, culture and knowledge entrepreneurship
Edited by Philip Cooke and Dafna Schwartz

34. European Cohesion Policy
Willem Molle

33. Geographies of the New Economy
Critical reflections
Edited by Peter W. Daniels, Andrew Leyshon, Michael J. Bradshaw and Jonathan Beaverstock

32. The Rise of the English Regions?
Edited by Irene Hardill, Paul Benneworth, Mark Baker and Leslie Budd

31. Regional Development in the Knowledge Economy
Edited by Philip Cooke and Andrea Piccaluga

30. Regional Competitiveness
Edited by Ron Martin, Michael Kitson and Peter Tyler

29. Clusters and Regional Development
Critical reflections and explorations
Edited by Bjørn Asheim, Philip Cooke and Ron Martin

28. Regions, Spatial Strategies and Sustainable Development
David Counsell and Graham Haughton

27. Sustainable Cities
Graham Haughton and Colin Hunter

26. Geographies of Labour Market Inequality
Edited by Ron Martin and Philip S. Morrison

25. Regional Innovation Strategies
The challenge for less-favoured regions
Edited by Kevin Morgan and Claire Nauwelaers

24. Out of the Ashes?
The social impact of industrial contraction and regeneration on Britain's mining communities
Chas Critcher, Bella Dicks, David Parry and David Waddington

23. Restructuring Industry and Territory
The experience of Europe's regions
Edited by Anna Giunta, Arnoud Lagendijk and Andy Pike

22. Foreign Direct Investment and the Global Economy
Corporate and institutional dynamics of global-localisation
Edited by Jeremy Alden and Nicholas F. Phelps

21. Community Economic Development
Edited by Graham Haughton

20. Regional Development Agencies in Europe
Edited by Charlotte Damborg, Mike Danson and Henrik Halkier

19. Social Exclusion in European Cities
Processes, experiences and responses
Edited by Judith Allen, Goran Cars and Ali Madanipour

18. Metropolitan Planning in Britain
A comparative study
Edited by Peter Roberts, Kevin Thomas and Gwyndaf Williams

17. Unemployment and Social Exclusion
Landscapes of labour inequality and social exclusion
Edited by Sally Hardy, Paul Lawless and Ron Martin

16. Multinationals and European Integration
Trade, investment and regional development
Edited by Nicholas A. Phelps

15. The Coherence of EU Regional Policy
Contrasting perspectives on the structural funds
Edited by John Bachtler and Ivan Turok

14. New Institutional Spaces
TECs and the remaking of economic governance
Edited by Martin Jones and Jamie Peck

13. Regional Policy in Europe
S. S. Artobolevskiy

12. Innovation Networks and Learning Regions?
James Simmie

11. British Regionalism and Devolution
The challenges of state reform and European integration
Edited by Jonathan Bradbury and John Mawson

10. **Regional Development Strategies**
A European perspective
Edited by Jeremy Alden and Philip Boland

9. **Union Retreat and the Regions**
The shrinking landscape of organised labour
Ron Martin, Peter Sunley and Jane Wills

8. **The Regional Dimension of Transformation in Central Europe**
Grzegorz Gorzelak

7. **The Determinants of Small Firm Growth**
An inter-regional study in the United Kingdom 1986–90
Richard Barkham, Graham Gudgin, Mark Hart and Eric Hanvey

6. **The Regional Imperative**
Regional planning and governance in Britain, Europe and the United States
Urlan A. Wannop

5. **An Enlarged Europe**
Regions in competition?
Edited by Louis Albrechts, Sally Hardy, Mark Hart and Anastasios Katos

4. **Spatial Policy in a Divided Nation**
Edited by Richard T. Harrison and Mark Hart

3. **Regional Development in the 1990s**
The British Isles in transition
Edited by Ron Martin and Peter Townroe

2. **Retreat from the Regions**
Corporate change and the closure of factories
Stephen Fothergill and Nigel Guy

1. **Beyond Green Belts**
Managing urban growth in the 21st century
Edited by John Herington

Regional Worlds

Advancing the geography of regions

Edited by
Martin Jones and Anssi Paasi

LONDON AND NEW YORK

First published 2015 by Routledge

2 Park Square, Milton Park, Abingdon, Oxon OX14 4RN
711 Third Avenue, New York, NY 10017, USA

Routledge is an imprint of the Taylor & Francis Group, an informa business

First issued in paperback 2017

British Library Cataloguing in Publication Data
A catalogue record for this book is available from the British Library

ISBN 13: 978-1-138-85260-0 (hbk)
ISBN 13: 978-1-138-06024-1 (pbk)

Typeset in Bembo
by RefineCatch Limited, Bungay, Suffolk

Publisher's Note
The publisher accepts responsibility for any inconsistencies that may have arisen during the conversion of this book from journal articles to book chapters, namely the possible inclusion of journal terminology.

Contents

Citation Information

The following chapters were originally published in *Regional Studies*, volume 47, issue 1 (January 2013). When citing this material, please use the original page numbering for each article, as follows:

Chapter 1
Regional World(s): Advancing the Geography of Regions
Martin Jones and Anssi Paasi
Regional Studies, volume 47, issue 1 (January 2013) pp. 1–5

Chapter 3
Arguing with Regions
John A. Agnew
Regional Studies, volume 47, issue 1 (January 2013) pp. 6–17

Chapter 4
Conceptualizing the Region – In What Sense Relational?
Krisztina Varró and Arnoud Lagendijk
Regional Studies, volume 47, issue 1 (January 2013) pp. 18–28

Chapter 5
New Localities
Martin Jones and Michael Woods
Regional Studies, volume 47, issue 1 (January 2013) pp. 29–42

Chapter 6
Experienced Regions and Borders: The Challenge for Transactional Approaches
Maano Ramutsindela
Regional Studies, volume 47, issue 1 (January 2013) pp. 43–54

Chapter 7
Configuring the New 'Regional World': On being Caught between Territory and Networks
John Harrison
Regional Studies, volume 47, issue 1 (January 2013) pp. 55–74

Chapter 8
Crafting the Region: Creative Industries and Practices of Regional Space
Nicola J. Thomas, David C. Harvey and Harriet Hawkins
Regional Studies, volume 47, issue 1 (January 2013) pp. 75–88

Chapter 9
Unusual Regionalism in Northern Europe: The Barents Region in the Making
Kaj Zimmerbauer
Regional Studies, volume 47, issue 1 (January 2013) pp. 89–103

Chapter 10

Between Regional Spaces and Spaces of Regionalism: Cross-border Region Building in the Spanish 'State of the Autonomies'
Jacobo García-Álvarez and Juan-Manuel Trillo-Santamaría
Regional Studies, volume 47, issue 1 (January 2013) pp. 104–115

Chapter 11

(Small) Differences that (Still) Matter? Cross-Border Regions and Work Place Governance in the Southern Ontario and US Great Lakes Automotive Industry
Tod D. Rutherford and John Holmes
Regional Studies, volume 47, issue 1 (January 2013) pp. 116–127

Please direct any queries you may have about the citations to clsuk.permissions@cengage.com

Introduction: Regional World(s): Advancing the Geography of Regions

MARTIN JONES* and ANSSI PAASI†
*Department of Geography, The University of Sheffield, UK.
†Academy of Finland and University of Oulu, Oulu, Finland.

INTRODUCTION

> But what, after all, is 'the regional'? A region can be as large as the European peninsula. Within the political enterprise that is the European Union, however, regions subdivide a continent already sliced up into nation-states – and even then what counts as a region is far from certain. According to the latest *Map of European Regions*, a region might be an abstract geographical area like 'Mid East Ireland'; a subnational cultural and political unit like Bavaria; or a national but substate territory like Scotland or Wales. England appears to present a different problem altogether: the Assembly of European Regions divides it into some eighty-seven portions, including counties, parts of counties, and metropolitan authorities. Things are hardly more clear at the level of literary history, where 'region' is used to describe something as diverse as multilingual and multi-national literatures of the Caribbean archipelago and as specific as 1960s 'Liverpool Scene' poetry. If we are fully to grasp the implications of regionalism as a thematic and generic trend in English fiction of the interwar years, then we must first be clear about the protean nature of this thing called a region.
>
> (HART, 2009, p. 89)

Matthew Hart is neither a geographer, nor a spatial planner, political scientist or sociologist. He is a scholar of English and comparative literature, from the United Kingdom (currently based in North America) and, as the above quotation indicates, somewhat fascinated (and confused) by the variable, changeable, mutable, adjustable, fluctuating, erratic and somewhat inconsistent use of the word 'region', such that 'region' means so many things that, by itself, it means nothing. Hart goes on to discuss different interpretations of the region in English fiction of the interwar years. Authors such as George Orwell, H. G. Wells and Winifred Holtby are briefly examined and their use of spatial metaphors and regional deployments are unpicked. HART (2009) draws particular attention to a tension between 'exceptionality' and 'typicality' running through these established writing – an observation that, of course, has run through geographical analysis and regional studies for the last century (AGNEW, 2013; HARRISON, 2013; THOMAS *et al.*, 2013). Regions, for Hart, are 'points of difference' and their 'being' is thus linked to processes of nation-state formation, international and transnational movements. Hart, then, is depicting a territorial and relational world, one that can be read in and through literature (HART, 2013).

THE RESURGENCE OF REGIONS

Hart is definitely not alone in his search for the meanings of regions in literature. Indeed, 'literary regionalism' has a long and diverse tradition around the world (cf. GILBERT, 1951; PRYSE, 2004; PRESCOTT, 2011). Yet, it is a sort of a paradox how not only the region or regionalism, but also regional borders and identities rapidly have become important keywords in social science since the 1990s. And this occurred not only in academic discourse, but also in governance, planning and politics, at and *across* various spatial scales of the international geopolitical and economic landscape (PAASI, 2009; MOISIO and PAASI, 2013). Regions became important elements in making sense of the rapid transformation and rescaling of state spaces in this landscape (cf. JESSOP *et al.*, 2008). Debates and practices related to multilevel governance in the 'Europe of the Regions' industry are fitting illustrations of these developments (STUBBS, 2005), but sub-state, supra-state, and cross-border regions and regionalisms have become topical around the world: from Europe (KEATING, 1998) to Latin America (RIGGIROZZI and TUSSIE, 2012), from East Asia (BEESON, 2007) to Africa (GRANT and SÖDERBAUM, 2004). Some key tendencies can be identified behind these developments (JONES *et al.*, 2008). These include, for example:

- Accelerating globalization of economy, culture and 'consciousness' after the collapse of the Cold War divide between the capitalist and socialist worlds (KEATING, 1998; AGNEW, 2013).

- New regionalist claims for competitiveness, social cohesion and identity in promoting regional development (for example, BRISTOW, 2010; PAASI, 2012a; THOMAS *et al.*, 2013).
- Reorganization of regional governance around the world, especially through devolution and/or mergers (for example, HARRISON 2013; RIGGIROZZI and TUSSIE, 2012; JONES and MACLEOD, 2004).
- Regionalization and region-building processes at and across various spatial scales, often progressing from abstract discourses to concrete plans, maps and ultimately political and governmental action. Often such processes cross the existing state borders (for example, Baltic Sea or Barents region) (METZGER and SCHMITT, 2012; GARCÍA-ÁLVAREZ and TRILLO-SANTAMARIA, 2013; RUTHERFORD and HOLMES, 2013; ZIMMERBAUER, 2013).
- Region/place marketing, promotion and 'branding' (PIKE, 2011).

Inside academe and the 'intellectual industry', regions have gained currency not only in geography, but also in international relations, political science, history, and cultural and literary studies (PAASI, 2009). Regional worlds certainly exist, yet at the same time 'region' remains a vague category, set within a deep geographical lineage, interpreted and understood in many ways (HART, 2009). Scale also matters. If the region is for geographers archetypally a sub-state unit, among international relations scholars it refers rather to the supra-state institutional arrangements (HETTNE *et al.*, 1999; BEESON, 2007) of economies and governance (for example, the European Union, the North American Free Trade Agreement (NAFTA) or Mercado Común del Sur (MERCOSUR)). Cross-border regions, for their part, have become important for economists, geographers and political scientists (RUTHERFORD and HOLMES, 2013; ZIMMERBAUER, 2013). We therefore continue to live in interesting times and regional studies remain important around the world.

A resurgence of the region has thus occurred in both academic research and practical politics and governance. This has been a sort of contradiction, since the demise of the region – as well as community, culture or locality – that should follow from the deepening modernity and consolidating state-centric spatiality, has been predicted since the nineteenth century (WATNER, 2010). While regionalism has emerged around the world, this has not occurred similarly everywhere. Neither are the meanings of regional concepts singular in various contexts. Both these facts are clearly displayed by this international collection of papers.

In Europe regionalism and integration have been typically generated by the states and the European Union, whereas in Asia integration has been driven by markets than by governments. Cooperation among national authorities is a more recent phenomenon (cf. BEESON 2007). The following papers show that in some contexts (for example, in Finland) the interest and emphasis on regions and 'regionality' reflects the endurance of a long, gradually transforming tradition where regions or regional borders do not matter significantly even if both can be mobilized in the service of tourism or regional planning activities (for instance, PAASI, 2012a). Contrary to this, in some other contexts (for example, Spain or South Africa) emphasis on regions is often tied to ethno-cultural identities and ideologies. The resurgence of regions and regional borders is thus related to politics. Respectively, the meanings associated with regions and regional borders matter and are often contested (GARCÍA-ÁLVAREZ and TRILLO-SANTAMARIA, 2013; RAMUTSINDELA, 2013).

The interpretations of the concept of region have also altered perpetually. Traditional views of regions as bounded, homogeneous units have been mostly rejected and new conceptual alternatives developed accordingly. If the 1980s witnessed the rise of social constructionist views accentuating the role of human agency in regional construction, the 1990s witnessed new relational tunes in the deliberations on regions. After the turn of the millennium, new keywords such as 'competitiveness', 'resilience' or 'assemblage' have been deployed, often in a relational spirit, to broaden the regional concept (PIKE, 2007; PAASI, 2010). The region thus seems continually to reanimate the understanding of the spatialities of contemporary societies. Simultaneously, new conceptual interpretations also have emerged that bring together several spatial dimensions (JESSOP *et al.*, 2008).

Relational thinking suggests that regions should be seen as non-bounded in the current mobile, globalizing world. Relational approaches have a long history in social sciences. In geography relational views on the region were firstly proposed by economic geographers, but this idea soon extended to cultural and political geography (JONES, 2009). Such thinking is attractive also in planning circles (HAUGHTON *et al.*, 2010). In terms of politics, seeing regions as bounded is labelled then as 'regressive', while seeing them as open is 'progressive' (following the work of MASSEY, 1994; see also JONES and WOODS, 2013). Accordingly, regions are seen to 'stretch' in space so that their social contents and relations are networked across borders and this networking indeed constitutes both regions and their borders – regional boundaries and identities need not be exclusive (THOMAS *et al.*, 2013; RUTHERFORD and HOLMES, 2013; VARRÓ and LAGENDIJK, 2013).

In spite of these dynamic and progressive ideas, in some contexts the importance of regions and boundaries as catalysts for regionalist movements and for planning strategies is nevertheless obvious (JONES and MACLEOD, 2004; GARCÍA-ÁLVAREZ and TRILLO-SANTAMARIA, 2013; RAMUTSINDELA, 2013). This is evident in the case of many ethno-territorial groups around the world, but identity narratives produced and reproduced, for example, by regional activists, media and governmental bodies, are also typical examples of this politics of distinction, often mobilized in the name of 'strategic essentialism' (cf. SPIVAK, 1987). The next step has been a search for a balance between the relational and territorial approaches, and the papers in the special issue contribute to this terrain. MCCANN and WARD (2010) (cf. PAASI, 2012b) have noted how regional policy-making (and regional borders) has to be understood as both relational *and* territorial; as both in motion and simultaneously fixed, or embedded in place. JONAS (2012) suggested, in turn, that the distinction between territorial and relational can be 'registered obsolete' if critical attention is paid to matters of territory and the nature of territorial politics, both of which are products of bounded and unbounded forces. This special issue offers further insights on all this.

AIMS OF THE SPECIAL ISSUE

The key motive of this *Regional Studies* special issue is to push the debate and empirical research further. The Guest Editors are very interested in the evolution of the conceptualizations and practical uses of the idea of 'region'. Hence, both the intellectual *and* the practical development of regional studies is a priority and there is a deep trajectory of scholarship on which to build. Respectively the papers in this issue aim at advancing the theoretical and empirical understanding of regions by stressing, firstly, the complex forms of agency/advocacy that are always involved in the production and reproduction of both regional spaces and spaces of regionalism (and the meanings attached to them); and secondly, by stressing the importance of geohistory and context in making sense of both 'regional worlds' and the words used contextually to interpret them. The last, but not least, aim of this issue is to take the debate on regions and regional borders *beyond* the territorial/relational divide that has characterized debates since the 1990s (cf. PAASI, 2012b). The argument here is that this requires the fusion of conceptual work and contextual, geohistorical concrete study. Ontologically tuned either/or debates, so common in the past, are clearly a dead end for regional studies.

The majority of the papers published in this issue were presented, through two paper sessions, at the 2008 Association of American Geographers Conference, held in Boston, Massachusetts, USA. The key idea behind these sessions, and a panel that followed (involving J. Nicholas Entrikin, Alec Murphy, Anssi Paasi, Andy Jonas, Gordon MacLeod and Ray Hudson), was to bring together an international group of political, economic, and cultural geographers to reflect on and scrutinize the resurgence of the idea of 'region' in both geographical thought and societal practice. The panel was transcribed, edited by the session convenors (Martin Jones and Anssi Paasi) and the contributors, and appears as Chapter 2 of this book. Invited papers were presented by John Agnew (AGNEW, 2013), Mark Goodwin (his paper will be published in another issue of *Regional Studies*), Maano Ramutsindela (RAMUTSINDELA, 2013), Krisztina Varró and Arnoud Lagendijk (VARRÓ and LAGENDIJK, 2013), Jacobo García-Álvarez and Juan-Manuel Trillo-Santamaria (GARCÍA-ÁLVAREZ and TRILLO-SANTAMARIA, 2013), Tod Rutherford and John Holmes (RUTHERFORD and HOLMES, 2013), and Nicola Thomas, David Harvey and Harriet Hawkins (THOMAS *et al.*, 2013). Additional papers were solicited from Martin Jones and Mike Woods (JONES and WOODS, 2013), Kaj Zimmerbauer (ZIMMERBAUER, 2013), and John Harrison (HARRISON, 2013), both to broaden out the contextual features displayed by this special issue and to highlight the importance of scalar dimensions and related agencies for regional thinking. Collectively, the aim here is to build on the excellent and important 'Whither Regional Studies?' special issue edited by Andy Pike (PIKE, 2007), which offered an 'in retrospect' and 'in prospect' a take on notions of the region and regional studies. The contributions in the present special issue aim at answering the following questions from different conceptual and concrete-contextual angles:

- How should one understand the continual importance of the region in geographic discourse and how should current debates be pushed further?
- How should one conceptualize place, region, territory, locality, etc. in an increasingly mobile world characterized by all kinds of flows and networks?
- Are relational and territorial views overlapping, complementary or competing, antagonistic, ontological and epistemological concerns and how should one move beyond this conceptual divide?
- How does the region 'become' or how is it produced and how do power and politics become constitutive in and constituted by region-building processes?
- What are the 'boundaries' of regions, and what are their social and political functions and consequences in various contexts?
- What does it mean in practice and in different contexts to claim that 'regions are social constructs'?
- What is the role of context (and, indeed, what is this context) in the becoming of regions?
- How does the context modify one's understanding of the region (for example, the European Union, the state, regional and local contexts)?

The contributors provide contextual answers to these questions and it is hoped collectively they will motivate readers to reflect on the perpetual significance of regional concepts and how they are mobilized by various actors to maintain or transform the contested spatialities of societal power relations.

REFERENCES

AGNEW J. (2013) Arguing with regions, *Regional Studies* **47**, 6–17.

BEESON M. (2007) *Regionalism and Globalization in East Asia.* Palgrave, London.

BRISTOW G. (2010) *Critical reflections on Regional Competiveness.* Routledge, London.

GARCÍA-ÁLVAREZ J. and TRILLO-SANTAMARIA J.-M. (2013) Between regional spaces and spaces of regionalism: cross-border region-building in the Spanish 'State of the Autonomies', *Regional Studies* **47**, 104–115.

GILBERT E. W. (1951) Geography and regionalism, in TAYLOR G. (Ed.) *Geography in the Twentieth Century*, pp. 345–371. Methuen, London.

GRANT J. A. and SÖDERBAUM F. (2004) *The New Regionalism in Africa.* Ashgate, London.

HARRISON J. (2013) Configuring the new 'regional world': on being caught between territory and networks, *Regional Studies* **47**, 55–74.

HART M. (2009) Regionalism in English fiction between the wars, in CASERIO R. L. (Ed.) *The Cambridge Companion to the Twentieth-Century English Novel*, pp. 89–102. Cambridge University Press, Cambridge.

HART M. (Forthcoming 2013) *Extraterritorial: Transnational Culture and the Question of the State.* Cambridge University Press, Cambridge.

HAUGHTON G., ALLMENDINGER P., COUNSELL D. and VIGAR G. (2010) *The New Spatial Planning: Territorial Management with Soft Spaces and Fuzzy Boundaries.* Routledge, London.

HETTNE B., INOTAL A. and SUNKEL O. (1999) *Globalism and the New Regionalism.* Macmillan, London.

JESSOP B., BRENNER N. and JONES M. (2008) Theorizing socio-spatial relations, *Environment and Planning D: Society and Space* **26**, 389–401.

JONAS A. (2012) Region and place: regionalism in question, *Progress in Human Geography* **36**, 263–272.

JONES M. (2009) Phase space: geography, relational thinking, and beyond, *Progress in Human Geography* **33**, 487–506.

JONES M. and MACLEOD G. (2004) Regional spaces, spaces of regionalism: territory, insurgent politics and the English question, *Transactions of the Institute of British Geographers* **29**, 433–452.

JONES M., PAASI A., MURPHY A., ENTRIKIN N., MACLEOD G., JONAS A. and HUDSON R. (2008) Panel discussion and audience questions undertaken at the Regional World(s) Session, Annual Meeting of the Association of American Geographers, Boston, MA, USA. [Copy of transcript available from Martin Jones, Institute of Geography and Earth Sciences, Aberystwyth University, Aberystwyth, UK.]

JONES M. and WOODS M. (2013) New localities, *Regional Studies* **47**, 29–42.

KEATING M. (1998) *The New Regionalism in Western Europe.* Elgar, Cheltenham.

MASSEY D. (1994) *Space, Place and Gender.* Polity, Cambridge.

MCCANN E. and WARD K. (2010) Relationality/territoriality: toward a conceptualization of cities in the world, *Geoforum* **41**, 175–184.

METZGER J. and SCHMITT P. (2012) When soft spaces harden: the EU strategy for the Baltic Sea Region, *Environment and Planning A* **44**, 263–280.

MOISIO S. and PAASI A. (Forthcoming 2013) From geopolitical to geoeconomic: the changing political rationalities of state space, *Geopolitics* **18(2)**.

PAASI A. (2009) The resurgence of the 'region' and 'regional identity': theoretical perspectives and empirical observations on the regional dynamics in Europe, *Review of International Studies* **35**, 121–146.

PAASI A. (2010) Regions are social constructs but 'who' or 'what' constructs them? Agency in question, *Environment and Planning A* **42**, 2296–2301.

PAASI A. (2012a) Regional planning and the mobilization of 'regional identity': from bounded spaces to relational complexity', *Regional Studies* iFirst article, dx.doi.org/10.1080/00343404.2012.661410.

PAASI A. (2012b) Border studies reanimated: going beyond the territorial–relational divide, *Environment and Planning A* **44**, 2303–2309.

PIKE A. (2007) 'Whither Regional Studies?', *Regional Studies* **41(9)** [Special Issue].

PIKE A. (Ed.) (2011) *Brands and Branding Geographies.* Elgar, Cheltenham.

PRESCOTT S. (2011) 'That private shade wherein my Muse was bred': Katherine Philips and the poetic spaces of Welsh retirement, *Philosophical Quarterly* **8**, 345–364.

PRYSE M. (2004) Literary regionalism and global capital: nineteenth-century US women writers, *Tulsa Studies in Women's Literature* **23**, 65–89.

RAMUTSINDELA M. (2013) Experienced regions and borders: the challenge for transactional approaches, *Regional Studies* **47**, 43–54.

RIGGIROZZI P. and TUSSIE D. (2012) *The Rise of Post-Hegemonic Regionalism: The Case of Latin America.* Springer, Dordrecht.

RUTHERFORD T. D. and HOLMES J. (2013) (Small) differences that (still) matter? Cross-border regions and work place governance in the Southern Ontario and US Great Lakes automotive industry, *Regional Studies* **47**, 116–127.

SPIVAK G. (1987) *In Other Worlds: Essays in Cultural Politics.* Routledge, London.

STUBBS P. (2005) Stretching concepts too far? Multi-level governance, policy transfer and the politics of scale in South East Europe, *Southeast European Politics* **11**, 66–87.

THOMAS N., HAWKINS H. and HARVEY D. (2013) Creative networks of the south-west: reconciling the relational region and territorial region, *Regional Studies* **47**, 75–88.

VARRÓ K. and LAGENDIJK A. (2013) Conceptualizing the region – in what sense relational?, *Regional Studies* **47**, 18–28.

WATNER C. (2010) The territorial assumption: rationale for conquest, *Journal of Libertarian Studies* **22**, 247–260.

ZIMMERBAUER K. (2013) Unusual regionalism in Northern Europe: the Barents Region in the making, *Regional Studies* **47**, 89–103.

Bounded vs. Open Regions, and Beyond

Critical Perspectives on Regional Worlds and Words

ALEXANDER B. MURPHY[1], J. NICHOLAS ENTRIKIN[2], ANSSI PAASI[3], GORDON MACLEOD[4], ANDREW E.G. JONAS[5] and RAY HUDSON[6]

[1]*Department of Geography, University of Oregon;* [2]*Department of Sociology, University of Notre Dame*
[3]*Department of Geography, University of Oulu;* [4]*Department of Geography, University of Durham;*
[5]*Department of Geography, Environment and Earth Sciences, University of Hull;*
[6]*Department of Geography, University of Durham.*

ABSTRACT

This chapter is based on an edited and revised transcript of a panel discussion that was organized in 2008 during the Association of American Geographers Annual Meeting in Boston. The panellists were given a list of themes that the organizers encouraged them to reflect in their interventions. The themes were related to the ongoing debates on how we should understand regions in a globalizing world where all kinds of border crossing are the order of the day. The panellists reflect the history of regional thinking, the specific issue of the bounded versus open character of regions, current 'new regionalism(s)' and challenges of sustainable and resilient regions under capitalism. All contributions question the taken-for-grantedness that often characterizes the role of regions in basic and especially applied research and the authors provide tools for understanding the contemporary complexity of regions. Collectively, they advance our understanding of the 'geography of regions' (MacLeod and Jones, 2001, cf. Jonas, 2012).

The Case for (Somewhat) Bounded Regions

Alexander B. Murphy

Despite the longstanding interest of geographers and others in the concept of the region (Whittlesey, 1954), until recent decades the region was largely treated as something to be identified and described rather to be analyzed critically. Moreover, one type of region – the territorial state – received far more attention than all others, a reflection of the 'territorial trap' that captured the modern geographical imagination (Agnew, 1994). This state of affairs began to change in the 1970s and 1980s, as new regional forms – substate, suprastate, and transstate – became more visible; as new technologies and mobilities challenged the coherence of discrete regional spaces, especially the state; and as scholars began to bring new concepts (e.g., human territoriality) and new theories (e.g., post-structuralism) to bear on the study of regions (Pudup, 1988; Gilbert, 1988; Murphy, 1991). Regions increasingly came to be treated as socially constructed and dynamic, as arrangements that are made and remade as political, economic, social and environmental processes play out.

The intellectual trajectory set in motion during the 1970s and 1980s has led to wide-ranging theoretical and empirical critiques of the notion that regions can be usefully conceptualized simply as fixed, bounded spatial units. Many studies now treat regions as ephemeral representations produced by relationships; as partially or even wholly unbounded; and as defined more by the networks in which they are embedded than by their internal coherence (e.g., Amin, 2004). These ways of thinking have opened up new avenues of research and understanding, and they have demonstrated the limitations of regional conceptions rooted in simplistic notions of bounded spaces. Yet for all the intellectual and hermeneutic advantages of conceptualizing regions in these terms, there is some danger that the regional concept will lose fundamental coherence.

The regional idea has long been rooted in the notion that phenomena on Earth's surface are sometimes spatially grouped into clusters of functional or formal significance (Grigg, 1965), and that the human striving to make order out of the world leads people to attach meaning to discrete chunks of the planet's surface (Entrikin, 1994). The power of the regional idea lies in probing the nature and meaning of these clusters and chunks – at different scales, in different contexts, and in various historical periods. It clearly makes sense to modify our conceptions of regions in the face of empirical evidence challenging the coherence of particular regional orders and theoretical understandings that highlight the contingent, relational character of all regions, whether functional, formal, or perceptual. Yet in the rush to unbundle and unbound the region, it is arguably vital that we retain some focus on the nature and power of regions as bounded spaces that reflect and shape geographic processes (accord, MacLeod and Jones, 2001).

There are at least three reasons for keeping the region tethered to some kind of spatially distinct construct, whether perceptual, aspirational or tangible. The first is that the concept of the region risks becoming so malleable that it loses much of its communicative power. Consider, for example, the claim made by proponents of methodological nationalism that regions lose significance in the wake of deepening modernity and consolidation of state-centric territorial control (discussed in PAASI, 2009). Among the challenges that can be levelled against such an approach is that it is based on a chaotic conception of what constitutes a region. The state can be excluded as a region only if one adopts a narrow functionalist definition that treats regions solely as manifestations of developments unfolding at a specific (non-state) scale. Yet a generation of work on regions has shown that they are the product of processes operating at a variety of different scales – including the state scale – and that the relationships among regions at different scales can profoundly shape economic, social and cultural processes (e.g., PAASI, 1991; BRENNER, 2004).

A second reason for retaining some notion of regions as bounded (though not necessarily unchanging) spaces is that only by taking the spatial fixity of regions over discrete time periods seriously can we grasp their constitutive potential in the political, social and ideological realms. Consider the current situation in Belgium. The polarization between the Flemish North and the Walloon South is not simply a product of social and economic relations that have unfolded over time; the institutionalization of Flanders and Wallonia as significant formal regions shaped the spatial organization of people, economy and politics in that country in ways that brought into being the dichotomous ethnoregional identities that dominate political life today (MURPHY, 1988). Understanding the increasing polarization of Belgian politics requires considering the ways reified, institutionalized regions shape how people think about themselves and the places where they live (PAASI, 2003). Of course relationships are fundamental to the constitution of regions and their evolution over time, but if we lose track of the potential of regions to construct issues and problems, we limit our ability to identify and assess the power of regions of all sorts – including the state – to structure the world around us (MURPHY, 2013).

Finally, retaining some focus on regions as bounded entities provides an important counterpoint to the contemporary emphasis on networks. The explosion of interest in networks has brought a rich set of insights into the workings of the contemporary world, yet networks often end up becoming spatially fixed as they interact with perceptually and functionally bounded regions – with important implications for economic, social and political processes (a corollary to the second point noted above). For example, patterns of resource development and conflict in the U.S. Pacific Northwest during the mid- to late twentieth century cannot be understood simply as the product of the convergence of a set of networks in a particular place; they were shaped by a regionalist conception promulgated by the Pacific Northwest Regional Planning Commission in 1935 that led to the creation of a functionally, perceptually and eventually legally bounded 'Pacific Northwest' that was knit together by shared Columbia River hydropower: transmission lines, uniformly inexpensive power rates, and a federal power agency (VOGEL, 2008). That region, in turn, fostered political identities and infrastructural arrangements that fundamentally influenced the fortunes of the peoples, places and environments making up the region. Recognizing such dynamics requires looking at the interactions between fluidity and fixity, networks and regions – not writing regional fixity out of the picture.

There is no question that regions mean different things in different contexts, that they are the product of different circumstances, and that they are always in some ways unbounded. But since no amount of mobility or interaction is ever likely to produce a completely fluid or geographically undifferentiated world, there is value in keeping the region tethered to some kind of spatial or territorial construct. As any member of a repressed ethnic minority movement can attest, the spatial chunks of Earth's surface that possess some kind of functional or perceptual significance (however fleeting) can have profound impacts on the evolving geography of the planet. It follows that we cannot afford to ignore them in the rush to embrace the unbounded.

To Undo Regions

J. Nicholas Entrikin

The sociologist Louis Wirth once wrote that, 'We must always, especially in modern times, reckon with the power of communication and transportation – with the mobility of men and ideas – to undo regions' (WIRTH, 1951, pp. 388–389). Wirth recognized the value of regionalism as a counteragent to the excesses of social standardization and homogenization, but saw regionalism, in large part, as a barrier to progressive social change. Others have since used his words as a sign of the end of the region and regionalism as an academically significant cultural and social theme. An interesting quality of the so-called 'new regionalism' and some of the themes raised by this panel is that the long-standing criticism is, in fact, no longer a criticism at all. Proponents of new geographical orientations in geography that emphasize movement, networks and, more generally, process-oriented approaches have begun to use the concept of region in ways that push the concept into new intellectual territory. The region has been a remarkably adaptable concept. Are there limits to this adaptability?

Questions about bounding regions and the fixity of these boundaries have linked the various approaches and perspectives presented in this panel session on 'Regional World(s)'. Having addressed questions about the region through various stages of my career as a geographer, I found that beginning to consider this topic again was like preparing for a visit with an old and slightly eccentric friend, who each visit appears in a new guise and speaks of a new beginning. One listens patiently, hopefully, but with a degree of scepticism. For, with every new start, there is inevitably a similar ending.

The many guises of the regional concept in geography since the end of the nineteenth century suggest that the concept defies simple definition or association with particular theories or methodologies. Its persistence as a core geographical concept is thus unexplained through comprehensive analysis of its use or intellectually strenuous attempts at semantic clarification. The most ambitious attempt at identifying the essence of the region remains Richard HARTSHORNE's (1939) in his classic volume, *The Nature of Geography*. The regional approach's purported role in geography's rational and progressive march forward offered a grounding of the region through the logical foundation of a real differentiation and integration. The many new uses that geographers have proposed for the region since the publication of Hartshorne's volume have made his arguments seem more quaint than rigorous and more representative of a particular moment in the history of geographic thought than transcendent of his era. During the early twentieth century the region was central to the theoretical, or at least the meta-theoretical, literature of geography as an intellectually viable means of bridging the troublesome disciplinary gap between human and physical geography. This chorological moment in disciplinary history has long passed.

The region, however, continues to come back into the geographical literature by different scholarly routes and in different forms. Debate about the region was once equivalent to debate about the nature of geography. Today, however, discussion about the region is unevenly distributed in geography and is found widely scattered among increasingly independent, sub-fields of geography. As the discipline itself has fragmented, geographers have apparently given up, with some notable exceptions, the practice of offering arguments about the nature of the field as a unified academic discipline.

So the rise, fall and return of the regional concept has mirrored the movement of modern geographic thought. It has largely been detached from the idea of regional geography as a methodology, so central a concern of early twentieth-century geography. In recent years, regional geography has been presented through a variety of largely negative caricatures. It has been described darkly, as the great retreat from a more socially progressive geography; pathetically, as a misguided turn away from the powerful logic of science; conservatively, as an ideological defence of traditional ways of life; imperialistically, as an intellectual tool for hiding projects of cultural and political dominance; and, on rare occasion, heroically, as defending the spirit of the humanities and a humanistic perspective within a scientistic age.

This incomplete listing of the various interpretations of the regional approach sheds light on the reason for the regional concept's persistence and seemingly infinite adaptability to new intellectual circumstances. The region represents a particular way of viewing the world rather than a systematic research agenda. It is atheoretical and above all useful in the flexibility that it offers researchers to adapt it to the kinds of question that become prominent in any particular era. For example, we now see the regional concept re-emerging around particular sets of empirical questions associated with topics such as globalization, the crisis of the nation-state, increased movements of people, and fluid and overlapping territorial identities, not to mention environmental activism.

Not surprisingly, geographers currently rediscovering the region often stumble into the old logical demons of chorology. Questions of ontology, functional coherence, bounding, constructivism, scale and contingency are old ones that take on different significance when couched in relation to the pressing empirical issues and shared theoretical assumptions of current regional practitioners. I suspect that the failure to acknowledge this lineage is in part a function of the radically different content of contemporary regional work and the ways in which this new content obscures logical similarities in use and misuse of the concept.

One of the central themes addressed in this panel, however, does appear to move the regional concept from familiar territory to significantly different intellectual ground. The distinction to which I am referring is one stated as a 'relational' versus a 'territorial' view of the region, which can be simplified as spatially bounded areas versus unbounded networks of flows. The ideological shading added to this distinction typically colours the former as atavistic and the latter as progressive.

The mobility of ideas and peoples has far surpassed what Louis Wirth could have ever imagined and the magnitude would seem to lead to a profound questioning about the significance of regions and regionalism. Instead, it has led to yet a further testing of the semantic flexibility of the regional concept. The turn toward process-oriented approaches, such as actor-network theory and the geography of mobilities, in discussions of place and region resurrects the old Bergsonian theme of the misleading use of spatial concepts to describe temporal flow, or *durée*. To put the issue in the form of a question, when do geographers reach the limit of reasonable use of a concept, even one as semantically capacious as the region? At what point does the geographer's emphasis on processes so 'undo' the region (or place) that it becomes largely an expendable concept, easily replaced by more commonly used and more descriptively accurate terms? My own assessment is that the so-called 'relational' approach ('so-called' because there are competing and very different ideas of a relational approach) to regions and regionalism appears to have already passed that point.

Crossing Borders: Problematizing (and Moving Beyond) the Relational vs. Territorial Divide

Anssi Paasi

It is been an exciting task to follow the debate on relational and territorial spaces which has gradually moved from rather strong emphasis on the inevitability of relational instead of territorial approaches to more nuanced interpretations highlighting the need to move beyond such a dichotomy (JONES and PAASI, 2013). I will problematize here the relational/territorial 'dichotomy' by reflecting on what the 'boundedness' of regional spaces in general means by looking at three issues. Respectively, my key argument is that a major problem in the whole territorial/relational divide is a narrow view on what regional borders and 'boundedness' actually mean and that advancing this debate requires that scholars pay attention to the parallel discussions in political geography on the future and current roles of state borders.

First, this dichotomy that characterized early debates implied a relatively straightforward division between 'old' bounded (= territorial) and 'new' open (= relational) views on regions. This issue was not completely new: geographers have criticized 'bounded regions' and presented relational ideas for more than a half of century. Second, some commentators were ready to abandon the view on regions as bounded units and to replace it with a relational, non-bounded spatial ontology. This view implied that relational and territorial perspectives were alternatives, one of which can simply be chosen, a view that passes the ambivalent and context-bound meanings of both regions and borders. Third, I will approach the relational/territorial issue by discussing the problems of contextuality in social science. My argument is that a division between relational 'open regions' and territorial 'bounded regions' is not productive because it tends to universalize the complexities of socio-spatial practice that are contextual, which in most cases reflect both relational and territorial dimensions.

BORDERS AND REGIONS

While this theme became powerfully on agenda along with the rise of relational thinking, the problem of regional borders is not a new one. Already traditional regional geographers criticized 'given' regional borders. HARTSHORNE (1939, p. 275), for example, wrote that:

> The problem of establishing the boundaries of a geographic region represents a problem for which we have no reason to even hope for an objective solution. The most that we can say is that any particular unit of land has significant relations with all the neighboring units and that in certain respects it may be more closely related with a particular group of units than with others, but not necessarily in all respects.

He suggested that the tendency to overlook the relative location of things results 'from consideration of a region as a relatively closed unit in itself' and, further, that 'regions do not have relations to each other as units – only particular elements and complexes of elements within regions are related to those in others' (HARTSHORNE, 1939, pp. 281–282). KIMBLE (1951) was even more straightforward when suggesting that regional geographers may perhaps be trying to put boundaries that do not exist around areas that do not matter.

Such comments were critical of the supposed coherence of 'geographical regions' that were 'constructed' as part of the research process by geographers. Attributes such as synthesis, uniqueness, individual, totality, organism or personality etc. were widely used to accentuate the holistic understanding of regions. Respectively, borders were 'dividing lines' that distinguished such 'wholes' from each other. This view on borders as dividing lines is deeply rooted in the memories of some key relational thinkers. MASSEY (1993, p. 64), for example, wrote: 'I remember some of my painful times as a geographer have been spent unwillingly struggling to think how one could draw a boundary around somewhere like "the East Midlands".'

Early relational critique implied that such 'old thinking' has been dominant up to recent times and that new thinking was challenging it. Yet most contemporary human geographers probably have 'territorial jurisdictions' in their mind, i.e., administrative units, rather than such 'drawing exercises' on the borders of geographical regions. Administrative regions have been regarded as 'social constructs' to be made and mobilized in governance for decades. This also holds with their boundaries (PAASI, 2010). Contemporary 'regional geographers' are not searching for a 'unity' and 'coherence' but see regions as contested socio-spatial processes that may be simultaneously open and bounded, depending on the social practices and discourses in question. Politics, regional planning, marketing and identity building, for example, may operate in diverging regional registers. 'Boundedness' is for border scholars a contextual-empirical rather than an ontological issue. Planners and regional developers or entrepreneurs often operate with such ambiguous borders (PAASI, 2013). Indeed, also MASSEY (2011), in line with many other scholars, recognizes today the importance of both relational and territorial perspectives, i.e., territories are constituted relationally.

WHAT AND WHERE ARE THE BORDERS?

Much of relational thinking thus implies that borders are dividing lines between social entities. Yet regions (and especially jurisdictional territories) acquire their borders in institutionalized practices. Rather than being fixed lines used, for example, in governance, borders are social processes, practices, discourses, forms of knowledge, narratives, symbols and institutions. This is crucial for both a political and regional geographic understanding of borders/regions and helps to comprehend their persistence. Borders may 'locate' practically everywhere in a region (or as political geographers argue with state borders, everywhere in the state). Everywhere should not be taken literally since borders and bordering manifest themselves in diverging localized social practices, ideologies and discourses and come into being in diverging ways in regional governance, media, festivals, museums, archives, education, electoral districts, voting practices, tax paying, health care systems and even in sports events (cf. PAASI, 2009, 2010). These are all practices that may stretch across 'borders' but may be simultaneously constitutive of the region, identity building and – borders! Regional borders are thus not 'cutting' social practices in some abstract way, but rather it is the relational social practices and discourses that produce and reproduce boundaries as part of the perpetual region-building process. Respectively, the inside and outside are not separate but part of the same relational process. Thus, it is crucial to study how difference is established in material and discursive practices. A search for how, why and by whom distinctions are produced and reproduced may be more fruitful than simply denying the role of 'boundedness' in social life or taking such borders for granted. Both borders and regions require perpetual contextual conceptualization and analysis.

POLITICAL ROLES

An open, relational and cosmopolitan world without bounded territories is certainly a most laudable ideal. Yet, in practice, territorial and relational practices and discourses characterize social life and politics simultaneously. In some spatial contexts (especially those dominated by political and ethnic relations), territorial dimensions can be significant. In some other contexts and spheres (like economy) networks/connections may be much more significant. Recognition of their inseparability is crucial to understanding the contextual features of social practice and to the struggle to transform such practices. Relations and regions are not 'universals', but are socially constructed in different ways in different contexts, in different relations of power.

Actors involved in state-level governance and politics have, in spite of the perpetual 'rescaling' processes occurring in governance and politics, an interest in the regulation and governance of space economy, social life, cohesion, well-being and the 'minds' of citizens. The transformation of the form and content of regional governance and regional policies is a key medium in this process. Without fetishizing them, territories are one medium in this process, a medium that results from and operates in and through the networks of activities. The number of states has quadrupled since the end of World War II, but the number of sub-national regional units has multiplied even more (LOVERING, 2007). At the same time, an opposite tendency is occurring around the world, where mergers of regional spaces are the order of the day in the current economic decline. At the same time the world is continuously characterized by regionalist movements, ideologies and struggles, whether this is seen as progressive or regressive development. Thus, whether we like it or not, people incessantly tend to identify themselves, for various individual, collective and institutional reasons, with local, regional and state levels (PAASI, 2013).

Regions thus matter in many ways and we cannot simply write them off or decide universally whether they are relational, territorial or, more likely, both at the same time. Instead of ignoring them, regions provide us with a set of exciting and challenging questions: what, why, where and under what power relations they are produced, reproduced, removed or merged?

Regional Worlds: Institutionalizations, Incongruities

Gordon MacLeod

John Agnew opened these sessions with a presentation on diverse 'arguments with regions', and I am going to begin with a reference to his book, *Place and Politics in Italy*, where he identified an 'intellectual standoff' between those who maybe overstate the novelty and impact of networks in the conceptualization of regions and spatiality more generally and those who remain overly committed to the enduring significance of territorial spheres. For Agnew, '[P]art of the problem is the way the debate is posed, as if networks invariably stand in opposition to territories [and, further, as if . . .] networks are seen as a completely new phenomenon without geographical anchors' (AGNEW, 2002, p. 2). Perhaps these sessions have been helpful in narrowing this 'intellectual standoff'.

On one level, all expressions of territory – regional, urban, national, cross-border – are, to varying degrees, orchestrated through myriad trans-territorial mobilities and relational webs of connectivity. And, to be sure, it is hard to dispute the contention that globalization and the restructuring of the state's administrative and political spheres have been a cause and consequence of cities and regions being more permeable to 'external' influences, whether through the mobile trafficking of people, money, capital or ideas. All of which is unsettling the landscape of governance and everyday life, for politicians, practitioners and citizens. In an insightful paper, ALLEN and COCHRANE (2007) reveal how the governance of a rapidly growing urban region like Milton Keynes in southern England is increasingly being orchestrated around and through an assemblage of practices, affiliations and networks – mobile and connective rather than 'global' scale (ONG, 2007) – that stretches across and beyond the official boundaries of Milton Keynes and the South East region. However, crucially, they also demonstrate how this unfolding 'regional assemblage' is itself being choreographed around and through the institutional landscape inherited from certain administrative lines, not least Milton Keynes's former New Town Development Corporation.

It is when interpreting such a historical-geography that I believe PAASI's (1986, 1996) pioneering work on the institutionalization of regions – as a socio-spatial process through which a territorial unit emerges and becomes identified in everyday consciousness and practice – to become most compelling. Paasi and others were pivotal to the formulation of a 'new regional geography' in the late 1980s that can be viewed as a precursor to a 'politics of scale' approach (MacLeod and Jones, 2001), a fundamental premise of both being that geographical territories such as nation-states and regions are socially constructed rather than ontologically pre-given, but that, in turn, such territories themselves become implicated in the constitution of social, economic and political processes (Delaney and Leitner, 1997). And here I want to register a frustration about how certain contributions advocating a topological approach to regions have been culpable of caricaturing a scalar or territorial perspective to be guilty as charged of interpreting places as fixed, static and closed. In riposte, it needs to be acknowledged how the contributions of a new regional geography and those on a politics of scale have been pioneering relational readings to regions and spatiality: Smith and Swyngedouw brilliantly opened the door for such interpretations, the latter crucially offering an ontological guide to research the mobile processes generative of territorial units rather than pre-defined territories (global, national, local) themselves as the starting point for analysis (Smith, 1992; Swyngedouw, 1997; Brenner, 2001; Paasi, 2004).

In an insightful contribution to the scale debate, Katherine Jones (1998, p. 26) also informed us how the relational processes of place-making are actively performed through a 'politics of representation', whereby political, economic and cultural agents discursively re-present their struggles, visions and strategies for change around and through particular scales and often across and beyond territorial scales, to 'jump scale' so to speak. Acknowledgement of this enables us to remain appreciative of how so many instances of *realpolitik* – as in the case of a central government delimiting a particular region as a 'problem' space in need of 'renewal', or of groups of aspirant citizens seeking political and cultural rights – often distinguish what Cox (1998) terms a territorially articulated 'space of dependence' through which to conduct their politics of engagement. These concepts are deployed imaginatively in García-Alvarez and Trillo-Santamaría's presentation on cross-border regionalization in Galicia and North Portugal. Varro and Lagendijk's paper also reveals how the Northern Way in England represents a pan-regional space imagined and forged through a multi-nodal city-regional network, and with the explicit aim of reducing the combined and uneven development that is Britain's North–South divide. So in this perspective, places, regions and scales function as important frames of reference for what Bob Jessop refers to as state strategy and the strategic selectivity of the state.

The upshot of all this is that the degree to which we interpret regions as territorial and scalar or topological and networked ought to remain an open question, perhaps more appropriately resolved *ex post* and empirically rather than *a priori* and theoretically (Hudson, 2006; MacLeod and Jones, 2007). I think this principle has guided several papers presented in the sessions such as Mark Goodwin's (2013) analysis of the governance of climate change, and some of the key concerns in the debate are expressed cogently by Kevin Morgan in a previous special issue of *Whither Regional Studies* back in 2007:

> To overcome the debilitating binary division between territorial and relational geography we need to recognise that political space is bounded *and* porous: *bounded* because politicians are held to account through the territorially-defined ballot box, a prosaic but important reason why we should not be so dismissive of territorial politics; *porous* because people have multiple identities and they are becoming ever more mobile, spawning communities of relational connectivity that transcend territorial boundaries.
>
> (Morgan, 2007, p. 33; original emphases)

These communities of relational connectivity may tread the tramlines of voluntary or forced migration, or they could be connected via cyberspace, or be enrolled through public policy, politics and governance. I think that it is in this sense that – for all its ability to shed light on the geography of mobility and trans-territorial connectivity in everyday life – perhaps a network or topological perspective is less adept at locating the evolutionary form, endurance, resilience of regions and also, crucially, the asymmetrical geometries of power, geographies of immobility and place dependence, and geographies of possession and dispossession.

In thinking more generally about the various territorial imaginaries that are defined as or mobilized as regions – highly prized creative economic spaces, regional political administrations, spaces of cultural identity and vernacular – while they may share some land mass, they may not readily correspond in terms of symbolic and territorial shape (Paasi, 1986). And, of course, the tangled, overlapping territorial systems, and incompatible maps of regionalism are only intensified when we consider the case of cross-border regions, as outlined in Garcia-Alvarez and Trillo-Santamaria. In a crucial sense, then, as Painter (2008) contends, the boundaries characterizing various regionalisms and regionalizations old and new are often 'incongruous'. The challenge to map and interpret such incongruities will doubtless inform and motivate scholars of regional studies for years to come. But crucially, such incongruities will also inspire, frustrate and motivate politicians, entrepreneurs, planners, citizens and those aspiring to gain such political membership. As Massey (2004, p. 9) reminds us, '[I]n this world so often described as a space of flows, so much of our formal democratic politics is organized territorially'.

The New Regionalism in Question

Andrew E. G. Jonas

My interest in regionalism has developed out of my ongoing research into the changing geography of the state in capitalism. One particular aspect of that geography which I choose to highlight here is the emergence of new regional structures of the state in and around major metropolitan agglomerations. My research on the new regionalism has involved empirically grounded case studies of the reorganization of the geography of the local state in the United States. This includes, most recently, work on regional collaboration in metropolitan areas such as Denver and Detroit, alongside a longer-standing interest in regionalism and regional planning in California. In the latter case, I have been following California's new regionalism, which emerged in the early 2000s as a self-styled non-political movement led by business organizations in response to various planning and governance challenges in regions throughout the State of California (JONAS and PINCETL, 2006). I have also been interested in different approaches to regionalism and city-regionalism in the European context (WARD and JONAS, 2004). The theme of this panel therefore represents an opportunity to reflect critically on some of that work.

Re-examining that work in the context of this panel, I am especially struck by the diversity of regionalisms operating in different national contexts. Kevin Ward and I referred explicitly to this diversity when we drew on our research on regionalism in the United Kingdom and the United States, respectively, to talk about 'worlds of regionalism' (JONAS and WARD, 2002). Yet I remain a little bit troubled by the fact that we have often fixed our attention on the region without always recognizing the diverse political-geographic contexts in which regionalism operates. In comparison to the recent attention given to regionalism and sub-national governance processes, we seem rather less preoccupied with understanding the territorial structures of the (national) state which might (or might not) engender regionalism (new or old).

I have some concerns insofar as the study of the state territoriality at a variety of scales – upwards and downwards (if one prefers to think hierarchically) or laterally (if you prefer to think relationally) – has always been very central to the sub-discipline of Political Geography. Yet we seem to be in this age of uncertainty as regards the changing content and form of state territoriality. This uncertainty is conveyed by the proliferation of concepts, such as state 'hollowing out' (and the reciprocal process of state 'filling in') or the Castellsian idea of global 'spaces of flows'. Such relational thinking seems to be a reaction against thinking about state territoriality as a quasi-fixed feature in an otherwise fast-changing landscape of regionalism (ALLEN and COCHRANE, 2007). It is as if we are latching on to regions because they give us certainty in these uncertain times. So my question for you today is: can knowledge of regionalism and regionalist struggles nevertheless help to shed light on the changing territoriality of the state?

Perhaps the analysis of state territoriality need not be the starting point for this kind of investigation but we should at least recognize that the analysis of regionalism – or more specifically the new regionalism – can help to shed light on the contingent and necessary properties of state territoriality. We need to have some *a priori* knowledge of the properties of state territorial structures in order to understand the generative conditions for the new regionalism, its diverse forms, and the spaces of the state which it colonizes. Of course, it does depend on the kind of new regionalism we might be interested in: economic governance and inter-firm relationships; a social movement; or perhaps a state governance project. In all of these cases, state territoriality is a crucial part of the explanatory context.

Joe Painter recently commented critically about how the desire to draw boundaries around regions reflects a 'cartographic anxiety' in Geography (PAINTER, 2008). Nevertheless, if new regions have fairly loose boundaries or encompass spaces well beyond existing local jurisdictional arrangements, then let us map them. Maybe those boundaries are porous and malleable but they are boundaries nonetheless. For example, the way the new regionalism has evolved in the United States is grounded in certain ideals and material realities with respect to how the U.S. state organizes and operates across territory. Here we can highlight the problem of metropolitan political fragmentation. Accordingly, new regionalism's proponents in the United States talk quite explicitly about circumnavigating (local) political geography; for them the geography of the (local) state is the problem. Moreover, what has emerged concretely in places like California is very different in form to what has arisen out of ostensibly similar new regionalist processes in the United Kingdom (or even other regions of Europe), and this must be due to profound differences in state territorial structures. So in developing our abstract propositions about regions and changing state spaces, we need to continue to hold on to these differences.

An alternative way of approaching the new regionalism it is to think of regions as consisting of particular spaces of interests. By focusing on interests – those of, for instance, capital, labour and the state – rather than regions, we can begin to think about regionalism as a contested process rather than a fixed economic or political outcome. Regionalism is a moment in the contestation of state territoriality. The recent debates in Human Geography about scale are relevant here (JONAS, 2006). Scale refers to the notion that social relations are not just spatial but also organized into various patterns and hierarchies that, more or less, correspond with the territorial structures of the state, i.e., local, the regional, the national, the international and so forth. The writings of scholars like BRENNER (1998) have been extremely important in showing how capital accumulation both produces and disrupts such taken-for-granted scalar categories. But does 'scale' itself explain how interests in regions take shape? I think that is an open question. Following Kevin Cox's lead (COX, 1998), there is no necessary correspondence between scales of material interests and scales of political engagement; regions can materialize from non-regionalist political interests. Having said this, I do find a bit perplexing that some scholars dismiss altogether the concept or category of scale (MARSTON *et al.*, 2005). Just as some geographers are abandoning scale, anthropologists, sociologists and even some economists have embraced the concept. Perhaps we should be using grounded knowledge of scalar politics to shed light on the new regionalism.

In Economic and Political Geography, we are naturally drawn to the analysis of different varieties of competitive regionalism or city-regionalism (HARRISON, 2007). This has encouraged JONES and MACLEOD (2004) to draw an important distinction between regional economic spaces and spaces of political regionalism. While helpful, I feel such a heuristic distinction could be difficult to sustain as it does encourage one to look for examples of economic and political regionalism separately rather than together. In my experience, and drawing on evidence from places in California, the new regionalism is a political movement that has an identifiable set of economic (class) interests. In approaching the new regionalism, I have drawn a conceptual distinction between those aspects of regionalism which I would take to be examples of territorial governance projects inside the state and those that are struggles for control of the territorial resources of the state. Both types of struggle might be at work. But the common factor is thinking about regionalism in terms of struggles around particular spaces (of distribution) inside the state, which may or may not be regionally bounded. So in conclusion, regionalism offers a starting point for thinking about the processes producing state geographies of strategic interest to different economic and social factions, and which might or might not correspond to the kinds of neatly self-contained regions that once preoccupied the minds of regional scientists and human geographers.

Regions, Resilience and Sustainability

Ray Hudson

There are five points that I want to make in this brief intervention. The first concerns the impacts of human activity, particularly the increase in CO_2 emissions, on the global environment, with over 25 per cent of all CO_2 emissions resulting from transport. This clearly has serious ecological impacts but it also has quite profound implications for how we should think about models of regional development. Following from this, my next point relates to dominant conceptions of regional development in a neoliberal world. As patterns of regional inequality became more sharply etched in recent decades, concepts of regions and what constitutes regional development also changed (for example, see PIKE *et al.*, 2007). The dominant meaning of regional development altered as the concept was re-worked as part of the narrative of a neoliberal globalizing economy. Regions and city-regions came to be seen as key nodes in global economic networks. There was also a growing emphasis on endogenous processes, utilizing regional assets, institutions and knowledges and promoting intra-regional links via cluster policies as the key to regional economic success in a global political economy. At the same time, there was an emphasis on improving material process efficiencies, more effectively transforming materials and reducing wastes to enhance competitiveness under the rubric of 'lean production'. However, the focus was on the efficiency of individual plants and companies and on linear flows leading to end-of-pipe wastes. Consequently, these wastes become externalities, disposed of at a minimal cost to the company and dumped into the global commons.

This changed neoliberal conception of regions and development is reflected both in policy discourse and academic literature. For example, consider the burgeoning academic literatures on global commodity chains, global value chains, global production networks and so on (SMITH *et al.*, 2002; HUDSON, 2008a). In the realm of policy discourse, development became defined as the successful repositioning of regions within those networks or chains. To develop became to move up the value chain, to become core rather than peripheral within global networks. However, this model of development is predicated on increasing volumes of material flows into and out of regions; growing volumes of inputs sourced from all around the world, outputs sold on global markets. As the volume of commodities rose, so too did the environmental costs of their transportation. However, scant, if any, regard was paid to the ecological costs or the ethical implications of such a model of regional development. Continuing with it is increasingly problematic and, in fact, will become increasingly – if it isn't already – unsustainable.

The third step in my argument therefore is that we need to recover a serious consideration of materiality into the way in which we think about the political economy of regional development (HUDSON, 2008b). Until recently, political economy of virtually all political and theoretical stripes had little to say about the implications of the material grounding of the economy in nature and this absence needs to be addressed in the context of regional development. The implications of the laws of thermodynamics and the limits that they set for how we think about development and regional development must be acknowledged. As BENTON (1989) noted, to recognize these limits and acknowledge that people cannot conquer nature in some unproblematic fashion is emancipatory in thinking about development. We also need to recognize that all economic activity necessarily involves material transformations that have unintended as well as – or on occasion instead of – intended consequences. The unintended consequences create outputs that are often referred to as 'wastes'. Consequently, the economy must be understood as a complex, socio-technical or a socio-ecological system, in which wastes are endemic, the unavoidable by-products of every stage in an economic process. Since every economic activity involves energy, those activities that depend on carbon-based fossil fuels as their energy source unavoidably produce CO_2 emissions.

The fourth point I want to make relates to how we might begin to think about recent economic development and a transition to more sustainable, self-reliant and resilient regions in light of those unavoidable material limits via the concept of resilience (Hudson, 2010). Resilient entities have three properties which are helpful in thinking differently about regions and regional development: the amount of change that a region can undergo while retaining its basic form, structure and functions; the degree to which a region is capable of reorganization; the degree to which a region can learn and build adaptive capacity. This raises some key questions. How might a transition to more resilient regional economies, with a greater degree of intra-regional closure, reducing their ecological footprint, be brought about? How can we construct models of development that maximize intra-regional rather than inter-regional transactions and mobility and movement? There are many examples of ways in which regions can be made more sustainable, more resilient, via reorganizing production, exchange and consumption.

My final point is this: While the repertoire of technologically feasible options is far from exhausted, the extent to which moving towards greater regional resilience and sustainability is systemically possible within the capitalist social relationships remains unclear. Capitalism is an inherently contradictory and uneven mode of development, concerned with maximizing profits and value creation rather than creating sustainable, resilient regions. Can the pursuit of profitability be made compatible with the pursuit of resilient and sustainable regions? Eco-modernist optimists would argue 'yes we can' – a green capitalism is feasible. Personally, I'm not convinced that the challenge can be met so easily in that way, which leaves unanswered the question 'how *can* it be met?' Can the social relations of the economy be configured in ways that make them compatible with resilient and sustainable regions? Can the social relations of regions be constructed in ways that make them compatible with a sustainable and resilient economy?

REFERENCES

Agnew J.A. (1994) The territorial trap: the geographical assumptions of International Relations theory, *Review of International Political Economy* **1**, 53–80.

Agnew, J. (2002) *Place and Politics in Modern Italy*. University of Chicago Press, Chicago.

Allen J. and Cochrane A. (2007) Beyond the territorial fix: regional assemblages, politics and power, *Regional Studies* **41**, 1161–1176.

Amin, A. (2004) Regions unbound: towards a new politics of place, *Geografiska Annaler Series B* **86**, 33–44.

Benton, T. (1989) Marxism and natural limits: an ecological critique and reconstruction, *New Left Review* **178**, 51–86.

Brenner, N. (1998) Between fixity and motion: accumulation, territorial organization and the historical geography of spatial scales, *Environment and Planning D: Society and Space* **16**, 459–481.

Brenner, N. (2001) The limits to scale? Methodological reflections on scalar structuration, *Progress in Human Geography* **15**, 525–548.

Brenner, N. (2004) *New State Spaces: Urban Governance and the Rescaling of Statehood*. Oxford University Press, Oxford.

Cox, K.R. (1998) Spaces of dependence, spaces of engagement and the politics of scale, or: looking for local politics, *Political Geography* **17**, 1–23.

Delaney, D. and Leitner, H. (1997) The political construction of scale, *Political Geography* **16**, 93–97.

Entrikin, N. (1994) Place and region, *Progress in Human Geography* **18**, 227–233.

Gilbert, A. (1988) The new regional geography in English and French-speaking countries, *Progress in Human Geography* **12**, 208–228.

Goodwin, M. (2013) Regions, territories and relationality: exploring the regional dimension of political practice, *Regional Studies* **47**, 1181–1190.

Grigg, D. (1965) The logic of regional systems, *Annals of the Association of American Geographers* **55**, 465–491.

Harrison, J. (2007) From competitive regions to competitive city-regions: a new orthodoxy, but some old mistakes, *Journal of Economic Geography* **7**, 311–332.

Hartshorne, R. (1939) *The Nature of Geography.* The Association of American Geographers, Lancaster, PA.

Hudson, R. (2006) Regional devolution and regional economic success: enabling myths and illusions about power, *Geografiska Annaler* **88B**, 159–171.

Hudson, R. (2008a) Cultural political economy meets global production networks: a productive meeting?, *Journal of Economic Geography* **8**, 421–440.

Hudson, R. (2008b) Material matters and the search for resilience: re-thinking regional and urban development strategies in the context of global environmental change, *International Journal of Innovation and Sustainable Development* **3**, 166–184.

Hudson, R. (2010) Resilient regions in an uncertain world: wishful thinking or practical reality?, *Cambridge Journal of Regions, Economy and Society* **3**, 11–25.

Jonas, A.E.G. (2006) Pro scale: further reflections on the scale debate in human geography, *Transactions of the Institute of British Geographers* **31**, 399–406.

Jonas, A.E.G. (2012) Region and place: regionalism in question, *Progress in Human Geography* **36**, 263–272.

Jonas, A.E.G. and Pincetl, S. (2006) Rescaling regions in the state: the New Regionalism in California, *Political Geography* **25**, 482–505.

Jonas, A.E.G. and Ward, K. (2002) A world of regionalisms? Towards a US-UK urban and regional policy framework comparison, *Journal of Urban Affairs* **24**, 377–401.

Jones, K. (1998) Scale as epistemology, *Political Geography* **17,** 25–28.

Jones, M. and MacLeod, G. (2004) Regional spaces, spaces of regionalism: territory, insurgent politics and the English question, *Transactions of the Institute of British Geographers* **29**, 433–452.

Jones, M. and Paasi, A. (2013) Regional worlds: Advancing the geography of regions, *Regional Studies* **47**, 1–5.

Kimble, G.H.T. (1951). The inadequacy of the regional concept, in Stamp L.D. and Woolridge S.W. (Eds) *London Essays in Geography*, pp. 151–174. Longmans, Green, London.

Lovering, J. (2007) The new imperial geography, in Baghni-Sen S. and Lawton-Smith H. (Eds) *Economic Geography: Then, Now and the Future*. Routledge, London.

MacLeod, G. and Jones, M. (2001) Renewing the geography of regions, *Environment and Planning D: Society and Space* **19**, 669–695.

MacLeod, G. and Jones, M. (2007) Territorial, scalar, networked, connected: in what sense a 'regional world'?, *Regional Studies* **41**, 1177–1191.

Marston, S., Jones III, J.P. and Woodward, K. (2005) Human geography without scale, *Transactions of the Institute of British Geographers* **30**, 416–432.

Massey, D. (1993) Power-geometry and a progressive sense of place, in Bird J., Curtis B., Putnam T., Robertson G. and Tickner L. (Eds) *Mapping the Futures: Local Cultures, Global Change*, pp. 59–69. Routledge, London.

Massey, D. (2004) Geographies of responsibility. *Geografiska Annaler B* **86**, 5–18.

Massey, D. (2011) A counterhegemonic relationality of place, in Mccann E. and Ward K. (Eds) *Mobile Urbanism: Cities and Policymaking in the Global Age*, pp. 1–14. University of Minnesota Press, Minneapolis.

Morgan, K. (2007) The polycentric state: new spaces of empowerment and engagement?, *Regional Studies* **41**, 1237–1251.

Murphy, A.B. (1988) The regional dynamics of language differentiation in Belgium: a study in cultural-political geography, Geography Research Paper No. 227, University of Chicago, Chicago.

Murphy, A.B. (1991) Regions as social constructs: the gap between theory and practice, *Progress in Human Geography* **15**, 23–35.

Murphy, A.B. (2013) Territory's continuing allure, *Annals of the Association of American Geographers* **103**, 1212–1226.

Ong, A. (2007) *Neoliberalism as Exception: Mutations in Citizenship and Sovereignty*. Duke University Press, Durham, NC.

Paasi, A. (1986) The institutionalization of regions: a theoretical framework for understanding the emergence of regions and the constitution of regional identity, *Fennia* **16**, 105–146.

Paasi, A. (1991) Deconstructing regions: notes on the scales of social life, *Environment and Planning A* **23**, 239–256.

Paasi, A. (1996) *Territories, Boundaries and Consciousness: The Changing Geographies of Finnish-Russian Border*. Wiley, Chichester.

Paasi, A. (2003) Region and place: regional identity in question, *Progress in Human Geography* **27**, 475–485.

Paasi, A. (2004) Place and region: looking through the prism of scale, *Progress in Human Geography* **28**, 536–546.

Paasi, A. (2009) The resurgence of the 'region' and 'regional identity': theoretical perspectives and empirical observations on regional dynamics in Europe, *Review of International Studies* **35**, 121–46.

Paasi, A. (2010) Regions are social constructs, but who or what constructs them? Agency in question, *Environment and Planning A* **42**, 2296–2301.

Paasi, A. (2013) Regional planning and the mobilization of 'regional identity': from bounded spaces to relational complexity, *Regional Studies* **47**, 1206–1219.

Painter, J. (2008) Cartographic anxiety and the search for regionality, *Environment and Planning A* **40**, 342–361.

Pike, A., Rodrigues-Pose, A., and Tomaney, J., (2007) What kind of regional development and for whom?, *Regional Studies* **41**, 1253–1269.

Pudup, M.B. (1988) Arguments within regional geography, *Progress in Human Geography* **12**, 369–390.

Smith, N. (2002) Geography, difference and the politics of scale, in Doherty J., Graham E. and Malek E. (Eds) *Postmodernism and the Social Sciences*, pp. 57–79. Macmillan, Basingstoke.

Smith, A., Rainnie, A., Dunford, M., Hardy, J., Hudson, R. and Sadler, D. (2002) Networks of value, commodities and regions: reworking divisions of labour in macro-regional economies, *Progress in Human Geography* **26**, 1, 41–63.

Swyngedouw, E. (1997) Neither global nor local: 'glocalization' and the politics of scale, in Cox K. (Ed) *Spaces of Globalization*, pp. 137–166. Guilford Press, New York.

Vogel, E. (2008) Regional power and the power of regions: resistance to dam removal in the Pacific Northwest, in Goodman, M. Boykoff M., and Evered K. (Eds) *Contentious Geographies: Environment, Meaning, Scale*, pp. 165–186. Ashgate, Surrey.

Ward, K. and Jonas, A.E.G. (2004) Competitive city regionalism as a politics of space: a critical reinterpretation of the New Regionalism, *Environment and Planning A* **36**, 2119–2139.

Whittlesey, D. (1954) The Regional Concept and the Regional Method, in James P.E. and Jones C.F. (Eds) *American Geography: Inventory & Prospect*, pp. 30–68. Syracuse University Press, Syracuse, NY.

Wirth L. (1951) The limitations of regionalism, in Jensen M.J. (Ed) *Regionalism in America*, pp. 381–393. University of Wisconsin, Madison.

Arguing with Regions

JOHN A. AGNEW
Department of Geography, University of California – Los Angeles, Los Angeles, USA.

AGNEW J. A. Arguing with regions, *Regional Studies*. An analytical survey of how regions have entered into the arguments of the social sciences serves to highlight the uses and limitations of different understandings of regions and their various theoretical biases. It also provides a way of introducing the articles in the rest of this special issue. It considers how regions have come to be used as a classificatory device across the social sciences, discusses the various meanings given to regions in empirical research, and examines the main philosophical and theoretical controversies that have been sparked by their use. Matching regions to purpose and avoiding a singular conception of 'region' that claims to fit all arguments are the main conclusions.

AGNEW J. A. 争论区域，*区域研究*。对于区域如何进入社会科学争论的分析性研究，得以强调不同理解区域方式的使用与限制，及其互异的理论偏见。该分析同时提供做为此一专题中其他文章的引文。它考虑区域如何成为社会科学中分类的机制、探讨经验研究中赋予区域的各种意涵，并检视此一使用在哲学上与理论上引发的主要争论。将区域与目的相互配对，并避免宣称适用于所有主张的单一概念化区域，是为本文的主要结论。

AGNEW J. A. Discuter avec les régions, *Regional Studies*. Une étude analytique de comment les régions sont entrées dans la polémique des sciences sociales permet de mettre en lumière l'emploi et les limites des divergences d'interprétation de ce que c'est une région et de leurs biais théoriques particuliers. Elle fournit aussi un moyen de présenter les articles qui font figurent dans ce numéro spécial. On considère comment les régions sont devenues un classement à travers les sciences sociales, discute des diverses interprétations dans la recherche empirique de ce que c'est une région, et examine les principales polémiques philosophiques et théoriques qui en découlent. Les principales conclusions à en tirer sont les suivantes: adapter les régions à l'objectif et éviter une notion unique de la 'région' qui prétend s'adapter à tous les arguments.

AGNEW J. A. Die Kontroverse der Regionen, *Regional Studies*. Eine analytische Untersuchung der Frage, wie die Regionen zum Streitpunkt der Gesellschaftswissenschaften geworden sind, ermöglicht eine Herausarbeitung der Verwendungen und Grenzen der unterschiedlichen Auffassungen der Regionen sowie ihrer verschiedenen theoretischen Verzerrungen. Ebenso bietet diese Untersuchung eine Einführung in die übrigen Artikel dieser Sonderausgabe. Es wird untersucht, wie die Regionen in den Gesellschaftswissenschaften zu einem Mittel der Klassifizierung geworden sind, es werden die verschiedenen Bedeutungen von Regionen in der empirischen Forschung erörtert, und es werden die wichtigsten philosophischen und theoretischen Kontroversen analysiert, die sich aus dieser Nutzung ergeben haben. Die wichtigsten Schlussfolgerungen lauten, dass die Regionen an ihren Zweck angepasst werden müssen und dass die Nutzung einer einzigen Auffassung der 'Region', die für sich in Anspruch nimmt, zu sämtlichen Argumenten zu passen, zu vermeiden ist.

AGNEW J. A. La polémica con las regiones, *Regional Studies*. Un estudio analítico donde se cuestiona cómo han entrado las regiones en la polémica de las ciencias sociales sirve para destacar el uso y las limitaciones de las diferentes interpretaciones de las regiones y sus sesgos teóricos. También ofrece una forma de presentar los otros artículos de este número especial. Se aborda el modo en que las regiones se han empezado a utilizar como un método de clasificación en las ciencias sociales, analizando los diferentes significados que se han dado a las regiones en el estudio empírico, y examinando las principales controversias filosóficas y teóricas que se han generado por su uso. Las principales conclusiones son que hay que ajustar las regiones a su finalidad y evitar un concepto singular de la 'región' que pretende encajar en todas las discusiones.

INTRODUCTION

This article starts with a once widely accepted example of arguing with regions. It was recently popular to divide the world as a whole into three parts: the so-called Three Worlds. Since 1989, however, the world has lived through a period of regional 'extinction'. The Second World of the Soviet Union and its allies disappeared from the global political and intellectual radar because the socio-political order that region represented disappeared. At the same time, the 'Other Worlds' this Second World held in place – the First World and the Third World – have necessarily lost their raison d'être. As in any classification scheme based on totalizing the differences between units, once that which the others were defined against disappears, the old regional labels and what they stand for no longer make much sense (PLETSCH, 1981). In other words, regions of whatever scale or definition are neither immediately self-evident as geographical designations nor meaningful outside of the historical context and theoretical frame of reference in which they are used.

But what if the geographical scale of regionalization represented by the Three Worlds had either long since failed to or never ever did capture the complex geography of the world in the twentieth century? From this point of view, the emerging regional 'reality' has been of a world either of meso-scale regions based around world cities challenging the division of the world into a set of mutually exclusive state territories (for example, SCOTT, 1998, 2001) or a world whose shape is increasingly complex and difficult to define according to a single regional measure or a limited set of criteria because of globalization and increased geographical differentiation of cultural and economic processes at a range of scales (for example, SCHWARZ and DIENST, 1996; COX, 1998, 2009; MACLEOD, 2001; BRENNER, 2004, 2009). Of course, such representations do not go unchallenged nor do they supersede attempts at stabilizing the world intellectually and politically by reasserting the power of old global–regional schemes of one sort or another such as civilizational blocs or Eurasia as the cockpit of world–political conflict (for example, HUNTINGTON, 1993; BRZEZINSKI, 1997; KELLY, 1997). Arguing with regions is always historically contingent.

Beyond the global scale and perhaps even as a response to the declining relevance of the regional schemas at that scale there has been a recent revival of interest in thinking with regions at other scales. Classifying the world by geographical areas seemingly cannot be avoided if one is both to make sense of it and acknowledge that many people also think about the world in terms of regional divisions at various scales. This revival extends well beyond the confines of geography as a field, so necessarily this survey must also. Regions are used to make arguments in a large number of fields. The main concern in this article in the context of this special issue is with how regions have come to be used as a classificatory device across the social sciences and history (from sociology and political science to geography and economic history), the various meanings given to regions in empirical research, and the main philosophical and theoretical controversies that have been sparked by their use. This is not primarily a survey of specific disputes about regions among geographers. Down the years others have had much to say about this (for example, HARTSHORNE, 1939; KIMBLE, 1951; MASSEY, 1979; NEUMANN, 2010; ENTRIKIN, 2011; JONAS, 2011). However, as the more general points related to arguing with regions are examined in this article, the endeavour is to situate the subsequent articles in this issue in relation to the more general overview of how regions have figured in arguments made by social scientists and historians of various casts.

This overview of the regional problematic in the social sciences first turns to how regions can qualify as classificatory devices for investigating a range of social, political and economic phenomena. It then considers four ways in which regions have been used in social science arguments (as so-called macro-regions in 'total history', functional regions and specific phenomena, geographical areas of similarity, and sub-national regional identities). The third section addresses seven controversies that have arisen over arguing with regions, a number of which are pursued explicitly and implicitly in other articles in this special issue: the region as a territorial or relational concept, the region as an idea versus a real object, regions as persistent over the *longue durée* or not, regions as particular contexts versus containers for case studies, some regions as 'modern' versus others as 'backward', regions as opposed to mobility, and regions as a feature of the past in a nationalizing world. Finally, it concludes by suggesting four ways in which regions can be thought of within the pluralistic conception of regional studies being championed: as communities, territories, networks and societies, giving brief examples of each and how they match different disciplinary and epistemological imperatives.

USING REGIONS AS GEOGRAPHICAL CLASSIFICATION DEVICES

In much popular usage and in many academic fields, the 'region' typically conjures up the idea of a homogeneous block of space that has a persisting distinctiveness due to its physical and cultural characteristics. The claim is that it exists 'out there' in the world, even if there is a prior requirement to think that the world is divided up in this way. This combination of a claim to real existence and the necessity for prior thought so as to define a region has caused untold problems for those trying to have their regionalization schemes accepted as more 'real' than others. It also leads to the opposition in contemporary geography between those who claim the mantle 'real' for their regions and those who regard all regions as mere inventions of an observer whose definitions say more about the political–social position of that observer than the phenomena the regions purport to classify. Thus, there are conflicts between realists and constructionists, empiricists and postmodernists.

The idea of the region typically goes against that of the nation-state as the fundamental geographical unit of account that has been at the heart of the humanities and social sciences as a whole since the late nineteenth century (DUARA, 1995). Yet, the 'view from below', or that of social groups marginalized in orthodox political history and often associated with, for example, social history and anthropology as fields of study, rests on the premise that the national scale typically represents the privileging of attention to the institutions associated with the interests and outlooks of modern political élites more than the reality of an homogeneous and enclosed society conforming to the political boundaries imposed by the modern system of territorial states. Moreover, not only have the world's political boundaries been unstable over even relatively short periods of time – consider how 'Poland' has moved across the map of Europe in this century – but also the geographical patterning of social life is by no means successfully captured by a singular focus on the national scale. Social networks, cultural influences, and economic linkages often transcend borders as well as cluster regionally inside them.

Of course, this is not to say that national-state-based processes of political and economic regulation are without substance in European social history. Since the nineteenth century in particular nation-states have played influential roles both in reinforcing and in changing various social phenomena. Rather, it is to suggest that the national is only one geographical scale among several in terms of relevance to understanding the long-term structuring of such phenomena as household and family organization, economic growth, industrial development, literacy, social protest, social-class formation, and political ideologies. Consequently, regions at a sub-national level and regions at a supra-national level are often invoked by social scientists, depending on the phenomenon in question, to provide more appropriate territorial units than the putative nation-state upon which to base their empirical investigations. As Otto Dann expressed the point with respect to social history:

> With the region, social history, liberated for some time from the weight of the national state, finally has found a more adequate concept of space. The region is the territory of the social historian, varying in its size and structure depending on the object of research.
>
> (DANN, 1989, p. 117)

Usage of the term 'region' is often without much conscious motivation other than either to group together nations that are apparently similar and thus to simplify a greater complexity or to ground local studies within a larger meso-regional/sub-national field of reference. The drawing of regional differences above and below the national scale also frequently involves deploying such familiar, and often theoretically unexamined, conceptual oppositions as modern–backward, capitalist–feudal and core–periphery, depending upon the theoretical orientation of the author in question. In this light, regions are often viewed as geographical units in narratives that are incidental to more fundamental processes operating across space and time.

The region, whatever its precise geographical and social parameters, however, is increasingly important in a range of fields, even when it is not rigorously defined as an inherent feature of a particular study. In recent years, however, there has been a resurgence of studies explicitly engaging with sub-national regions, not least because of the regional–ethnic revivals going on around Europe, from Spain and the British Isles to the former Yugoslavia and the former Soviet Union. Regions as geographical units with which to define the *contexts* of study of a wide range of social structures and processes are therefore important both implicitly and explicitly in the contemporary humanities and social sciences.

Some 'schools' of history, particularly that associated with the *Annales* in interwar and immediate post-war France, have been explicitly devoted to avoiding the privileging of the state as the primary unit of geographical context. Perhaps the close link between Geography and History in France led to a greater recognition by social and economic historians of the importance of assumptions about the spatial units used in research that is largely missing in the English-speaking world where an abstract sounding but usually nationally oriented Sociology has tended to be more influential than Geography among historians. FERNAND BRAUDEL's classic study, *La Méditerranée et Le Monde Méditeranéen* (1949), is an excellent example of the use of an alternative geographical frame of reference, in this case an ocean basin, to the nation-states that had dominated historical research during the nineteenth and for much of the twentieth centuries. For Braudel's long-term total history the relatively short histories of European states posed a significant barrier to the historical understanding that only a larger regional entity, such as the Mediterranean world, could adequately convey. Of course, even Braudel eventually succumbed to the allure of national history in his *L'identité de la France* (1986), though this work remains more sensitive than the typical national history to the physical geography and regional distinctions of the territory that later became France as it is known today. In addition, according to Lynn Hunt:

> Despite the enormous prestige of *La Méditerranée*, Braudel's example did not elicit many works within the French historical community on cross-national networks of commercial exchange. Rather, French historians of the third *Annales* generation focused largely on France, and usually on one region of France. The best known of these great *theses* were *Les Paysans de Languedoc* (1966) by Emmanuel Le Roy Ladurie and *Beauvais et le Beauvaisis* (1960) by Pierre Goubert.
>
> (HUNT, 1986, p. 212)

More recently, world-systems frameworks, such as that of Immanuel Wallerstein (WALLERSTEIN, 1974), based on distinguishing the dynamic economic–geographical core macro-regions, such as Northwest Europe after 1700, from relatively peripheral or exploited ones, such as Eastern and Southern Europe; theoretical frameworks such as that of E. W. Fox (FOX, 1971) posing an opposition between 'commercial' and 'feudal' regions within countries such as France; and internal–colonial or mode of production arguments, such as those of Michael Hechter (HECHTER, 1976) and William Brustein (BRUSTEIN, 1988), identifying different types of regions within states with respect to political and social characteristics, represent different ways of explicitly incorporating regions into social–historical or economic analysis. Even greater emphasis on the role of regions as contexts for social invention and political affiliation can be found in the work of the economic historians Sidney Pollard (POLLARD, 1981) and Gary Herrigel (HERRIGEL, 1996), of economic sociologists such as Arnaldo Bagnasco (BAGNASCO, 1977) on local economic development and the social construction of the market, and of economic geographers such as Michael Storper (STORPER, 1995) and Allen Scott (SCOTT, 2001) on the importance of regionalized agglomeration economies to the overall geography of economic growth. Much research, however, tends to operate on an implicit rather than an explicit conception of region. Even as they adopt regional frameworks in their research, scholars are not always very self-conscious about the nature of the geographical divisions that they use.

ARGUING WITH REGIONS

Using mainly European examples, it could be said that five modes of usage of regions tend to have dominated across the social sciences. The first consists of *macro-regions* as units for the pursuit of total history. The *locus classicus* of this approach is BRAUDEL's *La Méditerranée et Le Monde Méditerranéen* (1949). The claim is that over long periods of time regions emerge based on functional linkages that then continue to distinguish one from the other. Such regions need not be ocean basins such as the Black Sea, the Indian Ocean or the Mediterranean. They can be units determined by their relative orientations towards certain modes of production and exchange.

The example of FOX's *History in Geographic Perspective: The Other France* (1971) illustrates this case, as the logic of the argument need not be restricted to a single national setting. Struck by a France that seemed repeatedly to divide itself since the Revolution of 1789 into two socio-political divisions around 'order' and 'movement', Fox states that 'For an American, it was natural to begin by seeking to identify these societies in sectional terms' (p. 13). Unlike the United States, however, France has had nothing like a regional–sectional civil war since at least the medieval Albigensian Crusade. Fox finds the regional division in the different communications orbits that have emerged down the years between a Paris-oriented interior France and an externally oriented commercial France along the coasts. He gives the argument a transcendental appeal by claiming that the opposition between an agricultural–military society, on the one hand, and a commercial–seagoing society, on the other, can be found in ancient Greece and in medieval Europe as much as in the modern world. What Fox is distinguishing between is a subsistence society dependent on control of territory and a waterborne commercial society dependent on access to flows of goods and capital. The two 'types' of society achieved their most characteristic forms during the 'long' century between the revolutions of the sixteenth century and the French Revolution. The social commentators of the time, such as Charles-Louis Montesquieu, clearly recognized them. Fox uses the dichotomous model as a framework for exploring the course of French social history since 1789, but accepts that by the Fifth Republic the opposition between two societies had largely run its material course, even if the legacy of the two Frances still 'left its imprint upon the political preferences of their members' (FOX-GENOVESE and GENOVESE, 1989, p. 237).

Fox's regionalization rests on what can be called a fixed spatial division of labour between two different modes of production which though present within the boundaries of the same state nevertheless have both fractured that state and led to distinctive social orders (class struggles, inheritance systems, religious and political affiliations, etc.) within it. Thus, the history of France (and, Fox suggests, many other states) cannot be understood satisfactorily as a singular whole but only in terms of the opposition and interaction between 'two Frances' based upon competing principles of social and economic organization. Though articulated in the setting of a specific (perhaps the quintessential) nation-state, Fox's argument is similar to other macro-regional ones in pointing to the *persistence* of regional patterns of social and political behaviour as the foundation for interpreting other social phenomena. Whether such phenomena can be invariably reduced to the opposition is, of course, another thing entirely.

The second and perhaps most common mode of use is that of dividing up Europe into *functional regions* to examine specific phenomena such as class transitions and transformations of rule, industrialization, urbanization, and trade. Sometimes these regions are at a macro-scale, as with the divisions between Western and Eastern Europe (or between Western, Central/Middle and Eastern Europe) in such works as BARRINGTON MOORE, JR's *Social Origins of Dictatorship and Democracy* (1960) (although this study extends in scope well beyond Europe per se), PERRY ANDERSON's *Lineages of the Absolutist State* (1974), and WILLIAM MCNEILL's *The Shape of European History* (1974), and sometimes the regions are more fine-grained and sub-national, as in GARY HERRIGEL's study of German industrialization, *Industrial Constructions* (1996), CHARLES TILLY's work (for example, *Coercion, Capital, and European States, AD 990–1992*, 1991) on the logics of coercion and capital in European urbanization and state formation, and work on regional differences in artistic production as in CASTELNUOVO and GINZBURG's (1994) work on Italy.

Stein Rokkan's geographical template for Europe as a whole with respect to rates and degrees of state formation (for example, ROKKAN and URWIN, 1983), is an example of work that brings together the main west–east division of the continent with the centre–periphery differences that have developed within the emerging states. Among other things, Rokkan noted that adjacent states tended to develop similar forms of government and that there was a fairly systematic north–south and east–west dimensionality to this variation. He represented spatial variation between states in a series of schematic diagrams transforming Europe into an abstract space by drawing on crucial periods and processes in European socio-political history. Three periods/processes are seen as crucial. The first is the pattern of the peopling and vernacularization of language in the aftermath of the Roman Empire. This produces a geo-ethnic map of Europe based on the south–north influence of the Romans and a west to east physical geography/ethnic geography of the settlement of new groups and their differentiation from one another. The second is the pattern of economic development and urbanization in medieval/early modern Europe, distinguishing a south–north axis drawn largely with reference to the impact of the Protestant Reformation and the Catholic Counter-Reformation and an east–west axis with strong seaward states to the west, a belt of city-states in the centre, and a set of weak landward states to the east. The third is the way in which recent democratization has produced different responses in different regions with smaller, unitary states in the extreme west, larger, unitary states flanking them to the east, a belt of federal and consociational states in the centre, and a set of 'retrenched empires' and successor authoritarian states yet further to the east.

This geographical template draws attention to systematic geographic variation in the forms of European states and how they arose out of different combinations of social and economic processes. It is particularly original in pointing out the distinctiveness of a long-established urbanized region running from Italy in the south to Flanders in the north. But this use of regionalization neglects the ways in which the social divisions to which Rokkan refers (ethnic identities, city-states versus territorial states and empires, religious affiliations) are translated into political power and how this in turn affects the character of state formation. An entire stage in the process of creating the political map of Europe is missing. As TILLY (1991) put it, perhaps a little too forcefully:

> It is hard to see how Rokkan could have gotten much farther without laying aside his maps and concentrating on the analysis of the mechanisms of state formation.
>
> (p. 13)

The third use is to aggregate together lower-level units (counties, departments, etc.) without much regard for national boundaries to identify persisting patterns of demographic, social and political behaviour. Regions are thus *geographical areas of similarity* extending across space and time. This inductive approach to regionalization is most common in studies of demography, literacy, land tenure, economic growth and the development of political ideologies. This very different approach to the use of regions uses local government areas in different countries as the basis for identifying clusters of units that can cross national boundaries and that define formal regions sharing particular attributes to one degree or another. Maps can be made of such phenomena as family types, fertility and mortality rates, rates of suicide, types of land holding, modes of agrarian organization (share cropping, peasant proprietorship, capitalist agriculture, etc.), literacy, religious practice (for example, attendance at Catholic mass), levels of industrial employment, civic culture, and levels of support for ideological parties of the right and the left (for example, GOODY *et al.*, 1976; LE BRAS, 1979; GRAFF, 1981; PUTNAM, 1993). These maps can also be correlated to see to what extent the various phenomena co-vary spatially with one another. For example, high suicide rates correlate highly in some places with high rates of illegitimate births and high female autonomy (for example, much of Sweden and Finland), but elsewhere, as in Southern Portugal, they seem to correlate more with something absent in the rest of Europe, perhaps going back to the recovery of the region from Islamic conquest, matrilineal inheritance of names, equal relations in families between parents, and a nuclear ideal of family (TODD, 1990, pp. 56–61).

EMANUEL TODD's *L'invention d'Europe* (1990) can be taken as a good example of this genre of usage. Various hypotheses about secularization of European society, the impact of industrialization, and the persisting effects on politics and social life of historic forms of household and family organization have been investigated by

Todd and others taking this approach. Todd is perhaps the most forceful in his claim for basing the incidence of a wide range of social phenomena on the prior spatial distribution of family types. He shows quite convincingly that family types (communal, nuclear, stem, etc.), inheritance customs, parent–child relations, and certain features of fertility in Europe do not conform to national-level patterns. Rather, there are both localized clusters within countries and regional groupings which criss-cross national boundaries. What is less convincing is the degree to which other social phenomena are truly the outcome of the 'underlying' demographic and familial characteristics rather than mediated regionally by a range of economic and social pressures that have extra-regional rather than historically accrued local sources. The tendency is to interpret rigidly regional patterns of 'higher-level' phenomena (such as political ideologies or civic cultures) as arising from long-term regional patterns of familial and demographic features (for example, SABETTI, 1996).

Fourth is the usage associated with the so-called *new regionalism*. This refers to those theoretical and policy perspectives that directly relate the relevance of regions to the economic restructuring of national economies in the face of globalization and supranational regionalization (above all with the European Union). The overall focus is on the 'hollowing out' of national economies and the regulatory response to this as manifested in the growth of regional-level initiatives to manage economic challenges. The new regionalism literature has a number of strands. One strand emphasizes newly empowered regions arising as a consequence of central government and cross-national border initiatives in response to economic restructuring, sometimes seeing these as a direct administrative response (for example, BRENNER, 2004) sometimes more as a political response to the dilemmas facing states in contemporary circumstances (for example, LAGENDIJK, 2007). Other strands stress either the development of global-city regions (for example, SCOTT, 1998) or the emergence of metropolitan-level political coalitions pursuing resolutions to local economic challenges (for example, COX, 2010). All these approaches tend to share economic–functionalist logic in that regions are seen as a 'response' to the 'need' for a new regulatory framework in the face of economic change (AGNEW, 2012). Other major criticisms include a tendency to reify regions as fixed containers rather than seeing them in relational terms as only operational in relation to the networks and flows that define them (for example, ALLEN and COCHRANE, 2007) and the dissolution of the state as a continuing defining actor in their formation and operation (for example, THERBORN, 2011). Nevertheless, the new regionalism can still be seen as an important vehicle for the introduction of regions into ongoing debates about globalization. Indeed, this literature serves as an important source for many of the arguments deployed by the articles in this issue.

Finally, the explosion of regionalist and separatist movements in Europe has stimulated considerable interest in the emergence and roots of regional identities in relation to national ones. *Sub-national regional identities* have become the focus for social historians and others concerned with the history and restructuring of European political identities (for example, APPLEGATE, 1999). Nations and regions are typically understood as categories of practice that are reified or given separate existence by people struggling to define themselves as members of this or that group. Much work seeks to identify the diversity of group identities in contemporary Europe and how they have arisen. A distinctive current, however, tries to relate regional to national identities as they have arisen over the past several hundred years. The basic premise is that regional and national identities are often intertwined rather than necessarily oppositional and that only with the rise of globalization and the emergence of supranational agencies such as the European Union have these connections undergone significant challenge (for example, MURPHY, 1993; KEATING, 1995).

Charlotte Tacke, for example, in comparing the historical construction of French and German national identities, claims that

> the individual's identification with the nation ... rests on a large variety of social ties, which simultaneously forge the links between the individual and the nation.
>
> (TACKE, 1994, p. 698)

The most important ties are those constituted in regions, which serve as 'cultural and social space' for 'civic communication'. Local bourgeoisies in both countries created renewed regional identities at precisely the same time that the symbols they selected (honouring ancient heroes in statues, for example) were made available for appropriation by nation-building elites. In these cases, therefore, regional identities fed into the national ones and were thus frequently lost from sight.

Elsewhere in Europe, however, regional identities, particularly those coming to the fore recently, appear more as acts of opposition than of accommodation to national ones (AGNEW, 1995; PAASI, 2002). This is the message not only of the internal–colonial and mode of production approaches, but also of constructivist approaches that emphasize the tendency of region and nation to become synonymous in some social–cultural contexts. Resistant regional identities, such as the Irish and Basque ones, have taken shape around claims to nationhood. Unlike the French and German cases, they have tried to develop alternative spatial mythologies to the dominant nations within their respective states (the English and the Castilian, respectively), but are often forced into terms of debate and the use of institutional forms that signify the inevitability of at least a degree of accommodation to the territorial status quo. Of course, the resistant regional identities suggest that the word 'region' in political usage is itself dependent on the prior existence of nation-states of which the regions are presently part but could possibly become their own nations in the future.

One lesson is clear: if all of the other meanings of the term discussed previously are neglected in pursuit of the currently fashionable interest in political regionalism and regional identities, then one will be left with thin intellectual gruel indeed – regions are only potential nations in the making. The attempt to find an alternative regional accounting system to that of the dominant national one would then have come full circle.

CONTROVERSIES ABOUT THE USES OF REGIONS

Down the years, seven disputes or controversies about regions have episodically flared up both to challenge and to enliven the generally consensus view of regions as homogeneous, self-evident blocks of terrestrial space. This article cannot hope to cover each of these in great detail. The purpose is to give the flavour of what has been at stake in arguing with regions as a modus operandi in social science research and show how the various disputes show up in subsequent articles in this special issue.

The first controversy has been about the ways in which the areas designated as regions at whatever geographical scale (local, sub-national, continental or global) are integrated and/or exhibit homogeneous characteristics. Typically, regions are thought of as areas exhibiting uniformity with respect to one or more characteristics. This view has been challenged by scholars who claim that such regions are often purely *formal*, in the sense that they are the result of aggregating smaller geographical units (census districts, municipalities, provinces, etc.) according to statistical similarity without attending to what it is that binds the region together with respect to *functional* ties. Functional ties include the network/circulation linkages (transport, migration, trade and capital flows) and central-place (settlement hierarchy) links that create distinctive regions and from which their other characteristics are derived (as described, for example, in HOHENBERG and LEES, 1994).

Of course, regions are often politically defined by governments (PATRIARCA, 1994) and political movements (such as separatist ones). They can also have affective meaning for local populations (APPLEGATE, 1999). In such cases, the absolute formal/functional opposition fails to account for the subjective identifications that people can have with formal regions even if it continues to serve a useful analytic purpose more generally in questioning the territorial homogeneity assumption on which much regionalization tends to rely (LÈVY, 1997). Institutionalization of regions as legitimate political forms seems particularly crucial in underpinning their role in building regional political identities and in persisting as effective agents of economic development (see Garcia-Alvarez and Trillo-Santamaria, in this issue). As Zimmerbauer (in this issue) emphasizes for the Barents Sea supranational region, however, top-down designations rarely seem enough for either. There must be some impetus from local actors.

The recent call to think of geographic space in entirely relational and non-territorial terms can be thought of as extending the idea of functionality, but also perhaps brings into doubt the entire idea of regionalizing at all (JONES, 2009). Functionality relies on a relative view of space in which the objects and processes of interest are differentiated in some way by how they relate in one region from how they do in another. From this viewpoint, regions are still territorial entities, even though they are integrated differently than when they are thought of as absolute spaces, as with the formal sense of a region. On a relational view, regions can no longer be ascribed either a classificatory or a political–economic–cultural role in themselves, but only as clusters of nodes and flows that regions are held to represent. In this perspective, all that counts is connectivity across space (for example, AMIN, 2004). Dividing space territorially misses precisely what space does: it relates objects and has no meaning apart from them. Yet, of course, as much of the research discussed by AMIN (2004) attests, 'regions' are powerful sources of social and political identification and social life remains bounded and regionalized in ways that defy the presumed total 'openness' of space on a relational basis. An epistemological obsession with the nature of space can miss the ontological significance of regions for practical life (ENTRIKIN, 2011; MUSSO, 2003; see Ramutsindela, in this issue).

The uses and limitations of the 'relational debate' are examined at some length by Varró and Lagendijk (in this issue). In identifying two groups of scholars subscribing to 'radical' and 'moderate' positions on relationality, they suggest that the groups tend to argue past one another because the former tend to have an ontological understanding of relationality, whereas the latter see it in terms of empirical connectedness. The solution, they say, is to think of regions when defined as possible instruments for economic policies and political representation, as being 'constituted relationally through agonistic struggles'. In other words, regions come to exist and take on significance only in the context of their wider political and institutional settings. Harrison (in this issue) reaches a somewhat different conclusion when in surveying the course of the 'debate' over the years he argues that in the case of a North West England region a spatial development strategy initially configured around a network conception could not escape 'the territorial mosaic of politico-administrative units' inherited from the past. To the extent that the relational view relies on the practical character of networks, therefore, it cannot ever escape from the equally practical constraints exercised by the powers of existing territorial–administrative arrangements (also see Zimmerbauer, in this issue).

Another dispute, mentioned at the outset, and going back to Immanuel Kant, concerns the belief that regions are real in the sense of marking off truly distinctive bits of the Earth's surface versus the view that they are the product solely of political and social conventions that impose regions on a much more geographically variegated world. There is a visceral tension between the idea that something is *real* and that is *constructed*. But are they indeed as mutually exclusive as the dispute suggests? The opposition between the real and the conventional has once again arisen to prominence in recent disputes among geographers over the character of region and place (ENTRIKIN, 1996, 2011; SACK 1997; LEWIS and WIGEN, 1997). On the one hand, the real is like the body in Philosophy's mind–body problem. It is tangible, touchable and empirically visible. On the other hand, the constructed is like the mind making sense of itself and the body. Consciousness is prior to how the body works. Each of these positions rests on the same confusion between an object (a region) and an idea about that object (regional schemes). Regions both reflect differences in the world and ideas about the geography of such differences. They cannot be reduced simply to one or the other (AGNEW, 1999). As Varró and Lagendijk (in this issue) argue, this confusion continues to bedevil much recent writing about regions.

A third controversy has focused on the tendency to see regions as fixed for long time periods rather than mutable and subject to reformulation, even over relatively short periods. Leading figures in the *Annales* school, such as Marc Bloch and Fernand Braudel, world-systems theorists, and demographic historians have been particularly drawn to the idea of macro-regions as the settings for long-term structural history. At the same time others, particularly local historians and regional geographers, have invested heavily in the idea of fixed regional divisions and unique regional entities within countries, owing their uniqueness to 'internal' characteristics. One thinks, for example, of such an influential study as ROBERT PUTNAM's *Making Democracy Work* (1993) which posits a set of Italian regional differences in political mores more or less immutable since the tenth century AD. In recent years, however, with the increased sense of a world subject to time–space compression, following the opening of national borders to increased trade, capital, and labour mobility and the shrinkage of global communication and transportation costs, regions are increasingly seen as *contingent* on the changing character of the larger contexts in which they are embedded rather than dependent on *unique* features of a more-or-less permanent nature (JOHNSTON *et al.*, 1990; GUPTA and FERGUSON, 1997). This understanding animates Rutherford and Holmes (in this issue), who show how shifts in the organization of automotive industry workplaces within the Ontario (Canada)–Great Lakes (United States) cross-border region owe as much to the rapidly changing dynamics of demands on labour force characteristics as to relatively stable national–institutional traditions.

Less noted but perhaps more importantly with respect to the meaning of regions for social history and economic geography, a debate has periodically erupted over regions as fundamental *contexts* for social life as opposed to mere accounting devices or *case study settings* taken as examples of national or Europe-wide norms and standards. With respect to industrialization, for example, POLLARD (1981) has argued that regions are the relevant entities for considering the processes whereby different industries developed. Each brings different combinations of attributes crucial to the establishment of specific industries. In like manner, social and political processes relating to household structures, class formation, and political movements can all be thought of as embedded in regional and local contexts, 'the physical arenas in which human interaction takes place' (WEITZ, 1995, p. 291), rather than as abstract or national-level processes only manifesting themselves regionally, as presumed by the idea of the regional case study. The case study is always of something that is presumably not regional as such, hence the reference to 'case study'. MARTIN and SUNLEY (1996) made much the same point when criticizing the conception of region in the 'new' geographical economics for reducing regions entirely to externality containers rather than seeing them as also involving institutional and cultural contexts that can also systematically affect regional patterns of growth and change. An important contribution of Thomas (in this issue) is to show how much economic development in a region (in this case the South West of England) owes to harnessing the region's accumulated creative impulses for self-governance as much as the economic organization of the end-products for sale elsewhere.

A fifth controversy has involved the tendency to represent the character of regions by locating them along a temporal continuum from the *backward* or traditional at one end and the *advanced* or modern at the other. This conversion of time into space has been particularly important in historicizing and exoticizing certain subnational regions (such as the Italian South, the Scottish Highlands and Andalusia) and countries as a whole (such as Italy or Ireland) into a schema representing the historical trajectory of Europe as a whole (AGNEW, 1996). Thus, presumably isolated and remote regions with lower levels of economic growth than more central regions are viewed as lagging behind the more advanced ones, notwithstanding the long-term ties that bind such regions into their particular nation-states. This tendency has given rise to a contending view that poorer regions are poor because the richer ones have become rich at their expense (as in HECHTER, 1976, on the British Isles). In other words, it is not a temporal lag but rather spatial exploitation that lies behind regional differences in economic development and social change. Though also criticizing 'radical' relational conceptions of regions, Ramutsindela (in this issue) illustrates neatly how much the relative location of regions within a country, in this case South Africa, depends on coeval power relations across regions rather than on the inherent character of different regions judged according to a temporal scale categorizing differences in economic development.

A sixth controversy arises because regions are often seen as diametrically opposed in character to the realities of population movement that are such an evident part of many people's lives. In other words, regions are simple spatial containers that cannot possibly match the dynamism of mobility. This position animates many of the relativist and relational critiques of regionalizing mentioned previously. In fact, the conventional territorial sense of region need not be seen in such a light. Much recent attention to place as a concept has attempted to mediate between the relatively fixed and the relatively mobile in defining geographical contexts. In this construction, nomads, travellers, temporary migrants, commuters and other itinerants, even while inherently mobile, also define places (more specifically, locales) with which to move and in which to rest and interact. Thus, rather than the opposite to or disruptive of place or region, *mobility* is an inherent part of how many places are defined and operate (CRESSWELL, 2004).

For example, commuting paths are very much part of the experience of place of many people and migrants often maintain social ties over long distances and thus acquire different senses of place than those of their more spatially rooted neighbours. The kinship, migrant itineraries and ritual exchanges that form personhood do not necessarily require long histories of sedentary habitation. In a 'frontier region' of East Java, Indonesia, for example, the anthropologist RETSIKAS (2007) noted that place is a tool of sociality; by which he means that because people

> move and stop, settle, and move again … places are shifting and changing, always becoming through people's engagements – material as well as discursive – in, through, and with them. … In other words, place is not where social relations simply take place, but an inherent ingredient of their modalities of actualization.
>
> (pp. 971–972)

The relational views of regions discussed by Varró and Lagendijk and others in this issue seem particularly appropriate in taking population mobility into account in their approach to regions. Rather than fixed containers it is the relative openness/closedness of regions to the dynamics of population movement that defines one of the ways in which they mediate between established social routines and new possibilities introduced from outside.

From this point of view, contexts of place and time are perhaps not best thought of as invariably regional (in the sense of sub-national) or local, although they frequently have elements of one or both. Rather, they are best considered as always located somewhere with some contexts more stretched over space (such as means of mass communication and the spatial division of labour) and others more localized (school, workplace and residential interactions). The balance of influence on social and political choices between and among the stretched and more local contextual processes can be expected to change over time, giving rise to subsequent shifts in political outlooks and affiliations (for example, NICHOLLS, 2009). So, for example, as foreign companies introduce branch plants, trade unions must negotiate new work practices, which, in turn, erode long-accepted views of the roles of managers and employees. In due course, this sort of *configuration of contextual changes* can, for example, give an opening to a new political party or a redefined old one as interests, identities and political heuristics (yardsticks) shift and upset established political affiliations (for example, AGNEW, 2007; CUTLER, 2007). But changes must always fit into existing cultural templates and cleavages that often show amazing resilience as well as adaptation. Identities of regions can persist as influences on behaviour even as regional consciousness, in the sense of lives buried in singular regional contexts, weakens (PAASI, 2002). Indeed, much of the political regionalism increasingly found in different parts of the world reflects the former as much as or more than the latter. The overall point about the openness of places or regions is made well by Doreen Massey, when she wrote:

> This is a notion of place where specificity (local uniqueness, a sense of place) derives not from some mythical internal roots nor from a history of isolation – now to be disrupted by globalization – but precisely from the absolute particularity of the mixture of influences found together there.
>
> (MASSEY, 1999, p. 22)

Finally, perhaps the dominant sense of many scholars about regions, particularly of regions at the sub-national level, has been of entities destined to fade in significance with the creation of national markets, the emergence of national political parties with more or less uniform support across all regions, and the spread of national cultures robbing local and regional identities of their specificity. This *nationalization* or modernization thesis, articulated in works ranging from EUGEN WEBER's general study of late-nineteenth century France, *Peasants into Frenchmen* (1976), to SUSAN COTTS WATKINS's survey of demographic indicators (fertility rates, women's age at marriage, etc.) across Western Europe between 1870 and 1960, *From Provinces into Nations* (1991), relies on the premise that social organization in Europe has undergone a fundamental shift from local and regional levels to the national scale. This premise is a shaky one, however. Not only can some of the data in a study such as that of Watkins be interpreted to indicate re-provincialization after a period of nationalization, but also nationalization of demographic indicators need not indicate the substitution of regional sources of social influence by national ones. Rather, demographic behaviour may still be mediated through the regionally specific routines and institutions of everyday life yet yield increasing similarity of behavioural outcomes across regions. The same goes for religious affiliations, voting, consumption and other types of social behaviour, some of which betray regional patterns that conform little or at all with national political boundaries (TODD, 1990; AGNEW, 1987; CARTOCCI, 1994). All of the articles in this issue speak to the continuing relevance of regions in various guises as continuing the work of mediating various forms of social, economic and political behaviour.

CONCLUSION

Arguing with regions has been a major feature of social science of various genres for many years. This article has briefly traced the lineage of some perspectives that are avowedly 'regionalist'. This can involve adopting a certain kind of region as a case study for a specific phenomenon or using regions as the basis for undertaking comparative analysis. The use of regions as an alternative classificatory framework to states has become well established, particularly at a time when the world is perhaps less meaningfully thought of entirely in state-based terms. This article has described with examples how regions have been used in a number of distinctive ways in actual social science research: as macro-regions, functional regions, geographical areas of similarity and sub-national regional political identities. There is hardly a singular or overarching conception of region inspiring all of these approaches. This reflects the fact that there have been numerous philosophical and theoretical challenges to arguing with regions. This article has surveyed seven of these, from the formal/functional, real/conventional and relational space to case study/context, mobility/fixity, backward/modern, and nationalization of regions. In a sense these disputes are irresolvable, resting as they do on competing assumptions about the nature of space and time, the relative roles of thought and practice in designating regions, and the methodological traditions of different research fields. What they also suggest, however, is a lively and continuing debate about the 'regional question' that extends across a number of disciplines. The region is often pronounced dead in a particular guise only to be resurrected in another. Altogether, one cannot seem to avoid arguing with regions in one mode or another. The articles in this special issue provide some interesting and distinctive ways in which dialogue about the uses and limitations of regions in argument can be pushed forward outside the constraints imposed by the typical usages necessarily assumed in the empirical work that regularly appears in the pages of *Regional Studies*.

By way of conclusion, it seems clear that there is no single way of best arguing with regions, at whatever geographical scale is of interest, and there are plenty of plausible arguments about what regions are and how regions should be used. Usage is so diverse and disputes over the substance and philosophy of regions are too contentious to allow for application of a single principle of division. This being the case, four general conceptions of regions in theory and practice can be suggested. The first concerns that of distinctive regional *communities* which can share identities as well as other socio-political characteristics. This conception is most useful for those focusing on the vagaries of sub-national political regionalism as well as the persistence of socio-political traits from the past. The second is that of geopolitical *territories* under construction and challenge, often on the peripheries of states. Apparently less relevant to the interests of many sociologists and economic historians, this one is useful for those concerned with the tensions and conflicts associated with state formation and disintegration. As authors such as Rokkan and Tilly have suggested, historically based lines of geographical fracture both between and within states have emerged due to differences in state-organization and the divergent histories of capitalism. The third is that of geographical *networks* which tie together regions through hierarchies of cities and their hinterlands. This is most relevant to studies of industrialization, urbanization and trade. The fourth is that of regional *societies* which now share a wide range of social and cultural characteristics. This fits the needs of those interested in associating social indicators to examine hypotheses about trends in social phenomena such as classes, family types, secularization, economic development and political activities by identifying formal regions.

The main lesson to be drawn from this analysis is that we should collectively invest in the plural of 'regional logics', tailoring usage to the problems at hand, rather than in a singular logic that simply replaces the romance of the nation-state with an equally simple and one-size-fits-all alternative geographical unit of account such as the ocean basin, the civilization, the administrative region or the global city-region. All of these, if one can forgive the pun, have their place.

REFERENCES

AGNEW J. A. (1987) *Place and Politics: The Geographical Mediation of State and Society*. Allen & Unwin, London.

AGNEW J. A. (1995) The rhetoric of regionalism: the Northern League in Italian politics, 1983–94, *Transactions of the Institute of British Geographers* **20**, 156–172.

AGNEW J. A. (1996) Time into space: the myth of 'backward' Italy in modern Europe, *Time and Society* **5**, 27–45.

AGNEW J. A. (1999) Regions on the mind does not equal regions of the mind, *Progress in Human Geography* **23**, 91–96.

AGNEW J. A. (2007) Remaking Italy: place configurations and electoral politics under the Second Republic, *Modern Italy* **12**, 17–38.

AGNEW J. A. (Forthcoming 2012) The 'new regionalism' and the politics of the regional question, in LOUGHLIN J., KINCAID J. and SWENDEN W. (Eds) *The Routledge Handbook of Regionalism and Federalism*. Routledge, London.

ALLEN J. and COCHRANE A. (2007) Beyond the territorial fix: regional assemblages, politics and power, *Regional Studies* **49**, 1161–1175.

AMIN A. (2004) Regions unbound: towards a new politics of place, *Geografiska Annaler B* **36**, 33–44.

ANDERSON P. (1974) *Lineages of the Absolutist State*. New Left Books, London.

APPLEGATE C. (1999) A Europe of regions: reflections on the historiography of sub-national places in modern times, *American Historical Review* **104**, 1156–1182.

BAGNASCO A. (1977) *Tre Italie: la problematica territoriale dello sviluppo*. Il Mulino, Bologna.

BRAUDEL F. (1949) *La Méditerranée et Le Monde Méditerranéen à l'époque de Philippe II*. Armand Colin, Paris; English trans. by REYNOLDS S. (1972) *The Mediterranean and the Mediterranean World in the Age of Philip II*. HarperCollins, New York, NY.

BRAUDEL F. (1986) *L'identité de la France*. Editions Arthaud, Paris; English trans. by REYNOLDS S. (1989) *The Identity of France*, Vol. I: *History and Environment*. Harper & Row, New York, NY.

BRENNER N. (2004) *New State Spaces*. Oxford University Press, New York, NY.

BRENNER N. (2009) Open questions on state rescaling, *Cambridge Journal of Regions, Economy and Society* **2**, 123–139.

BRUSTEIN W. (1988) *The Social Origins of Political Regionalism: France, 1849–1981*. University of California Press, Berkeley, CA.

BRZEZINSKI Z. (1997) *The Grand Chessboard: American Primacy and its Geostrategic Imperative*. Basic Books, New York, NY.

CARTOCCI R. (1994) *Fra Lega e Chiesa: L'Italia in cerca di integrazione*. Il Mulino, Bologna.

CASTELNUOVO E. and GINZBERG C. (1994) Centre and periphery, in BURKE P. (Ed.) *History of Italian Art*, Vol. I, pp. 28–130. Polity, Cambridge.

COX K. R. (1998) Spaces of dependence, spaces of engagement and the politics of scale, or: looking for local politics, *Political Geography* **17**, 1–23.

COX K. R. (2009) 'Rescaling the state' in question, *Cambridge Journal of Regions, Economy and Society* **2**, 107–121.

COX K. R. (2010) The problem of metropolitan governance and the politics of scale, *Regional Studies* **44**, 215–227.

CRESSWELL T. (2004) *Place: A Short Introduction*. Blackwell, Oxford.

CUTLER F. (2007) Context and attitude formation: social interaction, default information, or local interests?, *Political Geography* **26**, 575–600.

DANN O. (1989) La regione. Una cornice elastica per la nuova storia sociale, in ANDREUCCI F. and PESCAROLO A. (Eds) *Gli spazi del potere*, pp. 116–134. Usher, Florence.

DUARA P. (1995) *Rescuing History from the Nation: Questioning Narratives of Modern China*. University of Chicago Press, Chicago, IL.

ENTRIKIN J. N. (1996) Place and region 2, *Progress in Human Geography* **20**, 215–221.

ENTRIKIN J. N. (2011) Region and regionalism, in AGNEW J. A. and LIVINGSTONE D. N. (Eds) *Sage Handbook of Geographical Knowledge*, pp. 344–356. Sage, London.

FOX E. W. (1971) *History in Geographic Perspective: The Other France*. Norton, New York, NY.

FOX-GENOVESE E. and GENOVESE E. D. (1989) Social classes and class struggles in geographic perspective, in GENOVESE E. D. and HOCHBERG L. (Eds) *Geographic Perspectives in History*, pp. 226–242. Blackwell, Oxford.

GOODY J., THIRSK J. and THOMPSON E. P. (1976) *Family and Inheritance in Rural Western Europe*. Cambridge University Press, Cambridge.

GRAFF H. J. (Ed.) (1981) *Literacy and Social Development in the West*. Cambridge University Press, Cambridge.

GUPTA A. and FERGUSON J. (Eds) (1997) *Culture, Power, and Place: Explorations in Critical Anthropology*. Duke University Press, Durham, NC.

HARTSHORNE R. (1939) *The Nature of Geography*. Association of American Geographers, Washington, DC.

HECHTER M. (1976) *Internal Colonialism: The Celtic Fringe in British National Development*. University of California Press, Berkeley, CA.

HERRIGEL G. (1996) *Industrial Constructions: The Sources of German Industrial Power*. Basic Books, New York, NY.

HOHENBERG P. and LEES L. H. (1994) *The Making of Urban Europe, 1000–1990*. Harvard University Press, Cambridge, MA.

HUNT L. (1986) French history in the last twenty years: the rise and fall of the *Annales* paradigm, *Journal of Contemporary History* **21**, 209–224.

HUNTINGTON S. P. (1993) The clash of civilizations, *Foreign Affairs* **72**, 23–49.

JOHNSTON R.J., HAUER J. and HOEKVELD G.A. (Eds) (1990) *Regional Geography: Current Developments and Future Prospects*. Routledge, London.

JONAS A. E. G. (2011) Region and place: regionalism in question, *Progress in Human Geography* **35(1)**, 76–93.

JONES M. (2009) Phase space: geography, relational thinking, and beyond, *Progress in Human Geography* **33**, 487–506.

KEATING M. (1995) Europeanism and regionalism, in JONES B. and KEATING M. (Eds) *The European Union and the Regions*, pp. 1–22. Clarendon, Oxford.

KELLY P. (1997) *Checkerboards and Shatterbelts: the Geopolitics of South America*. University of Texas Press, Austin, TX.

KIMBLE G. H. T. (1951) The inadequacy of the regional concept, in STAMP L. D. and WOOLDRIDGE S. W. (Eds) *London Essays in Geography*, pp. 151–174. Longman Green, London.

LAGENDIJK A. (2007) The accident of the region: a strategic relational perspective on the construction of the region's significance, *Regional Studies* **41**, 1193–1208.

LE BRAS H. (1979) *L'enfant et la famille dans les pays de l'OCDE*. Organisation for Economic Co-operation and Development (OECD), Paris.

LÈVY J. (1997) *Europe: une géographie*. Hachette, Paris.

LEWIS M. and WIGEN K. (1997) *The Myth of Continents: A Critique of Metageography*. University of California Press, Berkeley, CA.

MACLEOD G. (2001) The new regionalism reconsidered: globalization, regulation and the recasting of political–economic space, *International Journal of Urban and Regional Research* **25**, 804–829.

MARTIN R. and SUNLEY P. (1996) Paul Krugman's geographical economics and its implications for regional development theory: a critical assessment, *Economic Geography* **72**, 259–292.

MASSEY D. (1979) In what sense a regional problem?, *Regional Studies* **13**, 233–243.

MASSEY D. (1999) *Power-Geometries and the Politics of Space–Time*. Hettner Lecture 1998. Institute of Geography, University of Heidelberg, Heidelberg.

MCNEILL W. (1974) *The Shape of European History*. Harper & Row, New York, NY.

MOORE B. Jr (1960) *Social Origins of Dictatorship and Democracy: Lord and Peasant in the Making of the Modern World*. Beacon, Boston, MA.

MURPHY A. B. (1993) Emerging regional linkages within the European Community: challenging the dominance of the state, *Tijdschrift voor Economische en Sociale Geografie* **84**, 103–118.

MUSSO P. (2003) *Critique des réseaux*. Presses Universitaires de France, Paris.

NEUMANN R. P. (2010) Political ecology II: theorizing region, *Progress in Human Geography* **34**, 368–374.

NICHOLLS W. (2009) Place, networks, space: theorizing the geographies of social movements, *Transactions of the Institute of British Geographers* **34**, 78–93.

PAASI A. (2002) Bounded spaces in the mobile world: deconstructing 'regional identity', *Tijdschrift voor Economische en Sociale Geografie* **93**, 137–148.

PATRIARCA S. (1994) Statistical nation building and the consolidation of regions in Italy, *Social Science History* **18**, 359–376.

PLETSCH C. E. (1981) The three worlds, or the division of social scientific labor, circa 1950–1975, *Comparative Studies in Society and History* **23**, 565–590.

POLLARD S. (1981) *Peaceful Conquest: The Industrialization of Europe*, 1760–1970. Oxford University Press, New York, NY.

PUTNAM R. (1993) *Making Democracy Work: Civic Traditions in Modern Italy*. Princeton University Press, Princeton, NJ.

RETSIKAS K. (2007) Being and place: movement, ancestors, and personhood in East Java, Indonesia, *Journal of the Royal Anthropological Institute* **13**, 969–986.

ROKKAN S. and URWIN D. (1983) *Economy, Territory, Identity: Politics of West European Peripheries*. Sage, London.

SABETTI F. (1996) Path dependency and civic culture: some lessons from Italy about interpreting social experiments, *Politics and Society* **24**, 19–44.

SACK R. D. (1997) *Homo Geographicus: A Framework for Action, Awareness and Moral Concern*. Johns Hopkins University Press, Baltimore, MD.

SCHWARZ H. and DIENST R. (Eds) (1996) *Reading the Shape of the World: Toward an International Cultural Studies*. Westview, Boulder, CO.

SCOTT A. J. (1998) *Regions and the World Economy: The Coming Shape of Global Production, Competition, and Political Order*. Oxford University Press, Oxford.

SCOTT A. J. (Ed.) (2001) *Global City-Regions*. Oxford University Press, Oxford.

STORPER M. (1995) The resurgence of regional economies, ten years later: the region as a nexus of untraded interdependencies, *European Urban and Regional Studies* **2**, 191–221.

TACKE C. (1994) The nation in the region: national movements in Germany and France in the 19th century, in BERAMENDI J. G., MAIZ R. and NUNEZ X. N. (Eds) *Nationalism in Europe: Past and Present*, Vol. 2, pp. 681–698. Universidad de Santiago de Compostela, Santiago de Compostela.

THERBORN G. (2011) End of a paradigm: the current crisis and the idea of stateless cities, *Environment and Planning A* **43**, 272–285.

TILLY C. (1991) *Coercion, Capital, and European States, AD 990–1992*. Blackwell, Oxford.

TODD E. (1990) *L'invention d'Europe*. Seuil, Paris.

WALLERSTEIN I. (1974) *The Modern World-System*, Vol. I: *Capitalist Agriculture and the Origins of the European World-Economy in the Sixteenth Century*. Academic Press, New York, NY.

WATKINS S. C. (1991) *From Provinces into Nations: Demographic Integration in Western Europe, 1870–1960*. Princeton University Press, Princeton, NJ.

WEBER E. (1976) *Peasants into Frenchmen: The Modernization of Rural France, 1870–1914*. Stanford University Press, Stanford CA.

WEITZ E. D. (1995) The realms of identities: a comment on class and politics in Milan, *Social Science History* **19**, 289–294.

Conceptualizing the Region – In What Sense Relational?

KRISZTINA VARRÓ and ARNOUD LAGENDIJK

Department of Human Geography and Spatial Planning, Nijmegen School of Management, Radboud University Nijmegen, the Netherlands.

VARRÓ K. and LAGENDIJK A. Conceptualizing the region – in what sense relational?, *Regional Studies*. Recently, the question of how to conceptualize the region seems to have created a division in geographical scholarship between those propagating the primacy of a relational view, on the one hand, and those defending the relevance of a territorial view, on the other. This paper argues that two main factors have impeded a fruitful discussion, to the extent that even some points of convergence have been neglected. First, the two strands have drawn, sometimes implicitly, on incommensurable philosophical assumptions. Second, scholars in favour of a relational view have at times made statements that do not fit well (some of) their philosophical sources of inspiration. The paper suggests the task of conceptualization is readdressed by following consistently a discourse–theoretical relational ontology.

VARRÓ K. and LAGENDIJK A. 概念化区域-就什么而言是相关的？区域研究。目前关于如何能够概念化区域这个问题在地理学研究者中出现了分歧，一部分研究者坚持相对性视角，另一部分则坚持领域相关性观点。本文认为，有两个原因阻碍了有益的探讨，涉及到对两者的联性的忽略。首先，两种思路是建立在不同的哲学假设上的。其次，学者关注相关性观点在很多情况下其论点并未完全符合其哲学假设。本文认为，概念化这一任务需要建立在语境理论相关性存在论的基础上。

VARRÓ K. et LAGENDIJK A. La conceptualisation de la région – dans quel sens est-ce relationelle?, *Regional Studies*. Au cours des dernières années, la conceptualisation de la région semble avoir divisé les spécialistes de la géographie entre ceux qui prônent d'un côté la primauté de l'approche relationnelle et de l'autre côté ceux qui justifient la pertinence de l'approche territoriale. Cet article affirme que deux facteurs principaux ont empêché un débat fructueux, dans la mesure où des points de vue convergents même ont été négligés. Primo, les deux fils ont quelquefois puisé, de façon implicite, dans des suppositions philosophiques incommensurables. Secundo, les spécialistes qui prônent l'approche relationnelle ont quelquefois fait des déclarations qui ne correspondent pas bien à (quelques-unes de) leurs sources d'inspiration philsophiques. Cet article laisse supposer que l'on devrait aborder à nouveau la tâche de la conceptualisation en poursuivant systématiquement une ontologie relationnelle fondée sur un discours théorique.

VARRÓ K. und LAGENDIJK A. Die Konzeptualisierung der Region – in welchem Sinne relational?, *Regional Studies*. In letzter Zeit hat die Frage, wie sich eine Region konzeptualisieren lässt, offenbar zu einer Spaltung der geografischen Wissenschaft geführt, wobei sich ein Lager für das Primat einer relationalen Perspektive ausspricht und das andere die Relevanz einer territorialen Perspektive verteidigt. In diesem Beitrag wird argumentiert, dass vor allem zwei Faktoren einer fruchtbaren Diskussion im Wege stehen und sogar zur Vernachlässigung einiger Konvergenzpunkte geführt haben. Zum einen haben sich beide Richtungen – manchmal implizit – auf inkommensurable philosophische Annahmen bezogen. Zum anderen haben manche Wissenschaftler, die eine relationale Perspektive verfechten, teilweise Aussagen getroffen, die nicht gut zu ihren philosophischen Inspirationsquellen (oder einigen davon) passen. Wir schlagen vor, die Aufgabe der Konzeptualisierung neu anzugehen und dabei konsequent eine diskurstheoretische relationale Ontologie zu befolgen.

VARRÓ K. y LAGENDIJK A. La conceptualización de la región; ¿en qué sentido relacional?, *Regional Studies*. Recientemente, la cuestión de cómo conceptualizar la región parece haber creado una división en la ciencia geográfica entre, por una parte, los que abogan por la primacía de una perspectiva relacional, y por otra, los que defienden la relevancia de una perspectiva territorial. En este artículo sostenemos que existen dos principales factores que han impedido un provechoso debate, de forma que incluso se han descuidado algunos puntos de convergencia. En primer lugar, los dos grupos se han basado, algunas veces implícitamente, en suposiciones filosóficas inconmensurables. En segundo lugar, los académicos a favor de una perspectiva relacional a veces han hecho declaraciones que no encajan bien (algunas) de sus fuentes filosóficas de inspiración. En este artículo sugerimos que se considere de nuevo la tarea de la conceptualización siguiendo sistemáticamente una ontología relacional de discurso teórico.

INTRODUCTION

> At the moment only philosophical confusion reigns supreme in much writing about place, space and region.
>
> (Agnew, 1999, p. 93)

In the past decade, a relational perspective on regions seems to have become widely accepted in geographic scholarship. This growing acceptance has been undoubtedly due to perceptions of an increasingly mobile and globally interconnected world. On the other hand, 'the relational turn' has not remained uncontested, with scholars taking divergent stances on 'how far' one should go in thinking about regions relationally, and on how one should conceptualize territories, which are still very much part of one spatial realities. The above divergence of views became manifest in particular in the writings of a group of UK-based scholars, centred largely on the issue of England's (the UK's) 'regional problem', and the newly emerging structures of regional governance under the post-1997 Labour governments. However, in spite of their limited spatial–temporal empirical focus, the above writings have supplied theoretical–conceptual arguments that are relevant for 'regional thinking' more generally. While the present review of these various arguments necessarily reproduces the narrow focus on 'New' Labour's England (UK) to some extent, the aim is to contribute to the broader academic debate on the conceptualization of 'the region', that is, both beyond the electoral defeat of Labour in 2010 and beyond the confines of England (the UK).

So what divergence of views is at issue – what has the 'relational versus territorial debate' been really about? The authors propose to discuss the debate as an exchange between two camps of scholars. The label 'radicals' will be used to refer to the group of scholars that has – although without explicitly identifying itself as a collective – advocated a perspective from which regions are understood primarily in relational terms. The other group, that of the self-proclaimed propagators of 'moderate relationalism' (Jones, 2009, p. 487), will be referred to hereafter briefly as the group of 'moderates'. Moderates have persistently countered radicals' emphasis on the relationality of regions, arguing that radicals' view tends to ignore actual regional differences/particularities, and how/why these differences/particularities persist. In fact, however, considering that radicals have not responded to moderate relationists' repeated criticisms, one cannot even speak of a real debate. Possibly, others share the authors' puzzlement about what radicals and moderates have really disagreed about, and how one can come to grips with the conceptualization of the region. This paper is motivated by the authors' conviction that in order to have a fruitful debate about the above, important task of conceptualization, the vocabulary of radicals and moderates needs to be reconsidered. Above all, more clarity is needed about the *kind of relations* that are said to be implicated in the construction of regions.

Based on the careful re-reading of some of the key writings of radicals and moderates, the authors of the present paper wish to argue that two main factors have acted against gaining greater clarity. First, moderate and radical relationists have been inspired by different – and incommensurable – meta-theoretical frameworks, namely (critical) realism, on the one hand, and various strands of post-structuralist thought, on the other hand. With scholars often not making their meta-theoretical choices explicit, it has been difficult, both for 'outsiders' and 'insiders' of the 'debate', to appreciate the arguments made. Second and importantly, the apprehension of various statements has become further complicated by the fact that some scholars, in particular radicals, have not consistently adhered to the assumptions of post-structuralist frameworks.

Although moderates' fervent criticism of radicals might suggest otherwise, this paper argues that on the whole the gap between the two strands is actually much smaller than one might think at first sight. Radicals and moderates have largely converged on emphasizing the inherently constructed character of regions, and adherents of both strands have done so on the basis of a shared concern with spatial justice. The authors conclude by arguing that the nexus between the construction of regional spaces and spatial justice can be adequately addressed through a consistently applied discourse-theoretical ontology.

RELATIONAL VERSUS TERRITORIAL: THE CONTOURS OF THE 'DEBATE'

The 'radical' versus 'moderate' 'debate' originates primarily in radical relationists' call to think of regions in relational terms. The above call is rooted in turn in radicals' concern with the 'regional problem' of the UK, that is, the persisting dominance of the South East vis-à-vis the rest of the UK. From the late 1990s on, radical scholars have claimed more and more ardently that one has to think of the UK's geography in relational terms if the UK's regional problem is to be addressed adequately (ALLEN *et al.*, 1998; AMIN *et al.*, 2003a; MASSEY, 2001, 2007). Actually, Doreen Massey, one of the leading figures of the radical group, already argued in 1979 that the lagging behind of certain regions cannot be explained in terms of characteristics internal to those areas; as she put it, 'inequalities do not result from a simple absolute deficiency' (MASSEY, 1979, p. 57). Accordingly, regional policy can only diminish spatial inequalities effectively if it is addressing the relations through which these inequalities are produced. Massey's above remarks were part of a broader effort of Marxist scholarship from the 1970s on to challenge the hegemonic positivist 'spatial science' that was inclined to assume an autonomous sphere of the spatial in which 'spatial relations' and 'spatial processes' produced spatial distributions. Marxist scholars stressed that all these spatial relations and spatial processes were actually social relations taking a particular geographical form. The aphorism of the 1970s was then that 'space is a social construct', meaning that space is constituted through social relations and material social practices. Actually, as MASSEY (1992) noted, the above seemed soon an inadequate characterization of the social/spatial relation. For although

> it is surely correct to argue that space is socially constructed, the one-sidedness of that formulation implied that geographical forms and distributions were simply outcomes, the end point of social explanation. Geographers would thus be the cartographers of the social sciences, mapping the outcomes of processes which could only be explained in other disciplines – sociology, economics, and so forth. [...] The events taking place all around us in the 1980s – the massive spatial restructuring both intra-nationally and internationally as an integral part of social and economic changes – made it plain that, in one way or another, 'geography matters'. And so, to the aphorism of the 1970s – that space is socially constructed – was added in the 1980s the other side of the coin: that the social is spatially constructed too, and that it makes a difference.
>
> (p. 70)

The above-mentioned, dialectical conceptualization of socio-spatial relations, as well as the understanding of regional spatiality through plural spatial interconnections, was carried forward by the seminal work of ALLEN *et al.* (1998) entitled *Rethinking the Region*. The above authors' drive to challenge the thinking of regions in terms of self-enclosed entities was rooted in the authors' deep-going discontent with the (un)treatment of the regional problem under Thatcherism. In particular, Allen *et al.*'s main message was that the celebration of the South East by the neoliberal right as a region that – in contrast to the North – had successfully adapted to the requirements of global market forces is based on a fundamentally wrong view of socio-spatial relations. Echoing MASSEY's (1979) above-mentioned point that lagging regions' position does not result from those regions' absolute deficiency, ALLEN *et al.* (1998) stressed that the South East 'in itself' does not possess any potential that explains its success. Rather,

> [t]he form of growth which took place in the south east was fundamentally influenced by state intervention and emergent forms of regulation, even if they sometimes appeared in the guise of 'deregulation'. State policy has been fundamental to the construction of the south east as 'growth region'.
>
> (p. 125)

Accordingly, Allen *et al.* proposed that the growth of the South East – and regions more generally – is rethought as existing in mutually constitutive interrelations with other regions. In line with this proposition, the above-mentioned authors argued that they did not draw precise boundaries to delimit their object of research (that is, the South East), because

> [o]nce drawn, such lines of containment convey the impression that all the social relations relevant to an understanding of growth in the region fall neatly within the boundaries. The result, effectively, is to empty the region of meaning and to fix its changing geography.
>
> (p. ix)

Ironically, following the 1997 election defeat of Conservatives, which was interpreted by the above scholars as resulting from the public discontent with the growth-oriented policies favouring the South East, soon it proved that making a case for relational spatial thinking is still timely. In fact, New Labour's evolving, territorially framed apparatus of spatial interventions made protagonists of relational thinking increasingly 'fed up' (MASSEY, 2001) and reassert their point about the inherent relationality of regions and places. Actually, it was as a response to this reasserted position that the stance of moderate relationists began to take shape. To turn back to Labour's spatial policies, it goes beyond the scope of this paper to give an extensive overview of the above-mentioned spatial interventions that targeted most notably the scale of neighbourhoods and (standard) regions. Briefly, considering the first, community-focused policy initiatives of neighbourhood renewal became considered central to tackling micro-scale territorial disparities. As analysts have noted, under New Labour, 'communities of place' became not only a priori assumed to exist, but also they have been given an ontological status as agents of (local) governance (RACO, 2003), expected to be mobilized, shaped and activated in the pursuit of the broader agenda of efficient service delivery (COCHRANE, 2003; IMRIE and RACO, 2003). Importantly, under New Labour, a container-view of socio-economic processes – or as AMIN (2005) aptly put it, the 'repackaging of the economy and society as a series of territorial entities' (p. 614) – was characteristic not only of interventions at the neighbourhood level. Regions became imagined also as

> a jurisdiction beyond which the actors have no real business or influence, and as a political community that, through mechanisms of deliberation, partnership, and shared interest, knows what is best for the locality and can deliver solutions that work for the common good.
>
> (AMIN, 2005, p. 618)

Scholars propagating a view on space as produced through interrelations have strongly criticized the shaping 'local boosterism' under New Labour. As the 'radical' scholars in question stressed, it is not devolution to various sub-national scales per se that they oppose. Rather, they disapproved the apparent assumption underlying new regional and urban policies according to which

> there is a defined geographical territory out there over which local actors can have effective control and can manage as a social and political space.
>
> (AMIN, 2004, p. 36)

As Amin argued, the public sphere is trans-territorial by its very definition, for

> [a]ny particular geographical site can only ever be a nodal connection in a hydra-like network space that never coheres into a local public sphere.
>
> (p. 38)

According to radical relationists, the above, relational reading of places and regions should lead to the rethinking of the understanding of local (regional) democratic politics. The framework of the *relational politics of place* propagated by radicals has built on the acknowledgement that spatialities of connectivity and transitivity constitute the local (regional). Accordingly, democratic local (regional) politics should not be seen as based on a territorially given, regional 'inside'; rather, the regional 'inside' has to be negotiated through public debate (AMIN, 2004).

With leaving the regional 'insides', on the basis of which devolution is (was) to unfold, unquestioned, the Labour government's regionalization agenda has been regarded by radical relationists as offering only an imitative model of democracy (AMIN, 2004). In particular, scholars have dismissingly pointed out that Labour's devolution agenda (in particular for England) had failed to engage with the power dynamics that underlie the UK's London-biased geography: a dynamic that continues to return London and the South East as the centre of the nation (AMIN *et al.*, 2003a). Instead of the misleading celebration of self-reliant regions that actually remain entangled in centrally orchestrated policy frameworks, radicals have called for a more radical revision of the UK's territorial management. Summarizing their arguments in the pamphlet entitled *Decentering the Nation: A Radical Approach to Regional Inequality* (AMIN *et al.*, 2003a), radicals have asked more specifically – and evoking traditional, that is, Keynesian regional policy measures – for a dispersal of state investments, including public sector institutions.

As to moderate relationists, they have expressed their sympathy with especially the way radicals have challenged the asymmetrical power geometries that continue to shape devolution arrangements (JONES and MACLEOD, 2004). Also, moderates have welcomed radicals' relational reading of regions as opening up 'innovative ways of conceptualizing contemporary economic and political spatialities' (JONES and MACLEOD, 2004, p. 448). At the same time, however, moderates have pointed out the need to be aware of the persisting relevance of the territorial dimension of socio-spatial processes. In the words of JONES (2004a):

> regions are made through *the territorial specificities of social struggle* between political society and civil society, which involves several integrated components.
>
> (p. 163, original emphasis)

In similar vein, JONES and MACLEOD (2004, p. 437) referred to the example of Cornwall's struggle for regional autonomy to support a claim that 'many everyday *realpolitik* acts of regionalization and/or regionalism continue to be framed in territorial terms.'

In fact, moderates have regarded regional territories as key manifestations of the institutionalization of regions, where 'institutionalization' is understood, following Paasi's seminal work, as the process in which regions acquire a 'status in the spatial structure and the social consciousness of society' (PAASI, 1991, p. 246). For moderates, clinging to a territorial perspective has been a way of acknowledging the 'spatial relations of permanence' (JONES, 2009, p. 493); in other words, a way of remaining aware of the solidified ways of thinking and acting in 'regional terms'. On the whole, moderates have argued in favour of a combination of territorial and relational readings. As HUDSON (2007) put it, the relational and the (hierarchically scalar) territorial are not either/or conceptions, but both/and conceptions. 'Territorially embedded' and 'relational and unbounded' conceptions of regions are complementary alternatives, and actually existing regions are a product of a struggle and tension between territorializing and de-territorializing processes. Consequently, for moderates, the main task is to elaborate

> a conceptual middle road between space as territorial anchorage and fixity *and* conceptions of space as topological, fluid and relationally mobile.
>
> (JONES, 2009, p. 496, original emphasis)

The present authors agree with moderates' stress concerning the persisting importance of the territorial dimension of spatiality. But have radicals ever stated the opposite? Have radicals, as JONES (2009) claimed, discarded the territorial view because they are uncomfortable with acknowledging 'the spatial relations of permanence'? Have territories, as PAASI (2008) contended, been 'like a red rag to a bull for many relationalists' (p. 406)? The authors would like to argue that radicals are incorrectly accused of the neglect of territorial structures. These incorrect accusations are in turn, it is further suggested, at least partly due to the inattentive reading of radical accounts by moderates. To begin with, MASSEY (2007) seems to echo moderates' call for a combined territorial–relational approach when arguing in favour of a 'territorially grounded politics that is responsive to relational space' (p. 156). Furthermore, while the South East and London often figure central to their writings, scholars ascribing to the radical agenda do emphasize that their arguments are not specifically about these territories. As AMIN (2004, p. 34) put it, London is not any more relationally constituted than any other place. ALLEN and COCHRANE (2007) similarly underlined the fact that they did not argue

> that the South East of England was simply 'unbounded', but that it, indeed any region, is made and remade by political processes that stretch beyond it and impact unevenly.
> (p. 1172)

In spite of the above explicit remarks, a recurring comment from the moderate side is that given its long-standing involvement in international networks, London/the South East is a very specific English region, and as such an inappropriate base for generalization (JONES and MACLEOD, 2004; JONES, 2009).

However, it is not only the inattentiveness of moderates that can be blamed for making the standpoints of the two camps appear to be irreconcilable. The seeming disagreement concerning the question 'What kind of a region is London?' (or, 'Is London a more relational kind of a region than others?') is a good entry point to discuss those philosophical divergences that prevent moderates from appreciating the actual message of radicals. It is this issue that the next section explores in more detail.

THE DIFFERENT 'FACES' OF RELATIONALITY

Mapping the underlying philosophical assumptions of the radical and moderate standpoints is not a straightforward task, as proponents of both stances have made only few if any explicit statements that would help position them philosophically. Nonetheless, based on the sporadic explicit comments that they have made, and their general line of argumentation, the positions in question can be sketched.

As to moderates, they have tended to adhere to (critical) realism. Two quotes from Jones, one of the most prominent representatives of moderates, are illustrative here. According to Jones,

> [f]or *realist relationists* [such as moderates], true statements about space are made true by *facts about material bodies* and the way they related, which can involve detailed and diverse empirical observations and abstractions from reality.
> (JONES, 2009, p. 496, original emphasis)

Furthermore, Jones emphasizes that '[a]ll things [relations] considered potential does not necessarily become an actual' (p. 493) and that, consequently, it is crucial to attend to those 'forces that restrict, constrain, contain, and connect the mobility of relational things' (p. 496). Or, using the conceptual vocabulary of critical realism, one should 'distinguish between necessary and contingent [empirically observable] spatial relations' (p. 495). More concretely, moderates caution that it is wrong to assume, on the basis of the empirical observation concerning the rising prominence of networks of flows in times of globalization, that all regions (spaces) can be thought of in relational terms. Actually, moderates argue that radicals, by focusing predominantly on a global city such as London, make the mistake of drawing this false conclusion. False because London/the South East is 'a very specific English region [...] given its long-established networks into the internationalizing economy' (JONES and MACLEOD, 2004, p. 437). By developing their relational perspective on the basis of the example of London/the South East, radicals run the risk of 'translating uniqueness into one-region-tells-all-scenarios' (JONES, 2009, p. 493).

The authors would like to argue that this accusation of radicals is unjust and stems from an undue acknowledgement of radicals' philosophical sources of inspiration. Radicals have conceptualized relationality by drawing on various lines of post-structuralist thought, most notably actor–network theory (ANT) and discourse theory. Before considering how these lines of thought have entered the arguments of radicals, their central assumptions will be briefly discussed. As to ANT, it is a relational and process-oriented sociology that treats agents, organizations and devices as interactive effects, that is, as an effect of stable arrays or networks of relations (LAW, 2002, 2003). As to discourse theory, it can be seen as a framework of enquiry starting out from the assumption that meaning in the social world depends on contingently constructed rules and differences (for example, TORFING, 1999, 2005). What is particularly relevant in view of the argument of this paper is that – in contrast to (critical) realism – the fundamental concern of ANT and discourse theory is not to make true statements about material reality in the vein of 'What kinds of objects and relations are there?'. Importantly, in spite of recurrent affirmations of the opposite by critics, this lack of concern does not imply the denial of materially existing objective relations. ANT and discourse theory are, however, interested in '*how* "what is" *is*' (ELDEN, 2005, p. 16). ANT's and discourse theory's concerns lie not with the concrete relations between people or entities that are implicated in (re)constructing particular objects (including spaces). Rather, their focus is on the *existential preconditions* that make the existence of objects possible or effective (for example, GLYNOS and HOWARTH, 2007). Thus, contrary to common misinterpretations, ANT 'has very little to do with the study of social networks' (LATOUR, 1996, p. 369) in the narrow sense of studying actual relations between ('given') human actors. Instead, by advancing that objects are network effects enacted by humans *and* non-human materials, ANT wishes to stress that the latter materials, as mediators, have a crucial role in constituting socio-spatial order. Within the framework of discourse theory in turn, the primary understanding of relationality is rooted in Saussurean linguistics, in particular in the assumption that the meaning of signs lies in their systematic relation to each other. Accordingly, from a discourse–theoretical perspective, objects come into existence as they become meaningful through relational systems of signifying discursive practices (for example, TORFING, 1999). Clearly, the two perspectives allow for different conceptualizations of 'the region': from an ANT perspective, any region is an interactive effect of humans and non-human materials; from a discourse–theoretical standpoint, any region's significance is constituted by the articulation (and institutionalization) of a range of differential meanings. However, it is rather evident that from both ANT's and discourse theory's perspective, not only is every region 'relational', but also no region is 'more' relational than any other region; London/the South East is thus *just as (relational as) any other region*.

But why assert the 'relational sameness' of regions, which are on the other hand so obviously different? And, accepting that regions can be seen as interactive effects of human and non-human materials, or as articulations of differential meanings, which mechanisms shape and structure those interactions and articulations? Furthermore, if the heterogeneous networks and the web of differential meanings that constitute regions are principally fluid and never-ending, then how to account for the boundaries that unquestionably delimit regional territories? Re-reading moderate scholars' accounts, it seems that it is these interrogations that underlie their dismissive comments on radicals' views. According to MACLEOD and JONES (2007, p. 1186), 'a network–topological perspective is less adept at locating the asymmetrical geometries of power', and it should be recognized that in many cases, territorially bounded spaces are spaces of dependence for various actors. JONES (2009) elsewhere wrote of the risks of spatial voluntarism and stresses repeatedly the importance of power relations.

As noted above, however, drawing on ANT or discourse theory does not imply that one denies materially existing relations, thus the fact that social reality is shaped by power, and is characterized by fixity. On the contrary, LAW (2003) emphasized that the objective of ANT is exactly to characterize the above interactive networks in their heterogeneity, and to 'explore how it is that they come to be patterned to generate effects like organisations, inequality and power' (p. 3). Discourse theorists recognize that 'the world around us appears for the most part to be rather decided and unambiguous' (TORFING, 1999, pp. 64–65). In other words, meanings – of what and where a region is – seem to be rather fixed than floating, and discourse theory's key concern is to show how power works through limiting the potentially endless re-articulations of meaning.

An ANT or a discourse–theoretical perspective is particularly apt for stressing that no matter how solid ('fixed') and unquestioned power relations and structures seem to be, fundamentally (that is, ontologically) they are always unstable. The emphasis on 'flat' ontological relationality and on the ultimate instability of structures is of crucial importance here. Ascribing to a flat ontology does not entail ascribing to an 'empty ontology' (JONES, 2009). Rather, it is a way of making sure that one avoids the trap of essentialism, that is, the assumption that patterns of actual – definitely 'non-flat' – relational interdependencies and power geometries are preordained through some transcendental logics. Furthermore, the ultimate precariousness of object-constituting relations is seen by discourse theorists as a condition of being able to conceive of social change. From a discourse–theoretical point of view, meanings might be, and indeed are, fixed durably, but without assuming that they are inherently unstable, one would exclude the possibility of politics, and ultimately suppress the room for social change. Arguing that one needs to conceive of meaning as inherently unfixed for politics to be possible, LACLAU and MOUFFE (1985/2001) rejected the (normative) idea that diverging social demands could be reconciled for good on the basis of rational consensus. Rather, Laclau and Mouffe asserted that without conflict and division, a pluralist democratic politics would be impossible (p. xvii). MOUFFE (2005) elsewhere further emphasized that the very condition of possibility of the formation of political identities is at the same time the condition of impossibility of a society from which antagonism has been eliminated. According to Mouffe, one should not take policy ambitions concerning more cohesion in terms of development at face value, but work towards an agonistic democracy that recognizes the inevitability of conflict in political life, and the impossibility of identifying rational decision-making procedures. '[F]ar from jeopardizing democracy, agonistic confrontation is the very condition of its existence' (MOUFFE, 2005, pp. 29–30). Therefore, discourse theory is especially helpful for underlining the fact that the construction of regional particularities is of an inherently *political* nature – this is also why it will be argued that it serves as a good basis for readdressing the conceptualization of 'the region'. Before this argument is developed, however, this section will now briefly reconsider how the above assumptions of ANT and discourse theory have become incorporated in radicals' standpoints. According to MURDOCH (1998, p. 359), by stating that 'each place is the focus of a distinct mixture of wider and more local relations', MASSEY (1991) has already echoed actor–network theorists. MASSEY (2004) referred to Latour by saying that

> [i]f space is really to be thought relationally, and also if Latour's proposition is to be taken seriously, then 'global space' is no more than the sum of relations, connections, embodiments and practices.
>
> (p. 8)

Similarly, AMIN (2004) has also drawn on ANT's insights in order to underpin his view that in current times of globalization, whatever is seen as local economic activity is always part of, and inseparable from, proximate and distanciated transactions; ultimately, it is a product of varied spatial practices.

As to inspiration by discourse theory, Massey, for example, connects her view of the 'continuous becoming of space' with the discourse theory of Laclau, in particular discourse theory's assumption that one can engage in any serious notion of politics only if the future is conceived as open. Accordingly, for MASSEY (2005), space is

> neither a container for always–already constituted identities nor a completed closure of holism. ... *For* the future to be open, space must be open too.
>
> (pp. 11–12, original emphasis)

AMIN's (2004) statement that there is no 'defined geographical territory out there over which local actors can have effective control and can manage as social and political space' (p. 36) is also expressive of the point that territorial boundaries as social structures are always incomplete. It is thus not, as critics (for example, JONES, 2009) mistakenly have tended to interpret it, signalling a neglect of the *actual* 'givenness' of territorially defined regulatory frameworks, strategies of intervention or identity narratives. Rather, it wishes to underline that such frameworks, strategies and narratives, no matter how well-entrenched and of benevolent appeal, embody particular claims of inclusion and exclusion that are and should remain open to contestation. ALLEN *et al.* (1998) explicitly noted that what they meant is not

> that there are no lines or boundaries in social space. But – like all the other relations which together form social space – they are social constructions, put there for specific purposes and within particular sets of power relations; they are in principle contested, and they may be used in the course of social contests.
>
> (p. 54)

Furthermore,

> [t]his is not to say that such boundaries will never adequately define a region, nor that they can be assumed not to be important; rather it is merely to stress that they should never be taken unquestioningly as adequate definitions.
>
> (p. 137)

Ultimately – and seemingly aligning with the insights of discourse theory – radicals emphasize the inherent openness of spaces in order to uphold the possibility of questioning any (institutionalized) claim concerning regional unity and coherence. In view of radicals' ambition to 'shake up the manner in which certain political questions are formulated' (MASSEY, 2005, p. 9), the degree to which one interprets cities or regions as territorial and scalar or topological and networked is definitely *not* 'a matter to be resolved ex post and empirically rather than a priori and theoretically' (MACLEOD and JONES, 2007, p. 1186; also Hudson, cited by JONES and MACLEOD, 2004, p. 448). In order to remain alert to the ways cities and regions embody actual spaces of exclusion, one always has to start out from the (ontological) relationality of all – territorial, scalar and networked – spaces. In other words, the assumption that those excluded can effectively challenge established ways of regional thinking necessarily presupposes that regions are constituted in a field of claims and counterclaims, that is, in a field of agonistic engagement (AMIN, 2004). One should thus not take the region

> as a practical and 'prescientific' bounded territorial space that has [...] become 'identified' as such a discrete territory in the spheres of economics, politics and culture.
>
> (JONES and MACLEOD, 2004, p. 437)

Boundedness as a real feature of spatiality namely might pre-exist scientific analysis, but critical scholarship should be focused exactly on the power relations that make it (appear) not only real, but also natural (cf. PAINTER, 2008).

Actually, the open and contested character of regions as social constructs has been also repeatedly stressed by those supporting a moderate viewpoint concerning relationality. PAASI (2001), for example, argued that regions are not independent actors, but 'exist and "become" in social practice and discourse' (p. 16). Furthermore, PAASI (2002) stressed that the boundaries, symbols and institutions of regions

> are not results of autonomous and evolutionary processes, but expressions of a perpetual struggle over the meanings associated with space, representation, democracy and welfare.
>
> (p. 805)

In fact, moderate accounts have commonly asserted the 'becoming' of regions, and that political struggles are inherently implicated in the construction of regions (for example, HUDSON, 2007; JONES and MACLEOD, 2004; MACLEOD and JONES, 2007). Also, HUDSON (2005) seems to echo the above-mentioned point made by Amin concerning local (regional) politics as a field of agonistic engagement when he notes that regions should be rethought as the products of agonistic politics.

A further parallel that can be observed between radical and moderate accounts is that the latter have, just as the former, been critical of the territorial framing of spatial interventions of the post-1997 Labour governments. JONES (2004b), for example, seemed also dismissive of England's new regionalism, where Regional Development Agencies (RDAs) have appeared as institutional sites through which national state power, defined as the ability to exercise intervention through a *territorial* programme of action (the regionalist project), can be realized (JONES, 2004b, p. 195, original emphasis). As Jones noted, RDAs have become designated as 'territorial managers' of change, promoting an associationalist form of coherence at the regional scale. HUDSON's (2005) account is also evocative of radicals' writings at several points. According to Hudson, perhaps the most important task is to rethink the region:

> to escape the limitations of the myth of a unified (and unifying) regional interest and explicitly acknowledge the existence of different – and at times openly competitive, grounded in different class structural positions and other sources of social power – interests held by individuals and social groups living in the same space.
>
> (p. 624)

Arguably, thus radicals and moderates have largely converged on emphasizing the inherently constructed character of regions. However, they arrive at this principally shared standpoint from divergent philosophical assumptions, and this is arguably a key source of still persisting disagreements or, rather, misunderstandings. As noted above, (critical) realism on the one hand and strands of post-structuralist thought on the other hand are motivated by fundamentally different enquiries. In connection with that, the above perspectives not only take a different ontological perspective, but also embody a fundamentally different – and irreconcilable – view of what ontology *is*. While for (critical) realists ontology refers to the independently existing world, for post-structuralists ontology is the plane for the relational constitution of the existence of any object (space). In view of this elementary difference, it becomes finally understandable why moderates could not apprehend radicals' insistence on seeing relationality as a fundamental dimension of spatiality. At the same time, it could be argued that the incommensurability of philosophical inspirational sources has not been the sole reason for the moderate–radical disagreement (misunderstanding). While drawing on post-structuralist frameworks, radical relationists have namely not always consistently adhered to the assumptions of the above frameworks. The point here is not that piecemeal borrowing is illegitimate. Neither of the two camps forms a homogenous whole, and scholars 'belonging' to either camp have developed their own frameworks by drawing on a wide range of intellectual sources. However, even though all theoretical frameworks are born through a combination of perspectives, it is believed crucial that any such combination is ontologically and epistemologically consistent. Only this way can the 'philosophical confusion' observed by AGNEW (1999, p. 93) be overcome. As to the inconsistent line of radicals' arguments, it is regarded as the second obstacle to clarity in the moderate versus radical 'debate' and it is examined in more detail in the next section.

TOWARDS A 'TRULY' RELATIONAL ONTOLOGY

As discussed above, radical relationalists have argued that all spaces should be regarded as relationally constituted. Insights of various strands of post-structuralist thought, in particular ANT and discourse theory, have been key – and explicitly mentioned – sources of inspiration for the claims of radicals. On closer inspection, however, it appears that radicals' accounts do not build firmly on the main assumption underlying the above strands of thought, notably that relationality is first and foremost an ontological concept, capturing the fundamental condition of being of any object. Instead, radicals have tended to see relationality (also) in terms of actual relations – and have, thus rather absurdly, paralleled moderates' view. AMIN (2002), for example, referred explicitly to ANT, but argued that 'the very ontology of place and territoriality itself is altered by the rise of world-scale processes and transnational connectivity' (p. 387). However, from the perspective of both ANT and discourse theory, the ontology of place and territoriality has *not* changed with the proliferation of actual relationships and with the increase in observable interdependencies. Possibly, the formation of ANT and discourse theory as conceptual–theoretical frameworks can be linked to the growing awareness of the above-mentioned relationships and interdependencies. However, following both strands, relationality *has been always–already* constitutive of objects.

Similarly, radicals actually do not seem to ascribe to discourse theory's ontological understanding of 'difference', and the view that the existence of all objects depends on contingently constructed differences. For Massey, for example, the term 'difference' designates *actual* difference, and figures as a synonym for heterogeneity/multiplicity/plurality. The emphasis on what she calls 'positive multiplicity' is important for Massey in order to do away with the Western/Northern-biased perspective in defining what is development/progress/modernization. The above perspective implies namely that places are not genuinely different, but simply 'behind' or 'advanced' within the same story of progress. MASSEY (1999) wishes to challenge this powerful imaginary geography that according to her obliterates, among others, the 'real differences' between the global South and the global North. As she says, 'a fuller recognition of difference would entertain the possibility of the existence of a multiplicity of trajectories' (p. 271).

In connection with Massey's arguments in favour of a fuller recognition of 'real difference', the question arises why there cannot be multiple regional trajectories, corresponding to real regional differences *within* nation-state territories? Why should one acknowledge macro-regional differences above the national scale, and assume the possibility of a more coherent trajectory for the development of national territories, overwriting local/regional differences? A possible answer can be traced in a more recent publication by Massey entitled *World City* (2007) in which Massey notes that

> [t]he biggest interests of ordinary people, in both London and 'the regions', are in common. Neither regional inequality nor poverty within London/South east will be seriously addressed without a shift in the national model of economic growth.
>
> (MASSEY, 2007, p. 155)

In line with that, Massey holds a politics of place desirable that recognizes 'the commonality of interests in spite of the very different geographical positioning within the wider geographies' (p. 156). Again, there is a striking parallel between moderates arguing that under certain circumstances the region can be taken as a practical and 'prescientific bounded territorial space' (JONES and MACLEOD, 2004) and radicals who seem to take national territories as a given object of analysis.

To be sure, MASSEY (2001) acknowledges that the isomorphism between space and society embodied in the nation-state has been an outcome of, and a support for, particular forms of power and politics. Also, Massey is well aware of the fact that relations constituting spaces stretch over national boundaries (MASSEY, 2007). But can the commonality of interests within a nation be assumed? What about those – by MASSEY (2007) much-criticized – claims of policy-makers who assert the necessity of privileged state support for London and the South East by arguing that this also serves the nation's common interest? Here it is useful to refer to CRITCHLEY (2004), according to whom:

> the main strategy of politics is to make itself invisible in order to claim for itself the status of nature or a priori self-evidence. In this way, politics can claim to restore the fullness of society or bring society into harmony with itself.
>
> (p. 114)

In other words, the political character of claims is often concealed by the appeal that such claims attempt to make to some natural, harmonic state of affairs. Paradoxically, while Massey recognizes that claims supporting London's privileged treatment and those picturing regional inequality as 'natural' are political claims, she seems unaware of the fact that her assumptions of a national common interest are not apolitical ones either.

On the whole, it is suggested here that it is imperative to recognize – and one can do so by following more consistently the postulations of discourse theory – that national development is, just as regional development, also a *politics* that can be best apprehended as a field of agonistic engagement. It is thus not only the case that choices of regional development interventions cannot be grounded in a presumption of a unified regional interest. Also, one should avoid seeing these choices as rooted in a unified national interest. Recognizing the impossibility of an ultimate consensus on spatial justice at *any* scale is a precondition for addressing spatial justice in a democratic way.

CONCLUSIONS

This paper set the objective of bringing more clarity into what could be called the relational versus territorial 'non-debate' that has unfolded in the past years about the conceptualization of the region. Based on a careful re-reading of texts, it was argued that the critique expressed by moderates that radicals disregard *actual* regional differences/particularities does not hold. 'Radicals' might be seen as such by others because they – in an attempt to ground their agenda on a new politics of space – have drawn upon various insights based on forms of post-structuralist relational ontology. Taken out of context, statements based on such insights indeed might appear as 'bending the stick too far' (JONES and MACLEOD, 2004, p. 437). However, thinking about regions through post-structuralist ontologies does not in any way imply a neglect of concrete regional differences/particularities. Rather – and this is what radicals wish to direct one's attention to – the above way of thinking enables an awareness, and also a critique, of the constructed character of any regional particularity. Radicals thus cannot be simply accused of falling into the 'non-territorial trap' (JONES, 2009).

In an attempt to trace the sources of – what are in the authors' view erroneous – accusations of radicals by moderates, it was found useful to review the deeper (ontological) philosophical anchoring of both strands. This review showed that arguably a key source of disagreements (misunderstandings) between radicals and moderates has been that the understanding of relationality as a fundamental condition of being of any object, on the one hand, has become confused with relationality in terms of actually existing relations, on the other hand. For while radicals have, by drawing on actor–network theory (ANT) and discourse theory, (seemingly) aligned with the former view of *ontological relationality*, moderates have continued to interpret relationality in the latter sense of *empirical connectedness*. Regarding the divergence of their (mostly implicit) meta-theoretical inspiration, the above camps might be surely seen as two worlds apart. A close reading of their accounts reveals actually that purported radicals do not embrace fully any post-structuralist ontology. In fact and rather paradoxically, radicals' standpoint bears much resemblance with that of moderates and, eventually, it is arguably only (some of) radicals' propositions for concrete state spatial reforms in England/the UK that would warrant the 'radical' label.

Although both radicals and moderates have largely focused on how regions are (and should be) thought of in England/the UK, it is contended here that the review of their 'non-debate' is giving clues to the conceptualization of 'the region' more generally. More specifically, it could be argued that the way forward in conceptualizing the region is to think of regions, and by extension, of all – thus also national – spaces as constituted relationally through agonistic struggles. Admittedly, an agonistic democracy still needs consensus concerning the institutions through which such struggles can take place (MOUFFE, 2005), and it is highly questionable whether the appropriate institutions – in the broad sense – are in place to move towards an agonistic engagement with the spatiality of development. Concerning the UK more specifically, many have pointed out, for example, that the lack of a National Spatial Planning Framework for England seriously impedes the establishment of an open debate about the 'what we want to do, why we want to do it, and what the implications might be' (SHEPLEY, 2005a, p. 263; also SHEPLEY 2005b; TOWN AND COUNTRY PLANNING ASSOCIATION, 2006). Certainly, a wide range of structural institutional constraints stand in the way of the elaboration of such a framework, including the fact that thinking about British political space in London-centric terms seems to be 'deeply engrained in the national psyche' (AMIN *et al.*, 2003b, p. 271). Addressing and changing such constraints is of course a great challenge that can surely use the efforts of critical scholarship. It could be suggested that such efforts should be best grounded in the assumption of the fundamental relationality of all spaces: this assumption is namely the condition for being able to conceive of change at all.

Acknowledgements – The authors are thankful for a grant provided by the Dutch Organisation for Scientific Research NWO [Nederlandse Wetenschappelijke Organisatie] – Shifts in Governance (Grant Number 450-04-142 once more).

REFERENCES

AGNEW J. (1999) Regions on the mind does not equal regions of the mind, *Progress in Human Geography* **24**, 23–36.

ALLEN J. and COCHRANE A. (2007) Beyond the territorial fix: regional assemblages, politics and power, *Regional Studies* **41**, 1161–1175.

ALLEN J., MASSEY D. and COCHRANE A. (1998) *Rethinking the Region*. Routledge, London.

AMIN A. (2002) Spatialities of globalisation, *Environment and Planning A* **34**, 385–399.

AMIN A. (2004) Regions unbound: towards a new politics of place, *Geografiska Annaler* **86 B**, 33–44.

AMIN A. (2005) Local community on trial, *Economy and Society* **34**, 612–633.

AMIN A., MASSEY D. and THRIFT N. (2003a) *Decentering the Nation: A Radical Approach to Regional Inequality*. Catalyst, London.

AMIN A., MASSEY D. and THRIFT N. (2003b) Rethinking the regional question, *Town and Country Planning* **October**, 271–272.

COCHRANE A. (2003) The new urban policy: towards empowerment or incorporation? The practice of urban policy, in IMRIE R. and RACO M. (Eds) *Urban Renaissance? New Labour, Community and Urban Policy*, pp. 223–234. Policy, Bristol.

CRITCHLEY S. (2004) Is there a normative deficit in the theory of hegemony?, in CRITCHLEY S. and MARCHART O. (Eds) *Laclau: A Critical Reader*, pp. 113–122. Routledge, London.

ELDEN S. (2005) Missing the point: globalization, deterritorialization and the space of the world, *Transaction of the Institute of British Geographers* **30**, 8–10.

GLYNOS J. and HOWARTH D. (2007) *Logics of Critical Explanation in Social and Political Theory*. Routledge, London.

HUDSON R. (2005) Region and place: devolved regional government and regional economic success?, *Progress in Human Geography* **29**, 618–625.

HUDSON R. (2007) Regions and regional uneven development forever? Some reflective comments upon theory and practice, *Regional Studies* **41**, 1149–1160.

IMRIE R. and RACO M. (2003) Community and the changing nature of urban policy, in IMRIE R. and RACO M. (Eds) *Urban Renaissance? New Labour, Community and Urban Policy*, pp. 3–36. Policy, Bristol.

JONES M. (2004a) Social justice and the region: grassroots regional movements and the English question, *Space and Polity* **8**, 157–189.

JONES M. (2004b) The regional state and economic governance: regionalized regeneration, or territorialized political mobilisation?, in WOOD A. and VALLER D. (Eds) *Governing Local and Regional Economies. Institutions, Politics and Economic Development*, pp. 177–204. Ashgate, Aldershot.

JONES M. (2009) Phase space: geography, relational thinking, and beyond, *Progress in Human Geography* **33**, 487–506.

JONES M. and MACLEOD G. (2004) Regional spaces, spaces of regionalism: territory, insurgent politics, and the English question, *Transactions of the Institute of British Geographers* **29**, 433–453.

LACLAU E. and MOUFFE C. (1985/2001) *Hegemony and Socialist Strategy. Towards a Radical Democratic Politics* [1985]. Verso, London.

LATOUR B. (1996) On actor–network theory: a few clarifications, *Sociale Welt* **4**, 369–381.

Law J. (2002) Objects and spaces, *Theory, Culture and Society* **19**, 91–105.

Law J. (2003) *Notes on the Theory of the Actor Network: Ordering, Strategy and Heterogeneity*. Centre for Science Studies, Lancaster University, Lancaster (available at: http://www.comp.lancs.ac.uk/sociology/papers/Law-Notes-on-ANT.pdf).

MacLeod G. and Jones M. (2007) Territorial, scalar, networked, connected: in what sense a 'regional world'?, *Regional Studies* **41**, 1177–1191.

Massey D. (1979) In what sense a regional problem?, *Regional Studies* **13**, 233–243.

Massey D. (1991) A global sense of place, *Marxism Today* **24–29 June**.

Massey D. (1992) Politics and space/time, *New Left Review* **I/196**, 65–84.

Massey D. (1999) Space–time, 'science' and the relationship between physical geography and human geography, *Transactions of the Institute of British Geographers* **24**, 261–276.

Massey D. (2001) Geography on the agenda, *Progress in Human Geography* **25**, 5–17.

Massey D. (2004) Geographies of responsibility, *Geografiska Annaler* **86 B**, 5–18.

Massey D. (2005) *For Space*. Sage, London.

Massey D. (2007) *World City*. Polity, Cambridge.

Mouffe C. (2005) *On the Political*. Routledge, London.

Murdoch J. (1998) The spaces of actor–network theory, *Geoforum* **29**, 357–374.

Paasi A. (1991) Deconstructing regions: notes on the scales of spatial life, *Environment and Planning A* **23**, 239–256.

Paasi A. (2001) Europe as a social progress and discourse. Considerations of place, boundaries and identity, *European Urban and Regional Studies* **8**, 7–28.

Paasi A. (2002) Place and region: regional worlds and words, *Progress in Human Geography* **26**, 802–811.

Paasi A. (2008) Is the world more complex than our theories of it? TPSN and the perpetual challenge of conceptualization, *Environment and Planning D: Society and Space* **26**, 405–410.

Painter J. (2008) Cartographic anxiety and the search for regionality, *Environment and Planning A* **40**, 342–361.

Raco M. (2003) New Labour, community and the future of Britain's urban renaissance, in Imrie R. and Raco M. (Eds) *Urban Renaissance? New Labour, Community and Urban Policy*, pp. 235–250. Policy, Bristol.

Shepley C. (2005a) A National Spatial Planning Framework for England? I – Context and need, *Town and Country Planning* **September**, 261–264.

Shepley C. (2005b) A National Spatial Planning Framework for England? II – Options and mechanisms, *Town and Country Planning* **October**, 305–308.

Torfing J. (1999) *New Theories of Discourse: Laclau, Mouffe and Žižek*. Blackwell, Oxford.

Torfing J. (2005) Introduction. Discourse theory: achievements, arguments, and challenges, in Howarth D. and Torfing J. (Eds) *Discourse Theory in European Politics, Identity, Policy and Governance*, pp. 1–31. Palgrave, New York, NY.

Town Country Planning Association (2006) *Connecting England. A Framework for Regional Development*. Town and Country Planning Association, London.

New Localities

MARTIN JONES and MICHAEL WOODS

Wales Institute of Social and Economic Research, Data and Methods (WISERD) and Institute of Geography and Earth Sciences, Aberystwyth University, Aberystwyth, UK.

JONES M. and WOODS M. New localities, *Regional Studies*. During the mid-to-late 1980s, 'locality' was *the* spatial metaphor to describe and explain the shifting world of regional studies. The paper argues that the resulting 'localities debate' threw this baby out with the bathwater and rather than invent new concepts to capture socio-spatial relations in the twenty-first century, the paper urges a 'return to locality' to enlighten regional studies. The paper offers three new readings of locality, which when taken together constitute the basis for thinking about regions, society and space through the lens of 'new localities'. It further suggests that for locality to have analytical value it must also have both an imagined and a material coherence, and it puts a 'new locality' framework to work in research on devolved regional economic and social geographies.

JONES M. and WOODS M. 新的地域性，*区域研究*。1980 年代中期至晚期，"地域性"的概念便做为区域研究描绘并解释世界变迁的象征。本文认为其所导致的"地域性辨论"如同将可取之处与废物一同丢弃一般，与其创造新的概念来捕捉二十一世纪的社会空间关系，本文则主张以 "回到地域性" 启迪区域研究，并提供有关地域性的三种新式阅读，三者整合起来将形成以 "新的地域性"之视角思考区域、社会与空间的基础。本文并进一步提议，地域性的概念若要具有分析价值，则必须同时拥有想象与物质层面的连贯性，"新的地域性"并将成为研究中央权力下放下的区域经济和社会地理的崭新研究架构。

JONES M. et WOODS M. De nouvelles localités, *Regional Studies*. Du milieu à la fin des années 1980, la notion de 'localité' constituait la métaphore pour décrire et expliquer l'évolution des études régionales. L'article affirme que 'le débat sur la notion de localité', qui en a résulté, a jeté ce bébé avec l'eau de bain et, plutôt que d'inventer de nouveaux concepts afin de capter les relations socio-géographiques du vingt-et-unième siècle, l'article prône en faveur d'un 'retour à la notion de localité' pour améliorer les études régionales. Cet article fournit trois nouvelles appréciations de la notion de 'localité' lesquelles, prises ensemble, constituent le bien-fondé des opinions sur les régions, la société et l'espace dans l'optique des 'nouvelles localités'. De plus, on propose que la notion de localité doit avoir une cohérence à la fois imaginaire et réelle pour justifier une valeur analytique, et on met en branle un cadre de 'nouvelle localité' dans la recherche au sujet des géographies économiques et sociales régionales dévolues.

JONES M. und WOODS M. Neue Lokalitäten, *Regional Studies*. In der zweiten Hälfte der achtziger Jahre handelte es sich bei der 'Lokalität' um *die* räumliche Metapher zur Beschreibung und Erklärung der veränderlichen Welt der Regionalwissenschaft. In diesem Beitrag wird argumentiert, dass in der daraus resultierenden 'Lokalitätsdebatte' das Kind mit dem Bade ausgeschüttet wurde; statt neue Konzepte zur Erfassung der sozioräumlichen Beziehungen im 21. Jahrhundert zu erfinden, wird eine 'Rückkehr zur Lokalität' zur Aufklärung der Regionalwissenschaft gefordert. Angeboten werden drei neue Lesarten der Lokalität, die gemeinsam die Grundlage für die Betrachtung von Regionen, Gesellschaft und Raum durch das Objektiv der 'neuen Lokalitäten' bilden. Ebenso wird argumentiert, dass die Lokalität nur dann einen analytischen Wert bietet, wenn sie sowohl eine imaginäre als auch eine materielle Kohärenz aufweist, und es wird ein Rahmen der 'neuen Lokalitäten' zum Einsatz in der Forschung über dezentralisierte regionale Wirtschafts- und Sozialgeografien geschaffen.

JONES M. y WOODS M. Nuevas localidades, *Regional Studies*. De mediados a finales de los ochenta, la 'localidad' era la metáfora espacial preferida para describir y explicar el mundo cambiante de los estudios regionales. En este artículo sostenemos que el 'debate de localidades' resultante acabó tirando el grano con la paja; en vez de inventar nuevos conceptos para captar las relaciones socio-espaciales en el siglo XXI, aquí instamos a 'volver a la localidad' para esclarecer los estudios regionales. En este artículo ofrecemos tres nuevas lecturas de localidad que juntas constituyen la base para reflexionar sobre las regiones, la sociedad y el espacio a través del objetivo de las 'nuevas localidades'. Además sugerimos que para que el concepto de localidad ofrezca un valor analítico, también debe tener una coherencia imaginada y material, y establecemos una estructura de 'nueva localidad' para la investigación sobre geografías regionales con las competencias transferidas desde una perspectiva económica y social.

INTRODUCTION

> Locality has suddenly emerged as one of the more popular ideas in social science, especially in sociology, geography, urban and regional studies, and political science. A content analysis might reveal the term vying for place with structure, and cause, if not yet approaching the use levels of class, status or gender. But it is an *infuriating idea.* It is one that seems to signify something important, and indeed most people seem to know – roughly – what it signifies for them. *Yet few would care to explain what locality (or is it a locality or even the locality) actually is.* Even fewer, I suspect, would agree on the result – even if there was one.
>
> (DUNCAN, 1989, p. 221; added emphasis)

'What is locality?' asked Simon Duncan in 1989 when commenting on the locality debates of the previous five years. As discussed below, these were certainly productive and extensive debates on social and spatial relations, occurring at a time of intense economic restructuring and written across landscapes of deindustrialization. 'Locality' was that buzz-word of the mid-1980s, even a 'new geography' (COCHRANE, 1987), used to frame research on economic geography. It filled the pages of human geography journals and, it could be argued (also COOKE, 1990), contributed to the intellectual development of regional studies. Reflecting on this, COOKE (2006) went as far as to argue that this was

> the most heated yet illuminating wrangles in human geography since those over 'environmental determinism' in the 1950s and the 'quantitative revolution' in the 1960s. The soul of the discipline seemed to be at stake ....
>
> (p. 1)

For Duncan, locality was being used as a catch-all term, somewhat misleading and unsupportive (or even that 'infuriating idea'), to describe the local autonomy of areas, case study areas, spatially affected process (social, political, economic, cultural), spaces of production and consumption, the local state, and so on. In a classic paragraph, DUNCAN (1989) wrote that:

> Localities in the sense of autonomous subnational social units rarely exist, and in any case their existence needs to be demonstrated. But it is also misleading to use locality as a synonym for place or spatial variation. This is because the term locality inevitably smuggles in notions of social autonomy and spatial determinism, and this smuggling in excludes examination of these assumptions. *It is surely better to use terms like town, village, local authority area, local labour market or, for more general uses, place, area or spatial variation.* These very useable terms do not rely so heavily on conceptual assumptions about space vis-à-vis society.
>
> (p. 247; added emphasis)

Social science debates rapidly moved on (post-Fordism, post-modernism, new regionalism, politics of place) ... this material was not advanced, theoretically or empirically, few cared to continue with locality, and instead today there are other spatial concepts such as territory, place, scale and network to capture the regional world of socio-spatial relations. As charted below, the locality concept baby was effectively thrown out with the locality studies bathwater to make space for new ways of seeing the regional world.

This paper argues that 'locality' remains an important vehicle in and through which to conduct social science research and when re-energized through a multilayered theoretical framework locality can enlighten and energize regional studies. The authors would like to suggest that recent exchanges over the nature of socio-spatial relations in the social sciences (JESSOP *et al.*, 2008; JONES, 2009; JONES and JESSOP, 2010; MERRIMAN *et al.*, 2012), and the ongoing debate between territorial versus relational perspectives on this, notably in human geography (JONAS, 2012; MACKINNON, 2011; MCCANN and WARD, 2010, 2011; PAASI, 2010), but also related concerns in the social sciences, arts and humanities (BRENNER, 2004; HART, 2010; JONES, 2010; SASSEN, 2006; SMITH and GUARNIZO, 2009), would benefit significantly from returning to this missing spatial metaphor.

The paper discusses the 'locality debate' of the 1980s, then turns to discuss the new regionalism in the 1990s, which extended some of this ground, before focusing on relational notions of space that have stretched the regional geographical imagination further, and the debates and counter debates on relationality. It takes stock and reintroduces locality as a bridging concept, whereby through three readings, the 'new localities' lens offers a way forward for regional studies by firstly reconciling some of the tensions in the current use of spatial metaphors and, secondly, offering a research agenda and methodological framework for advancing this.

The paper argues that, firstly, locality can be seen as bounded territorial space, which is recognized politically and administratively for the discharge and conduct of public services, and for the collection and analysis of statistical data. Secondly, locality represents a ways of undertaking comparative research analysis, linked to processes occurring within the locality and also processes shaping the locality from the outside, and most importantly connecting localities. This also allows for the historical analysis of a given locality over time. Thirdly, locality can be used to read spaces of flows for numerous policy fields, which in turn exhibit spatial variations due to interaction effects. The object of analysis here is the policy field and not the locality per se. This reading of locality is sensitive to localities being defined by their cores rather than by the total area, such that the boundaries might be flexible and fuzzy. In addition to this, it is argued here that for any given locality to have analytical value it must have both a material coherence and an imagined coherence, and this distinction is unpacked.

The paper concludes by briefly illustrating how the 'new locality' framework has been put to work in a research programme exploring the contemporary economic and social geographies of Wales, undertaken by the Wales Institute of Social and Economic Research, Data and Methods (WISERD).[1] The paper does not discuss the research programme or its findings in detail (HELEY *et al.*, 2012; HELEY, 2012; HELEY and JONES, 2012b; HELEY and MOLES, 2012), but rather it seeks to move from the particular to the general and highlights how principles from the 'new localities' approach have been engaged to allow meaningful representations of 'locality' to be constructed and mobilized through the research.

REMEMBERING SOCIETY AND SPACE: CURS AND THE LOCALITY DEBATE

MASSEY's *Spatial Divisions of Labour* (1984) was pivotal to starting what became the locality debate. This was written during an era of intense economic restructuring and challenged how geographers thought about 'the local' in an increasingly internationalizing and globalizing world fuelled by the collapse of Fordist–Keynesian compromises. The economic background is critical with five trends taking place in manufacturing across local areas in North America and Western Europe: slowing productivity, declining output, trade deficits, collapsing profitability and reductions in employment (MARTIN and ROWTHORN, 1986). This was happening at the same time as changes in the monetary conditions of exchange (inflationism to anti-inflationism). Added to this, Massey emphasized three interrelated mechanisms driving local economic restructuring under advanced capitalism: intensification (increasing labour productivity and obtaining the same output with a reduced workforce), rationalization (cutting capacity in response to intensification and/or relocating capacity elsewhere geographically), and technical change (labour-saving methods of production such as mechanization and manufacturing improvement). This, in turn, influenced three spatial structures of production: locationally concentrated and vertically integrated, cloning branch-plants, and part processing systems. The net impact of all this was inevitably job losses, with a geographical anatomy of uneven development and distinctive localities emerging under globalization and economic restructuring, which MASSEY (1984) (also LOVERING, 1989) sought to uncover by way of a 'restructuring approach' based on five principles:

- Linkages need to be made between local economies and processes operating at regional, national and international scales.
- Local economic factors and economic changes need to be linked to constellations of social, political, technical and cultural concerns.
- Critical focus has to be placed on the role of labour (and class relations) in the location imperatives of firms.
- Analysis of local and regional economic change should begin with broad economic processes and then examine impacts on localities, thereby identifying a two-way relationship between local conditions and broader processes (the specific and the general).
- Over time, and across space, the links between 'the local' and 'the global' produce different 'rounds of investment', which build up in layers and influence the role 'the local' plays in the next wave of restructuring and investment.

The intellectual goal was to tease out the dialectic between space and place by looking at how *localities* were being positioned within, and in turn help to reposition, the changing national and international division of labour. For MASSEY (1991), 'the local in the global', of course, is not simply an area one can draw a line around; instead, it is defined in terms of sets of social relations or processes under consideration. This highly influential 'new regional concept of localities' (JONAS, 1988) influenced two government-sponsored research initiatives in the UK, delivered through the Economic and Social Research Council (ESRC): the Social Change and Economic Life programme and the 'Changing Urban and Regional Systems' (CURS) programme. Both were given substantial funding and charged with remits to uncover the effects of international and global economic restructuring on local areas and why different responses and impacts were reported in different places. Locality research, independent of these programmes, was already taking place at Lancaster University (MURGATROYD *et al.*, 1985) and at Sussex University (DUNCAN, 1989), which fuelled an interest in this important topic, although as BARNES (1996) highlighted, notions of 'locality' differ across all these interventions and focusing on the CURS programme is most helpful in getting behind the meaning of locality.

In seeking to put 'the local' into 'the global', the CURS initiative set out to undertake theoretically informed empirical research in seven localities between 1985 and 1987. The goal was to examine the extent to which localities themselves could shape their own transformation and destiny as agents and not be passive containers for processes passed down from above. A series of mainly metropolitan de-industrializing towns/regions and rural areas being encroached by restructuring were selected as case studies for this analysis – Swindon, Thanet, Cheltenham, Middlesbrough, East Liverpool and South Birmingham – with the results being published in two edited books (COOKE, 1989a; HARLOE *et al.*, 1990). Each book contained detailed chapters on each locality, with research teams uncovering (with varying degrees of success) the impacts of globalization and economic restructuring on 'the local' through different 'rounds of investment' occurring over time and with local politics producing locality interactions.

Particularly worthy of note here was the work of HUDSON (1989, 1990) and BEYNON *et al.* (1989), whose research closely followed Massey's theoretical and interpretative framework. Their account of economic change in Teesside seemed to demonstrate a 'locality effect' of local particularities in global times, that is, the different ways in which 'rounds of investment' can be read in the local economic landscape, how local politics played a role in international investment decisions, and in turn how attempts to cope with de-industrialization by either building a service-based economy or using state-sponsored local economic initiatives to create employment opportunities were working themselves out on the ground. This economic strategy, of course, had questionable sustainability due to the volatility of global production regimes (HUDSON, 2000; SADLER, 1992).

As argued by GREGSON (1987), DUNCAN and SAVAGE (1991), and BARNES (1996), there is a fundamental difference between locality research (the CURS findings) and the resulting 'locality debate' across human geography and the social sciences, which was fuelled by a rethinking of how one theorized socio-spatial relations across these disciplines (itself bound up with a transition from Marxist to poststructuralist research enquiry) and shifting research methodologies and practices (such as the rise and fall of critical realism; PRATT, 2004).

With all this in mind, things were inevitably going to be messy and the journal *Antipode*, between 1987 and 1991, published a series of often-heated exchanges on the whereabouts of localities (for summaries, cf. COOKE, 2006; and PRATT, 2004).

The initial assault came from North America by SMITH (1987), who bemoaned the perceived shift away from (Marxist) theory to a critical realist-inspired regional world of empirics, worthy of nothing more than a 'morass of statistical data'. Smith famously said:

> like the blind man with a python in one hand and an elephant's trunk in the other, the researchers are treating all seven localities as the same animal.
>
> (p. 63)

This was supported, to a differing degree, by HARVEY (1987), who saw these projects as refusing to engage in any theoretical or conceptual adventures, the consequences of which, for SCOTT (1991), encourage

> a form of story-telling that focuses on dense historical and geographical sequences of events, but where in the absence of a strong interpretative apparatus, the overall meaning of these events for those who live and work in other places is obscure.
>
> (pp. 256–257)

In a more balanced manner, the resume by DUNCAN (1989) saw locality – in the wrong hands – as a form of reified uniqueness and 'spatial fetishism', that is, in what sense can localities act, or is it the social forces within these spaces that have this capacity? Duncan then questioned the relationships within a defined territorial unit and in two brilliant papers with Savage made of the first serious interventions on the relationships between spatial scales (SAVAGE and DUNCAN, 1990). Duncan concluded with some thoughts on three ways forward for research on locality: considerations of spatial contingent effects (processes contained in places), propositions on local causal processes (locally derived forces of change), and the notion of locality effects (the combination of the previous two, affording a capacity to localities to act). WARDE (1989) recognized the value of locality for empirical research but also highlighted that the scale of locality changes according to the object of analysis under question. COOKE (1987, 1989b), the Director of CURS, took a more defensive and ultimately pragmatic line, arguing that CURS was about seeking to make some general claims from multi-site case-study research, even if this was about nothing more than local labour markets and its boundaries. The CURS findings were, therefore, empirical and not empiricist (COOKE, 2006).

A special issue of *Environment and Planning A* offered further critique and extension, and showed that locality was still a valuable concept to be grappled with. For JACKSON (1991), unsuccessful and at times dangerous attempts were being made to read cultural change and political change from the economy, rather than seeing these as being embedded in each other's presence. PRATT (1991) took a similar line and suggested that one needs to look at the discursive construction of localities and their material effects. PAASI (1991), much inspired by the 'new regional geography' material that the locality debate uncovered and which brought regions back into the room as a consequence, encouraged scholars to take 'geohistory' more seriously and offered the idea of 'generation' to distinguish between the concepts of locality, place and region. DUNCAN and SAVAGE (1989, 1991) pushed what they saw as the missing agenda of place formation and class formation and the interconnections of these within and between localities. COX and MAIR (1988, 1991) offered an interesting US account of localities as arenas for economic development coalitions and ways of exploring the fixing and scaling of socio-spatial relations. They took the debate forward and brought agency and scale to the fore through notions of 'local dependency', the 'scale division of labour' and the 'scale division of the state' – concepts that highlighted the location and mobility of actors at different times. Cox and Mair claimed this avoided 'spatial fetishism' (a criticism levelled by SAYER, 1991) as locality is seen not in physical terms but as a 'localised social structure'. COX (1993) pushed this further in work on the new urban politics. This claimed that capital was not as hyper-mobile as globalization theory was arguing at the time due to the territorial organization of the (probably peculiar in relation to capital–labour relations in Ohio) US local state system. Cox, however, probably pushed things too far by claiming that localities could ultimately act, as opposed to the social relations in these strategically selected spaces acting (MACLEOD and JONES, 2011).

As COOKE's (2006) excellent retrospective commentary notes, because CURS and the locality debate became so quickly conflated in these debates, jettisoning the notion of locality for some twenty-five years was somewhat inevitable. Debates moved on and during the mid-1990s economic geographers became preoccupied not so much with localities per se but rather with the links between space and place as a way of looking at the 'local in the global'. BEYNON and HUDSON (1993), reviewing the locality debate and noting the gaps over missing politics, made some interesting points on our local–global times: 'space' for these authors captures the rather abstract domain of capital, with 'place' being 'meaningful' situations established by labour. 'Meaningful' was never fully defined or demonstrated, apart from reference to historically contingent economic identities and attachments, and the important point that 'place-based' is not necessarily reducible to notions of 'place-bound' (cf. MASSEY, 1991).

MASSEY, commenting on related themes, wrote an extension to the debate in the journal *Marxism Today*, reprinted in his collection of essays entitled *Space, Place and Gender* (1994). This was an early application of the 'thinking space relationally' approach. For Massey, of course, globalization is happening, but probably not as we know it. Time–space compression (the shrinking-world thesis) is socially and spatially differentiated due to the different mobility potentially of people in place. 'Power geometries', a metaphor for capturing geographies of power, exist and therefore constrain some and enable others. This makes generalizations about the powerlessness of 'the local' in a globalizing world unwise: one needs instead to understand and see localities as 'global senses of place' – they are interconnected nodes in spaces of flows, stretching back and forth, ebbing and flowing according to how these are positioned by, and positioning, socio-spatial relations. Localities as 'global senses of place' are *relational* in the sense of seeing the local as an unbounded mosaic of different elements always in a process of interaction and being made. In short, one cannot explain locality or place only by looking inside it, or outside it; the 'out there' and 'in here' matter *together* and are dialectically intertwined (MASSEY, 2005, 2007).

TOWARDS 'NEW LOCALITIES': THE NEW REGIONALISM AND RELATIONAL SPACE

In the early 1990s, 'region' certainly replaced locality as the spatial metaphor for doing economic and political geography. Academic trends tend to mirror closely political and policy events (COOKE, 1995, 1998; COOKE and MORGAN, 1998) and economic geographers started to get very excited about what they saw as the re-emergence of regional economies and new spaces of economic governance across the globe. These spaces had, of course, been initially flagged by writers talking about post-Fordism and the geographies of flexible accumulation. The pace of generalizing from this though, to paint a 'regional world' (STORPER, 1997) picture, increased. SCOTT, for instance, in his *New Industrial Spaces* (1988) offered a new way of looking at agglomeration and the development of distinct local territorial production complexes or industrial districts. Whereas Fordist accumulation was favoured by and grew in accordance with economies of scale and vertical integration, economic development after-Fordism was seen to be linked to spatially specific economies of scope resulting from the vertically disintegration of production and the development, amongst other things, of flexible working practices and shared support mechanisms. The geographical extent of this phenomenon and its reproducibility and sustainability was discussed at length in various edited collections (STORPER and SCOTT, 1992) and, inspired by this, debates gradually shifted throughout the 1990s to examine the governance of local economies in global contexts through a 'new regionalist' perspective – as part of a broader 'institutional-turn' in economic geography. A parallel set of debates, also drawing on 'new regionalist' thinking, took place in political science on 'multilevel governance' – driven by the so-called hollowing out of the national state and the 'Europe of the Regions' thesis (KEATING, 1998; SCOTT, 2001) – advancing these scalar claims further. For COOKE (2006) this was important for locality studies.

> Probably the longest-lasting legacy of locality studies has been the rise of so-called 'new regionalism'. Already spotted around the time of his return from Australia by Nigel Thrift (1983) this theorised regional political economy analysis was gaining ground rapidly as we have seen, in the new times of 'global localisation.
>
> (p. 10)

This orthodoxy and alleged theoretical coherence referred to above by Cooke has, of course, been subjected to piercing academic critiques. In a similar manner to some of the critiques of locality, philosophically (via critical realism) the new regionalism is deemed guilty of 'bad abstraction' – it ignores the role of multiple and contingent factors (both economic and non-economic) that produce regions. For this reason LOVERING (1999) argued that the region is becoming a 'chaotic conception'; generalized claims are being made based on selective empirical evidence to support the centrality of this scale for stimulating economic growth. Consequently, Lovering argues, this approach is a theory led by selective empirical developments and recent public policy initiatives. It is

> a set of stories about how *parts* of a regional economy *might* work, placed next to a set of policy ideas which *might* just be useful in *some* cases.
>
> (LOVERING, 1999, p. 384; original emphasis)

These arguments have been developed and extended by others (MACLEOD, 2001a, 2001b; HADJIMICHALIS, 2006a, 2006b; HARRISON, 2008, 2010; PAINTER, 2008) and the present paper will return to issues of 'regional method'.

New regionalist thinking on what one might want to call 'socio-spatial relations' has, in turn, been challenged by relational approaches to space, where – building on the work of MASSEY (1991, 1994) above – geographies are made through stretched-out and unbounded relations between hybrid mixtures of global flows and local nodal interactions that are interconnected (for a summary, see MURDOCH, 2006). No longer is space a container or independent backdrop for existence, nor is there a concern for a distance between points; instead, uncovering networked, nodal and open place-based relationships is where it is at. This argument, of course, has been clearly articulated by those advocating a 'thinking space relationally' approach to geography (AMIN, 2004; AMIN *et al.*, 2003; also MARSTON *et al.*, 2005). In the 'unbounded' or 'relational region' thesis there is no automatic promise of territorial integrity. An 'alternative regional geography' of 'jostling' (MASSEY, 2007, p. 89) is argued for, where spatial configurations and boundaries are no longer necessarily or purposively territorial or scalar, since the social, economic, political, and cultural inside and outside are constituted through the topologies of actor networks which are becoming increasingly dynamic and varied in spatial constitution (AMIN, 2004).

This take certainly stretches the imagination of economic geography in local–global times, but those working within state theoretic frameworks and more grounded approaches to economic geography have taken issue with the *realpolitik* of 'the local' grappling with the challenges of globalization. For example, it is important to consider the ways in which cities and regions can be categorized as a 'problem' by the state and those seeking to direct resources to different geographical areas. It is also important not to lose sight of the ways in which 'contentious politics' (LEITNER *et al.*, 2008) are being played out across the globe. One instance of this in recent years has seen the distinguishing of territorially articulated spaces by those campaigning for devolved government and cultural rights. These spaces are not out there waiting to be found, but they are being mobilized and managed in the era of the post-national political constellation. Such spaces become central for conducting territorial political struggles over economic and cultural identities (JONES and MACLEOD, 2004; MACLEOD and JONES, 2007). Pushing this further, for TOMANEY (2007) and MORGAN (2007) localities are more than the local articulation of global flows and concerns with territorialized culture need not necessarily be atavistic, archaic or regressive.

JONAS (2012) suggested that the distinction between territorial and relational can be 'registered obsolete' if critical attention is paid to matters of territory and the nature of territorial politics, both of which are products of bounded and unbounded forces and the balance/form this takes is contingent and requires empirical investigation. The way forward, then, is 'further examples of both relational thinking about territorial politics and of territorial thinking about relational processes' (JONAS, 2012, p. 270). This requires some empirical hard work, which is welcome, and there are good examples of how this might be conducted (BEAUMONT and NICHOLLS, 2007; GONZÁLEZ, 2009; JONES and MACLEOD, 2011; SAVAGE, 2009; MCCANN and WARD, 2010, 2011).

Significant outstanding issues remain when dealing with socio-spatial relations since the inception of the locality debate, and it would foolish to suggest that notions of 'locality' can provide a solution to all the remaining concerns of space and spatiality in human geography, regional studies and the social sciences more broadly. It could be contended, though, that when fused and energized by the material contained within debates since then, locality can be taken forward with analytical value and clarity to answer the challenges thrown up by the rise and fall of the new regionalism, the relational turn and the territorial–relational backlash. It could be concurred, in part, that the power of locality rests on its regional method. Locality offers a 'comparative methodology that allow[s] spatial variety to be explained within a coherent and satisfying theoretical framework' (COOKE, 2006, p. 10).

To summarize the position to this point, there are two key issues at stake. First, following a line from critical realism, if locality or any other substantive spatial concept as it happens is to the explanation of action of any kind, it is because it constitutes a context, or configuration, which delimits such actions.

> The emergent properties of the spatial distribution of social objects with causal powers appear as contexts for action. Context doesn't determine action, but it delimits action.
>
> (WARDE, 1989, p. 280)

Second, localities, like regions, are only ever semi-coherent in their concrete realizations. Localities are always constructed out of the tensions and grapples between spatial fixity and flow. MASSEY's (2011) recent statement on this is a helpful resume.

> Territories are constituted and are to be conceptualized, relationally. Thus, interdependence and identity, difference and connectedness, uneven development and the character of place, are in each pairing two sides of the same coin. They exist in constant tension with each other, each contributing to the formation, and the explanation, of the other.
>
> (p. 4)

Going beyond Massey, the issue is to think not so much of the processes that help bound space into discrete localities, but rather to undertake research that investigates where, why and how the processes of 'locality making' are negotiated, constructed and contested, becoming semi-permanently fixed or, equally, dissolving together (JONAS, 2012). These agendas are taken forward to the next section, which discusses a 'new localities' research agenda.

A 'NEW LOCALITIES' RESEARCH AGENDA

SAVAGE *et al.* (1987, p. 30) argued that '[g]reater clarification of the concept 'locality' should start with an analysis of the significance of space in general'. This approach has certainly been lacking – with the exception of relational space, but at the same time this reading is disconnected from other philosophical positions (JONES, 2009) – from all the debates discussed so far in the paper. The authors agree fully and offer three readings of 'new locality' which can initially be formulated from the three commonly understood notions of space in general – absolute, relative and relational – which, as HARVEY (1969, 1973) has highlighted, can coexist at the same time. In absolute understanding of space, the local in the global, for instance, is treated independently, that is, locality is a discrete space around which a line can be drawn and where a loose spatial determinism has some purchase. Concerns with *relative space* then lead one to consider the relationship between localities in an increasingly internationalizing world of processes and patterns. Last, as noted above, *relational space* is a truly radical attempt to collapse analysis into networked concerns such that there is no global and local to talk about, only unbounded and networked geographies of 'jostling' (MASSEY, 2007), 'throwntogetherness' (MASSEY, 2005) and becoming (WOODS, 2007). Sites become the sources of analysis, but how sites relate to each other is not clear, such that research needs to pay attention to power and policy relations flowing through localities.

It could be argued that these three notions of space can be deployed to inform different ways of identifying localities as objects of research. Three readings of 'new locality' follow:

- From the perspective of absolute space, localities can be presented as bounded territories, such as local authority areas, which are recognized politically and administratively for the discharge and conduct of public services, and for the collection and analysis of statistical data. They are not naturally occurring entities (though some may be contiguous with natural features such as islands), but they do have a stable and precisely delimited materiality that can form the focus for traditional, single-place-based or comparative case study research (BENNETT and MCCOSHAN, 1993).
- From the perspective of relative space, localities can be seen as connected containers for spatial analysis. Here localities are identified by their cores, not their edges, and are not necessarily consistent with formal administrative geographies. In this perspective, the boundaries of localities are relative, fuzzy and sometimes indeterminate, contingent on the processes and phenomena being observed, and shaped by dynamics within, outside and between localities. Such a notion of locality forms the basis for research sensitive to connective forms of enquiry, including, for example, work on city-regions and nested hierarchies (ETHERINGTON and JONES, 2009).
- From the perspective of relational space, localities are nodes or entanglements within networks of interaction and spaces of flow. They are not bounded in any conventional understanding of the term, but have a topography that is described by lines of connectivity and convergence. Localities transgress inscribed territories and are not necessarily discrete, sharing points of coexistence. Such a conceptualization of locality lends itself to counter-topographical research (KATZ, 2001; also HELEY and JONES, 2012a), or the practice of a 'global ethnography' (BURAWOY, 2000).

Unlike earlier locality debates, the 'new localities' approach does not seek to adjudicate between these different representations of locality, but rather recognizes that all are valid ways of 'talking about locality', and each captures a different expression of locality. New localities are, therefore, multifaceted and multidimensional. They are 'shape-shifters' whose form changes with the angle from which they are observed. As such, the identification of localities for research can be freed from the constraints of the rigid territoriality of administrative geography and should move beyond the reification of the local authority scale that was implicit in many previous locality studies. WARDE's (1989) comments of twenty plus years ago on this remain critical:

> Deciding on an appropriate spatial scale depends initially on the research problem. If we want to know about foreign policy we might choose states; if voting behavior, constituencies; if material life, perhaps the labour market; if everyday experience, maybe the neighbourhood. Greater

> difficulty arises if we want to know about the intersection of several of these, the burden of the restructuring thesis. (p. 277)

In recognizing the relationality, contingency and impermanence of localities, it is those notions of 'intersection' that are important to uncover. The new localities approach accordingly focuses attention on processes of 'locality-making', or the ways in which semi-stabilized and popularly recognized representations of locality are brought into being through the moulding, manipulation and sedimentation of absolute, relative and relational space within ongoing social, economic and political struggles (JONAS, 2012; PIERCE *et al.*, 2010). Indeed, it is in these 'acts of locality-making' that localities are transformed from mere points of location (a description of where research was conducted) to socio-economic–political assemblages that provide an analytical framework for research.

For the concept of locality to have analytical value, it must be possible to attribute observed processes and outcomes to social, economic and political formations that are uniquely configured in a given locality, and this, it is argued, requires a locality to possess both material and imagined coherence.[2] By material coherence the authors refer to the social, economic and political structures and practices that are uniquely configured around a place. Thus, material coherence may be provided by the territorial remit of a local authority, by the geographical scope of an economic development initiative, by the catchment area of a school or hospital, by a travel-to-work area, by the reach of a supermarket or shopping centre, or by any combination of the above and other similar structures and practices. Material coherence hence alludes to the institutional structures that hold a locality together and provide vehicles for collective action. By imagined coherence it is meant that residents of the locality have a sense of identity with the place and with each other, such that they constitute a perceived community with shared patterns of behaviour and shared geographical reference points. Imagined coherence therefore makes a locality meaningful as a space of collective action. There are territorial units that exhibit material coherence but lack a strong imagined coherence – notably artificially amalgamated local authority areas – and there are territories with an imagined coherence but only a weak material coherence, either through fragmentation between local authority areas or integration into larger socio-economic–administrative structures. The authors would not consider areas falling into either of these categories to be strongly functioning localities.

Both material coherence and imagined coherence are also important in fixing (through multiple intersections) the scale at which localities can be identified. The imagined coherence of a locality is framed around perceived shared behaviours (such as using the same schools, hospitals, railway stations, supermarkets; being served by the same local authority; supporting the same football or rugby team; or attending the same 'local' events or joining the same 'local' branches of organizations) and shared geographical/historical reference points (recognition of landscape features; knowledge of local 'characters'; memories of events in 'local' history), but it is 'imagined' in that it is not founded on direct inter-personal connection (cf. ANDERSON, 1991). In this it differs from the social coherence of a neighbourhood – which may share some of the above attributes but is framed around the probability of direct interaction between members – and from the imagined coherence of a region – which is a looser affiliation that draws more on perceived cultural and political identities and economic interests.

Similarly, the material coherence of a locality should be denser and more complex than that found at a neighbourhood or regional scale, since the material coherence of a neighbourhood will be restricted by its situation within a larger geographical area for employment, administrative and many service provision functions, and the material coherence of a region will be fragmented by the inclusion of several different labour markets, local authority areas, sub-regional shopping centres, etc. SAVAGE's (2009) work on 'granular space' is illustrative of these concerns. Savage argued that

> People do not usually see places in terms of their nested or relational qualities: town against country: region against nation, etc. but compare different places with each other without a strong sense of any hierarchical ordering. I further argue that the culturally privileged groups are highly 'vested' in place, able to articulate intense feelings of belonging to specific fixed locations, in ways where abstract and specific renderings of place co-mingle. Less powerful groups, by contrast, have a different cultural geography, which hives off fantasy spaces from mundane spaces.
>
> (p. 3)

The attributes of localities outlined above though do not easily translate into discrete territorial units with fixed boundaries. Labour market areas overlap, as do shopping catchment area; residents may consider themselves to be part of different localities for different purposes and at different times; the reach of a town as an education centre may be different to its reach as an employment centre; and so on. The boundaries that might be ascribed to a locality will vary depending on the issue in question (WARDE, 1989).

All this has a bearing on how localities are identified, defined and constructed for case study research. The authors note here the argument of BEAUREGARD (1988) on the 'absence of practice' in locality research, which was a call for both methodological and political interventions to strengthen locality research. The application of the approach discussed logically leads the authors to start by identifying localities by their cores – whether these be towns or cities or geographical areas – rather than as bounded territories, and working outwards to establish an understanding of their material and imagined coherence. This process will necessarily require mixed methods, combining cartographic and quantitative data on material geographies with qualitative evidence of imagined coherence and performed patterns and relations. However, the authors do not envisage this as an exercise in boundary-drawing. Whilst it may be possible to identify fixed territorial limits for the reach of a locality with respect to certain governmental competences or policy fields, the authors anticipate that all proxy boundaries will be permeable to a degree, and that localities may be configured differently depending on the object of inquiry. The following section provides an illustration of this process as applied to locality research in Wales.

DOING 'NEW LOCALITIES' RESEARCH

This final section provides a short illustration of how the principles of the 'new localities' approach might be deployed in practice in localities research by briefly describing the establishment of a 'Knowing Localities Research Programme' by the Wales Institute of Social and Economic Research, Data and Methods (WISERD).[3] The consolidation of Wales as a regional/national space of social and economic governance with increasingly sharp territorial definition since the introduction of devolved government in 1999 has refocused attention on the dynamics of spatial difference within Wales. Persistent uneven geographies of socio-economic performance as well as seemingly entrenched geographies of political and cultural difference suggest the existence of locality effects within Wales and present challenges for the delivery of policy. However, the shape of the constituent localities is far from clear. Although Wales has a sub-regional tier of twenty-two local authorities, these have only been in existence since 1995 when they replaced a two-tier local government system established in 1974. Moreover, the administrative map is overlain and cross-cut by a plethora of other governmental bodies including health boards, police authorities, transport consortium and economic development partnerships – to name a few – that work to their own territorial remits. An attempt to produce a more nuanced and process-led representation of Wales's internal geography was made with the Wales Spatial Plan in 2004 (updated in 2008), but subsequent efforts to align the initially 'fuzzy' boundaries of the spatial plan regions with the hard boundaries of local authority areas demonstrates the accretional power of fixed institutional geographies in shaping the representation of localities (cf. HAUGHTON *et al.*, 2010; HELEY, 2012; HELEY and JONES, 2012b; WELSH ASSEMBLY GOVERNMENT, 2004, 2008).[4]

The Knowing Localities Research Programme was designed to develop understanding of the form and effects of localities in Wales. In keeping with the wider objective of WISERD to build social science research capacity, the programme aimed to develop analyses of localities that could serve to contextualize future case study research, and to test locality effects in the processes and practices of policy-making and delivery and in wider social and economic experiences and dynamics through a series of focused pilot studies. The programme incorporated elements of the 'new localities' approach from the outset, including the need to examine both the material and imagined coherence of localities, as reflected in its key research questions (Table 1).

The programme was, however, immediately faced with a paradox. Although studying the shape and constitution of localities was intrinsic to the research design, it was also necessary to select the geographical areas in which the research would be undertaken. This was resolved by adopting the strategy proposed above of defining localities by their cores, with the limits initially undetermined. In this way, three localities were selected as the foci for the programme, none of which was based on a single local authority. The *Central and West Coast* locality was loosely based on the 'Central Wales' region described in the Wales Spatial Plan, and included the local authority areas of Ceredigion and Pembrokeshire, and the historic county of Montgomeryshire, each of which could be potentially be identified as a locality in their own right (HELEY *et al.*, 2012). The *North Wales* locality took as its core the A55 transport corridor, with an influenced

Table 1. Implementing a new localities research strategy: research questions for the Wales Institute of Social & Economic Research, Data & Methods (WISERD) Knowing Localities Research Programme

How do people come to 'know' locality?
What are the relationships and barriers between universal, public, elite and local knowledges and how are these articulated and acted upon in everyday discourse, policy and practice?
How does locality condition and contextualize knowledge production and utilization? And how does this lead (or not lead) to effective local-level community action in tackling regeneration?
What are the possibilities for generalizing local knowledge and experience?
How can we map communities of knowledge and the related interrelationships between economic and social welfare within local settings?
How do knowledge of locality and local knowledge shape practices of citizenship and community participation, and contribute to the development of new 'localist' forms of governance through 'place-shaping'?
How is local knowledge and experience enrolled in strategies for economic development, regenerations skills capacity building, and how does knowledge of locality shape engagement with exogenous capital and fluid labour market dynamics?
How can knowing of locality and local knowledge be harnessed in addressing questions of sustainability?
How do the ways in which people 'know' localities in intersect with ways of knowing national and regional identities and territorialities, and how do these shape practices of citizenship and civic engagement?

potentially extending across territories of the five local authority areas that it transected, as well as neighbouring Wrexham (MANN *et al.*, 2011). The *Heads of the Valleys* locality in South Wales focused on a 'place' whose cultural identity had grown since the opening of the Heads of the Valley road in the 1980s, and which had been recently territorially defined as part of the establishment of a regeneration initiative, but which was not consistent with formal administrative boundaries. Responsibility for research in the three areas was led by a different participating university and this short discussion focuses on the *Central and West Coast* locality studied by Aberystwyth University.

The next stages of the research followed the principles of the 'new localities' approach by assembling and examining evidence for the material and imagined coherence of the locality, as well as for the networks, flows and relations that transgressed its proxy boundaries. Firstly, published secondary data were collated to test the material coherence of the locality. These included information on the scale, remit and boundaries of local authorities and other governmental agencies; the territories and provisions of economic development designations; the pattern and focus of strategic and policy delivery partnerships; and the fit of statistical units used to approximate socio-economic dynamics, such as travel-to-work areas. In Central and West Coast Wales this evidence pointed to a fragmented material coherence. 'Central Wales' itself, as represented in the Wales Spatial Plan, exhibited limited material coherence, with no coterminous administrative authority, and an economy differentiated by only partial inclusion in the European Union Convergence Region of West Wales and the Valleys. The individual local authority areas within the Central Wales and West Coast locality certainly held a greater material coherence; but in practice this is being increasingly destabilized by an increasing tendency for inter-authority partnership working. Driven forward in accordance with the desire to increase efficiency (in terms of both cost and accountability), the extent to which joint-authority models of service delivery have been forged and implemented varies according to policy area – as does the geographical orientation of these relationships. For example, Ceredigion and Powys work together as the Central Wales Waste Partnership, where the neighbouring authorities share landfill sites, and facilities for food waste collection and recycling.[5] The highways departments in these two authorities also have a memorandum of understanding and maintain a close operational agenda. By contrast and in respect to children's services, Ceredigion County Council works rather more closely with Pembrokeshire County Council, and the two authorities have established a joint advocacy service catering for the needs of young people in need and in residential care.[6]

Secondly, interviews were conducted with key stakeholders in a variety of public and private organizations to examine the significance of institutional geographies in shaping practice and to explore perceptions of imagined coherence. Again, the interviews produced differentiated results. Institutional settings exerted significant influence over individuals' spatial imaginaries, such that interviewees – perhaps unsurprisingly – tended to identify spatially with the territory of the organization for which they worked. However, at the same time, individuals acknowledged discrepancies between administrative territories and the imagined coherence of the local population (including popular attachment to historical entities such as Montgomeryshire), as well as expressions of imagined coherence with neighbouring areas, in some cases forged through experiences of partnership working. For example, interview data collected by the Knowing Localities Research Programme supported those claims made in official policy releases regarding a strong working relationship between Ceredigion and Pembrokeshire in the area of children's services. With stakeholders working for both authorities making reference to heightened levels of communication and the sharing of resources, this was widely attributed to a shared physical landscape. Specifically, stakeholders made marked references to the predominately rural character of both counties, and to the particular aspects of community, culture and accessibility.

Thus, thirdly, the interview data, together with other secondary sources, provided evidence of the extended relational geographies of the localities concerned. Interviewees asserted the material and imagined coherence of their institutional territory, but they also described narratives of engagement in their everyday work that reached out beyond this delimited space to multiple external sites. For example, interviewees in Ceredigion talked not only about places within the county, but also about neighbouring areas of Pembrokeshire and Gwynedd, the administrative centres of adjacent local authorities, and the Welsh capital, Cardiff. Furthermore, detailed geographical information system (GIS) analysis (ORFORD, 2012) reveals that these described relational geographies varied between policy sectors: being most constrained for crime, and most extensive for education; skewing to the north for language and culture, but to the south for employment and training.

Highlighting the highly fluid and contingent nature of localities, their representation and their ongoing (re) production, it is also important then to reflect on the legacy of past institutional and policy forms, and the role of these forms in shaping and mediating current spatial imaginaries. For example, a considerable number of interviewees working in the Central and West Coast Locality referred to the ongoing influence of Dyfed County Council. Broken up in 1996 under the terms of the Local Government (Wales) Act; with the ancient counties of Carmarthenshire, Pembrokeshire and Cardiganshire (renamed Ceredigion) being restored for administrative purposes; the influence of Dyfed is still felt beyond its ceremonial retention as a

Lord Lieutenancy. Thus, stakeholders working for Ceredigion and Pembrokeshire authorities across a range of policy areas recognized the agency of Dyfed in terms of creating lasting organizational ties (although many council workers of the Dyfed era have retired or left post), and as a lasting, semi-coherent, spatial imaginary. In this way, we are reminded of the importance of ostensibly 'past' political spaces, the creation of boundaries and institutions through of simultaneous rounds of restructuring and sedimentation, and their role in shaping the form and function of their successors (MACKINNON and SHAW, 2010).

CONCLUSIONS: 'REHEATING THE PUDDING'[7]

> [S]electing a pudding requires considerable thought. Cooke's pudding, the heavily battered one made with self-raising flour, is a bit shapeless. Duncan and Savage's alternative recipe seems to have overlooked the sugar and spice, a rather insipid dish of nouvelle cuisine proportions, scarcely pudding at all. A good pudding should have substance, which requires careful choice of ingredients. Probably Cox and Mair's not-quite-frozen jelly is the best on the menu. But beware, too much pudding can make you sick.
>
> (WARDE, 1989, p. 280)

The above quotation is from Warde's classic 'recipes for pudding' analysis of the different menus on offer for doing locality. The analysis offered for the opening night of 'New Localities' will be that whilst concepts such as 'region' and 'place' have been resurrected and reinvigorated by the injection of new theoretical perspectives, 'locality' has been largely neglected. Yet, it is argued here that locality still has potential as an explanatory tool to analyse dynamics and contexts that are not adequately captured by 'region' or 'place'. In short, locality still matters; it is tasty and good for you.

This paper has proposed a new approach to thinking about localities. This recognizes that localities not only exist in absolute space as bounded territories, but also have expression in relative space and relational space where boundaries are at best 'fuzzy' and permeable. Whilst each representation may be legitimately employed to frame localities in particular contexts, taken together they point to a new understanding of localities as multifaceted, dynamic and contingent entities that change shape depending on the viewpoint adopted. These arguments are analogous to the thinking of relational space by authors such as MASSEY (2011). This paper's contribution is to advance this further by recognizing that constructing localities as frames for the analysis of social, economic or political phenomena requires investigation of actual 'acts of locality-making' using the vehicles of imagined coherence and their material coherence, which collectively make a locality meaningful and create a capacity for action. The paper explored this empirically and has moved from the seemingly specific to the broad-ranging. The world is much more complicated than other theories of it (PAASI, 2008) and this paper has thus tried to bridge the divides between theory, methodology and empirics in the analysis of 'thinking space relationally'. The current research is developing this further to 'do space relationally' and one could point to the importance of qualitative GIS analysis being conducted by ORFORD (2012) and others (DODGE *et al.*, 2009) to get a handle on those 'intersections', 'jostlings' and 'granular' descriptions of the regional world. In short, one needs the new locality concept primarily to free the study of places from the shackles of fixed boundaries, but at the same time extreme versions of relational space, where 'all is flow and connectedness' (MASSEY, 2011, p. 4), only tell part of the story. New localities emphasize contingency *and* relationality and this paper has discussed some of the ways in which this can be uncovered.

To summarize, then, the 'new localities' approach has at least three implications for geographical research. Firstly, it provides a revised model for understanding locality effects that does not take localities as a given bounded spatial unit, but which instead emphasizes the contingency and relationality of localities. Secondly, it therefore requires the identification and description of the locality to be incorporated as a core part of the research process, rather than treating locality as a taken-for-granted context that can be lifted off the shelf. This approach further recognizes that the shape, reach and orientation of a locality might differ according to the research questions being examined. Thirdly, it consequently demands a new body of research concerned with establishing the material and imagined coherences of localities, employing mixed-method strategies and framed around the kind of questions described in Table 1. The challenge is to uncover 'knowledge regimes' on the locality-making process and, paraphrasing JONAS (2012, p. 265), to investigate the ways in which these are 'negotiated, constructed and contested', and whether localities become 'semi-permanently fixed' or, conversely, 'dissolve together'. Through these mechanisms, it is argued here, 'locality' can be reclaimed as a meaningful and useful concept in social and economic research. In its resurrected guise 'locality' can be freed from the shackles of fixed boundaries and take on new life as a dynamic shape-shifter, which means that any return to locality studies must recognize that locality boundaries will also be indefinite and permeable. As such, whilst locality research can be spatially focused, it should not be spatially constrained, and needs to be prepared to follow networks and relations across scales and spaces in order to reveal the full panoply of forces and actors engaged in the constitution of a locality. This requires detailed and careful empirical work and the brief study of devolved Wales has sought to demonstrate the possibilities of thinking about new localities.

Acknowledgements – This paper develops ideas explored in 'The local in the global', a chapter by Martin Jones published in LEYSHON A., LEE R., MCDOWELL L. and SUNLEY P. (Eds) (2011) *The Sage Handbook of Economic Geography* (Sage, London). This paper is based on research supported by the Wales Institute of Social & Economic Research, Data & Methods (WISERD). WISERD is a collaborative venture between the universities of Aberystwyth, Bangor, Cardiff, Glamorgan and Swansea. The research to which this publication relates was funded by the Economic and Social Research Council (ESRC) (Grant Number RES-576-25-0021) and the Higher Education Funding Council for Wales (HEFCW). The authors would like to thank the three anonymous referees for their insightful comments and also Andy Pike for his brilliant editorial steer. The authors would also like to thank the Research Fellows at Aberystwyth University – Jesse Heley, Laura Jones and Suzie Watkin – for stimulating discussions on the notion of locality. The usual disclaimers apply.

NOTES

1. Established in 2009, WISERD brings together five universities in Wales with the proviso of developing the quantitative, qualitative and mixed-method research infrastructure. Part of the WISERD work programme is the 'Knowing Localities Research Programme', which considers the way in which place-based embedded experiences impacts on personal, public and professional knowledge regimes. This strand is being driven around primary data collection in and across three localities, which have been chosen to reflect the diversity of contemporary Wales. The findings in this paper are derived from interviews undertaken mainly with local government stakeholders.
2. In positing the notions of material and imagined coherence, the authors are drawing inspiration from, but not seeking to deploy fully, cultural political economy. Cultural political economy emphasizes the interplay of economic and cultural 'imaginaries', that is, narrative elements that provide senses of coherence and identity. The 'imaginary' is not to be understood as opposed to or distinct from reality; it structures a landscape in which individual goals are situated and political projects can be pursued (JESSOP and SUM, 2001).
3. See note 1.
4. The six 'area visions' of the Wales Spatial Plan are: Central Wales; North East Wales (Border and Coast); North West Wales (Eryi a Môn); Pembrokeshire (The Haven); South East Wales (Capital Network); and Swansea Bay (Waterfront and Western Valleys).
5. See http://www.midwaleswaste.org.uk/partners.php/.
6. 'Children and Young People's Plan and Child Poverty Strategy 2011–2014', Ceredigion Children and Young People's Partnership.
7. This subtitle was suggested, with our thanks, by Gordon MacLeod.

REFERENCES

AMIN A. (2004) Regions unbound: towards a new politics of place, *Geografiska Annaler* **86B**, 33–44.

AMIN A., MASSEY D. and THRIFT N. (2003) *Decentering the Nation: A Radical Approach to Regional Inequality*. Catalyst, London.

ANDERSON B. (1991) *Imagined Communities: Reflections on the Origin and Spread of Nationalism*. Verso, London.

BARNES T. (1996) *Logics of Dislocation: Models, Metaphors, and Meanings of Economic Space*. Guilford, New York, NY.

BEAUMONT J. and NICHOLLS W. (2007) Between relationality and territoriality: investigating the geographies of justice movements in the Netherlands and the United States, *Environment and Planning A* **39**, 2554–2574.

BEAUREGARD R. A. (1988) In the absence of practice: the locality research debate, *Antipode* **20**, 52–59.

BENNETT R. J. and MCCOSHAN A. (1993) *Enterprise and Human Resource Development: Local Capacity Building*. Paul Chapman, London.

BEYNON H. and HUDSON R. (1993) Place and space in contemporary Europe: some lessons and reflections, *Antipode* **25**, 177–190.

BEYNON H., HUDSON R., LEWIS J., SADLER D. and TOWNSEND A. (1989) 'It's all falling apart here': coming to terms with the future in Teesside, in COOKE P. (Ed.) *Localities: The Changing Face of Urban Britain*, pp. 267–295. Unwin Hyman, London.

BRENNER N. (2004) *New State Spaces: Urban Governance and the Rescaling of Statehood*. Oxford University Press, Oxford.

BURAWOY M. (2000) *Global Ethnography*. University of California Press, Berkeley, CA.

COCHRANE A. (1987) What a difference the place makes: the new structuralism of locality, *Antipode* **19**, 354–363.

COOKE P. (1987) Clinical inference and geographical theory, *Antipode* **19**, 69–78.

COOKE P. (Ed.) (1989a) *Localities: The Changing Face of Urban Britain*. Unwin Hyman, London.

COOKE P. (1989b) Locality-theory and the poverty of 'spatial variation', *Antipode* **21**, 261–273.

COOKE P. (1990) *Back to the Future: Modernity, Postmodernity and Locality*. Routledge, London.

COOKE P. (1995) Introduction: Regions, clusters and innovation networks, in COOKE P. (Ed.) *The Rise of the Rustbelt*, pp. 1–19. UCL Press, London.

COOKE P. (1998) Introduction: Origins of the concept, in BRACZYK H. J., COOKE P. and HEIDENREICH M. (Eds) *Regional Innovation Systems: The Role of Governances in a Globalized World*, pp. 2–25. UCL Press, London.

COOKE P. (2006) *Locality Debates*. Mimeograph. Centre for Advanced Urban Studies, Cardiff University, Cardiff.

COOKE P. and MORGAN K. (1998) *The Associational Economy: Firms, Regions, and Innovation*. Oxford University Press, Oxford.

COX K. (1993) The local and the global in the new urban politics: a critical view, *Environment and Planning D: Society and Space* **11**, 433–448.

COX K. and MAIR A. (1988) Locality and community in the politics of local economic development, *Annals of the Association of American Geographers* **78**, 307–325.

COX K. and MAIR A. (1991) From localised social structures to localities as agents, *Environment and Planning A* **23**, 197–213.

DODGE M., KITCHIN R. and PERKINS C. (Eds) (2009) *Rethinking Maps: New Frontiers in Cartographic Theory*. Routledge, London.

DUNCAN S. (1989) What is locality?, in PEET R. and THRIFT N. (Eds) *New Models in Geography: Volume Two*, pp. 221–254. Unwin Hyman, London.

DUNCAN S. and SAVAGE M. (1989) Space, scale and locality, *Antipode* **21**, 179–206.

DUNCAN S. and SAVAGE M. (1991) New perspectives on the locality debate, *Environment and Planning A* **23**, 155–164.

ETHERINGTON D. and JONES M. (2009) City-regions: new geographies of uneven development and inequality, *Regional Studies* **43**, 247–265.

GONZÁLEZ S. (2009) (Dis)connecting Milan(ese): deterritorialised urbanism and disempowering politics in globalising cities, *Environment and Planning A* **41**, 31–47.

GREGSON N. (1987) The CURS initiative: some further comments, *Antipode* **19**, 364–370.

HADJIMICHALIS C. (2006a) Non-economic factors in economic geography and in 'new regionalism': a sympathetic critique, *International Journal of Urban and Regional Research* **30**, 690–704.

HADJIMICHALIS C. (2006b) The end of Third Italy as we knew it?, *Antipode* **38**, 82–106.

HARLOE M., PICKVANCE C. and URRY J. (Eds) (1990) *Place, Policy and Politics: Do Localities Matter?* Unwin Hyman, London.

HARRISON J. (2008) The region in political economy, *Geography Compass* **3**, 814–830.

HARRISON J. (2010) Networks of connectivity, territorial fragmentation, uneven development: the new politics of city-regionalism, *Political Geography* **29**, 17–27.

HART M. (2010) *Nations of Nothing But Poetry: Modernism, Transnationalism, and Synthetic Vernacular Poetry*. Oxford University Press, New York, NY.

HARVEY D. (1969) *Explanation in Geography*. Arnold, London.

HARVEY D. (1973) *Social Justice and the City*. Arnold, London.

HARVEY D. (1987) Three myths in search of a reality in urban studies, *Environment and Planning D: Society and Space* **5**, 367–376.

HAUGHTON G., ALLEMENDINGER P., COUNSELL D. and VIGAR G. (2010) *The New Spatial Planning: Territorial Management with Soft Spaces and Fuzzy Boundaries*. Routledge, London.

HELEY J. (2012) Soft spaces, fuzzy boundaries and spatial governance in post-devolution Wales, *International Journal of Urban and Regional Research* DOI: 10.1111/j.1468-2427.2012.01149.x.

HELEY J., GARDNER G. and WATKIN S. (2012) Cultures of local economy in a Celtic fringe region, *European Urban and Regional Studies* DOI: 10.1177/0969776411431102.

HELEY J. and JONES L. (2012a) Relational rurals: some thoughts and relating things and theory in rural studies, *Journal of Rural Studies* **28**, 208–217.

HELEY J. and JONES M. (2012b) Devolution in Wales – fiddling with spatial governance while the economy burns, in WARD M. and HARDY S. (Eds) *Changing Gear – Is Localism the New Regionalism?*, pp. 56–64. Smith Institute, London.

HELEY J. and MOLES K. (2012) Partnership working in regions: reflections on local government collaboration in Wales, *Regional Science Policy and Practice* DOI: 10.1111/j.1757-7802.2012.01061.x.

HUDSON R. (1989) *Wrecking a Region: State Policies, Party Politics and Regional Change in North East England*. Pion, London.

HUDSON R. (1990) Trying to revive infant Hercules: the rise and fall of local authority modernization policies on Teesside, in HARLOE M., PICKVANCE C. and URRY J. (Eds) *Place, Policy and Politics: Do Localities Matter?*, pp 62–86. Unwin Hyman, London.

HUDSON R. (2000) *Production, Places and Environment: Changing Perspectives in Economic Geography*. Prentice-Hall, London.

JACKSON P. (1991) Mapping meanings: a cultural critique of locality studies, *Environment and Planning A* **23**, 215–228.

JESSOP B., BRENNER N. and JONES M. (2008) Theorizing sociospatial relations, *Environment and Planning D: Society and Space* **26**, 389–401.

JESSOP B. and SUM N. L. (2001) Pre-disciplinary and post-disciplinary perspectives in political economy, *New Political Economy* **6**, 89–101.

JONAS A. (1988) A new regional concept of localities, *Area* **20**, 101–110.

JONAS A. (2012) Region and place: regionalism in question, *Progress in Human Geography* **36**, 263–272.

JONES M. (2009) Phase space: geography, relational thinking, and beyond, *Progress in Human Geography* **33**, 487–506.

JONES M. (2010) Limits to thinking space relationally, *International Journal of Law in Context* **6**, 243–255.

JONES M. and JESSOP B. (2010) Thinking state/space incompossibly, *Antipode* **42**, 1119–1149.

JONES M. and MACLEOD G. (2004) Regional spaces, spaces of regionalism: territory, insurgent politics, and the English question, *Transactions of the Institute of British Geographers* **29**, 433–452.

JONES M. and MACLEOD G. (2011) Territorial/relational: conceptualizing spatial economic governance, in PIKE A., RODRIGUES-POSE A. and TOMANEY J. (Eds) *Handbook of Local and Regional Development*, pp. 259–271. Routledge, London.

KATZ C. (2001) On the grounds of globalization: a topography for feminist political engagement, *Signs* **26**, 1213–1234.

KEATING M. (1998) *The New Regionalism in Western Europe*. Elgar, Cheltenham.

LEITNER H., SHEPPARD E. and SZIARTO K. M. (2008) The spatialities of contentious politics, *Transactions of the Institute of British Geographers* **33**, 157–172.

LOVERING J. (1989) The restructuring approach, in PEET R. and THRIFT N. (Eds) *New Models in Geography: Volume One*, pp. 198–233. Unwin Hyman, London.

LOVERING J. (1999) Theory led by policy: the inadequacies of the 'new regionalism' (illustrated from the case of Wales), *International Journal of Urban and Regional Research* **23**, 379–395.

MACKINNON D. (2011) Reconstructing scale: towards a new scalar politics, *Progress in Human Geography* **35**, 21–36.

MACKINNON D. and SHAW J. (2010) New state spaces, agency and scale: devolution and the regionalisation of transport governance in Scotland, *Antipode* **42**, 1226–1252.

MACLEOD G. (2001a) Beyond soft institutionalism: accumulation, regulation, and their geographical fixes, *Environment and Planning A* **33**, 1145–1167.

MACLEOD G. (2001b) New regionalism reconsidered: globalization, regulation, and the recasting of political economic space, *International Journal of Urban and Regional Research* **25**, 804–829.

MACLEOD G. and JONES M. (2007) Territorial, scalar, networked, connected: in what sense a 'regional world'?, *Regional Studies* **41**, 1177–1191.

MACLEOD G. and JONES M. (2011) Renewing urban politics, *Urban Studies* **48**, 2443–2472.

MANN R., PLOWS A. and PATTERSON C. (2011) Civilising community? A critical exploration of local civil society in North West Wales, *Voluntary Sector Review* **2**, 317–335.

MARSTON S. A., JONES J. P. III and WOODWARD K. (2005) Human geography without scale, *Transactions of the Institute of British Geographers* **30**, 416–432.

MARTIN R. and ROWTHORN B. (Eds) (1986) *The Geography of De-industrialisation*. Macmillan, Basingstoke.

MASSEY D. (1984) *Spatial Divisions of Labour: Social Structures and the Geography of Production*. Macmillan, Basingstoke.

MASSEY D. (1991) The political place of locality studies, *Environment and Planning A* **23**, 267–281.

MASSEY D. (1994) *Space, Place and Gender*. Polity, Cambridge.

MASSEY D. (2005) *For Space*. Sage, London.

MASSEY D. (2007) *World City*. Polity, Cambridge.

MASSEY D. (2011) A counterhegemonic relationality of place, in MCCANN E. and WARD K. (Eds) *Mobile Urbanism: Cities and Policymaking in the Global Age*, pp. 1–14. University of Minnesota Press, Minneapolis, MN.

MCCANN E. and WARD K. (2010) Relationality/territoriality: toward a conceptualization of cities in the world, *Geoforum* **41**, 175–184.

MCCANN E. and WARD K. (Eds) (2011) *Mobile Urbanism: Cities and Policymaking in the Global Age*. University of Minnesota Press, Minneapolis, MN.

MERRIMAN P., JONES M., OLSSON G., SHEPPARD E., THRIFT N. and TUAN Y.-F. (2012) Space and spatiality in theory, *Dialogues in Human Geography* DOI: 10.1177/2043820611434864.

MORGAN K. (2007) The polycentric state: new spaces of empowerment and engagement?, *Regional Studies* **41**, 1237–1252.

MURDOCH J. (2006) *Post-Structuralist Geography: A Guide to Relational Space*. Sage, London.

MURGATROYD L., SAVAGE M., SHAPIRO D., URRY J., WALBY S., WARDE A. and MARK-LAWSON J. (1985) *Localities, Class, and Gender*, pp. 245–250. Pion, London.

ORFORD S. (2012) Mapping interview transcript records: theoretical, technical and cartographical challenges. Paper presented at the Wales Institute of Social & Economic Research, Data & Methods (WISERD) Conference, Bangor, UK, March 2012.

PAASI A. (1991) Deconstructing regions: notes on the scales of spatial life, *Environment and Planning A* **23**, 239–256.

PAASI A. (2008) Is the world more complex than our theories of it? TPSN and the perpetual challenge, *Environment and Planning D: Society and Space* **26**, 405–410.

PAASI A. (2010) Regions are social constructs, but who or what 'constructs' them? Agency in question, *Environment and Planning A* **42**, 2296–2301.

PAINTER J. (2008) Cartographic anxiety and the search for regionality, *Environment and Planning A* **40**, 342–361.

PIERCE J., MARTIN D. G. and MURPHY J. T. (2010) Relational place-making: the networked politics of place, *Transactions of the Institute of British Geographers* **36**, 54–70.

PRATT A. C. (1991) Discourses of locality, *Environment and Planning A* **23**, 257–266.

PRATT A. C. (2004) Andrew Sayer, in HUBBARD P., KITCHIN R. and VALENTINE G. (Eds) *Key Thinkers on Space and Place*, pp. 245–250. Sage, London.

SADLER D. (1992) *The Global Region: Production, State Policies and Uneven Development*. Pergamon, Oxford.

SASSEN S. (2006) *Territory, Authority, Rights: From Medieval to Global Assemblages*. Princeton University Press, Princeton, NJ.

SAVAGE M. (2009) *Townscapes and Landscapes*. Mimeograph. Department of Sociology, University of York, York.

SAVAGE M., BARLOW J., DUNCAN S. and SAUNDERS P. (1987) Locality research: the Sussex programme on economic restructuring, social change and the locality, *Quarterly Journal of Social Affairs* **3**, 27–51.

SAVAGE M. and DUNCAN S. (1990) Space, scale and locality: a reply to Cooke and Ward, *Antipode* **22**, 67–72.

SAYER A. (1991) Behind the locality debate: deconstructing geography's dualisms, *Environment and Planning A* **23**, 283–308.

SCOTT A. J. (1988) *New Industrial Spaces: Flexible Production Organisation and Regional Development in North America and Western Europe*. Pion, London.

SCOTT A. J. (1991) Book Review: Philip Cooke (ed.), *Localities: The Changing Face of Urban Britain*, *Antipode* **23**, 256–257.

SCOTT A. J. (2001) Globalization and the rise of city-regions, *European Planning Studies* **9**, 813–826.

SMITH M. P. and GUARNIZO L. E. (2009) Global mobility, shifting borders and urban citizenship, *Tijdschrift voor Economische en Sociale Geografie* **100**, 610–622.

SMITH N. (1987) Dangers of the empirical turn: some comments on the CURS initiative, *Antipode* **19**, 59–68.

STORPER M. (1997) *The Regional World: Territorial Development in a Global Economy*. Guilford, New York, NY.

STORPER M. and SCOTT A. J. (Eds) (1992) *Pathways to Industrialization and Regional Development*. Routledge, London.

THRIFT N. (1983) On the determination of social action in space and time, *Environment and Planning D: Society and Space* **1**, 23–57.

TOMANEY J. (2007) Keep a beat in the dark: narratives of regional identity in Basil Bunting's Briggflatts, *Environment and Planning D: Society and Space* **25**, 355–375.

WARDE A. (1989) A recipe for a pudding: a comment on locality, *Antipode* **21**, 274–281.

WELSH ASSEMBLY GOVERNMENT (2004) *People, Places, Futures: The Wales Spatial Plan*. Welsh Assembly Government, Cardiff.

WELSH ASSEMBLY GOVERNMENT (2008) *People, Places, Futures: The Wales Spatial Plan 2008 Update*. Welsh Assembly Government, Cardiff.

WOODS M. (2007) Engaging the global countryside: globalization, hybridity and the reconstitution of rural place, *Progress in Human Geography* **31**, 485–507.

Experienced Regions and Borders: The Challenge for Transactional Approaches

MAANO RAMUTSINDELA

Department of Environmental & Geographical Science, University of Cape Town, South Africa.

RAMUTSINDELA M. Experienced regions and borders: the challenge for transactional approaches, *Regional Studies*. This paper appreciates the intellectual value of relational thinking but cautions that dismissing 'region' as a meaningful territorial entity and concept, and asserting that borders are irrelevant in a supposedly borderless world, severely limits one's understanding of how both regions and borders are constructed, interconnected and experienced on the ground where they become 'real' to people. The paper affirms the region–border nexus as a promising theoretical avenue for analysing the ways in which regions are not only social constructs that are contingent and contested, but also having a material basis that profoundly shapes human consciousness and action.

RAMUTSINDELA M. 经验区域与边界：来自交易方式的挑战，区域研究。本文在相对论思考的基础上，一方面避免将区域贬抑为一个有意义的领域整体及概念，同时指出边界在无界时间中的非相关性会制约人们对区域及边界是如何被建构、相互关联以及在特定场合中对于人们的'真实性'经验的理解。文章肯定了区域边界联合体这一理论视角对于区域不仅仅是耦合且充满矛盾的社会构建体方式的分析，同时具备影响人们意识与行为的物质基础。

RAMUTSINDELA M. Les régions et les frontières expérimentées; le défi pour les approches transactionnelles, *Regional Studies*. Cet article se rend bien compte de la valeur intellectuelle de la pensée relationnelle mais avertit que refuser de considérer la 'région' comme une entité et une notion territoriales significatives, et affirmer que les frontières sont hors du sujet dans un monde qui est censé être sans frontières, limite sensiblement la compréhension de comment à la fois les régions et les frontières sont construites, entrelacées et expérimentées sur le terrain où elles deviennent de 'vrais' pour la population. L'article affirme que l'interconnexion région-frontière constitue une possibilité théorique prometteuse pour analyser les façons dont les régions sont non seulement des constructions sociales mais ont aussi une base matérielle qui influe profondément sur la conscience et l'action humaines.

RAMUTSINDELA M. Erlebte Regionen und Grenzen: die Herausforderung für Transaktionsansätze, *Regional Studies*. In diesem Beitrag wird der intellektuelle Wert von relationalem Denken gewürdigt, doch zugleich davor gewarnt, dass durch ein Verwerfen der Region als aussagekräftiger territorialer Einheit und Konzept und durch die Behauptung, Grenzen seien in einer angeblich grenzenlosen Welt irrelevant, das eigene Verständnis der Frage, wie Regionen und Grenzen aufgebaut und miteinander verbunden sind und wie sie von den Menschen vor Ort als Realität erlebt werden, erheblich eingeschränkt wird. Stattdessen wird die Verknüpfung zwischen Region und Grenze als vielversprechender theoretischer Weg zur Analyse der Frage bestätigt, inwiefern Regionen nicht nur gesellschaftliche Konstrukte darstellen, die kontingent und angefochten sind, sondern auch eine materielle Grundlage aufweisen, die das Bewusstsein und Handeln der Menschen grundlegend prägt.

RAMUTSINDELA M. Regiones y fronteras percibidas: el reto de los enfoques transaccionales, *Regional Studies*. En este artículo apreciamos el valor intelectual del pensamiento relacional, sin embargo también advertimos que al marginar el concepto de 'región' como una entidad territorial significativa, y al afirmar que las fronteras son irrelevantes en un mundo supuestamente sin fronteras, se limita gravemente la propia comprensión de cómo están construidas e interconectadas las regiones y fronteras y de qué modo se perciben sobre el terreno donde se convierten en algo 'real' para las personas. En este artículo afirmamos que el nexo región–frontera sirve de posibilidad teórica prometedora para analizar el modo en que las regiones no son solamente construcciones sociales contingentes y refutadas, sino también una base material que da forma fundamental a la conciencia y las acciones humanas.

INTRODUCTION: REGIONS AND BORDERS IN THE SOCIAL WORLD

> Lest [the Manifesto for a Relational Sociology] seems incomplete without one, I shall offer one final rallying-cry: Entities of the World – Relate! Both descriptive and prescriptive, with implications both causal and normative, this statement (despite slight interactional overtones) nicely captures the rich possibilities inherent in the relational, transactional vision of social reality.
>
> (EMIRBAYER, 1997, p. 312)

This quotation summarizes the core of conceptions of the social world by relational thinkers who believe that rather than consisting of substances or static 'things', the social world consists of dynamic and unfolding relations (EMIRBAYER, 1997; BOTTERO, 2009). Thus, substantialist and relationalist perspectives are underpinned by different views of the social world and how it should be understood and studied. A substantialist perspective:

> takes as its starting point of departure the notion that it is substances of various kinds (things, beings, essences, etc) that constitute the fundamental units of all inquiry
>
> (EMIRBAYER, 1997, p. 282)

thereby reducing process to static conditions (process reduction) (ELIAS, 1978). For its part, a relationalist perspective is guided by a view of the social universe as dynamic and continuous, and social phenomena that are fluid rather than fixed (ALLEN *et al.*, 1998; ALLEN and COCHRANE, 2007. It rejects any reifying concept, expression and form of thinking (DÉPELTEAU, 2008).

These perspectives account for much of the debate on regions and borders in the social sciences. ALLEN and COCHRANE (2007) have argued for a relational thinking of regions as open and discontinuous spaces that are produced by networked flows and relations that do not respect regional boundaries imposed upon them. Using the neo-liberal growth region in the South East of England as an example, they concluded that 'regions are being remade in ways that directly undermine the idea of a region as a meaningful territorial entity' (p. 1163). Similar sentiments have been made by relationalist thinkers on regional studies (ALLEN *et al.*, 1998; AMIN, 2004) and on borders in transnational context (BLATTER, 2001; ERNSTE *et al.*, 2009). In recent years, attempts have been made to caution the limits of relational thinking on regions and borders and to suggest new theoretical lenses that build on the merits of spatial and non-spatial perspectives instead of abandoning one in favour of the other. To this end, JONES (2009, p. 496) suggests the use of phase space as a conceptual middle ground between 'space as territorial anchorage and fixity and conceptions of space as topological, fluid and relationally mobile'. For Jones flow-like and fixities on space are compatible rather than mutually exclusive and:

> regions are non-essentialist entities that are, in the context of phase space, framed by the balance between different geopolitical, socio-economic, and cultural institutionalizing forces ... that can be activated in strategies, practices and discourses, some of which are bounded and others unbounded.
>
> (p. 499)

DARLING's (2010) work attempts to reconcile 'territorialized approaches' and relational thinking by arguing for the specificities of political projects (including content, spacing and practice) and the ways in which they mobilize varied spatialities. 'A relational account of place still has much to offer,' DARLING (2010, p. 128) maintains, 'when held alongside more place-based impulses.'

The purpose of this paper is to demonstrate the limits of relational thinking on regions and borders, especially when these are experienced and perceived by people on the ground. In working towards this objective, the first part of the paper reflects on new ways of thinking about regions and borders that are often missed when statements that regions have no territorial integrity are made. This is followed by a detailed discussion of the changing dimensions of regions and borders and their stagnation in the South African context. The discussion specifically highlights how the nature, functions, and qualities of regions and borders sharpened residents' conceptions of the spaces in which they live. In the closing pages the paper summarizes the theoretical messages that the South African case study offers to debates on regions as an object of enquiry.

NUANCED UNDERSTANDINGS OF REGIONS AND BORDERS

A meaningful critique of regions should contend with advances in regional studies and border research, especially contemporary understanding of regions as fluid and dynamic rather than as discrete and pre-given units (PAASI, 1999; KIMBLE, 1996). Regions, as they are known, have multiple meanings; they are produced, constructed and practiced in various ways; and are impacted upon by boundless processes (PAASI, 2010; OVERMAN *et al.*, 2010). The new regionalism approach emphasizes regions as social constructions 'that do not arise in a vacuum but that are made in broader social practice' (PAASI, 2009, p. 133). The approach is also attentive to the ways in which state–society complexes and formal and informal actors influence, and respond to, the process of regionalization. In new regionalism, the state is not the only actor but it often competes or collaborates with other forces in shaping a regional space. Informal and illicit enterprises have created all sorts of regions and corridors through which they compete against formal enterprises and state agencies for the share of the market (WASSER *et al.*, 2004). Most of these features of regions are evident in cross-border regions which occur in the form of political and economic projects, a constellation of actor networks, cultural enclaves, and so forth (SÖDERBAUM and TAYLOR, 2008; PAASI, 2009). It has been suggested that cross-border regionalism in Africa has more to do with non-state actors than the state, and represents the continent as it is rather than some normative designs of regions (SÖDERBAUM and TAYLOR, 2008). In short, regions are central to, rather than derivative of, non-spatial processes (AGNEW, 2000) and are also a territorial sphere in which the politics of engagement is often articulated and political power contested (MACLEOD and JONES, 2007).

Equally important is the observation that contemporary border research conceives of borders in their socio-political milieus and, rather than essentializing them, the research has paid adequate attention to the material functions of borders, their symbolic and metaphoric meanings, and to borders as sets of practices and discourses in society (ANDERSON and O'DOWD, 1999; PAASI, 2005; see also PARKER and VAUGHAN-WILLIAMS, 2009). Borders facilitate or obstruct interactions, and the ways in which 'borders are demarcated and managed are central to the notion of border as process and border as institution' (NEWMAN, 2006, p. 148). Thus, border scholars are attentive to the bordering process and its effects on people's daily lives; appreciate that borders are opening but also closing; acknowledge the fact that there is a close relationship between borders and identities; know that borders have spatial and non-spatial qualities; and that they are barriers but at one and the same time theatres of opportunities (NUGENT and ASIWAJU, 1996; AGNEW, 2008). These observations are a test for the 'borderless world' thesis and its emphasis on the deterritorializing tendencies of globalization (OHMAE, 1990; BLATTER, 2001). Indeed, it was the claim of a borderless world that spurred the renaissance of border studies (NEWMAN and PAASI, 1998; DIENER and HAGEN, 2010). Contemporary border studies challenge the borderless thesis, especially the way it accentuates the flow of capital and goods across state borders as if borders do not matter.

Theoretical advances in the study of borders and regions referred to above provide avenues for conceptually linking borders and regions as mutually constitutive as evident in cross-border regions of various kinds. The 'region' and the 'border' in a cross-border region are not necessarily related in co-deterministic ways. Rather, they are both involved in producing spaces of various forms and texture on, and through which, multiple processes operate. As PAASI (2009) has noted, the institutionalization of regions involves borders of various kinds (that is, territorial shaping). Cross-border regions are not only a fitting example of how spaces of regionalism have evolved at sub-national and supra-national levels, but also demonstrate the role of the border in the evolution of regions (PAASI, 2009). The presence of the border is a necessary condition for the creation of trans-border spaces and interactions. In the environmental domain, the creation of cross-border regions is contingent on the reassessment of the implication of the border on the protection and management of biodiversity. The border in fact becomes a narrative through which trans-border conservation areas are constructed and marketed (FALL, 2005; RAMUTSINDELA, 2007a). The recent development of cross-border regions in Europe is linked to, among other things, the creation and expansion of the border of the European Union (MARCU, 2009). These examples highlight that borders create meanings of space (PAASI, 1999) and also congeal flows into regional spatial forms. The next section illustrates that conceptions of regions are inseparable from those of borders and that this situation prevails in both official and civil society circles.

REGIONS AND REGIONALIZATION IN THE SOUTH AFRICAN CONTEXT

ANDERSON (1996) has suggested that questions of the proper size of the territory of sub-national governments and their boundary functions are linked to three theories, namely: constitutional theory about the distribution of power; theories about the relationship of governments to economic performance; and the propositions about the capacity of government below the national level to deliver services. These theories are useful but do not sufficiently explain the regionalization of the state space as a political project and the ways in which regions assume different territorial status and meanings, as amplified by South Africa's sub-national regions. This paper focuses on South Africa's sub-national regions and internal borders from 1910, a year in which the South African state as it is known today took concrete shape in the form of the Union of South Africa. The scope of this paper is therefore limited to the intersection between sub-national regions and borders since the time of the Union and how these could contribute to the debate on relational thinking in regional studies. The paper differentiates sub-national regions in the country into apartheid and post-apartheid phases. Each of these phases is characterized by processes of regionalism and bordering, and their consequent spatial and non-spatial manifestations. These phases exhibit the intricate relationships between borders and regions and also attest to the significance of regions as materialized spaces which hold meanings to people.

The Union Constitution of 1909 recognized political entities of the Cape, Orange Free State, Natal and Transvaal as strong regions[1] in a unitary state. Though the four polities were generally recognized as British (Cape and Natal) and Afrikaner (Orange Free State and Transvaal) colonies, they were not exclusive in terms of population distribution. Each of these regions had a provincial council, an administrator and an executive committee. The councils had the powers to develop their own administrative system, and these were retained when the Union became a Republic in 1961. The regions and their attributes (for example, population) provided the basis on which constituencies (electoral divisions) were delimited (Table 1).

By relegating the Cape, Natal, Orange Free State and the Transvaal to sub-national regions, the Union government not only attempted to unify the former English and Afrikaner polities into a nation-state, but also essentially applied a constitutional theory in which power was distributed between Afrikaners and the English as citizens of a common state (De Villiers, 1995). The creation of these sub-national regions is akin to transforming state borders into sub-national borders; a process of rescaling which has been experienced elsewhere (Marcu, 2009).

When those four polities became *de facto* regions of the Union, the process of forging a common white identity that transcends the historical division and conflict between the English and Afrikaners became an issue while regional borders per se were not contested. The move towards forging a white national identity included the use of landscapes and the Kruger National Park (Carruthers, 1995; Anker, 2001). The corollary to the promotion of a white nation was the accentuation of difference between races by means of territorial segregation. Schutte (1995) is of the view that:

> all white interest groups seemed to have agreed on the principle of territorial segregation of white and black after the unification of South Africa's four [polities] in 1910.
>
> (p. 35)

The passage of the Natives Land Act in 1913 by the Union government set in motion patterns of landownership and land dispossession which had racial undertones, hence 1913 is used as a cut-off date for land claims in post-apartheid South Africa (Ramutsindela, 2007b). These patterns were later to give shape to bantustans as regions for Africans that were politically separate from 'white' South Africa. It is argued here that the Act, together with subsequent legislation, became a cornerstone of apartheid's literal borders and also reflected other forms of bordering, namely, the creation of an exclusive white nation-state. Whereas the Natives Land Act of 1913 did not create hard literal borders around the reserves – as Africans in the reserves were provided for by the regions in which they lived – racial borders between whites and non-whites had already taken shape (Daverport and Saunders, 2000). The reserves were associated with Africans hence the Director on Native Agriculture, R. W. Thornton, considered deteriorating conditions in the reserves as not only leading to the 'colossal permanent poor [African] problem' but as also threatening white South Africa 'with calamity' (Dubow, 1989, p. 69).

It follows that the regionalization of the state space in the Union was not only limited to reconfiguring the polities that preceded the Union, but also aimed at transforming regional identities into a national white identity. This political project crumbled under the weight of Afrikaner nationalists who mobilized political support on the basis of difference; relying heavily on constituencies from their pre-1910 polities which had become regions (O'Meara, 1983; Dubow, 1994; Lemon, 2003; Giliomee, 2009). This mobilization moved to a national gear in 1924 when Hertzog and other Anglo-Boer War veterans ascended to cabinet positions in the Union (Daverport and Saunders, 2000). The resurgence of Afrikaner nationalism in the Union attests to the fact that national identity cannot simply be formed by redefining regions, more so because the spatial legacies of borders are hard to erase. In terms of the theme of this paper the creation of regions in the Union and the consequent exclusion of Africans, together with the remobilization of Afrikaner national identity at regional and national levels, illustrate a seamless connection between borders and regions which is often missed in analyses that seek to undermine regions and borders as useful conceptual tools. This connection is not limited to certain scales as the discussion below will make clear.

Table 1. Electoral divisions per region, 1973–1983

Date of delimitation	Cape	Natal	Orange Free State	Transvaal	Total
1910	51	17	17	36	121
1913	51	17	17	45	130
1919	51	17	17	49	134
1923	51	17	17	50	135
1928	58	17	18	55	148
1932	61	16	16	57	150
1937	59	16	15	60	150
1942	56	16	14	64	150
1947	55	16	13	66	150
1953	54	15	13	68	150
1958	52	16	14	68	150
1965	54	18	15	73	160
1973[a]	55	20	14	76	165

Note: [a]The delimitation was valid for ten years (that is, 1973–1983).
Source: South Africa (1983), p. 133.

Following the emergence of the first purely Afrikaner government in 1948 (DAVERPORT and SAUNDERS, 2000), the reserves that had been set aside in 1913 and enlarged in 1936 in terms of the Native Trust and Land Act became core areas of bantustans where Africans 'owned' land under a communal tenure system as opposed to a private property regime used in 'white area'. The effort to purify the white state saw the apartheid state embarking on a rigorous programme of up-scaling regions occupied by Africans into pseudo-independent states with the passage of the Bantu Authorities Act of 1951 and the Promotion of Bantu Self-Government Act of 1959 (SOUTH AFRICA, 1960). These acts conferred legislative powers to bantustan governments.

When the Union became the Republic in 1961 questions about the powers of regions rather than their need in 'white' South Africa were brought to the fore. White liberals, in particular the Progressive Federal Party, advocated federalism as an essential check on central government. The National Party (NP) government opposed federalism which it saw as an obstacle towards creating a centricist state through which an apartheid agenda could be fully implemented. The NP governments' view on bantustans was not guided by a vision for one federal state for all South Africans. Instead, bantustans were a political project designed to promote ethnic identities by designating separate territories for each of the major linguistic groups. The attempt to incorporate nominally independent bantustans into the Constellation of Southern States was a strategy of Prime Minister P. W. Botha's government to maintain the apartheid state; gain Western acceptance of South Africa's domestic arrangements; and thwart external military threats to Pretoria and its interests in the region (PRICE, 1984; ONSLOW, 2009). Bantustans were institutionalized through the demarcation of territorial and conceptual borders; and some bantustans such as Venda and Bophuthatswana reflected the linguistic groups found in them. All bantustans had formal institutions such as territorial authorities and also promoted some form of regional consciousness. Conceptually, the acts referred to above hardened two types of borders: the border between whites and Africans and that between African linguistic groups. This is evident in the massive forced removals of Africans from 'white' areas (PLATZKY and WALKER, 1985) and new border conflicts that accompanied the creation of bantustans (RAMUTSINDELA and SIMON, 1999). The manipulation of borders and regions provides evidence that processes associated with regions and borders could be mutually supportive depending on the goal at hand.

In the 1980s the South African state was highly securitized due to political developments in the country and across its borders; leading to a highly centralized administration. Consequently, the regional legislatures in 'white' South Africa were abolished on 1 July 1986 and were replaced by Presidential appointees (SOUTH AFRICA, 1992). The apartheid state also created Regional Services Councils (RSCs) in 1985 to align local government structures with constitutional reforms that were initially aimed at incorporating Coloureds and Indians into the structures of the state but were later reframed to accommodate urban Africans. RSCs were neo-apartheid local government structures in that though they sought to coordinate and provide services on a regional basis (hard functions), the primary local authorities – which provided services for the locals (soft functions) and on which RSCs were anchored – were established along racial lines (SEETHAL, 1991). This division between 'hard' and 'soft' functions was to be reproduced later when district and local municipalities were created in post-apartheid South Africa. With the exception of Natal, RSC boundaries did not extend to bantustan areas and were rejected in KwaZulu as an imposition by Pretoria (MCCARTHY, 1988). However, 'the [borders] of the RSCs were not a source of great dispute' (HUMPHRIES and SHUBANE, 1992, p. 20). Though RSCs reproduced the apartheid city, CAMERON (1993, p. 425) sees them as 'the first fully multi-racial decision-making bodies at local level'. Viewed in the context of borders and regions, the RSCs served to distinguish rural Africans from those in urban areas, and how these two should relate to 'white' South Africa. The recognition of the distinction among Africans in terms of location and ethnicity contradicted the very category of race – which erases difference – on which apartheid South Africa was founded.

The wide-ranging regional dispensation that was launched in 1982 is also instructive with regard to borders and regions. In pursuing some form of inclusion in a racially segregated state, the apartheid government created nine development regions, which cut across the four (white) regions while also transcending the borders of the RSCs and the bantustans. These development regions were variously seen as a strategy for incorporating blacks within the central state institutions while retaining race and ethnicity as the basis for political dispensation and as a means for supporting bantustans while curbing black migration to urban areas (SAVAGE, 1986; CHRISTOPHER, 1994). Nonetheless, the symbolic shape of the regions signalled a move away from overt racial and ethnic connotations. For example, the regions were named after the letters of alphabet, A to J. And the borders of development regions were not contested. In summary, regions under apartheid were not static but their significance and functions changed as a result of shifts in the political landscape. Regions are indeed social constructs that are infused with meanings that are often unstable (PAASI, 1999). When the apartheid state finally collapsed in the early 1990s, the four regions that had been established under the Union and the nine development regions had gained acceptance. The borders of the four regions had, for instance, formed the international borders of the Republic. These regions, together with the politically unpalatable bantustans, were crucial for debates on regionalism in a democratic South Africa.

DEMOCRATIZING THE STATE: BORDERS AND THEIR REGIONAL DIMENSIONS

The apartheid-era regions underpinned the regional debate in the early 1990s, especially the form of the state in the new political dispensation; the bases on which new regions were to be demarcated; and the functions which these regions were to perform. Rather than flows or imaginations of some sort, regions were understood as an expression of the form of the state: a unitary state with weak regions or a federal state with strong regions. Led by the African National Congress (ANC), proponents of the unitary state argued that strong regions would weaken the power of the state and its ability to transform society. HUMPHRIES and SHUBANE (1992) claim that the ANC's vision for a unitary state was informed by:

> the extent to which the National Party itself was able, through its control of central government, to fundamentally shape South African society according to its own ideological vision.
>
> (p. 5)

The second view, which was championed by the NP government and white liberals, held that South Africa could achieve the political imperatives of diversity and unity through a federal state. The NP, which was opposed to a federal state in the past, saw federalism in post-apartheid South Africa as a vehicle for protecting minority rights and power in the ANC majority government (MUTHIEN and KHOSA, 1995; RAMUTSINDELA and SIMON, 1999). Its conception of regionalism was founded on the theory of consociational democracy in which elites from different segments share power over government decisions (HUMPHRIES and SHUBANE, 1992). To achieve its political objective, the NP used the notion of regions rather than federalism to suggest a milder form of federalism that would be acceptable to the ANC-led liberation movement. The combined effects of the influence of comparative international constitutional experiences and the need for winning the support of sympathetic bantustan administrations enticed the ANC to embrace strong regions (MUTHIEN and KHOSA, 1995). It is suggested in this paper that the NP and the ANC used the same language of regionalism for entirely different reasons. The ANC regarded regions as a means to end, meaning agreeing to the concept of a region as a stepping stone towards capturing the state. For its part, the NP and its allied groups viewed regions as a means for defending the status quo in the new political dispensation (RAMUTSINDELA and SIMON, 1999). The opposing views on regions raised the question of whether regions should first be created in order to allow people to identify with them or whether existing regions, which have some regional consciousness, should be used as a stepping stone towards a new regional dispensation.

The debate on regions as a determinant of the form of the state reveals that conceptions of borders could be tied to that of region; further evidence that borders and regions are linked together in the conceptualization of space and power (PAASI, 2009). A telling example of this was the ANC's argument that regions were merely administrative units of the unitary state and that regional borders were peripheral to the restructuring of the state. It conceded that regional borders should not coincide with ethnic, racial and linguistic borders as this, in its view, could lead to the balkanization of the country (ANC, 1992). Despite this caution, the ANC embraced the four 'white' regions and nine development regions as a sound basis for the progressive re-integration of bantustans into the new South African state. Of significance to the discussion in this paper is that proponents of a unitary state considered the borders of regions as insignificant to the political project of developing a new national identity that transcends those borders. Such relational overtones are problematic as they ignore other forms of identity construction and the ways in which regions had impacted on people. The proposals for regional demarcation by some bantustan leaders are instructive on this. Though they were rejected by the liberation movement, bantustans had acquired a material reality, which could not be ignored in the restructuring of the state and the transformation of society. Unsurprisingly, bantustan leaders considered the demarcation of new regional borders as an opportunity for reconstituting their power bases and for advancing land claims. They pressed for new regional borders which either reflected or extended existing ethnically based bantustans and, in some cases, for demarcating borders that reflected entire pre-colonial kingdoms and chieftaincies (MUTHIEN and KHOSA, 1995). Like bantustan leaders, conservative Afrikaner groups argued for a regional dispensation that would promote some form of self-determination. In both counts there was an attempt to align literal and conceptual borders and to use this alignment as a basis for contesting power.

The contrasting views on borders and regions and their roles in transforming the state were considered by the Commission on the Demarcation/Delimitation of Regions (CDDR) that was charged with the task of demarcating regional borders in 1993. The demarcation process is well documented (MUTHIEN and KHOSA, 1995; RAMUTSINDELA and SIMON, 1999). It is nonetheless worth noting that the CDDR adopted and reaffirmed apartheid-era development regions as the basis for the post-apartheid state on the following grounds: first, the regions represented a hybrid of federalism and unitarism which made them a critical political compromise. Accordingly, DE VILLIERS (2007) has asserted that:

> it is fair to conclude that without the creation of [regions], the political compromises which gave rise to South Africa's democracy would not have been possible.
>
> (p. 4)

Second, the criteria used for demarcating regions were contradictory enough to prevent any radical reconceptualization of regions (RAMUTSINDELA and SIMON, 1999). Third, the two main parties in political negotiations, the ANC and NP, had accepted development regions as the basis for regional demarcation (MUTHIEN and KHOSA, 1995). Fourth, technical advisors to the CDDR such as De Villiers also supported the use of development regions (DE VILLIERS, 1995). Fifth, the development regions were acceptable because they originated from technical planning rather than overt political visions. Sixth, the regions appeared to represent an appropriate number of regions for a democratic South Africa (HUMPHRIES and SHUBANE, 1992; WELSH, 1994; DE VILLIERS, 1995). Both the interim (1993) and final (1996) constitutions conferred legislative powers to these regions as the second tier of the post-apartheid government – which made them resemble the four regions under the Union. These regions were largely institutionalized from 1994 onwards.

In addition to the reappearance of development regions in the form of the current provinces, post-1990 South Africa also inherited features of the RSCs discussed above. In 1990 the Thornhill Report recommended the creation of mini-RSCs with autonomous local authorities and local bodies as one of the models for non-racial local authorities in post-apartheid South Africa (SOUTH AFRICA, 1990). White local authorities used existing RSCs to consolidate their powers and to pre-empt local government structures in a democratic South Africa (CAMERON, 1993). Meanwhile, the Municipal Demarcation Board (MDB) was established in 1998 with the mandate to establish financially and administratively viable municipalities which integrate the citizens of the Republic (SOUTH AFRICA, 1998a). Of relevance to the theme of this paper is that the MDB established three categories of municipalities, namely: A (metros), B (local municipalities) and C (district municipalities) (MDB, 2004). Effectively, district municipalities took over the region-wide functions that were performed by apartheid-era RSCs while local municipalities performed 'soft' functions. For example, a district municipality is responsible for integrated development plans for the local municipalities falling within the jurisdiction of the district municipality, bulk supply of water and electricity, municipal roads, health services, and so on (SOUTH AFRICA, 1998b, 2000a). It:

> may levy and claim a regional services levy and a regional establishment levy referred to in section 12(1)(a) of the Regional Services Councils Act, 1985.
>
> (SOUTH AFRICA, 2000a, p. 13)

In brief, the attempt to redraw borders and create regions for a democratic state provided the platform on which official and non-official views and meanings of borders could be contested, as the next section will illustrate.

CONTESTING BORDERING AND REGIONALIZATION

In contrast to the 'borderless world' thesis and the tendency among relational thinkers to denounce the territorial significance of regions, borders and regions do matter to people affected by them. They are also useful concepts and sites for understanding the changing social world. In the context of the transformation of the South African society, the re-invention of new sub-national regions from the old, and the subsequent institutionalization of those regions, provided avenues through which ordinary citizens could contest the combined processes of bordering and regionalization for various reasons. First, the new regions entrenched inequalities in the country's space economy. For example, the municipal infrastructure is weakest in regions such as the Eastern Cape and Limpopo which inherited a greater portion of the former bantustans (GAFFNEY'S GROUP, 2006; MAIL & GUARDIAN, 2008; SOUTH AFRICA, 2009). Table 2 shows that regions differ significantly in terms of their development indices as measured by gross domestic product. The skewed distribution of resources implies that residents have unequal access to resources, hence protests over the borders of regions between 1993 and 2009 were couched in terms of resource access and the inequitable distribution of services (NARSIAH and MAHARAJ, 1997; RAMUTSINDELA and SIMON, 1999). The language of development and

Table 2. Population and gross domestic product (GDP) per the province

Province	Percentage of GDP[a]	Population estimates[b]	Percentage of the total population[b]
Eastern Cape	8.1	6 743 800	13.5
Free State	5.5	2 824 500	5.7
Gauteng	33.3	11 191 700	22.4
KwaZulu-Natal	16.7	10 645 400	21.3
Limpopo	6.7	5 439 600	10.9
Mpumalanga	6.8	3 617 600	7.2
Northern Cape	2.2	1 103 900	2.2
North West	6.3	3 200 900	6.4
Western Cape	14.4	5 223 900	10.4
Total	100	49 991 300	100

Notes: [a]2009 figures.
[b]Mid-year, 2010.

Sources: STATISTICS SOUTH AFRICA (2010a, 2010b); SOUTH AFRICA (2006).

resource endowment runs through grassroots campaigns for regional border changes that were variously organized by the Bushbuckridge Border Crisis Committee, the Matatiele Mass Action Organizing Committee, the Merafong Demarcation Forum, and the Moutse Demarcation Forum (HORNER, 2005; NARE, 2006; KOTLOLO, 2008; NTINGI, 2010). That is to say, border protests were about access to services in resource-endowed provinces such as Gauteng.

Second, while the demarcation process attempted to incorporate the voices of ordinary citizens – through submissions to the demarcation boards – most borders were imposed on residents. The ANC-led government dismissed requests for modest border changes by residents as amounting to destabilizing areas 'at the expense of the first and only legitimate, democratically elected and constituted African National Congress-led Government' (ANC, 1997). This attitude pervades official responses to the grassroots' demand for border changes, and also reveals the simplistic assumption that internal borders do not matter in a democratic South Africa. For example, former President Mbeki dismissed border protests in Khutsong (Fig. 1) as:

> mischievous efforts to elevate administrative issues, such as the demarcation of provincial boundaries, into important issues of the national democratic revolution, to divert attention away from the fundamental concerns of the masses of the people.
>
> (cited in VAN DER MERWE, 2005, p. 4)

Following the same logic, the former Premier of North West opposed the demands for border changes in Khutsong and suggested that:

> whether people fell in one or the other province should not be a critical matter ... what was important was that they belonged to one South Africa where all people were guaranteed their rights and services irrespective of where they lived.
>
> (PEETE, 2005, p. 5)

This is not true because regions have a constitutional mandate to provide services such as basic education and health to residents found in those regions (SOUTH AFRICA, 2007).

It should be emphasized that border communities felt that they were marginalized from the demarcation process even when the majority of residents had voted in support of border changes. For example, it is reported that in Matatiele 5000 people opposed the reincorporation of the area into the Eastern Cape compared with eighty who were in favour (LAGANPARSAD, 2009). Despite this outcome, the government proceeded with the reincorporation which was sanctioned by the courts on procedural grounds. The point here is that border protests were about asserting community aspirations in a democratic state and a reaction to the illusion of democracy as epitomized by the demarcation process. As the Editorial of the SUNDAY TIMES (2007) put it:

> the people of Khutsong are justifiably angry that they were misled into believing that their views counted for anything. They feel betrayed by the party they voted into government, and now believe that democracy is just a theory.
>
> (p. 28)

Third, border protests were also incited by the attempt by government to solve border disputes by demarcating more borders in the form of cross-border municipalities that straddle regional borders. The official reasons for cross-border municipalities were that they would promote functional linkages across regional borders, consolidate the tax base and promote efficient administration (SOUTH AFRICA, 2000b). Conceptually, cross-border municipalities represent attempts to play down the significance of municipal borders and to promote spatial visions congenial to the ideal of common nationhood. It could, however, be argued that the main reasons for creating cross-border municipalities were attempts to manage the demands for border changes under the guise of administrative efficiency and to prepare for local government elections that were held in 2000. The evidence of this claim is that most of the cross-border municipalities were created in areas where the demarcation of regional borders was in dispute (RAMUTSINDELA, 2010).

Fourth, border protests were about territorial politics. Since the early 1990s regions have become crucial for national and political party elections and also impact on the organizational structures of political parties. In national elections political parties often target regions they regard as their power bases as the examples of the Democratic Alliance in the Western Cape and Inkatha Freedom Party in KwaZulu-Natal show. Provincial votes are crucial for ascension to party leadership and the presidency of the country, as the 2007 ANC presidential elections make this clear. Notwithstanding the importance of votes from ANC structures such as the Youth League and Women's League, the party's presidential elections are either won or lost in regions. It is on this basis that most analysts viewed the failure of former President Mbeki to win more than four provinces in the run up to the ANC presidential election in 2007 as a signal for his demise (CAPE ARGUS, 2007; TSEDU, 2007).

Fifth, some of the border disputes were tied up with strategies for consolidating power at the regional level with the hope of gaining a passage to high offices. This is clear when border protests are supported by a faction of a particular political party or by an opposition party. By way of example, border protests in Khutsong had a strong anti-Mbeki sentiment which fed into the wider pro-Zuma political campaign in the battle for the soul of the ANC (BENJAMIN and MPHUTHING, 2005; NDABA and MAPHUMULO, 2005). This explains why the former Minister of Defence and national chairperson of the ANC under the Mbeki leadership, Mosiua

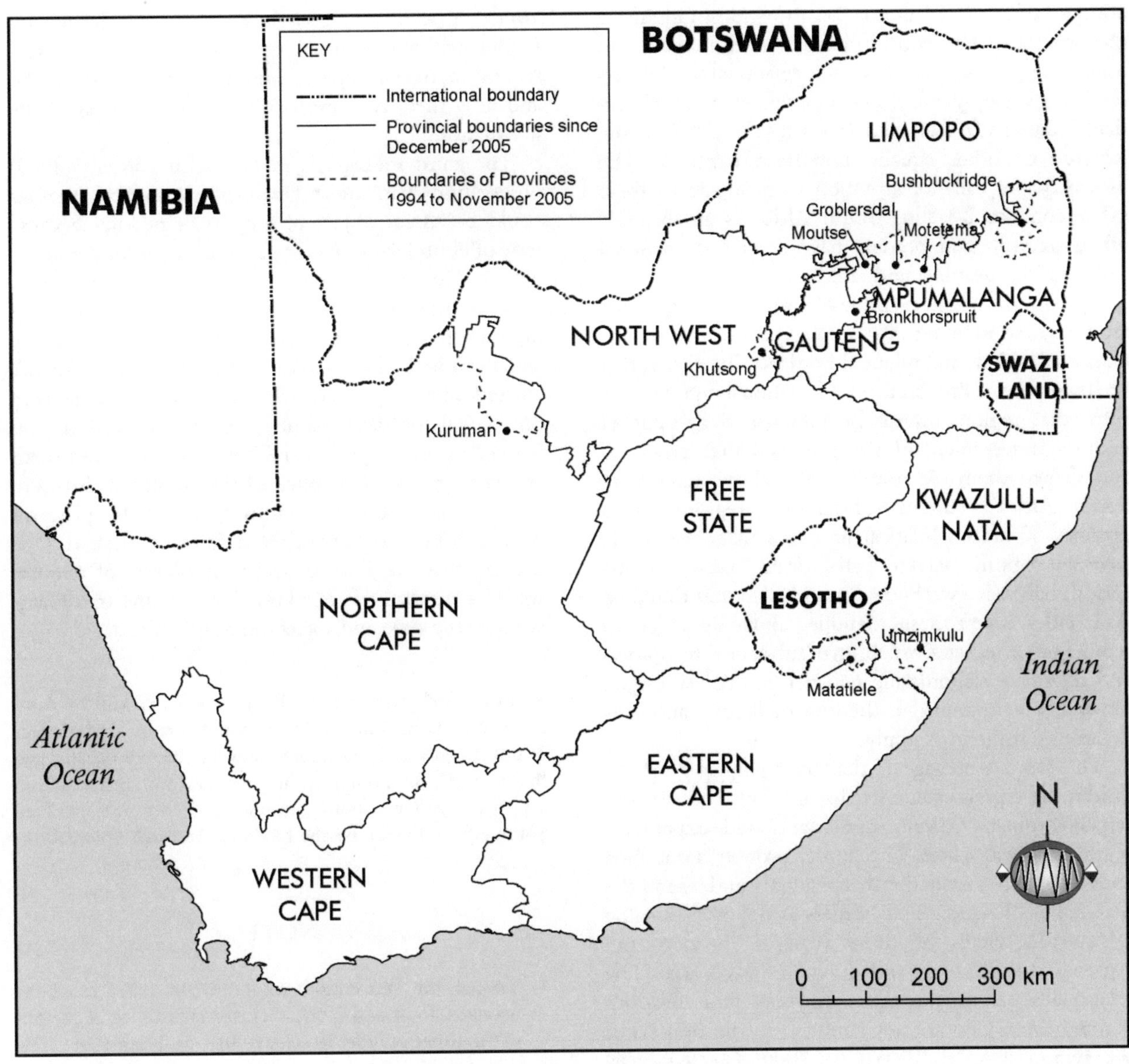

Fig. 1. Provincial boundaries and disputed areas
Source: Author

Lekota, was not even allowed in Khutsong. The first and only concession for border changes since Jacob Zuma became President of the Republic in 2009 was in Khutsong. It could be argued that the concession feeds into the image-building of the Zuma administration as one that listens to the masses when in actual fact it has ignored the voices of the people of Matatiele and Moutse whose border protests date back to political negotiations in the early 1990s.

CONCLUSION: MESSAGES FROM THE SOUTH AFRICAN EXPERIMENT

A growing body of work on regions and borders has moved away from substantialist perspectives to emphasize regions as products of complex processes (Agnew, 2000; Söderbaum and Taylor, 2008; Paasi, 2009; Jonas, 2011) and borders as both process and institution (Paasi, 2009; Newman, 2006). This literature nevertheless still considers the notion of territory as relevant for understanding regions. Relational spatial thinkers have misgivings about territorial viewpoints of regions and instead insist that regions should be understood in terms of 'interspatial relations, flows and networks' (Jonas, 2011, p. 1) rather than as bounded spaces. Others have attempted to bring territorial and relational approaches together and to relate these to questions of territory and territorial politics (Jones, 2009; Darling, 2010; Jonas, 2011). The present paper has attempted to contribute to the debate on regions in two ways. First, it has drawn insight on regions and borders to engage misgivings about territorial approaches. It has argued that critiques of territorial approaches to regions undermine the process of bordering inherent in the making and unmaking of regions. Second, relationalist thinkers tend to over-emphasize economic experiences of particular regions (ALLEN and COCHRANE, 2007) at the expense of other equally important contexts. The present paper calls for attention to be made to these other contexts by using South Africa as an example where regions and borders have significant material and political meanings and effects.

The South African example offers three messages that are worth considering in the debate about the redundancy of regions and regional borders. The first is that the trajectory of the country's sub-national regions confirms that regions cannot be understood as units of enquiry independent of the processes that produced and shaped them. As noted in the above discussion, South Africa's current sub-national regions are a product of various political processes that, over time, gave the regions concrete spatial forms. Inadequate historical analysis is a weakness of some relationist thinking. As in cities, the processes identified above do lay down sediments or legacies which give 'substance' to borders and regions – debordering and deterritorialization are never as unconstrained as theorists of fluidity and borderlessness sometimes imply.

The second message is that over-emphasis on the fluidity of regions contrasts sharply with the ways in which ordinary citizens understand and experience regions as lived spaces. The border protests mentioned above serve as a reminder that residents understand the materiality of regions and borders as opposed to some relationalist views of these (that is, borders and regions) as some open and discontinuous spaces. The relationalist argument that processes and relations shaping the region are not confined to the borders of the region is valid (BATHELT, 2006; MACKINNON and TETZLAFF, 2009) but does not answer the question why regional borders matter to ordinary citizens. The South African example shows that the debate on regions will benefit from paying attention to the intersection between regions and borders (PAASI, 2009) and how these two are involved in the process of co-production.

The third message is in line with JONES's (2009) observation that, under certain circumstances, regions could be useful object of enquiry, especially because they offer opportunities for performing practical politics. JONAS (2011) also emphasizes that the distinction between territorial and relational approaches does not hold when regions are viewed in the context of territory and territorial politics. This is true for South Africa's current nine regions which have become a platform on which political battles are waged within and between political parties and between the government and civic groups. For much of the country's history in the twentieth century regions provided the platform on which the ideology of the state was contested. Dismissing these regions as irrelevant objects of enquiry would severely limit our knowledge of the transformation of the state and society in South Africa.

Acknowledgements – The author is thankful to Anssi Paasi and Martin Jones for their comments on earlier drafts of this paper, and to the anonymous referees who challenged him to clarify his thoughts. This paper draws on material from a project on 'Cross-border municipalities in post-apartheid South Africa' funded by the National Research Foundation.

NOTE

1. Though the four entities were officially called provinces between 1910 and 1993, they are referred to as regions in this paper in order to achieve analytical clarity and consistency. The terms 'provinces' and 'regions' were used interchangeably during the historic negotiation for a new political dispensation in the early 1990s.

REFERENCES

AFRICAN NATIONAL CONGRESS (ANC) (1992) *ANC Regional Policy*. University of the Western Cape, Bellville.

AFRICAN NATIONAL CONGRESS (ANC) (1997) *Statement of the ANC on Bushbuckridge*. 23 June. ANC, Johannesburg.

AGNEW J. (2000) From the political economy of regions to regional political economy, *Progress in Human Geography* **24**, 101–110.

AGNEW J. (2008) Borders on the mind: re-framing border thinking, *Ethics and Global Politics* **1**, 175–191.

ALLEN J. and COCHRANE A. (2007) Beyond the territorial fix: regional assemblages, politics and power, *Regional Studies* **4**, 1161–1175.

ALLEN J., MASSEY D. and COCHRANE A. (1998) *Rethinking the Region*. Routledge, London.

AMIN A. (2004) Regions unbound: towards a new politics of place, *Geografiska Annaler* **86B**, 33–44.

ANDERSON J. and O'DOWD L. (1999) Borders, border regions and territoriality: contradictory meanings, changing significance, *Regional Studies* **33**, 593–604.

ANDERSON M. (1996) *Frontiers: Territory and State Formation in the Modern World*. Polity, Cambridge.

ANKER P. (2001) *Imperial Ecology: Environmental Order in the British Empire, 1895–1945*. Harvard University Press, Cambridge, MA.

BATHELT H. (2006) Geographies of production: growth regimes in spatial perspective – 3. Toward a relational view of economic action and policy, *Progress in Human Geography* **30**, 223–236.

BENJAMIN C. and MPHUTHING P. (2005) SACP, Cosatu rebel against boundary law, *Business Day (Johannesburg)* **9 December**, 3.

BLATTER J. (2001) Debordering the world of states: toward a multi-level system in Europe and a multipolicy system in North America. Insights from border regions, *European Journal of International Relations* **7**, 175–209.

BOTTERO W. (2009) Relationality and social interaction, *British Journal of Sociology* **60**, 399–420.
CAMERON R. (1993) Regional Services Councils in South Africa: past, present and future, *Public Administration* **71**, 417–439.
CAPE ARGUS (2007) Zuma will be President, *Cape Argus (Cape Town)* **26 November**.
CARRUTHERS J. (1995) *The Kruger National Park: A Social and Political History*. University of Natal Press, Pietermaritzburg.
CHRISTOPHER A. J. (1994) *An Atlas of Apartheid*. Routledge, London.
DARLING J. (2010) A city of sanctuary: the relational re-imagining of Sheffield's asylum politics, *Transaction of the Institute of British Geographers* **35**, 125–140.
DAVERPORT T. R. H. and SAUNDERS C. (2000) *South Africa: A Modern History*. Macmillan, London.
DE VILLIERS B. (1995) *A Constitutional Scenario for Regional Government in South Africa: The Debate Continues*. Konrad-Adenauer-Stiftung, Pretoria.
DE VILLIERS B. (2007) *The Future of Provinces in South Africa – The Debate Continues*. Konrad-Adenauer-Stiftung, Johannesburg.
DÉPELTEAU F. (2008) Relational thinking: a critique of co-deterministic theories of structure and agency, *Sociological Theory* **26**, 51–73.
DIENER A. C. and HAGEN J. (2010) Introduction: Borders, identity and geopolitics, in DIENER A. C. and HAGEN J. (Eds) *Borderlines and Borderlands: Political Oddities at the Edge of the Nation-State*, pp. 1–14. Rowman & Littlefield, Lanham, MD.
DUBOW S. (1989) *Racial Segregation and the Origins of Apartheid in South Africa,* 1919–36. Macmillan, London.
DUBOW S. (1994) Ethnic euphemisms and racial echoes, *Journal of Southern African Studies* **30**, 355–370.
ELIAS N. (1978) *What is Social Science?* Hutchinson, London.
EMIRBAYER M. (1997) Manifesto for a relational sociology, *American Journal of Sociology* **103**, 281–317.
ERNSTE H., VAN HOUTUM H. and ZOOMERS A. (2009) Trans-world: debating the place and borders of place in the age of transnationalism, *Tijdschrift voor Economische en Sociale Geografie* **100**, 577–586.
FALL J. (2005) *Drawing the Line: Nature, Hybridity and Politics in Transboundary Spaces*. Ashgate, Aldershot.
GAFFNEY'S GROUP (2006) *Local Government in South Africa, 2004–2006*. Gaffney Group, Northlands.
GILIOMEE H. (2009) *The Afrikaners: Biography of a People*, 2nd Edn. Tafelberg, Cape Town.
HORNER B. (2005) Town caught in a crossfire fights back, *Sunday Times (Johannesburg)* **9 October**.
HUMPHRIES R. and SHUBANE K. (1992) *A Delicate Balance: Reconstructing Regionalism in South Africa*. Centre for Policy Studies, Johannesburg.
JONAS A. E. G. (2011) Region and place: regionalism in question, *Progress in Human Geography* doi: 10.1177/0309132510394118.
JONES M. (2009) Phase space: geography, relational thinking, and beyond, *Progress in Human Geography* **33**, 487–506.
KIMBLE G. H. T. (1996) The inadequacy of the regional concept, in AGNEW J., LIVINGSTONE D. N. and ROGERS A. (Eds) *Human Geography: An Essential Anthology*, pp. 492–512. Blackwell, Oxford.
KOTLOLO M. (2008) Deliver us from poor Limpopo, *Sowetan (Johannesburg)* **4 November**.
LAGANPARSAD M. (2009) Matatiele voters likely to tick KZN, (available at: http://www.timeslive.co.za) (accessed on 12 May 2010).
LEMON A. (2003) The rise and fall of Afrikaner ethnic political mobilization, *South African Geographical Journal* **85**, 144–151.
MACKINNON D. and TETZLAFF D. (2009) Conceptualising scale in regional studies and catchment science – towards an integrated characterisation of spatial units, *Geography Compass* **3**, 976–996.
MACLEOD G. and JONES M. (2007) Territorial, scalar, networked, concerted: in what sense a 'regional world'?, *Regional Studies* **41**, 1177–1191.
MAIL & GUARDIAN (2008) The past still haunts us, *Mail & Guardian (Johannesburg)* **5–11 December**.
MARCU S. (2009) The geopolitics of the eastern border of the European Union: the case of Romania–Maldova–Ukraine, *Geopolitics* **14**, 409–432.
MCCARTHY J. J. (1988) The last metropolis – RSC stalemate, Indaba checkmate, *Indicator* **5**, 45–48.
MUNICIPAL DEMARCATION BOARD (MDB) (2004) *Shaping South Africa: Reflections on the First Term of the Municipal Demarcation Board, South Africa 1999–2004*. MDB, Hatfield.
MUTHIEN Y. G. and KHOSA M. M. (1995) 'The kingdom, the *volkstaat* and the new South Africa': drawing South Africa's new regional boundaries, *Journal of Southern African Studies* **21**, 303–322.
NARE S. (2006) Khutsong is on fire, *Sowetan (Johannesburg)* **24 April**.
NARSIAH S. and MAHARAJ B. (1997) The creation of 'real' spaces: regions and regionalism in the New South Africa, *Space and Polity* **1**, 225–248.
NDABA B. and MAPHUMULO S. (2005) Bullets, stones fly as Khutsong's rage boils over, *Star (Johannesburg)* **15 December**.
NEWMAN D. (2006) The lines that continue to separate us: borders in our 'borderless world', *Progress in Human Geography* **30**, 143–161.
NEWMAN D. and PAASI A. (1998) Fences and neighbours in the postmodern world: boundary narratives in political geography, *Progress in Human Geography* **22**, 186–207.
NTINGI A. (2010) Matatiele's provincial-based camps fight for economic aspirations, *City Press Business (Johannesburg)* **14 March**.
NUGENT P. and ASIWAJU A. (Eds) (1996) *African Boundaries: Barriers, Conduits and Opportunities*. Pinter, London.
O'MEARA D. (1983) *Volkskapitalisme: Class, Capital and Ideology in the Development of Afrikaner Nationalism, 1934–1948*. Cambridge University Press, Cambridge.
OHMAE K. (1990) *The Borderless World*. HarperCollins, New York, NY.
ONSLOW S. (Ed.) (2009) *Cold War in Southern Africa: White Power, Black Liberation*. Routledge, London.
OVERMAN H. G., RICE P. and VENABLES A. J. (2010) Economic linkages across space, *Regional Studies* **44**, 17–33.
PAASI A. (1999) Boundaries as social practice and discourse: the Finnish–Russian border, *Regional Studies* **33**, 669–680.

PAASI A. (2005) Generations and the 'development' of border studies, *Geopolitics* **10**, 663–671.

PAASI A. (2009) The resurgence of the 'region' and 'regional identity': theoretical perspectives and empirical observations on regional dynamics in Europe, *Review of International Studies* **35**, 121–146.

PAASI A. (2010) Commentary, *Environment and Planning A* **42**, 2296–2301.

PARKER N. and VAUGHAN-WILLIAMS N. (2009) Lines in the sand? Towards an agenda for critical border studies, *Geopolitics* **14**, 582–587.

PEETE F. (2005) All provinces are equal, says premier, *Star (Johannesburg)* **15 December**.

PLATZKY L. and WALKER C. (1985) *The Surplus People: Forced Removals in South Africa*. Ravan, Johannesburg.

PRICE R. M. (1984) Pretoria's southern African strategy, *African Affairs* **83**, 11–32.

RAMUTSINDELA M. (2007a) *Transfrontier Conservation Areas in Africa: At the Confluence of Capital, Politics and Nature*. CABI, Wallingford.

RAMUTSINDELA M. (2007b) The geographical imprint of land restitution with reference to Limpopo Province, South Africa, *Tijdschrift voor Economische en Sociale Geografie* **98**, 455–467.

RAMUTSINDELA M. (2010) The demarcation process and the resultant large non-metropolitan municipalities in South Africa, in STEYTLER N. (Ed.) *The First Decade of the Municipal Demarcation Board: Some Reflections on Demarcating Local Government in South Africa*, pp. 38–50. Municipal Demarcation Board, Pretoria.

RAMUTSINDELA M. and SIMON D. (1999) The politics of territory and place in post-apartheid South Africa, *Journal of Southern African Studies* **25**, 479–498.

SAVAGE M. (1986) *The Cost of Apartheid (Inaugural Lecture)*. University of Cape Town, Cape Town.

SCHUTTE G. (1995) *What Racists Believe: Race Relations in South Africa and the United States*. Sage, Thousand Oaks, CA.

SEETHAL C. (1991) Restructuring the local state in South Africa: Regional Services Councils and crisis resolution, *Political Geography Quarterly* **10**, 8–25.

SÖDERBAUM F. and TAYLOR I. (Ed.) (2008). *Afro-Regions: The Dynamics of Cross-Border Micro-Regionalism in Africa*. Nordic Africa Institute, Uppsala.

SOUTH AFRICA (1960) *South Africa Yearbook*. Government Printer, Pretoria.

SOUTH AFRICA (1983) *South Africa Yearbook*. Government Printer, Pretoria.

SOUTH AFRICA (1990) *Report and Recommendations of the Investigating Committee into a System of Local Government for South Africa*. Government Printer, Pretoria.

SOUTH AFRICA (1992) *South Africa Yearbook*. Government Printer, Pretoria.

SOUTH AFRICA (1998a) *Local Government: Municipal Demarcation Act 27*. Government Printer, Pretoria.

SOUTH AFRICA (1998b) *Local Government: Municipal Structures Act 117*. Government Printer, Pretoria.

SOUTH AFRICA (2000a) *Local Government: Municipal Structures Amendment Act 33*. Government Printer, Pretoria.

SOUTH AFRICA (2000b) *Cross-Boundary Municipalities Act 29*. Government Printer, Pretoria.

SOUTH AFRICA (2006) *Provincial Budgets and Expenditure Review 2002/03–2008/09*. National Treasury, Pretoria.

SOUTH AFRICA (2007) *Intergovernmental Co-operation and Agreements: An Introduction*. Department of Provincial and Local Government, Pretoria.

SOUTH AFRICA (2009) *State of Local Government in South Africa*. Department of Cooperative Government in South Africa, Pretoria.

STATISTICS SOUTH AFRICA (2010a) *Statistical Release (PO441)*. Statistics South Africa, Pretoria.

STATISTICS SOUTH AFRICA (2010b) *Mid-Year Population Estimates, 2010 (PO302)*. Statistics South Africa, Pretoria.

SUNDAY TIMES (2007) Mufamadi lit a fire in Khutsong, *Sunday Times (Johannesburg)* **20 May**.

TSEDU M. (2007) Mbeki's long walk to Polokwane, *City Press (Johannesburg)* **25 November**.

VAN DER MERWE J. (2005) Khutsong protests mischievous, *Sunday Times (Johannesburg)* **18 December**.

WASSER S. K., SHEDLOCK A. M., COMSTOCK K., OSTRANDER E. A., MUTAYOBA B. and STEPHENS M. (2004) Assigning African elephant DNA to geographic region of origin: applications to the ivory trade, *Proceedings of the National Academy of Sciences, USA* **101**, 14847–14852.

WELSH D. (1994) The provincial demarcation process, in DE VILLIERS B. (Ed.) *Birth of a Constitution*, pp. 223–229. Juta, Kenwyn.

Configuring the New 'Regional World': On being Caught between Territory and Networks

JOHN HARRISON

Department of Geography, Loughborough University, Loughborough, UK.

HARRISON J. Configuring the new 'regional world': on being caught between territory and networks, *Regional Studies*. Recent years have witnessed a tremendous appeal in debating the relative decline in 'territorially embedded' conceptions of regions vis-à-vis the privileging of 'relational and unbounded' conceptions. Nevertheless, the most recent skirmishes have seen some scholars emphasize how it is not the privileging of one or other that is important, but recognizing how it is increasingly different combinations of these elements that seem to be emerging in today's *new* 'regional world'. Here emphasis is being placed on a need to analyse how the different dimensions of socio-spatial relations (for example, territory, place, network, scale) come together in different ways, at different times, and in different contexts to secure the overall coherence of capitalist, and other, social formations. The purpose of this paper is to make visible the politics of transformation in North West England by uncovering the role and strategies of individual and collective agents, organizations and institutions in orchestrating and steering regional economic development. For it is argued that the unanswered question is not *which* socio-spatial relations are dominant, emerging or residual in any given space–time, but understanding *how* and *why* they are dominant, emerging or residual. The paper suggests the answer to this and other questions is to be found at the interface between emergent spatial strategies and inherited socio-spatial configurations.

HARRISON J. 配置新的"区域世界"：领土与网络，区域研究。近年来，"领土嵌入式"理念与日益受到垂青的区域"相关与无界"概念之间存在着激烈的讨论。然而，在近期的小规模碰撞中已出现部分学者不再强调支持某一方或反对另一方的观点，而是开始认识到在目前新"区域世界"中正出现越来越多上述要素的组合。重点在于有必要分析不同的社会－空间关系（例如，地区，地方，网络，尺度）是如何以不同方式、在不同的时间以及语境下进行组合，以保证资本主义以及其他社会形态的连续运转。本文的目的在于显像英格兰西北部转型的政治性通过解释个体以及集体行为者以及组织与机构在策划和督导区域经济发展中的作用。有待解决的问题并非是哪种社会经济空间关系在某特定时空占主导、出现或残留，而是需要了解他们是如何及为何占主导地位、新兴发展或残留。本文表明，这一问题与其他问题的答案通过综合新兴的空间战略与后继社会经济空间结构得以解答。

HARRISON J. La configuration du nouveau 'milieu régional': être coincé entre des territoires et des réseaux, *Regional Studies*. Au cours des dernières années on a porté un grand intérêt à discuter du déclin relatif des notions de régions 'ancrées dans les territoires' par rapport aux notions 'relationnelles et sans bornes'. Néanmoins, les escarmouches les plus récentes ont vu des spécialistes soulignent qu'il ne l'est ni l'un, ni l'autre qui importe, mais reconnaître que ce sont des combinaisons de plus en plus différentes qui semblent faire le jour dans le *nouveau* 'milieu régional' d'aujourd'hui. Ici on souligne le besoin d'analyser comment les diverses dimensions des rapports socio-géographiques (par exemple, le territoire, l'endroit, le réseau, l'échelle) se réunissent de façons différentes, à des moments différents et dans des contextes différents afin d'assurer la cohérence globale des formations capitalistes, parmi d'autres. Cet article cherche à améliorer la visibilité des politiques en faveur de la transformation dans le nord-ouest de l'Angleterre en dévoilant le rôle et les stratégies des agents, des organisations et des institutions individuels et collectifs quant à la direction et à la gestion de l'aménagement du territoire. On affirme que la question restée sans réponse n'est pas *quels* rapports socio-géographiques sont dominants, naissants ou résiduels, quels que soient l'espace ou le temps, mais comprendre *comment* et *pourquoi* ils sont dominants, naissants ou résiduels. Cet article propose que la réponse à cette question parmi d'autres est à trouver à l'interface entre des stratégies géographiques naissantes et des configurations socio-géographiques héritées.

HARRISON J. Konfiguration der neuen 'regionalen Welt': vom Gefangensein zwischen Gebiet und Netzwerken, *Regional Studies*. In den letzten Jahren hat sich eine Erörterung des relativen Rückgangs von Konzeptionen der 'territorialen Eingebettetheit' von Regionen zugunsten einer Privilegierung von 'relationalen und ungebundenen' Konzeptionen enormer Beliebtheit erfreut.

Dessen ungeachtet betonten einige Wissenschaftler bei den jüngsten Scharmützeln, dass nicht die Privilegierung der einen oder anderen Konzeption wichtig sei, sondern vielmehr eine Anerkennung der Tatsache, dass in der heutigen *neuen* 'regionalen Welt' zunehmend unterschiedliche Kombinationen dieser Elemente zu entstehen scheinen. Hierbei wird die Notwendigkeit betont zu analysieren, wie sich die verschiedenen Dimensionen der sozioräumlichen Beziehungen (z. B. Gebiet, Ort, Netzwerk, Maßstab) auf unterschiedliche Weise, zu unterschiedlichen Zeiten und in unterschiedlichen Kontexten miteinander verbinden, um die Gesamtkohärenz der kapitalistischen und sonstigen Gesellschaftsformationen zu sichern. In diesem Beitrag soll die Politik der Transformation in Nordwestengland sichtbar gemacht werden, indem die Rolle und Strategien der einzelnen und kollektiven Akteure, Organisationen und Institutionen bei der Orchestrierung und Steuerung der regionalen Wirtschaftsentwicklung verdeutlicht werden. Ich argumentiere nämlich, dass die unbeantwortete Frage nicht lautet, *welche* sozioräumlichen Beziehungen in einer bestimmten Raum-Zeit-Kombination dominant, im Entstehen begriffen oder noch verbleibend sind, sondern dass es darauf ankommt zu verstehen, *wie* und *warum* sie dominant, im Entstehen begriffen oder noch verbleibend sind. Im Beitrag wird die These aufgestellt, dass die Antwort auf diese und weitere Fragen an der Schnittstelle zwischen den entstehenden räumlichen Strategien und den übernommenen sozioräumlichen Konfigurationen zu suchen ist.

HARRISON J. Configuración del nuevo 'mundo regional': atrapados entre el territorio y las redes, *Regional Studies*. En los últimos años hemos sido testigos de un enorme interés por debatir el declive relativo de las concepciones de 'integración territorial' de las regiones, y también el privilegio de las concepciones 'relacionales e ilimitadas'. Sin embargo, las escaramuzas más recientes se deben a que algunos académicos han puesto de relieve que lo importante no son los privilegios de las concepciones, sino que hay que reconocer que en el *nuevo* 'mundo regional' de hoy día existen combinaciones cada vez más distintas de estos elementos. Aquí hacemos hincapié en la necesidad de analizar cómo las diferentes dimensiones de las relaciones socioespaciales (por ejemplo, territorio, lugar, red, escala) se combinan de distinto modo, en diferentes momentos, y en distintos contextos para asegurar la coherencia global de formaciones sociales capitalistas y otras. La finalidad de este artículo es hacer visible las políticas de la transformación en el noroeste de Inglaterra al revelar el papel y las estrategias de los agentes individuales y colectivos, las organizaciones y las instituciones en la orquestación y orientación del desarrollo económico regional. Y es que sostenemos que la cuestión sin responder no es *cuáles* son las relaciones socioespaciales dominantes, emergentes o residuales en cualquier espacio-tiempo determinado sino comprender *cómo* y *porqué* son dominantes, emergentes o residuales. En este artículo sugerimos que la respuesta a esta y otras cuestiones se halla en la interfaz entre las estrategias espaciales emergentes y las configuraciones socioespaciales heredadas.

INTRODUCTION: IN WHAT SENSE A *NEW* 'REGIONAL WORLD'?

> Advocates of a given turn are often tempted to focus on one dimension of spatial relations, neglecting the role of other forms of sociospatial organisation as presuppositions, arenas, and products of social action. Worse still, some scholars ontologically privilege a single dimension, presenting it as *the* essential feature of a (current or historical) sociospatial landscape. In most cases this overontologizes questions that are best resolved in more concrete–complex terms.
>
> (JESSOP *et al.*, 2008, p. 391, original emphasis)

> It could be argued that the relational and the (hierarchically scalar) territorial can be seen as both/and rather than either/or conceptions, that 'territorially embedded' and 'relational and unbounded' conceptions of regions are complementary alternatives, that actually existing regions are a product of a struggle and tension between territorializing and de-territorializing processes. Depending upon the circumstances and the specific situation of particular regions, policy and politics may be informed by a bounded territorial and hierarchical conception or by a relational conception that emphasizes a flat ontology of networked connections as the more appropriate perspective from which to view the region.
>
> (HUDSON, 2007, p. 1156)

A little over a decade ago the economic geographer Michael Storper famously declared that we are all now living in a 'regional world', where regions are the fundamental building blocks of a globally interconnected modern world (STORPER, 1997). Alongside this, the political geographer John Agnew argued that far from disappearing in globalization, 'regional economic and political differences seem, if anything, to be strengthening', implying that regions must be conceptualized as 'central rather than merely derivative of nonspatial processes' (AGNEW, 2000, p. 101). Symptomatic of a much wider academic debate and policy-related discourse known as the 'new regionalism' (cf. KEATING, 1998; LOVERING, 1999; MACLEOD, 2001; HADJIMICHALIS, 2006; HARRISON, 2006) these headline-grabbing claims are indicative of how regions were seen by many to be *the* pivotal sociospatial formation at the end of twentieth century (OHMAE, 1995; STORPER, 1997; SCOTT, 1998).

In large part this reflected a belief among economic geographers, institutional economists and economic sociologists that regions are focal points for knowledge creation, learning and innovation – capitalism's new post-Fordist economic form (MORGAN, 1997; SCOTT, 1998; STORPER, 1997). Part also reflected a belief among political and social scientists that regions are important sites for fostering new post-national identities, increasing social cohesion, and encouraging new forms of social and political mobilization (KEATING, 1998). And underpinning it all was a recognition that a select group of regional economies – the exemplars being California's Silicon Valley and the 'Four Motor Regions of Europe': Baden-Wurttemberg (Germany), Catalonia (Spain), Lombardy (Italy) and Rhône-Alpes (France) – were bucking the trend of national economic decline to emerge as early 'winners' in post-Fordism.

Lauded for its pioneering research, theory converged around the notion that regions represent the *only* scale through which order can be re-established following the collapse of the nationally configured Fordist–Keynesian institutional compromise. Nevertheless, the new regionalism is not without critics (LOVERING, 1999; MACLEOD, 2001; HADJIMICHALIS, 2006; HARRISON, 2006). One among many lines of critique is the failure of its proponents to define their object of study clearly. Often assumed, rarely defined, critics describe how the region remains 'conceptually vague' (LOVERING, 1999), an 'object of mystery' (HARRISON, 2006), and an 'enigmatic concept' (MACLEOD and JONES, 2007) in many new regionalist writings. Even in the work of the political scientist Michael Keating, one of the most consistently insightful scholars on this aspect of the new regionalism, while it is acknowledged that regions take various forms (for example, administrative, cultural, economic, governmental, historical) his and others' concern remains principally with regions as actual or potential sub-national political units – be they administrative or governmental (KEATING, 1998). Taking this one stage further, PAINTER (2008) acknowledges how this is symptomatic of regional geographer's 'cartographic anxiety': a tendency to want to present regions as integrated and bounded territorial wholes despite recognizing how they take various forms, which rarely (if ever) correspond, or have congruent geographies.

In an increasingly mobile world characterized by all kinds of flows and networks, this avowedly territorial and scalar logic is today challenged by those advocating a more radically 'relational' approach to the study of cities and regions (ALLEN and COCHRANE, 2007, 2010; ALLEN *et al.*, 1998; AMIN, 2004; AMIN *et al.*, 2003; MASSEY, 2007). Disturbing notions of regions as bounded territories, for these authors emerging sociospatial formations are not necessarily territorial–scalar but constituted through the spatiality of flow, juxtaposition, porosity and connectivity. Supported in policy terms by the emergence of an expanding plethora of 'unusual regions' – so called because they do not conform to any recorded territorial units (DEAS and LORD, 2006) – from this alternative perspective interpreting regions as spaces of movement and circulation (of goods, technologies, knowledge, people, finance and information) 'reveals not an "area", but a complex and unbounded lattice of articulations' (ALLEN *et al.*, 1998, p. 65).

All of which is leading to suggestions that we might now be living in a new relationally constituted 'regional world' (cf. STORPER, 1997) where capital accumulation and governance is

> about exercising nodal power and aligning networks in one's own interest, rather than about exercising territorial power … [for] there is no definable territory to rule over.
> (AMIN, 2004, p. 36)

But it is also prompting us to confront searching questions over the degree to which the relative decline in 'territorially embedded' conceptions of regions vis-à-vis the privileging of 'relational and unbounded' conceptions is part of some zero-sum either/or logic. For important differences continue to exist around the conception of 'the region'. In political science, the need to distinguish territorial (non-overlapping) governance from functional (overlapping) governance in theories of multilevel governance reflects a clear division between international relations scholars who came to view processes of global integration as producing a non-territorial vision of governance that challenges the autonomy of the nation-state, and scholars of federalism who point to processes of decentralization and regionalization as evidence of regional territories and jurisdictions formally administered or governed by the nation-state continuing to be strengthened by global integration (BLATTER, 2004; HOOGHE and MARKS, 2003). A related, albeit less pervasive, division can be seen in aspects of human geography. For the first decade of this new century can be characterized by a theoretical impasse between those steadfast in their view that the spatial grammar of flows and networks calls into question the usefulness of representing regions as territorially fixed 'in any essential sense' (ALLEN and COCHRANE, 2007), and those calling for a retention of territorially oriented readings of political economy and when appropriate their conjoining with this non-territorial, relational approach (HUDSON, 2007; MACLEOD and JONES, 2007; MORGAN, 2007).

Today, interventions by scholars more inclined toward the latter than the former are doing much to suggest the dawning of a new era in these debates (cf. BRENNER, 2009a, 2009b; JESSOP *et al.*, 2008; JONAS, 2011; JONES, 2009; JONES and JESSOP, 2010; JONES and MACLEOD, 2010; LEITNER *et al.*, 2008; MACLEAVY and HARRISON, 2010; MCCANN and WARD, 2010; PRYTHERCH, 2010). Most notable in this regard is JESSOP *et al.*'s (2008) attempt to devise a heuristic framework for theorizing sociospatial relations as 'inherently polymorphic and multidimensional'. Stimulated by their conviction that those who ontologically privilege a single dimension (for example, networks) and present it as the 'essential feature' of any given sociospatial landscape bend the stick too far and neglect the role of other forms of sociospatial organization (for example, territory, place, scale), Jessop *et al.* envision a future where the privileging of any single dimension is replaced by an understanding that what really matters is how the relative significance of the multiple dimensions of sociospatial relations come together in different ways, at different times, and in different contexts to secure the overall coherence of capitalist, and other, social formations. A proposition suggests that in future it will be important to see such conceptual development

> as a set of overlapping tendencies in which some ideas are residual (former dominant ideas that are losing their academic power), some are new dominant ideas and some are emerging, perhaps to challenge the dominant ideas in the future.
>
> (PAASI, 2008, p. 407)

All of which marks an important departure from the 'either/or' versus 'both/and' debate – itself the subject of much conjecture in this journals recent past (PIKE, 2007). Indeed, the current issue goes a long way to highlighting how it is already a catalyst for new enquiries into how best to conceptualize regions and regional change. But at the same time it serves up a number of new challenges for the regional researcher. Not least is that although Jessop *et al.* are successful in making visible the politics of transformation occurring in social scientific thinking and presenting a strong case for more systematic recognition of polymorphy in sociospatial theory, how one then translates this into practice, that is, more grounded and empirical research, is a key challenge currently facing those interested in interpreting spatial concepts such as the region.[1]

It is with this in mind that the current paper represents an initial endeavour to make visible the politics of transformation in an 'actually existing region': North West England. The aim is initially to demonstrate, then understand, how and why it is new combinations are emerging that appear more suited to stabilizing society in today's new 'regional world'. To achieve this task the empirical part of the paper examines the three 'key diagrams' produced as part of the regional strategy making process in North West England following the collapse in 2004 of the UK Labour government's territorially articulated 'new regional policy'. In adopting this approach the working assumption is that attempts to secure the overall coherence of regions is the goal of regional governance and, following THRIFT (2002, p. 205),

> to govern it is necessary to render the visible space over which government is to be exercised. This is not simply a matter of looking: space has to be represented, marked out.

The purpose of this paper then is to demonstrate how these 'key diagrams' represent a more than useful starting point for beginning to understand how these configurations are constructed politically. For it is clear they are not simply the outcome of capital accumulation strategies but are mediated through institutional forms and diverse social forces. The paper therefore seeks to uncover the role and strategies of individual and collective agents, organizations and institutions in actively structuring how the multiple dimensions of sociospatial relations are brought together in different ways, in different moments, to secure the overall coherence of regions such as North West England (JESSOP *et al.*, 2008). The unanswered question is not simply *which* sociospatial relations are dominant, emerging or residual in any given space–time, but understanding *how* and *why* they are dominant, emerging or residual.

CONCEPTUALIZING THE RESURGENT REGION: FROM ONE-DIMENSIONALISM TO POLYMORPHY?

With the crisis in North Atlantic Fordism prompting the demise of the nationally configured Fordist-Keynesian institutional compromise, the primacy afforded to territory–place is being challenged and replaced by scale network as the dominant sociospatial dimensions. In its broadest terms, this is seeing the a priori status of the nation-state as the arena in and through which economic management is conducted, social welfare delivered, and political subjects are treated as citizens challenged by the emergence and institutionalization of 'new state spaces' (BRENNER, 2004). Moreover, and alongside this, the intensification of globalization sees these new state spaces (but also firms, capital and knowledge) appear increasingly free from the regulatory control of national states and gives rise to what CASTELLS (1996) calls the 'network society', where the importance attached to *national* 'spaces of places' gives way to a *global* 'space of flows'.

It is against this backdrop that JESSOP *et al.* (2008) begin their call for a more systematic recognition of polymorphy in social scientific enquiry.[2] They identify how the search for a new spatiotemporal fix for capitalism has seen the privileging of four distinct sociospatial dimensions: territory (T), place (P), scale (S) and network (N). Each associated with its own explicit 'spatial turn', it was assumed that, for a time, this single dimension possessed some exclusive explanatory power and predictive value, only to be challenged and overtaken as consensus switched to a different dimension of sociospatial relations. Successful in making visible the politics of transformation occurring in social scientific thinking over the long-term, what follows constitutes an 'in retrospect' take on one-dimensionalism and how, perhaps unsurprisingly, it has characterized regional studies over the same period. The first part concludes by pinpointing how attempts to construct the 'new regionalism' as a new institutionalist paradigm for regional development in the 1990s revolved around a loose bundling together of these different dimensions, exhibiting all the weaknesses of one-dimensionalism identified by Jessop *et al.* The second part then looks at more recent developments in regional studies, illustrating how and why relational and territorial approaches are deemed compatible by some and incompatible by others, why it is necessary to think of regions as the product of fluid configurations of individual sociospatial relations, and how one might begin researching regions in this way.

Applying the TPSN framework to the 'new regionalism'

Despite a long and illustrious past, the 1950s and 1960s saw regions, regional studies, and regional geographers all deemed to be of diminishing importance and worth. This was due partly to industrial capitalist economies enjoying a long period of growth and the widely held assumption that the institutional mechanisms of spatial Keynesianism would ensure regional differences gradually disappear. Part also had to do with those political parties seeking regional autonomy or independence having little support and being increasingly marginalized from mainstream politics at this time. That was until the late 1970s when the crisis in the Fordist–Keynesianism institutional compromise and, in certain countries, an associated upsurge in regionalist politics signalled the birth of a 'new' regionalism.

Much of this work was undertaken by political geographers and political scientists working in Europe, and centred on regionalism as a political movement for greater territorial autonomy (ROKKAN and URWIN, 1982). In this way it formed the basis of what became the political strand of the new regionalism, and the work of its leading proponent, Michael Keating. Commenting on how the crisis and vulnerability of the state enabled certain groups and actors to permeate political discourse, Keating's intuitive analysis of the new regionalism in Western Europe identified how these conditions helped foster a territorially articulated politics at the regional level (KEATING, 1998). Empirically supported by the rise of regionalist and nationalist parties (prominent examples include the Lega Nord in Italy and the Scottish National Party) but more broadly by the European Commission's strategy for creating a 'Europe of the Regions', this version of the new regionalism is concerned principally with regions as actual or potential units – be they governmental or administrative. From this perspective regions are discrete bounded and non-overlapping spatial units, limited in number, the products of politico-administrative action, and are principally articulated through the spatial grammar of *territory*. Nevertheless, this representation of regions as static and fixed has been the subject of extensive critique over recent years, with many critical theorists now preferring to think of regions as dynamic, fluid and evolving social constructs which are always in the process of 'becoming' (PAASI, 2010). Such theoretical developments owe much to the importance of place in contemporary geography.

Place has been central to accounts documenting a regional resurgence but not always under the banner of 'new regionalism'. In fact, it was in the 'new regional geography' of the 1980s that place assumed prominence in the lexicon of regional geographers. At a disciplinary level, the turn toward a post-positivist paradigm among geographers and sociologists in the late 1970s and 1980s led to a re-examination of the specificity of places and interpretative understandings of people and place (PRED, 1984). Not of regions per se, it was only in the late 1980s and 1990s that non-essentialist accounts of regions emerged. A distinguished proponent of this 'new regional geography' was the Finnish geographer Anssi Paasi, who in drawing upon this new found emphasis on contingency and becoming, alongside recognition that places have a degree of integration and coherence, established principles for better understanding the emergence of regions 'not as static frameworks for social relations but as concrete, dynamic manifestations of the development of a society' (PAASI, 1986, p. 110). The move away from static frameworks was given further impetus in the 1990s when Massey's influential essay on a 'global sense of place' argued places and regions are constituted and reconstituted as the contingent outcome of interaction between diverse (often competing) economic, political and social forces operating both proximate to, and at a distance from, a particular locality (MASSEY, 1991). These ideas were then later incorporated into the new regionalist literature by the British state theorists Martin Jones and Gordon MacLeod, who, noting their despair at how much of the literature documenting a resurgence of regions had to that point concealed fundamental questions relating to how regions are historically constructed, culturally contested and politically charged, set about uncovering how regions were being socially and materially (re)constituted by the rescaling and reterritorialization of capital under globalizing conditions (MACLEOD and JONES, 2001).[3]

A more controversial turn to *scale* in the 1990s accompanied the recognition that spatial scale is not a nested hierarchy of fixed platforms for social activity, but a dynamic concept. In the same way regions and places are understood as both resources for, and outcomes of, social action, spatial scales came to be recognized as the outcome of those activities and processes to which they in turn contribute (SWYNGEDOUW, 1997). In the regional debates of the late 1990s and 2000s, the new lexicon of geographical scale proved conspicuous in tracing the development of what SCOTT (2001a) identified as

> the apparent though still quite inchoate formation of a multilevel hierarchy of economic and political relationships ranging from the global to the local.
>
> (p. 814)

Informed by new regionalist interventions and debates, it is within this context that regions came be seen as competitive and strategic territories in a complex system of multilevel governance (MacLeod and Jones, 2007). While some economic 'boosterist' accounts of globalization heralded this emergent multilevel hierarchy as signalling the death of the nation-state, more sophisticated accounts began registering how the relative decline in the power of the nation-state vis-à-vis the emergent power structures of regions is an 'attractive and persuasive story' (Lovering, 1999, p. 380), but one with only limited theoretical worth and whose empirical referents only tell part of the story. Critics of the new regionalist orthodoxy came to recognize how the rise of the regional state – and formation of a multiscalar institutional hierarchy more generally – was not necessarily or purposively at the expense of the state but an example of spatial selectivity by the state (MacLeod and Jones, 2001). To be sure, the literature on 'state rescaling' has drawn attention to how the state remains the primary orchestrator and enabler of change, engaging in ever more complex, tangled and diverse rescaling processes in pursuit of a multiscaled political–economic fix for organizing and structuring globalized forms of capital accumulation (Brenner, 2004).

These multiscalar territorial approaches adopted by both proponents and critics of the new regionalism alike are, however, being challenged of late by scholars whose focus is on emergent *network* geographies (Castells, 1996). Attaching particular significance to transnational relations, connections and flows, research on the geographies of networks has resulted in the growing attraction of an alternative, non-territorial, approach where space and regions are conceptualized as open, fluid and unbound (Amin, 2004). Nigel Thrift, for one, is unequivocal in his assessment that

> space is no longer seen as a nested hierarchy moving form 'global' to 'local'. This absurd scale-dependent notion is *replaced* by the notion that what counts is connectivity.
> (Thrift, 2004, p. 59, emphasis added)

Within the bounds of the new regionalism, this is allied, in part, to claims that a certain type of region – the 'global city-region' – now functions as *the* pivotal sociospatial formation in globalization (Scott, 2001a). Indicative of processes of deterritorialization, the global city-region discourse has extended the logic that saw 'global cities' defined by their external linkages to consider how processes of global economic integration and rapidly accelerating urbanization – the defining features of globalization – are producing large-scale urban formations that are networked externally on a global scale, as key staging posts for the operation of multinational corporations, and internally on a regional scale, as city expansion sees the functional economies of large cities extend beyond their traditional administrative boundaries to capture physically separate but functionally networked urban settlements in the surrounding hinterland. The emergence of transnational, trans-regional and trans-frontier economic spaces – prominent examples being Europe's 'Blue Banana', the Singapore–Johor–Riau Growth Triangle, and the 'Cascadia' region of Pacific North-West North America – are doing much to advance claims that city-regions comprising multiple functionally interlinked urban settlements are acting quasi-autonomously, that is, outside territorial structures formally administered or governed by nation-states (Scott, 2001b).

Taking stock of these developments, and acknowledging their own previous advocacy of a scalar turn, it is exactly this type of one-dimensionalism that Jessop *et al.* (2008) have come to disavow so much. For them the constant privileging of a single dimension contributes to the unreflexive 'churning' of spatial concepts and a series of troubling methodological tendencies, namely:

> theoretical amnesia and exaggerated claims to conceptual innovation; the use of chaotic concepts rather than rational abstractions; overextension of concepts and their imprecise application; concept refinement to the neglect of empirical evaluation; and an appeal to loosely defined metaphors over rigorously demarcated research strategies.
> (Jessop *et al.*, 2008, p. 389)[4]

Encompassed in claims that one-dimensionalism leads scholars to conflate a part (one dimension) with the whole (the totality of sociospatial organization), Jessop *et al.* argue for an approach that can grasp the inherently polymorphic, multidimensional character of sociospatial relations. For not only is it important to analyse how the relative importance attached to territory, place, scale and network varies across space–time, but also how increasingly it is the possible combination of some or all of these dimensions of sociospatiality that matters more in securing the coherence of spatio-temporal relations (Jones and Jessop, 2010).

This has important connotations for the new regionalism. During its period of orthodoxy the new regionalism was deemed a 'chaotic concept' (cf. Sayer, 1992), one that was guilty of bundling together too many diverse theories for it to be considered a coherent intellectual project (Lovering, 1999; Harrison, 2006). In this context critics referred to the way different theories were hastily coalesced under the banner of the 'new regionalism' with little consideration – other than some putative and loose attachment to the 'region' – of how, and in which contexts, they may be deemed complementary. In the current context a similar and related claim can be made that in the quest to present the new regionalism as a new institutionalist paradigm for development, academic and policy advocates were equally guilty of bundling together the different dimensions of sociospatial relations, that is, work on territorial restructuring, new regional geography, state rescaling and the network society (cf. PAINTER, 2008). Put like this, the new regionalism is an important example of the pitfalls of one-dimensionalism. But at the same time it provides a useful empirical test bed for considering the degree to which various dimensions of sociospatial relations can be deemed complementary alternatives.

Conceptualizing regions: both networked and territorial [5]

In regional studies, the debate over one-dimensionalism has its roots in a decade-long back-and-forth exchange between a group of relationalists who argue that territorial–scalar approaches should be jettisoned in preference for a wholly networked approach (ALLEN and COCHRANE, 2007, 2010; ALLEN *et al.*, 1998; AMIN, 2004; AMIN *et al.*, 2003; MASSEY, 2007) and those who wish to retain and further develop territorial–scalar approaches alongside, and in recognition of, the increased importance of geographical networks (HUDSON, 2007; JONAS, 2011; MACLEOD and JONES, 2007; MORGAN, 2007; HARRISON, 2010; MCCANN and WARD, 2010; PRYTHERCH, 2010). Underpinning arguments made by the latter are claims that relational approaches are at their most convincing when analysing cross-border economic flows, but they 'bend the stick too far' when relating this to acts of political mobilization and cultural identity which are often 'territorially articulated' (JONES and MACLEOD, 2004). In conceptual terms the degree to which regions are interpreted as territorial or relational must thus remain 'an open question: a matter to be resolved *ex post* and empirically rather than *a priori* and theoretically' (MACLEOD and JONES, 2007, p. 1186).

If, as PAASI (2008) suggests, territorial bounded spaces have been like a 'red rag to a bull' for many relationalists, then the pigeon holing of relational approaches as useful for analysing regional economies but only partly useful for interpreting the regional polities is only serving to irk them more. Keen to underline how relational approaches are equally applicable for issues of politics as they are economics, ALLEN and COCHRANE (2007) now acknowledge that while it might appear in their earlier work that relational approaches are at their most convincing when analysing cross-border economic flows (cf. ALLEN *et al.*, 1998), they are at pains to stress that more recent forms of networked regional governance evidence how

> regional polities no less than regional economies may be seen to take their shape from the open, discontinuous spaces that are called here 'the region'.
>
> (ALLEN and COCHRANE, 2007, p. 1163)

Here they point to the impressive array of non-standard regions and hegemonic discourse surrounding city-regions as clear evidence that regions are being remade in ways that 'directly undermine' the idea of a region as a 'meaningful territorial entity'. For albeit these new regional spaces are often defined in the first instance by a narrow set of empirical and theoretical issues relating to their economic logic (JONAS and WARD, 2007), the design and construction of more flexible and responsive frameworks of city-regional governance is providing a rich policy context from which relationalists can advance their claim that

> the governance of regions, and its spatiality, now works through a looser, more negotiable, set of political arrangements that take their shape from networks of relations that stretch across and beyond regional boundaries.
>
> (ALLEN and COCHRANE, 2007, p. 1163)[6]

While all can agree that there is undeniable logic to the relational argument that contemporary expressions of territory are being materially and experientially transformed by an untold myriad of trans-territorial flows and networks in the era of globalization, the final point relating to regional boundaries is of critical importance because it is here that the debate is currently being fought. Relationalists contend that with regional boundaries more porous than ever before and increasingly punctuated by trans-territorial networks and webs of relational connectivity, by its very nature this renders regional boundaries less important and increasingly redundant in the new 'regional world'. In very practical terms this is seeing 'regions' increasingly free to 'override purely political boundaries', with all the implications for regulatory supervision on the part of national states (SCOTT, 2001b, p. 4).

Doing little to appease critics of these most 'radical' relational approaches, for them, the indomitable appetite of relationalists to vanquish territorial–scalar approaches is leading them prematurely to erase regional boundaries, and by implication, territory and territorial politics from their enquiries. While this may be desirable for advancing a more progressive and effective spatial policies centred on cooperation and collaboration across regional boundaries (AMIN *et al.*, 2003), as JONAS and PINCETL (2006, p. 498) usefully note in their analysis of the new regionalism in California, in the end one still has

> to confront the hard reality of fiscal relations and flows between State and local government, jurisdictional boundaries, and distributional issues of each place in the State.

Drawing a similar conclusion, Kevin Morgan is unequivocal in his assessment that

> To overcome the debilitating binary division between territorial and relational geography one needs to recognize that political space is bounded and porous: *bounded* because politicians are held to account through the territorially defined ballot box, a prosaic but important reason why one should not be so dismissive of territorial politics; *porous* because people have multiple identities and they are becoming ever more mobile, spawning communities

> of relational connectivity that transcend territorial boundaries.
>
> (MORGAN, 2007, p. 33, original emphasis)

In urging this caution it is clear to see the logic and progression that has since led JESSOP *et al.* (2008) to take this a stage further and develop the TPSN framework as a heuristic device for conceptualizing not only two or more dimensions, but also multiple dimensions of sociospatial relations. In justifying the need for more systematic recognition of polymorphy, these authors are unequivocal in their condemnation of those who continue to privilege one dimension above all others, expressing surprise at how much work in sociospatial theory is dominated by what might usefully be called all-for-one rather than one-for-all approaches to conceptualizing sociospatial processes.

At one level, the sentiments expressed by these authors strike at the very heart of the 'practice' of sociospatial theorizing. But at another level they open the door to new and potentially fruitful ways of uncovering the different ways in which sociospatial relations are being organized in particular configurations across space–time, and for what purpose. For it is important to note that it is not only social scientists who are guilty of prioritizing one dimension of sociospatial relations. Not surprisingly, political leaders and policy-makers exhibit a similar tendency, often guilty of presenting a single dimension as the necessary solution to a whole host of deeply political issues ranging from uneven development and interregional competition to democracy and social justice. This is particularly evident in recent political praxis in the United Kingdom, and it is to this the paper now turns.

REDRAWING THE BOUNDARIES OF THE UK SPACE ECONOMY

Through most of the twentieth century national economies were described in regional terms to inform policy needs that were essentially territorialist in nature: in CASTELLS's (1996) thinking this was the national economy as a 'space of places'. In the UK this culminated in the Labour government's programme of Devolution and Constitutional Change (1997–1999) and the establishment of a new parliament in Scotland, elected assemblies in Wales and Northern Ireland, an assembly with an elected mayor in London, and (to work alongside Government Offices for the Regions) regional development agencies and indirectly elected regional assemblies in each of the eight English regions. In each case, the component territories of the UK were to find themselves in receipt of additional elected political representation, and by implication new institutional spaces through which to secure the 'new regionalist' promise of increased wealth *and* accountability. All except England that is; for when the English regions were presented with the opportunity to establish directly elected regional assemblies, the first (and only) referendum held in North East England saw the proposal rejected by 78% of voters in November 2004.

All of which left England as the 'gaping hole' in the devolution settlement once more (HAZELL, 2000). But in so doing it opened the door to a new era of 'relational regionalism' (HARRISON, 2008a). Triggered by the unravelling of Labour's 'new regional policy', but also the changing geography of the UK economy in the latest rounds of global restructuring, a remarkable shift in the policy discourse was observed. Compare, for instance, the UK government's take on sub-national policy in England just before and shortly after the North East referendum:

> We recognise the need to evolve our approach further to ensure that regional and local institutions have the capability, capacity and confidence to overcome regional economic disparities. Increasing institutional flexibility around targets, funding and central guidance, tied to stronger accountabilities and performance incentives, will help national, regional and local institutions work better together. The Regional Development Agencies, in particular, have an excellent understanding of what is needed to drive economic growth in the regions.
>
> (H. M. TREASURY, 2004, Foreword)

> Cities represent the spatial manifestations of economic activity – large, urban agglomerations in which businesses choose to locate in order to benefit from proximity to other businesses, positive spillovers and external economies of scale. This document sets out how successful cities can contribute to competitive regions, stimulating growth and employment, promoting excellence in surrounding areas and joining up separate business hubs to expand existing markets and create new ones.
>
> (H. M. TREASURY, 2006, p. 1)

Note that where politico-administrative regions remained as the organizing feature of the UK space economy in 2004, by 2006 they had disappeared to be replaced by city-regions. Related to this, where the spatial grammar is primarily (hierarchically scalar) territorial in 2004, focusing on regional disparities alongside centrally defined targets, funding, guidance and accountability, the equivalent extract from 2006 is explicitly couched in the new lexicon of geographical networks, with all the talk being of joining up separate business hubs, proximity and cities contributing to competitive regions. This suggests the privileging of territory as the predominant sociospatial dimension has been replaced by networks in the policy discourse – a point reinforced by a sustained period of city-region institution building in England.

In the months immediately after the North East referendum various alternative solutions were afforded a political hearing. Included in this were calls for an English Parliament, English votes on English laws, English independence, strengthened local government, elected mayors, a return to elected regional assemblies sometime in the future, and city-regions. Each was offering a territorially embedded alternative form of organization that, in principle, would plug the politico-institutional gap left by the failure to establish elected regional assemblies. That was all except city-regions. Couched in language extolling the virtues of more networked forms of governance for achieving competitiveness, city-regions successfully captured the imagination of an eclectic group comprising academics, policy think-tanks and individual government ministers/departments, all of who stressed the role city-regions could play in the future development of regional policy. The government soon agreed, signalling their intent to promote more networked forms of regional governance when in their enquiry into 'Is There a Future for Regional Government?' they dispensed with probing future directions for regions per se, choosing instead to focus solely on what role city-regions would play in the future development of regional policy (COMMUNITIES AND LOCAL GOVERNMENT (CLG), 2007).

The result has been a series of government-inspired policy measures designed to operate at a variously defined city-regional scale, including: The Northern Way growth initiative, comprising eight city-regions, each with its own city-region development programme; City Development Companies, city or city-region-wide economic development companies designed to drive economic growth and regeneration; Multi Area Agreements designed to enable local authorities to engage in more effective cross-boundary working across the economic footprint of an area; and the establishment of two statutory city-regions in Leeds and Manchester. With the incoming Conservative–Liberal Democrat coalition government signalling their intention to abolish Regional Development Agencies (RDAs) and support for Local Enterprise Partnerships – joint local authority–business bodies brought forward by groups of local authorities to support local economic development – in their place, compelling evidence exists to suggest these new state spatial strategies are compatible with a shift from a spatio-temporal fix organized around territory scale to one that now prioritizes

> a looser, more negotiable, set of political arrangements that take their shape from the networks of relations that stretch across and beyond given regional boundaries.
>
> (ALLEN and COCHRANE, 2007, p. 1163)

Nevertheless, the open question remains to what degree these more 'relational and unbounded' forms of regional governance are replacing inherited forms of 'territorially embedded' state spatial organization? And if as many argue they are not, then to what degree and in which contexts are these more networked forms of regional governance compatible with existing forms of 'territorially embedded' state spatial organization? To analyse these and other questions, the reminder of this paper examines the politics of transformation involved in securing the overall coherence of North West England following the unravelling of Labour's 'new regional policy' in 2004.

MAKING VISIBLE THE POLITICS OF TRANSFORMATION IN ENGLAND'S NORTH WEST[7]

A former industrial region, North West England has already proved to be an important lens through which to analyse the new regionalism (cf. DEAS, 2006; JONES and MACLEOD, 1999, 2002; HARRISON, 2008b). In part this reflects a history of institution building predating Labour's programme of Devolution and Constitutional Change (BURCH and HOLLIDAY, 1993; TICKELL *et al.*, 1995). But part has to do with the region being one of the most socioeconomically polarized. Recent figures measuring gross value added (GVA) suggest the regional economy is worth £119 billion per annum, making the North West the UK's largest regional economy outside London and the South East and larger than fifteen European Union countries. Having said that, GVA per head remains 6.2% below the England average, with the region containing fourteen of the twenty-five most deprived districts, including the five most deprived. Add to this the fact the region had the largest funded English RDA in gross terms, many believed Labour's 'new regional policy' would see the North West benefit more than most from the new regionalist policy orthodoxy.[8]

Today, much anecdotal evidence points to the North West being at the forefront of endeavours to build more networked forms of regional governance. Nationally, the region is home to three Northern Way city-regions (Manchester, Liverpool, Central Lancashire), two City Development Companies (Liverpool, Pennine Lancashire), four Multi-Area Agreements (Greater Manchester, Liverpool, Pennine Lancashire, Fylde Coast), one statutory city-region (Manchester), and five Local Enterprise Partnerships. Of more international note is the new Atlantic Gateway – a unique collaboration between the Manchester and Liverpool city-regions, the Atlantic Gateway constitutes a £50 billion strategic framework designed to create a growth area to rank alongside Europe's strongest metropolitan economies (NORTHWEST DEVELOPMENT AGENCY (NWDA), 2010a). Taken together, the North West offers a fertile terrain upon which to examine the politics underpinning attempts to secure coherence by reconfiguring the region in the face of territorializing and deterritorializing processes.

For the past decade, this task of bringing 'coherence' to the region has jointly fallen to the Northwest Development Agency (NWDA), the North West Regional Assembly (NWRA) and Government Office North West. In particular, the NWDA has had overall responsibility for orchestrating regional economic development, while the NWRA had responsibility for all aspects of regional spatial planning. Since their establishment in 1999, the NWDA has been responsible for producing the region's economic strategy (a visionary document that outlines specific regional priorities for driving economic growth in the region), while the NWRA had responsibility up until 2009 for the region's spatial strategy (a statutory planning document that provides a broad development strategy focused on infrastructure, housing and land-use activities). As regional institutions, the spatial coverage of these strategies and by implication their day-to-day activities are defined by the politico-administrative regional boundary, so not surprisingly the spatial visions produced in the period up to 2004 fit neatly within the formal structures of territorial governance. Yet all this was to change following the collapse of Labour's 'new regional policy'.

2004–2006: Territory → Network

In 2004 the North West was at the forefront of attempts to establish elected regional assemblies. A year previous the region recorded by some considerable distance the highest number of positive responses to a government consultation, welcoming the opportunity to vote on establishing an elected regional assembly. Not surprisingly the North West along with the North East, and Yorkshire and Humberside regions were nominated as the first regions to be offered a referendum. But the resounding rejection of the proposal in the North East meant the North West never got this opportunity. Like many regions, key actors in the North West subsequently switched tack and embarked on a path that was increasingly open to the possibilities of more networked forms of regional governance.

Nowhere was this more evident than in the political construction of *The Northern Way*. Published on 2 February 2004, *Making it Happen: The Northern Way* (OFFICE OF THE DEPUTY PRIME MINISTER (ODPM), 2004) outlined the UK government's vision to establish the North of England as an area of exceptional opportunity combining a world-class economy with a superb quality of life able to close the prosperity gap between Northern England and the UK average. First conceived on the campaign trail for elected regional assemblies in January 2004, *The Northern Way* was to dovetail the economic aspects of the regional agenda (tied to the work of RDAs) with the political and constitutional aspects (in the form of elected regional assemblies) across the three Northern regions. The initial spatial vision made visible plans for a new pan-regional growth strategy based around two growth corridors: one stretching from Liverpool in the west to Hull in the east; the other connecting Newcastle in the north to Sheffield in the south. Appearing without prior notice or consultation, the task of making the vision a reality fell to the three Northern RDAs.

On 26 February 2004 the three RDAs announced the formation of a Northern Way Steering Group, consisting of the Chairs of the three RDA, leaders of the three regional assemblies, representatives from three Core Cities (a group established in 1995 to represent England's eight leading regional cities, five of which are in Northern England), and representatives from housing, universities and developers. With extensive input from the RDAs, the result was a much revised second version, *Moving Forward: The Northern Way*, which appeared six months later (NORTHERN WAY STEERING GROUP (NWSG), 2004). Most striking was how the original spatial vision of growth corridors was substituted by a multi-nodal inter-urban networked based on eight interacting, but hierarchically differentiated, city-regions.[9] Looking increasingly like a relationally networked trans-territorial region, the magical disappearance of administrative boundaries, the identification of eight city-regions as key nodes in the space economy, and the recognition that the most prominent lines on the map identified important flows as opposed to politico-administrative boundaries ensured this map became synonymous with claims the UK space economy was not just being discussed in relational terms, but represented and defined as a relationally networked 'space of flows' (HARRISON, 2010).

With regional assemblies fulfilling a key role in the Steering Committee, the advent of The Northern Way posed a major dilemma for the NWDA/NWRA: how best to manage their statutory responsibilities for developing economic and spatial strategies based on territorially defined politico-administrative boundaries whilst at the same time driving forward new networked governance arrangements that stretch across and beyond their regions boundary. In other words, regional institutions were thrust to the forefront of contemporary debates on how best to manage the struggle and tension between territorializing and deterritorializing processes (cf. HUDSON, 2007). Speaking at the time, one well-placed interviewee reflected on the nature of the challenge they faced:

> There is a challenge which we are looking at and we haven't resolved. And it is up to the RDAs and to the subregional partnerships as to whether [their] subregional partnerships need to change to reflect those [city-regions], or whether subregional partnerships themselves can take the City-Region Plans, see what their implications are, and see what part of that plan they should be delivering. Subregional partnerships as they are set up do not reflect in the same way the regional economic geography, but they do represent established partnership-working patterns.
>
> (Senior Policy Official, Northern Way Steering Group)

Coming a little over twelve months after the North East referendum, the publication of the 2006 (draft) Regional Spatial Strategy provided clear evidence that the NWRA believed a networked 'spaces of flows' approach was now essential to bringing 'coherence' to the North West, and perhaps equally important, to maintaining their legitimacy for coordinating the region, its economy and polity (Fig. 1).

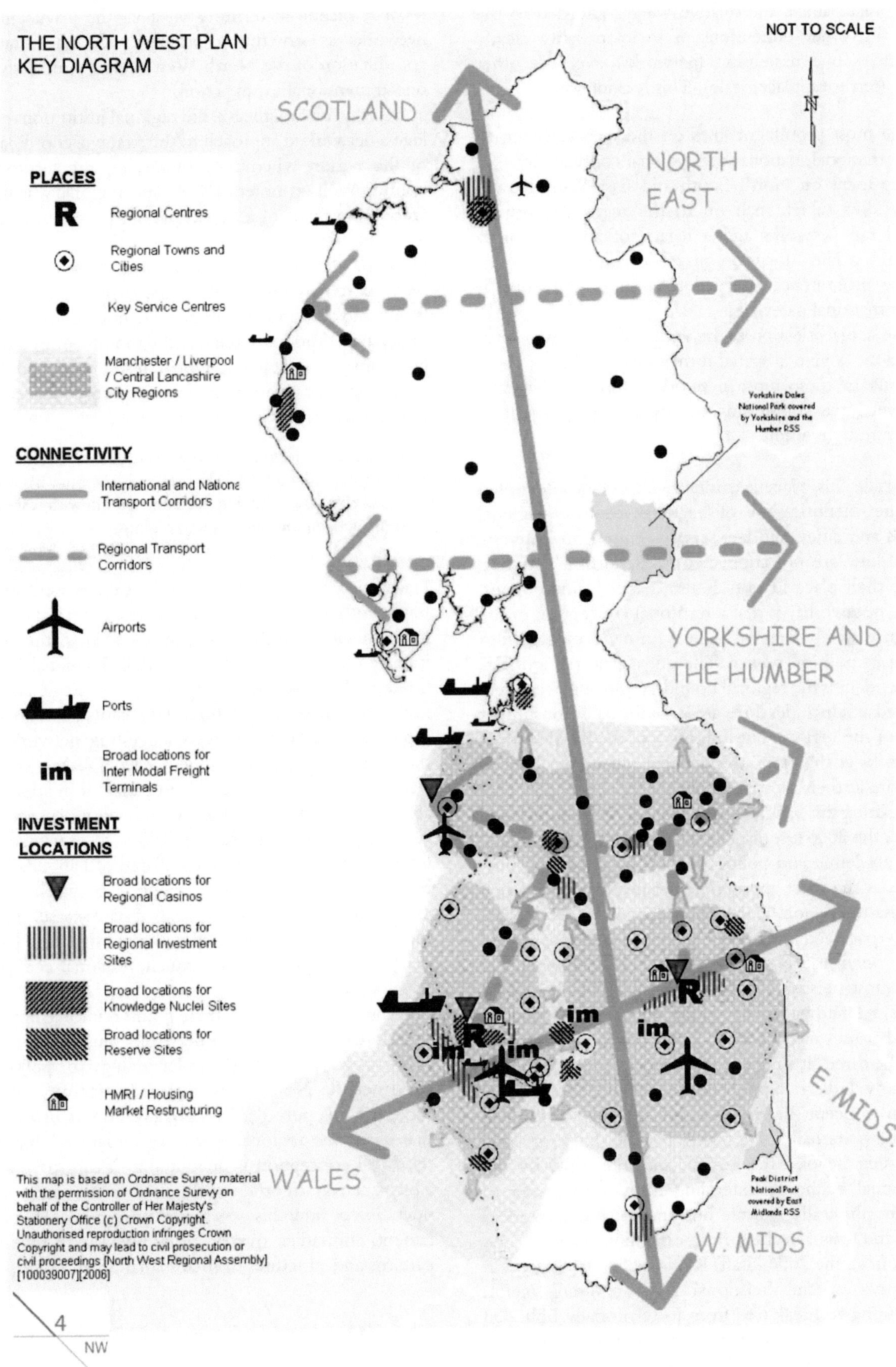

Fig. 1. Key diagram from the 2006 (draft) North West Regional Spatial Strategy

At first glance, the relative weight afforded to the four first-order dimensions of socio-spatiality clearly prioritizes one dimension (networks) over the other three (territory, place, scale). This is evidenced by:

- The most prominent lines on the map referring to international, national and regional connectivity.
- The focus on North–South and East–West growth corridors which map on to the major motorways and rail networks and a legacy of The Northern Way's original focus on growth corridors.
- The prominence afforded to airports and ports as international gateways.
- The spatial selection of the three Northern Way city-regions as pivotal spatial formations.
- None of these more networked forms of regional governance conforming to any known political or administrative unit.

Alongside this, place is evidently important as denoted by the identification of regional centres, regional towns and cities, and key service centres, but interestingly these are not connected up to form a network, while their place identity is also deemed unimportant. More noteworthy is that a territorial conception of the region is clearly deemed to be a former dominant idea losing its political power. The only territorial articulation evident is the regional boundary (albeit inaccurately defined as it includes three areas not formally constituent parts of the region), but indicative of the privileging of networks at this time, this is faded out where lines of flow are at their most pervasive.

Relating this back to the conceptual debates outlined above, the 2006 key diagram clearly reflects the tremendous academic and political appeal in presenting networks as the most appropriate perspective from which to view the region. Cities are privileged (as key nodes) in the space economy, the regional boundary is shown to be open and porous at points where flows are at their most pervasive, and new relationally networked spaces are shown to be cutting across the territorial map that prevailed in the twentieth century. Alongside this, the three city-regions are constructed in a way that is clearly indicative of SCOTT's (2001b) 'global city-region' concept. Each city-region is shown to be networked externally, illustrated by the lines of flow extending beyond the region, and internally, by the functional economy extending from a core area to capture physically separate but functionally networked cities and towns in the surrounding hinterland.

All in all the 2006 (draft) Regional Spatial Strategy is indicative of the 'relational and unbound' region attempting to break free from its territorially bounded politico-administrative regional straightjacket. As such, it could be used as evidence to support ALLEN and COCHRANE's (2007) contention that regions are being remade in ways that directly undermine the idea of a region as a meaningful territorial entity. Moreover, the relative decline in territory vis-à-vis the privileging of networks as structuring principles for the strategic coordination of the North West is clearly indicative of one-dimensionalism in action.

So why, one might ask, did regional institutions privilege a networked approach to the strategic coordination of the region when they themselves are territorially bound? Well, as noted, RDAs and regional assemblies were always part of a much grander plan. But coming so soon after the failure in the North East to approve plans for elected regional assemblies, these institutions were extremely vulnerable as the magnitude of defeat threw into question the validity of maintaining unelected regional institutions. Certainly the rhetoric from the UK government suggested regional institutions and their legitimacy for managing the economy was under threat, with the suggestion being that

> further devolution needs to encourage and reinforce this co-ordination and collaboration and so ensure maximum impact by better aligning decision-making with real economic geographies such as city-regions.
>
> (CLG, 2006, p. 73)

Place this alongside the emergence of new institutional frameworks of city-regional governance and it is not difficult to see how circumstances dictated to the actors involved in producing the 2006 draft Regional Spatial Strategy that a relational approach to strategic coordination was necessary at three levels: first, as part of a capital accumulation strategy suggesting networks are the essential feature of modern-day globalization and city-regions the pivotal sociospatial formation for anchoring and nurturing wealth-creating activity; second, as a response to the failure of previous state intervention, in this case the collapse of Labour's 'new regional policy'; and third, the link between RDAs and regional assemblies to this failed state spatial strategy meant it was key to maintaining their institutional legitimacy for continuing to coordinate regional economic development.

When taken together, these points reinforce how the one-dimensional swing to networks must be seen as a deliberate tactic, part of a wider strategy to politically construct the North West region in this way, at this time, for this purpose. It is equally important to note that albeit the regional boundary remains visible, this relational conception is presented as if this space were a blank canvas. In other words, there is little or no consideration of how this new spatial strategy would complement, contradict, overlap or compete with inherited patterns and structures of sociospatial organization.

2006–2008: Network → Territory and Network

By the time the 2008 (adopted) Regional Spatial Strategy was published the relative weight afforded to the four first-order dimensions of spatial relations had shifted (Fig. 2). Most notable is how territory re-

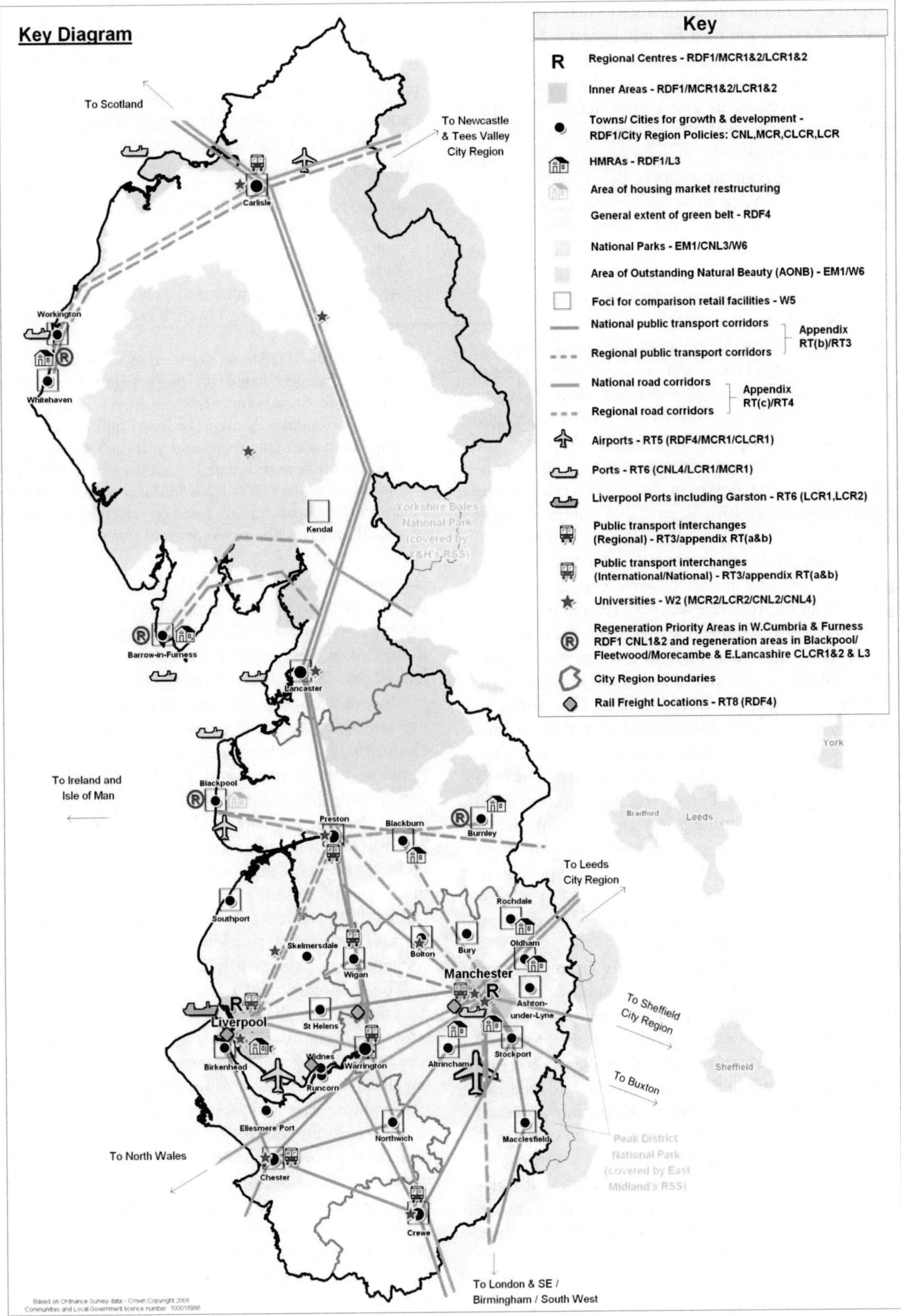

Fig. 2. Key diagram from the 2008 (adopted) North West Regional Spatial Strategy

emerged to challenge the dominance of networks. Illustrated in the first instance by the regional boundary (accurately defined) being the most prominent line on the map, perhaps more striking is how the three Northern Way city-regions are also clearly defined by hard, unambiguous lines on the map. Replacing the loose, ambiguous and schematic interpretation of global city-regions in the making from 2006, the spatiality of the regions Northern Way city-regions now map directly onto known political and administrative units, with each politically constructed around a coalition of local authorities and therefore bounded by local authority boundaries which extend to, but never beyond, the regional boundary.

In contrast, networks are now presented as former dominant ideas gradually losing some of their political appeal. Lines representing important flows become secondary to the aforementioned territorially articulated region and city-region boundaries. Airports and ports also assume less prominence as international connections are played down in favour of national and regional connections (that is, road and public transport corridors).

This is not, however, to suggest networks have been replaced by territory as part of some one-dimensional conception of the region. Networks are still important, as evidenced by the connecting up of regional centres to regional towns and cities to form a multi-nodal inter-urban network;[10] the identification of universities as spaces of knowledge production and key nodes in global circuits of knowledge circulation; and those connections beyond the region being to cities and city-regions. Important to note is how despite territorial boundaries becoming generally less visible (invisible in places) in the period immediately after the collapse of Labour's 'new regional policy', networks and their new institutional forms have clearly been unable to escape the existing territorial mosaic of politico-administrative units and their boundaries in the way that relationalists argue they can.

What can be seen in 2008 is an attempt to make more networked forms of governance compatible with existing forms of 'territorially embedded' state spatial organization. It is clear, for example, that networked forms of city-region governance are themselves politically constructed as the product of a struggle and tension between territorializing and deterritorializing processes (HARRISON, 2010). For sure, to make this more networked approach compatible with a territorially embedded conception of the region a different definition of the 'city-region' was required. In this case that meant jettisoning the 'global city-region' definition adopted in 2006 to promote a relational conception of the region, and replacing it instead with the definition used by the UK government – for which a city-region is

> a functionally inter-related geographical area comprising a central, or core city, as part of a network of urban centres and rural hinterlands. A little bit like the hub (city) and the spokes (surrounding urban/rural areas) on a bicycle wheel.
> (ODPM, 2005, n.p.)

That this was the beginning of a movement back toward a more territorial approach to configuring the North West was given further support by comments from two well-placed interviewees:

> It [mapping functional economic areas] is an endless task actually. Although it is true at a conceptual level that things work beyond those administrative boundaries it is in fact impossible to say what that area is; and that area, whatever it is, it doesn't have a political structure.
> (Planning Officer, North West Regional Assembly)

> Both we [the RDA] and the Regional Assembly have to deliver strategies based on those regional boundaries. Now within those boundaries there are very, very powerful political groupings. It might be based only on a line on a map but it is actually there, and you can't get away from that. So we have to interface with the real political institutions – and the real political institutions, even those that are 'city-regional', are still based on territorial boundaries.
> (Planning Officer, Northwest Development Agency)

Relating this to the theoretical debates outlined above, the notion of networks being unable to escape the existing territorial mosaic of politico-administrative units is indicative of how relational accounts have been challenged by those who contend that regions are the product of a struggle and tension between territorializing and deterritorializing processes (HUDSON, 2007). Conforming to conceptions of regions as both 'relational and unbounded' and 'territorially embedded' it also demonstrates how, far from 'escaping' regulatory supervision on the part of the national state (SCOTT, 2001b), the state retains a pivotal role in centrally orchestrating local and regional development. Indeed, this is crucial to any understanding of *why* the actors involved in producing the 2008 Regional Spatial Strategy saw it necessary to adopt a 'both/and' approach to conceptualizing the North West region.

The in vogue spatial scale among policy elites in England during 2004–2006, by late 2007 the city-region concept was occupying a less-than-glamorous role in the shadow of another spatial concept. Reflecting diminished enthusiasm on the part of the state for city-regions, key announcements coming as part of the UK government's major *Review of Sub-national Economic Development and Regeneration* in England saw 'city-regions' replaced by, or made a subset of, the broader, more politically neutral, and territorially embedded concept of the 'subregion' (H. M. TREASURY *et al.*, 2007). At one level, this responded to a growing recognition that although city-regions were the spatial concept at the heart of these new policy initiatives, the majority of new institutional frameworks established or planned were not in fact city-regional at all. Following on from the territorial articulation of The Northern

Way city-regions in 2008, it quickly became clear that most Multi-Area Agreements and City Development Companies were anything but city-regional. Rather, they were constructed around single or multiple local authorities formed by the scalar amplification or contraction of previous territorially articulated bodies. At another level, it was responding to accusations that a focus on city-regions was simply *too* city-centric – a case of 'picking winners' rather than the progressive approach to tackling uneven development that advocates of city-regions actively champion. Add to this cabinet reshuffles in May 2006 and June 2007, which saw key advocates move to positions in government where they could no longer drive the city-region agenda, and it was hardly surprising to observe how networks in general, and city-regions in particular, lost some of their political power (for more discussion, see HARRISON, 2011).

What this also did, however, was to present the NWDA with an opportunity to reassert their territorial control over regional economic development. The following quote is quite typical of what several interviewees observed to be happening in the region at this time:

> They [the NWDA] have now said that the subregional partnership will be the only point of contact. Now when I was a Local Authority Chief Executive I would have said to subregional partnerships, as I did then, well to hell with that I am going to go and see Steve Broomhead [Chief Executive of the NWDA] personally. I want to use the old pal's network. They have cut that off now, and it really has deflated the egos of some who think that they have got a direct line to him, who say, but you can't do this. Well if you want the [RDAs] money you go through the appropriate networks. So that will make local authorities in particular, engaged subregionally.
>
> (Chief Executive, Subregional Partnership)

When put like this, the politics underlying the decision to configure the North West as both territorial and relational reflects how networks were a former dominant idea losing some of their power. But perhaps more important than this, regional institutions were no longer so reliant on networks for securing the overall coherence of the region, and ultimately maintaining regulatory control and their own legitimacy for coordinating regional economic development. As one interviewee put it to the author, the open question arising from this was now whether this was part of some zero-sum, one-dimensional swing back toward the privileging of territory?

> It seems to me that we are at a tipping point in that we have got the RDAs who have been engaged in a process of regionalisation. They are trying to deal with that within their own regional strategies, and then they are trying to find the ways in which they influence the way things work on the ground to deliver the regional strategy. Now I actually think the right level to do these things is probably city-regionally – however you define city-regions – but it is very difficult to do that when you have still got a regional organisation operating with territorial structures.
>
> (Chief Executive, Economic Development Partnership)

2008–2010: Territory and Network → Polymorphy?

In 2010 the NWDA published the 'key diagram' for the 2010 (draft) Integrated Regional Strategy (Fig. 3).[11] What can be seen in 2010 is not evidence of a one-dimensional swing back to territory, but a North West region configured around a combination of the four first-order dimensions of sociospatial relations. Territory will first be taken. The territorial boundary of the region remains clearly evident, albeit less striking than in 2008, and once again including three areas not formally constituent parts of the political–administrative region. Alongside this one can clearly see how scale has been brought back in. In recognition of how networks are unable to escape the existing territorial mosaic of politico-administrative units and the UK government's focus of late on subregions, the five subregions are made visible for the first time since the collapse of Labour's 'new regional policy'. In so doing scale appears compatible with territory. A clear hierarchy of place – with subregions given first-order, cities second-order and towns third-order identification – is also seen. Finally, if territory-scale appears as the (re-) emerging and/or newly dominant sociospatial relations, then networks are a former dominant idea losing even more of their power. This is evidenced by the following:

- The disappearance of city-regions, universities, airports and ports, alongside all notions of virtual flows, networks and agglomeration.
- Connections to beyond the region no longer being to city-regions but to cities and regions.
- All flows being, in effect, truncated at or just beyond the regional boundary.
- Lip service being paid to international connectivity in the form of a blank map of 'England's Northwest in Europe' juxtaposed alongside the 'key diagram' in the published strategy, where the North West is identified as a single stand-alone territorial unit.[12]

What one has in 2010 then is a new approach to configuring the region – one that appears simultaneously *less relational* and *less territorial*. Therefore the question is why having gone for a networked approach in 2006, a territorial and networked approach in 2008, did the elements come together in 2010 to form this new configuration? One possible answer lies in the growing uncertainty surrounding regions. In the wake of the global economic downturn regions face an uncertain time. Economically, regions such as the North West face uncertainty as to what the impact of spending cuts will be, what business will look like post-recession (Will financial services again drive growth? Where will the jobs of the future come from?), how to develop a

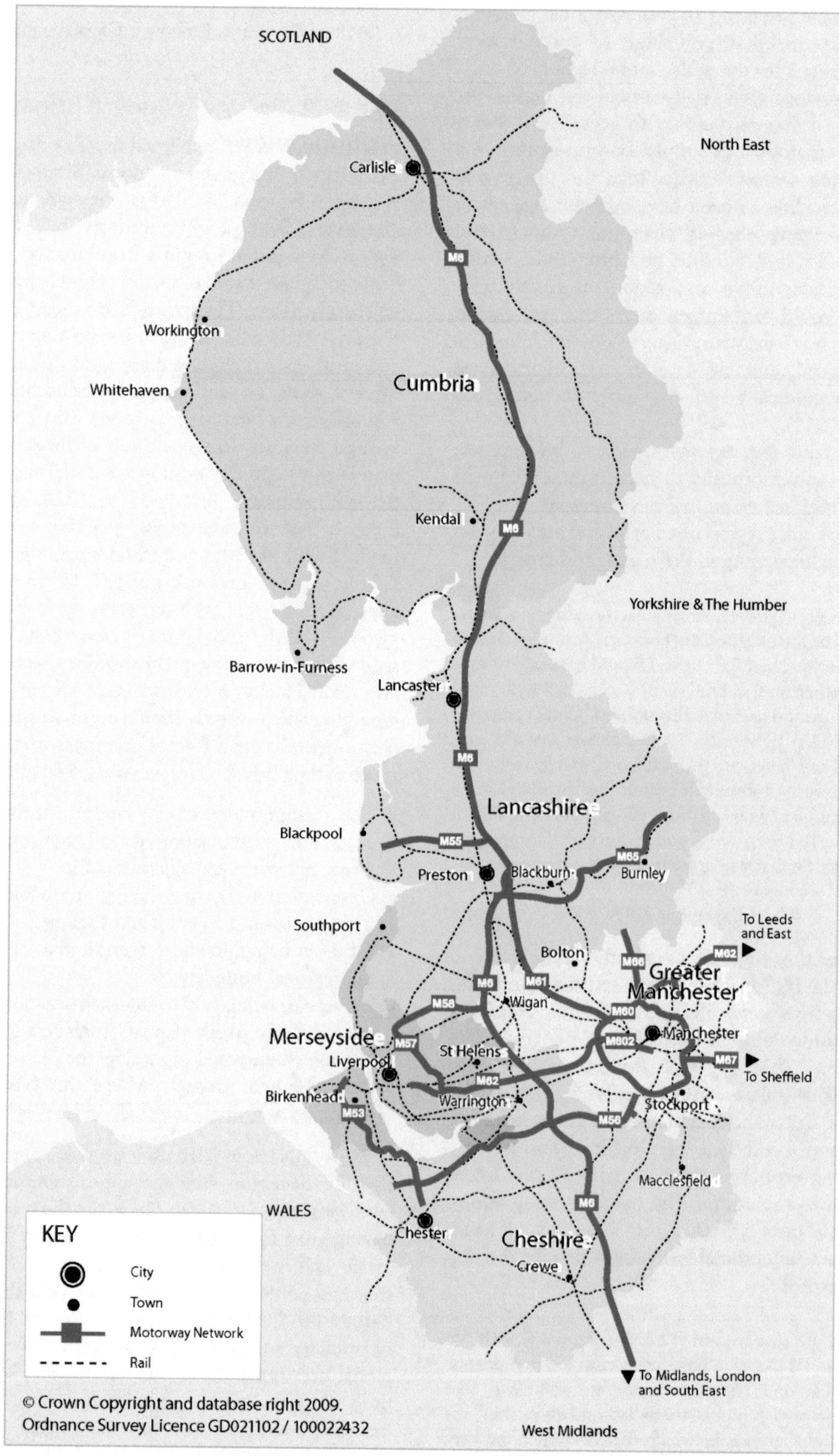

Fig. 3. Key diagram from the 2010 (draft) North West Integrated Regional Strategy

low-carbon economy and the role of new technologies therein, the opportunities and challenges posed by rapidly emerging markets in Brazil, Russia, India and China, and adaptation to increased flood risk and climate change. It is hardly surprising that all the talk then is of this being the 'right time' to think about the future economic drivers of the regional economy, to 'think carefully' about the nature of future growth, and to ask 'fundamental questions about how our economy and society work' (NWDA, 2010b, p. 3).

Politically, uncertainty surrounds the future of all things regional. The Labour government had already abolished unelected regional assemblies before the then opposition, soon to be lead-partners in a new coalition government, Conservative Party committed to abolishing RDAs and dangled the executioner's axe over anything vaguely regional during the 2010 General Election campaign and in the months immediately thereafter. Place this alongside the uncertainty surrounding city-regions and is it is hardly surprising that no clear sense of direction prevailed. All of which leads to an important question. To what extent are emerging configurations conducive to producing more effective spatial policies? For in the North West, if the emphasis on networks in 2006 and then territory and networks in 2008 was driven by a clear rationale and certainty amongst key actors as to why it was necessary to adopt this approach, the move to less territory and fewer networks in 2010 appears to be driven by a politics of increased uncertainty over the economic, political and institutional future of regions.

CONCLUSION

This paper set out to make visible the politics of transformation in an actually existing region: North West England. Using the three 'key diagrams' as a reference point, the paper documented the trial-and-error search for a new configuration capable of bringing stability to the region following the collapse of Labour's territorially embedded 'new regional policy'. What has been suggested is that since 2004 there have been three distinct moments, or periods, in this search. First, and triggered by the collapse of Labour's 'new regional policy', the 2006 map appears to indicate a one-dimensional swing from territory to network as *the* structuring principle for securing the overall coherence of the North West. Second, the 2008 map appears to reflect how the pendulum swing back toward territory in recognition that networks are unable to escape the existing territorial mosaic of politico-administrative units and the regulatory supervision of the state in the way many relationalists argue they can. Finally, what the 2010 map indicates is a situation where it could be suggested that the role of both territory *and* network as structuring principles currently appear in decline.

What can be distilled from this is two-fold. First and most obvious is how the three periods clearly mirror the development of academic debate in regional studies – with 2006 indicative of an 'either/or' conception of the region, 2008 a 'both/and' conception, and 2010 signalling an attempt to replace the privileging of a single dimension with an understanding that what is important is how the different dimensions can come together to secure the coherence of the region in that moment (HUDSON, 2007; JESSOP *et al.*, 2008). In this way the 'key diagrams' prove particularly useful in demonstrating how the relative significance of territory, place, scale and network as structuring principles vary in different socio-spatial fixes, while also providing evidence of how the search for a new socio-spatial fix is moving to ever more complex combinations (JESSOP *et al.*, 2008). But it also indicates a degree of movement of ideas and theories from inside to outside the academy.[13] This raises a number of important questions. Is the fit between academic conceptualization and on-the-ground developments really this neat? How does this play out in other contexts? Is this, as LOVERING (1999) might suggest, another example of theory led by policy? Do new and emerging conceptualizations of regions have any relationship to material and political interests? Are these conceptualizations imaginary constructions or real objects? Do they bring about coherence, however temporary this may be? These are questions that clearly warrant further critical enquiry.

Successful in making visible the politics of transformation, the second and more important step was to consider the politics underpinning how and why the relative significance of the different dimensions of sociospatial relations were dominant, emerging or residual in each moment. What the case study of the North West showed was that although the region was initially configured around an emergent spatial strategy centred on networks, what emerged thereafter was symptomatic of a struggle and tension not only between territory and network, but also between emergent spatial strategies and extant sociospatial configurations (BRENNER, 2009a). This observation is important for two reasons. First, and as BRENNER (2009b) usefully reminds us,

> the rescaling of state power never entails the creation of a 'blank slate' on which totally new scalar arrangements could be established, but occurs through a conflictual 'layering' process in which emergent rescaling strategies collide with, and only *partially* rework inherited landscapes of state scalar organization.
>
> (p. 134, emphasis added)

If this is placed alongside the evidence from the North West whereby the emergent spatial strategy of networks is unable to escape the existing territorial mosaic of politico-administrative units, one begins to see the logic behind the need for ever-more-complex configurations in order to make emergent strategies compatible with inherited landscapes of sociospatial organization, and for new conceptual frameworks capable of theorizing the 'inherently polymorphic and multidimensional' nature of sociospatial relations (JESSOP *et al.*, 2008). To this end, it suggests how going forward many of the answers to the questions being faced today around in what ways, and in what contexts, different sociospatial dimensions appear complementary, overlapping, competing or contradictory will be found at the interface between emergent spatial strategies and inherited landscapes of sociospatial organization. After all, and as one interviewee was keen to remind:

> In terms of delivering and creating our regional strategies, we have to interact with the world as it is rather than the world as we wish it were.
>
> (Planning Official, Northwest Development Agency)

Acknowledgements – Earlier versions of this paper were presented at the Regional Studies Association International Conference in Newcastle, UK, April 2011; and at the University of Manchester joint Planning and Landscape/Geography Research Seminar, October 2011. The author wishes to thank the organizers and audiences at these events; the Editors of the journal; and two anonymous reviewers for their constructive feedback. The usual disclaimers apply.

NOTES

1. Two of the original authors have since gone on to make a first attempt at this (JONES and JESSOP, 2010).
2. This is not an entirely new call; rather it has roots in earlier accounts on the polymorphic character of sociospatiality seen in the work of LEFEBVRE (1991, pp. 85–88), amongst others.
3. Often neglected in the accounts of radical relationalist scholars, this was done in a way 'befitting the current era of social complexity and ever more porous territorial boundaries' (MACLEOD and JONES, 2001, p. 671).
4. Readers will be reminded of the influential and thought-provoking paper by Ann Markusen on methodological and conceptual practice in regional analysis which made similar claims more than a decade ago (MARKUSEN, 1999).
5. The focus of this paper is on sub-national regions and for this reason the author limits this discussion to debates that have taken place within human geography. It is worth noting that albeit this debate has been informed and influenced by debates in political science, the focus of the former has been sub-national regions, whereas the latter often concerns itself distinguishing between sub-national and supranational forms of regionalism and regionalization. As this is a theme picked up by other papers in this issue (for example, by GARCÍA-ÁLVAREZ and TRILLO-SANTAMARÍA, 2012), the author focuses on the debates as they developed in human geography whilst recognizing the links to these broader debates.
6. LOVERING's (1999) shrill warning of the dangers of the 'policy tail wagging the analytical dog' should be remembered here. This suggests that the enthusiasm of policy-makers to adopt network approaches to regional governance leads to the construction of more networked forms of governance, which is then used as further evidence of networked spaces acting as autonomous political and economic spaces, thus elevating network approaches to a position of orthodoxy and fuelling further rounds of policy intervention.
7. The following two sections are based on empirical research undertaken by the author and funded by two research grants – 'Regions in Focus – A "New Regionalist" Interpretation of England's Northwest' (ESRC 2002–06) and 'Cities and Regions in Focus – Exploring the Evolution of City Development Companies in the English Regions' (British Academy 2008–09). This involved documentary research and interviews with key actors involved in regional economic development and regional policy in England in general, and the North West in particular. A selection of quotes is used to elucidate the discussion by offering insight into the role of political agency and territorial interests in the region over the period.
8. Recent figures seem to bear this out with the North West seeing the greatest rise in competitiveness of any English region since 1997 (CENTRE FOR INTERNATIONAL COMPETITIVENESS, 2010).
9. Available to view at http://www.thenorthernway.co.uk/downloaddoc.asp?id=418 (accessed on 15 September 2010).
10. Note that the key service centres identified in 2006 have now disappeared.
11. Integrated Regional Strategies were announced by the UK government in 2008 and require regions to combine the Regional Economic Strategy and Regional Spatial Strategy.
12. It would be wrong to say networks have disappeared completely – but where regional connectivity had been about *virtual* flows of knowledge, money and ideas in the years previous, in 2010 it now relates to *absolute* movements of people and goods via the regions' motorway and rail networks.
13. The author is indebted to the reviewers for raising this point, and for providing some of the questions.

REFERENCES

AGNEW J. (2000) From the political economy of regions to regional political economy, *Progress in Human Geography* **16**, 99–121.

ALLEN J. and COCHRANE A. (2007) Beyond the territorial fix: regional assemblages, politics and power, *Regional Studies* **41**, 1161–1175.

ALLEN J. and COCHRANE A. (2010) Assemblages of state power: topological shifts in the organization of government and politics, *Antipode* **42**, 1071–1089.

ALLEN J., MASSEY D. and COCHRANE A. (1998) *Rethinking the Region*. Routledge, London.

AMIN A. (2004) Regions unbound: towards a new politics of place, *Geografiska Annaler* **86B**, 33–44.

AMIN A., MASSEY D. and THRIFT N. (2003) *Decentering the Nation: A Radical Approach to Regional Inequality*. Catalyst, London.

BLATTER J. (2004) 'From spaces of place' to 'spaces of flows'? Territorial and functional governance in cross-border regions in Europe and North America, *International Journal of Urban and Regional Research* **28**, 530–548.

BRENNER N. (2004) *New State Space – Urban Governance and the Rescaling of Statehood*. Oxford University Press, Oxford.

BRENNER N. (2009a) A thousand leaves: notes on the geographies of uneven spatial development, in KEIL R. and MAHON R. (Eds) *Leviathan Undone? Towards a Political Economy of Scale*, pp. 27–49. University of British Columbia, Vancouver, BC.

BRENNER N. (2009b) Open questions on state rescaling, *Cambridge Journal of Regions, Economy and Society* **2**, 123–139.

BURCH M. and HOLLIDAY I. (1993) Institutional emergence: the case of the North West region of England, *Regional Politics and Policy* **3**, 29–50.

CASTELLS M. (1996) *The Rise of the Network Society*. Blackwell, Oxford.

CENTRE FOR INTERNATIONAL COMPETITIVENESS (2010) *UK Competitiveness Index 2010*. University of Wales Institute, Cardiff (UWIC).

COMMUNITIES AND LOCAL GOVERNMENT (CLG) (2006) *Strong and Prosperous Communities: The Local Government White Paper*. CLG, London.

COMMUNITIES AND LOCAL GOVERNMENT (CLG) (2007) *Is There a Future for Regional Government?* CLG, London.

DEAS I. (2006) The contested creation of new state spaces: contrasting conceptions of regional strategy building in north west England, in TEWDWR-JONES M. and ALLMENDINGER P. (Eds) *Territory, Identity and Spatial Planning: Spatial Governance in a Fragmented Nation*, pp. 83–105. Routledge, London.

DEAS I. and LORD A. (2006) From a new regionalism to an unusual regionalism? The emergence of non-standard regional spaces and lessons for the territorial reorganisation of the state, *Urban Studies* **43**, 1847–1877.

GARCÍA-ÁLVAREZ J. and TRILLO-SANTAMARÍA J.-M. (2012) Between regional spaces and spaces of regionalism: cross-border region building in the Spanish 'State of the Autonomies', *Regional Studies* (in this issue).

HADJIMICHALIS C. (2006) Non-economic factors in economic geography and in 'new regionalism': a sympathetic critique, *International Journal of Urban and Regional Research* **30**, 690–704.

HARRISON J. (2006) Re-reading the new regionalism: a sympathetic critique, *Space and Polity* **10**, 21–46.

HARRISON J. (2008a) The region in political–economy, *Geography Compass* **2**, 814–830.

HARRISON J. (2008b) Stating the production of scales: centrally orchestrated regionalism, regionally orchestrated centralism, *International Journal of Urban and Regional Research* **32**, 922–941.

HARRISON J. (2010) Networks of connectivity, territorial fragmentation, uneven development: the new politics of city-regionalism, *Political Geography* **29**, 17–27.

HARRISON J. (2011) Life after regions? The evolution of city-regionalism in England, *Regional Studies* DOI: 10.1080/00343404.2010.521148.

HAZELL R. (2000) *An Unstable Union: Devolution and the English Question, State of the Union Lecture*. Constitution Unit, London.

H. M. TREASURY (2004) *Devolving Decision Making 2 – Meeting the Regional Economic Challenge: Increasing Regional and Local Flexibility*. H. M. Treasury, London.

H. M. TREASURY (2006) *Devolving Decision Making 3 – Meeting the Regional Economic Challenge: The Importance of Cities to Regional Growth*. H. M. Treasury, London.

H. M. TREASURY, DEPARTMENT FOR BUSINESS ENTERPRISE REGULATORY REFORM (BERR) and COMMUNITIES AND LOCAL GOVERNMENT (CLG) (2007) *Review of Sub-national Economic Development and Regeneration*. H. M. Treasury, London.

HOOGHE L. and MARKS G. (2003) Unravelling the central state, but how? Types of multi-level governance, *American Political Science Review* **97**, 233–243.

HUDSON R. (2007) Regions and regional uneven development forever? Some reflective comments upon theory and practice, *Regional Studies* **41**, 1149–1160.

JESSOP B., BRENNER N. and JONES M. (2008) Theorizing sociospatial relations, *Environment and Planning D* **26**, 389–401.

JONAS A. (2011) Regionalism in question, *Progress in Human Geography* DOI: 10.1177/0309132510394118.

JONAS A. and PINCETL S. (2006) Rescaling regions in the state: the new regionalism in California, *Political Geography* **25**, 482–505.

JONAS A. and WARD K. (2007) An introduction to a debate on city-regions: new geographies of governance, democracy and social reproduction, *International Journal of Urban and Regional Research* **31**, 169–178.

JONES M. (2009) Phase space: geography, relational thinking, and beyond, *Progress in Human Geography* **33**, 487–506.

JONES M. and JESSOP B. (2010) Thinking state/space incompossibly, *Antipode* **42**, 1119–1149.

JONES M. and MACLEOD G. (1999) Towards a regional renaissance? Reconfiguring and rescaling England's economic governance, *Transactions of the Institute of British Geographers*, **24**, 295–313.

JONES M. and MACLEOD G. (2002) Regional tensions: constructing institutional cohesion?, *City of Revolution: Restructuring Manchester*, pp. 176–189. Manchester University Press, Manchester.

JONES M. and MACLEOD G. (2004) Regional spaces, spaces of regionalism: territory, insurgent politics, and the English question, *Transactions of the Institute of British Geographers* **29**, 433–452.

JONES M. and MACLEOD G. (2010) Territorial/relational: conceptualizing spatial economic governance, in PIKE A., TOMANEY J. and RODRIGUES-POSE A. (Eds) *Handbook of Local and Regional Economic Development*, pp. 259–271. Routledge, London.

KEATING M. (1998) *The New Regionalism in Western Europe: Territorial Restructuring and Political Change*. Edward Elgar, Cheltenham.

LEFEBVRE H. (1991) *The Production of Space*. Blackwell, Oxford.

LEITNER H., SHEPPARD E. and SZIARTO K. (2008) The spatialities of contentious politics, *Transactions of the Institute of British Geographers*, **33**, 157–172.

LOVERING J. (1999) Theory led by policy: the inadequacies of the new regionalism (illustrated from the case of Wales), *International Journal of Urban and Regional Research* **23**, 379–395.

MACLEAVY J. and HARRISON J. (2010) New state spatialities: perspectives on state, space and scalar geographies, *Antipode* **42**, 1037–1046.

MACLEOD G. (2001) New regionalism reconsidered: globalization and the remaking of political economic space, *International Journal of Urban and Regional Research* **25**, 804–829.

MACLEOD G. and JONES M. (2001) Renewing the geography of regions, *Environment and Planning D* **19**, 669–695.

MACLEOD G. and JONES M. (2007) Territorial, scalar, networked, connected: in what sense a 'regional world'?, *Regional Studies* **41**, 1177–1191.

MARKUSEN A. (1999) Fuzzy concepts, scanty evidence, policy distance: the case for rigour and policy relevance in critical regional studies, *Regional Studies* **33**, 869–884.

MASSEY D. (1991) A global sense of place, *Marxism Today* **June**, 24–29.

MASSEY D. (2007) *World City*. Polity, Cambridge.

MCCANN E. and WARD K. (2010) Relationality/territoriality: toward a conceptualization of cities in the world, *Geoforum* **41**, 175–184.

MORGAN K. (1997) The learning region: institutions, innovation and regional renewal, *Regional Studies* **31**, 491–503.

MORGAN K. (2007) The polycentric state: new spaces of empowerment and engagement?, *Regional Studies* **41**, 1237–1251.

NORTHWEST DEVELOPMENT AGENCY (NWDA) (2010a) *Atlantic Gateway*. NWDA, Warrington.

NORTHWEST DEVELOPMENT AGENCY (NWDA) (2010b) *RS2010 – Principles and Issues Paper*. NWDA, Warrington.

NORTHERN WAY STEERING GROUP (NWSG) (2004) *Moving Forward – The Northern Way*. NWSG, Newcastle.

OFFICE OF THE DEPUTY PRIME MINISTER (ODPM) (2004) *Making It Happen – The Northern Way*. ODPM, London.

OFFICE OF THE DEPUTY PRIME MINISTER (ODPM) (2005) *Planning Glossary*. ODPM, London.

OHMAE K. (1995) *The End of the Nation-State: The Rise of Regional Economies*. HarperCollins, London.

PAASI A. (1986) The institutionalization of regions: a theoretical framework for understanding the emergence of regions and the constitution of regional identity, *Fennia* **164**, 105–146.

PAASI A. (2008) Is the world more complex than our theories of it? TPSN and the perpetual challenge of conceptualisation, *Environment and Planning D* **26**, 405–410.

PAASI A. (2010) Regions are social constructs, but who or what 'constructs' them? Agency in question, *Environment and Planning A* **42**, 2296–2301.

PAINTER J. (2008) Cartographic anxiety and the search for regionality, *Environment and Planning A* **40**, 342–361.

PIKE A. (2007) 'Whither Regional Studies', *Regional Studies* **41(9)** [Special Issue].

PRED A. (1984) Place as historically contingent process: structuration and the time-geography of becoming places, *Annals of the Association of American Geographers* **74**, 279–297.

PRYTHERCH D. (2010) 'Vertebrating' the region as a networked space of flows: learning from the spatial grammar of Catalanist territoriality, *Environment and Planning A* **42**, 1537–1544.

ROKKAN S. and URWIN D. (Eds) (1982) *The Politics of Territorial Identity: Studies in European Regionalism*. Sage, London.

SAYER A. (1992) *Method in Social Science*. Routledge, London.

SCOTT A. (1998) *Regions and the World Economy: The Coming Shape of Global Production, Competition, and Political Order*. Oxford University Press, Oxford.

SCOTT A. (2001a) Globalization and the rise of city-regions, *European Planning Studies* **9**, 813–826.

SCOTT A. (Ed.) (2001b) *Global City-Regions: Trends, Theory, Policy*. Oxford University Press, Oxford.

STORPER M. (1997) *The Regional World: Territorial Development in a Global Economy*. Guildford, New York, NY.

SWYNGEDOUW E. (1997) Neither global nor local: 'glocalisation' and the politics of scale, in COX K. (Ed.) *Spaces of Globalisation*, pp. 137–166. Guildford, New York, NY.

THRIFT N. (2002) Performing cultures in the new economy, in DU GAY P. and PRYKE M. (Eds) *Cultural Economy*, pp. 201–234. Sage, London.

THRIFT N. (2004) Intensities of feeling: towards a spatial politics of affect, *Geografiska Annaler* **86B**, 57–78.

TICKELL A., PECK J. and DICKEN P. (1995) The fragmented region: business, the state and economic development in North West England, in RHODES R. (Ed.) *The Regions and the New Europe: Patterns in Core and Periphery Development*, pp. 247–272. Manchester University Press, Manchester.

Crafting the Region: Creative Industries and Practices of Regional Space

NICOLA J. THOMAS*, DAVID C. HARVEY* and HARRIET HAWKINS†
*Department of Geography, College of Life and Environmental Sciences, University of Exeter, UK.
†Department of Geography, Royal Holloway, University of London, UK.

THOMAS N. J., HARVEY D. C. and HAWKINS H. Crafting the region: creative industries and practices of regional space, *Regional Studies*. This paper draws on an analysis of craft-based networks in South West Britain to inform one's understandings of regional space; around thinking 'territorially' and thinking 'topologically'. It considers how the contemporary 'relational region' negotiates the historical context of sedimented practices and imaginaries of territory and authority. Through an analysis of micro-social relations, the paper examines how regionally based governance structures are negotiated through trans-local, inter-regional and international practices. It calls for attention to be placed on the planned and prosaic, conscious and unconscious practices, discourses and connections that are involved in the *becoming* of a region.

THOMAS N. J., HARVEY D. C. and HAWKINS H. 打造区域：创意产业与区域空间实践，*区域研究*。本文分析英国西南部的手工艺网络，以此增进理解区域空间之时间性与类别性的思考。本研究考量当代的"关系性空间"如何协商历史脉络中残留的对于领土和权力的想象与实践，透过分析微观的社会关系，检视植基于区域的治理结构如何透过跨地方、跨区域以及跨国之实践进行协商，并呼吁关注区域形构过程所涉及的计划与寻常之处、有意识与无意识的实践以及各种论述和连结。

THOMAS N. J., HARVEY D. C. et HAWKINS H. Élaborer la région artisanale: les industries et les pratiques créatives de l'espace régionale, *Regional Studies*. Cet article puise dans une analyse des réseaux à caractère artisanal dans le sud-ouest de la Grande-Bretagne afin de mieux comprendre la notion de l'espace régionale; articulé autour des réflexions à la fois 'territoriales' et 'topologiques'. On considère comment la 'région relationnelle' contemporaine négocie le contexte historique des pratiques et des imaginaires ancrées de territoire et d'autorité. À partir d'une analyse des relations micro-sociales, cet article cherche à examiner comment les structures de gouvernance régionales sont négociées par moyen des pratiques trans-locales, interrégionales et internationales. Il faut mettre l'accent sur les pratiques, les discours et les relations prévus et prosaïques, conscients et inconscients nécessaires à la *réalisation* d'une région.

THOMAS N. J., HARVEY D. C. und HAWKINS H. Gestaltung der Region: kreative Branchen und Praktiken des regionalen Raums, *Regional Studies*. In diesem Beitrag soll mit Hilfe einer Analyse der Kunsthandwerk-Netzwerke im Südosten Großbritanniens das Verständnis des regionalen Raums im Rahmen des 'territorialen' und 'topologischen' Denkens erweitert werden. Wir erörtern, wie in der heutigen 'relationalen Region' mit dem historischen Kontext der sedimentierten Praktiken und Imaginären von Gebiet und Autorität umgegangen wird. Durch eine Analyse der mikrosozialen Beziehungen wird untersucht, wie regionale Regierungsstrukturen über translokale, interregionale und internationale Praktiken ausgehandelt werden. Wir plädieren für eine Berücksichtigung der geplanten und prosaischen bewussten und unbewussten Praktiken, Diskurse und Verbindungen, die am *Entstehen* einer Region beteiligt sind.

THOMAS N. J., HARVEY D. C. y HAWKINS H. La creación de la región: industrias y prácticas creativas del espacio regional, *Regional Studies*. En este artículo analizamos las redes artesanales del suroeste de Gran Bretaña para informar de la comprensión individual del espacio regional en lo tocante al factor territorial y topológico. Consideramos cómo la 'región relacional' contemporánea negocia el contexto histórico de las prácticas sedimentadas y los imaginarios del territorio y la autoridad. Mediante un análisis de las relaciones microsociales, estudiamos cómo se negocian las estructuras de gobernanza a nivel regional a través de prácticas translocales, interregionales e internacionales. Abogamos por prestar atención a las prácticas, los discursos y las conexiones planificados y prosaicos, conscientes e inconscientes, que participan a la hora de *convertirse* en una región.

INTRODUCTION

This paper explores how the study of craft industries can inform one's understanding of regional space and, specifically, how practices of creative-makers and their supporting agencies provide a lens through which to examine the production of the region. In particular, this empirically rich investigation stresses the importance of historically situating debates about relational and territorial understandings of the region. Thus, the paper fills an empirical void by making space for the 'taking place' of creative governance alongside the associated activities of creative practitioners as practices of the region.

Understandings of regional space as practised space are well-established within the literatures. Such studies draw attention to the making and meaning of creative practices, with visual art, music, dance and fashion as practices of territory, place and identity (DANIELS, 1993; JACKSON *et al.*, 2007; JAZEEL, 2005; MATLESS, 1998; TOMANEY, 2007). Such work reinforces PAASI's (2001) observation that

> the region should not be regarded as merely a passive medium in which social action takes place. Neither should it be understood as an entity that operates autonomously above human beings. Regions are always part of this action and hence they are social constructs that are created in political, economic, cultural and administrative practices and discourses.
>
> (p. 16)

This paper, therefore, focuses on an analysis of the social worlds of creative practitioners alongside allied creative governance. Through an exploration of the Textile Forum South West (TFSW) and the crafts guilds within the South West of Britain, this paper examines the formal and informal networks of creativity and practice that have come, for many, to be a defining factor of the creative industries and cultural practices (CURRID and WILLIAMS, 2009; KONG, 2005; STORPER and VENABLES, 2004). Through the analysis of the geographies of these networks – their scope and extent – this paper considers the practices and imaginaries of the region that they negotiate. As PAASI (2010) noted,

> regions are performed and made meaningful ... in material and discursive practices and networks that cross borders and scales, often simultaneously giving shape to such borders and scales.
>
> (p. 2298)

The paper explores the ways in which these organizations are entangled within complex and multiple forms of territorial governance, working across scales. Examining the development and challenges of these different territorial configurations of creative governance brings to the surface the need to think about the multiplicity of territorial jurisdictions existing within regional spaces.

The paper is structured as follows. The first section situates this paper within the context of UK debates around new regionalism, the limited literature on the region and creative governance, and the broader theoretical debates concerning the thinking of regions territorially or topologically. The following two sections explore creative organizations that operate within the South West region: firstly, TFSW and, secondly, the Gloucestershire and Devon county-based crafts guilds. Grounded within these empirical case studies, an argument is developed that reflects calls by JONES (2009) and others (for example, ALLEN and COCHRANE, 2007) for a middle ground through which to comprehend the tensions between relational thinking and territorial fixity. Thus, the paper begins with a discussion of TFSW, interrogating the way in which this regional group manages its regional territory and organizes the networks of its membership. Exploring specific case studies, the way in which TFSW's socialities practise regional space is analysed. Crucially, however, the paper moves on from locating and exemplifying this 'middle ground', through the second case study, which seeks to situate these debates within an historical framework through an analysis of the complex territorial practices of the Devon Guild of Craftsmen and the Gloucestershire Guild of Craftsmen. Through a study of past and contemporary guild practices what emerges is the entangled nature of different territorial articulations over time, together with a series of different connections to governance in the delivery of creative policy and the practices of regions by creative-makers.

THE REGION, CREATIVE GOVERNANCE AND THEORY

The region of the South West (Fig. 1), which forms the focus of this paper, was created shortly after New Labour came to power in 1997, as part of what JONES and MACLEOD (2004, p. 433) called a comprehensive programme of constitutional 'modernization', which included a Scottish Parliament, Welsh and Northern Ireland Assemblies, an elected mayor and assembly for

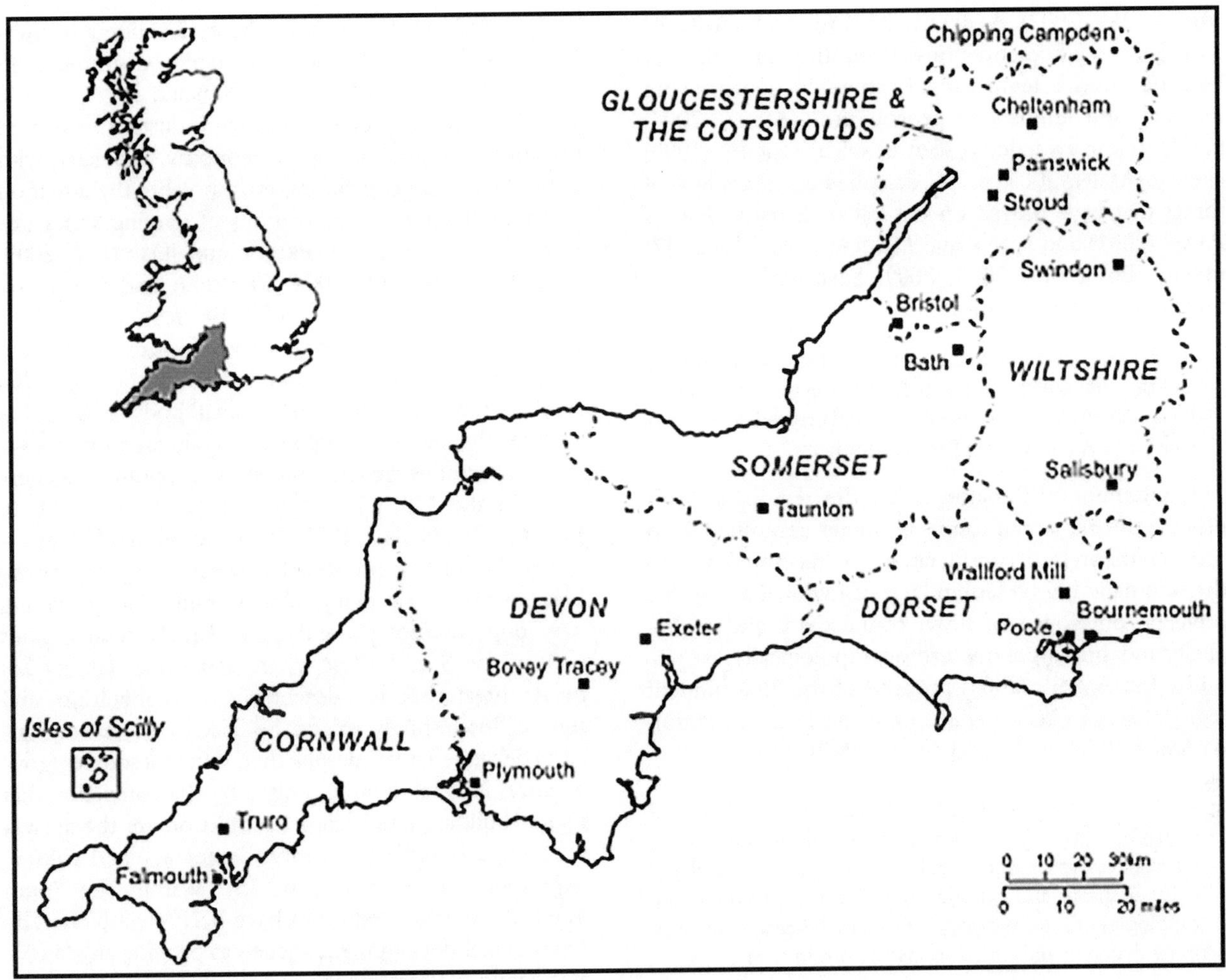

Fig. 1. Regional and county boundaries of the South West of Britain

London, and a further eight regional development agencies (RDAs) for the English regions. In England, this process saw RDAs, regional assemblies and regional Government Offices operating in parallel within a (supposedly) stable framework of regional units (JONES *et al.*, 2004). DEAS and GIODANO (2003, p. 235) noted that, despite meagre resources and limited powers, this rediscovery of regionalism by UK policy-makers 'can be seen as constituting something of a watershed in sub-national governance'. This scalar fix of economy and government authority has been seen by many as a crass exercise in 'functionalist boundary construction', exhibiting, as MACLEOD and JONES (2001, p. 671) continued, a 'gauche insensitivity to local civil society and a staggering lack of imagination' (also JONES *et al.*, 2004; TOMANEY, 2000). The UK government's 'compulsion to territory' should be contextualized within the geohistorical understanding of regions developed by PAASI (2001) and others (JONES and MACLEOD, 2004; SASSEN, 2006) – in which regions are performed, historically constructed, culturally contested and politically charged rather than existentially given and neutral. The UK governance-driven regionalization agenda has prompted a vibrant body of work, which explores the geographical imaginaries, ethical and political potential, contested territories, practical functionality, personnel and policy contradictions (AGNEW, 2000; ALLEN and COCHRANE, 2007; AMIN *et al.*, 2003; HARVEY *et al.*, 2011; JAYNE, 2005; JONES *et al.*, 2004; MACLEOD and JONES, 2001). Closely allied to this work has been neo-Foucauldian research that explores these newly created regional spaces as the locus of complex governance terrains, reinvigorating political participation and cultures of citizenship (GOODWIN *et al.*, 2005; JONES *et al.*, 2004; MACLEOD and GOODWIN, 1999). Through its interrogation of regional territorial practices, this paper responds to calls by Pike and others for empirical work that analyses how regional imaginaries of governance organizations work in practice (PIKE, 2007; MACLEOD and JONES, 2007). Whilst TFSW is an example of a cadre of regional governance organizations developed through this 'renewal of the regions' (MACLEOD and JONES, 2001), the analysis of the county-based craft guilds points towards the need for an historical sensitivity to these different territorial boundaries. This raises an awareness of the region as a spatial formation of 'continuously changing composition, character, and reach' (AMIN, 2004, p. 34; AMIN and THRIFT, 2002). As discussed below, such territorial articulations, whether regions or counties, can only ever be understood as 'temporary placements of ever-moving material and immanent geographies' (AMIN, 2004, p. 34). Clear evidence is seen of what THRIFT (1999, cited in AMIN, 2004, p. 34) described as 'hauntings' of things that have moved on but left their mark. For, as PAASI (2001) and JONES and MACLEOD (2004, p. 447) noted (also JONES, 2007, 2009; SASSEN, 2006), one must remain aware of the

> incessant processes of destabilization and re-stabilization, in and through which regions and territories are institutionalised, demarcated, contested and restructured at varying scales and at particular historical moments.

Contemporary thinking about the region, as with other territorial articulations, is closely enmeshed with broader theoretical considerations of relationality. On the one hand are understandings of regional space that privilege ontologies of flow, connectivity and multiplicity and thinking about territory topologically, as epitomized in AMIN's (2004) proposal of the 'unbounded' regional space (ALLEN *et al.*, 1998; AMIN *et al.*, 2003). As AMIN (2004, p. 33; also AMIN, 2002) argued,

> in this emerging new order, spatial configurations and spatial boundaries are no longer necessarily or purposively territorial or scalar, since the social, economic, political and cultural inside and outside are constituted through the topologies of actor networks which are becoming increasingly dynamic and varied in spatial constitution.

On the other hand, and often set in contrast to this imaginary of unfettered flows of people, objects and ideas, is research that emphasizes the importance of the territorial fix, together with a continued understanding of the region as a discrete space and a defined territory 'over which local actors can have effective control and can manage as a social and political space' (AMIN, 2004, p. 34). The present paper follows the work of Jones and others (ALLEN and COCHRANE, 2007; JESSOP *et al.*, 2008; JONES, 2009) in arguing for a middle ground in which thinking the region territorially and thinking the region topologically are reconciled.

Just as the most recent articulation of regionalism in the UK has been associated with the policies developed after 1997, so the collective term 'creative industries' has been closely associated with the rebranding of the creative economy under the New Labour government. Although the creative industries discourse has subsequently travelled internationally, under the hype of 'Cool Britannia', the New Labour government established a creative industries task force to 'analyse the needs of the creative industries and develop a policy across government' in support of the UK economy (DEPARTMENT OF CULTURE, MEDIA AND SPORT (DCMS), 2000, p. 4). Emerging at this point was the problematic thirteen subsectors of the creative industry bringing together advertising, architecture, art and antiques, computer games, crafts, design, designer fashion, film, music, the performing arts, publishing, software, television and radio. Commentators such as PRATT and JEFFCUTT (2009) and SCOTT (2000) articulated the rise of the creative industries as part of the contemporary knowledge economy, associated with a specific set of geographies, most notably the attention given to creative agglomerations of varying scales (for example, SCOTT, 2000; PRATT and JEFFCUTT, 2009; POWER and SCOTT, 2004; STORPER and CHRISTOPHERSON, 1987; PRATT, 2008; BASSETT *et al.*, 2002; BROWN *et al.*, 2000). In the context of research addressing the geographies of the creative industries, the region has received rather less attention. A small body of work has analysed the role of the region as a terrain for creative governance, creative practice and socio-economic regeneration in the UK (CHAPAIN and COMUNIAN, 2010; JAYNE, 2005; PRATT, 1997, 2004). As this work demonstrates, the creative industries have been recognized by the UK government as being of economic value, providing new opportunities particularly in largely rural regions such as the South West where economic stability has been threatened by downturns in agriculture and mining. Interestingly, this can be allied to the new regionalism debates that are, despite their different sources (governance, cultural–ethnic), united by the conviction that region-building and regional protection are the answer for local economic prosperity, democracy and cultural expression (AMIN, 2004, p. 35). Within the South West, the creative industries have been championed by the regional development agency to provide an alternative economic base for the region, alongside the role of culture, in developing sustainable communities.[1] More usually, however, creative practices and their governance have been analysed at the city scale (PRATT, 2006; TUROK, 2003; WAITT and GIBSON, 2009), or, occasionally, at the scale of the larger city-region, or problematized through the international translation of policy and concepts (LUCKMAN *et al.*, 2009; RANTISI *et al.*, 2006).

Through an empirical study of the issues and challenges of regional creative governance and an analysis of the complex articulations of regional governance over time, this paper reflects upon the manifold governance and social practices of these creative organizations that happen *within* and *beyond* regional territory. By historicizing the activities of these creative organizations, this paper responds to calls for work that challenges the historical blindness of much creative industries literature. Indeed, as KNELL and OAKLEY (2007) reminded readers:

> one of the besetting sins of creative industries policy-making is its obsession with the new, its insistence that everything is 'changed utterly,' and its seeming ignorance, of its own history.
>
> (p. 5)

Responding to Knell and Oakley's call for situated analyses of the creative sector, therefore, attention needs to be placed on appropriate methodologies, employing both historical and contemporary qualitative approaches. Thus, the empirical sections draw from ethnographic work that comprises interviews with key personnel within the organizations, repeated exchanges with their members and office holders, together with discourse analysis of policy documents, and web-based analysis of their activities.[2] This approach enables CASTREE's (2002) methodological call for researchers to step inside networks to be answered. The first step is taken by exploring the regional practices of TFSW. By examining the activities and experiences of TFSW's membership, the interweaving of craft networks across time and space is witnessed.

EXTENDING TEXTILE BOUNDARIES: TEXTILE FORUM SOUTH WEST (TFSW)

TFSW was formally established in February 2004 and it promotes itself as a

> contemporary 'textile hub' for the South West ... a point of exchange for people who love making, thinking or talking TEXTILES.
>
> (TFSW, 2009; original emphasis)

As a non-profit making organization, largely run by highly invested practitioner-volunteers, TFSW aims to 'promote and develop textiles in all forms for the educational, cultural and economic benefit of the region' (ANDREW, 2006, p. 7). TFSW was formed with the purpose of bringing together the varied elements of the textile sector in the South West under one umbrella, with funding secured from Arts Council England, South West, alongside member subscriptions (currently numbering seventy-five members). The membership is diverse and includes archivists, librarians and museum professionals; creative sector professionals; textile artists and designers; textile lecturers and teachers; and other amateur enthusiasts (ANDREW, 2006). TFSW is organized into five subgroups that provide a focus for different interest groups across the diverse textiles sector and facilitate the development of activities that are directed to the needs of the specific audience. A programme of meetings, exhibitions and an annual conference offers opportunities for all forum members to come together around specific themes and activities.

Stepping inside the TFSW network, two things become clear: first, that the inspiration to form the group came from within the rich textile community of the South West and was enabled by pre-existing practices of networking that demonstrated best practice; and secondly, that the forum suggestion was closely aligned with, and supported by, the newly emerging regional governance agenda, expressed through a regionally driven creative industries strategy. The seedbed for TFSW was the 2002 'Nomansland' conference, held in Bath and hosted by the Bristol-based textile group Brunel Broderers.[3] This conference enabled a forum for discussion, and Erica Steer, then Crafts Officer for Arts Council England – South West (ACE-SW) reflected:

> many of us spent much time musing on how valuable (and how rare) opportunities to get together were for textile practitioners.
>
> (STEER, 2006, p. 5)

The opportunity for 'textile specific dialogue at a higher education and professional practitioner level' (ANDREW, 2006, p. 9) was clearly signalled at the event, along with a desire to tap into 'learning, collaborating and networking opportunities linked to textiles that were generated outside the boundaries of traditional education' (p. 9). Members of the Brunel Broderers contributed to the early discussions (starting in 2003) around the formation of TFSW with Sonja Andrew, then a Senior Lecturer and course leader in Textiles at the University of West of England, playing a central role (ANDREW, 2006, p. 8). The initial steering group gathered together textile lecturers, curators, ACE-SW Crafts Officer (Steer) and textile practitioners. Members of this group had attended events hosted by the North West Textiles Forum and this provided the template for TFSW (Amy Houghton, interviewed 13 October 2008). At TFSW's opening conference, ANDREW (2006, p. 9) pointed to the success of the North West Textile Forum in 'initiating events that brought education and cultural benefits to their region', including hosting the European Textile Network conference. In the foundation of TFSW one therefore sees the mobilization of the regional agenda within the South West, but also linking across the English and European regions.

The negotiation of the geographies of the South West textile community has come to play a central part in the practices of TFSW. The title chosen by TFSW for their launch conference, held in March 2005, was 'At the Edge: Extending Textile Boundaries'. As the present authors have undertaken this research, the tensions that this title points towards have come into sharper focus. 'At the edge' indicates the South West regional territory that the forum negotiates: specifically, the challenge of networking its dispersed membership in a region that has been prescribed through regional governance strategies. The title also points towards their willingness to think within and beyond the region, or extending these boundaries and engaging with other regional, national, and European forums and textile practitioners. 'At the edge' directs attention to the more marginal position of textiles amidst the crafts sector, with TFSW aiming to

> develop the profile of textiles ... [a]nd raise awareness of new ideas, concepts, technology and practice in textiles, and how we can consider these within a wider critical framework.
>
> (ANDREW, 2006, p. 9)

Thus, members are encouraged to extend their own textile boundaries through the connections they make within the forum.

The regional scale of the forum mirrors the governance agenda of the time, with the desirability of networking the territorially bounded region (JAYNE, 2005; JONES *et al.*, 2004). The governance-orientated regional agenda had reconfigured bodies within the creative sector, most notably with the Arts Council reforming its boundaries to align with the English regions. New creative organizations emerged within this regional framework, offering opportunities for peer support and development of professional practice alongside (and enabling) networking opportunities to link professionals with practitioners in the creative sector.[4] The regional networking agenda that TFSW developed, therefore, was an explicit response to the governance terrain and the opportunities that were available through regional creative sector funding bodies such as ACE-SW.

The regional discourse permeates the founding objectives of TFSW in terms of promoting the region as a centre for innovative textile initiatives. The objectives indicate that TFSW aims to encourage debate about the region's textile culture: 'to raise the profile of textile heritage and culture within the region'; to promote 'its value within areas of economic development and tourism'; and to offer a coordinating approach 'to the development of textiles, promoting the interests, values and activities of textile communities within the region' (TFSW, 2009). As well as this strong 'regional' agenda, the objectives also point to TFSW's relations beyond the territorial region. The explicit need to

> collaborate with other organizations outside the region on jointly funded textile events and sharing of good practice (e.g. the North West Textile and European Textile Network).
> (ANDREW, 2009, p. 9)

alongside the desirability for the region to be recognized as a centre of excellence both within the UK and internationally, points to the outward looking nature of the group.[5]

Although the official discourse of TFSW speaks to a strong regional agenda, the authors were interested in talking to members about how the forum had developed since 2004 and, specifically, to discover how the *regional* spatialities of the forum were being negotiated by members. In discussion with committee member Amy Houghton (interviewed 13 October 2008), it was clear that TFSW had reached a critical moment: the coordinator's role was open; the volunteer base that supported the forum was beginning to get fatigued; and the ACE-SW grant that had helped to establish the forum was running out. In addition, the absence of support mechanisms to which TFSW had originally responded had also changed with Houghton noting that

> when Textile Forum was set up, there weren't so many bodies doing [the] sorts of things that we [were doing.] [O]ur aims were originally covering professional practice. [There is] so much around now … that are now fulfilling what we were [doing].

In response to this changing situation, TFSW started a process of reviewing its activity with the help of Audiences South West, a development agency that works with organizations to encourage engagement with the arts across the South West region. Through the review process Houghton (interviewed 13 October 2008) noted that TFSW identified the need to connect to the creative organizations in the sector:

> so what we need to do is a sort of re-jig … of creative relationships with those sorts of people in the right directions … [and make] sure we're filling the gaps and not duplicating what other bodies are now doing.

Another outcome has been an increased focus on the membership profile of TFSW, with the committee undertaking a mapping and survey exercise of interests, expertise, age and location.

This mapping exercise responds to a problem faced by TFSW in connecting its membership and enabling networking to take place beyond the physical meeting points that the forum sponsors (such as conferences and workshops). The practicalities of data protection have meant that membership lists have not been circulated, preventing members connecting with each other informally. This is something TFSW wishes to overcome, recognizing the benefits that will accrue from members being able to locate each other with ease. Houghton's aim is to build

> a website that's more user-led, so that there'll be a map, a sort of visual mapping system where you can put yourself … and actually have a gallery, so people can see who's near them, and say 'actually we could set up a little group ourselves because we're living in the same city or living in the same region, or that person down in Cornwall is doing some really interesting work that's really relevant to me; I might phone them up or email them and make a visit.
> (Amy Houghton, interviewed 13 October 2008)

This website idea has been received with enthusiasm by the Committee with Houghton stating:

> they really think that's needed, because the whole talk was the South West [being] too big to try and network across, physically, and needs to be done virtually as well.
> (Amy Houghton, interviewed 13 October 2008)

Social networking and online tools linked to Web 2.0 have been employed within a South West regional context to overcome problems of distance by other creative organizations, particularly those serving digital media practitioners. However, despite the emergence of a vibrant crafts-based online culture, this was an emerging area at the time of the authors' research reflected by TFSW embryonic plans.[6]

Such a need for mapping and surveying membership, however, also speaks strongly of disconnection within the region. Houghton indicated that membership had been dropping, and finding out about the membership was a way to ensure the forum 'talk[ed] to different groups' that come under TFSW umbrella. One TFSW member spoken to by the authors to represented such disconnection:

> There is a new Textile Forum South West, which has started. I've been to a few of their conferences but I find they're quite, I don't know, more into the critique and developing a critical framework for talking about textiles rather than actually making the work and getting the work out there … it seems to be more about meeting up and talking a lot. … I'm not sure I want to travel to Bath just to be in another meeting.
>
> (Anonymous, interviewed 2 March 2009)

Whilst the conference that this practitioner attended did not meet their practice-based needs, TFSW had responded to such concerns by finding ways for members to build practice-based networks. Events such as 'Tea and Textiles' offer an informal opportunity for people to come together in specific locations:

> Well people kept telling us they wanted to network … in a more informal way as opposed to perhaps a conference, … so we thought if people held [Tea and Textiles] in their studios and showed work. … It's often people who want to know more about the host's practice, and see their work and pick their brains.
>
> (Amy Houghton, interviewed 13 October 2008)

Such events are indicative of the role that networked socialities play in the creative sector (COE, 2000; COE and JOHNS, 2004; NORCLIFFE and RENDANCE, 2003; TUROK, 2003).

TFSW has tried hard to cover the region as it has developed its events programme over the last few years. Tea and Textile meetings have happened in Bristol and Bath and some in Devon, 'but we haven't had any in Cornwall' (Amy Houghton, interviewed 13 October 2008). The conference has been held at Taunton; workshops have taken place in Falmouth and Bristol; selling exhibitions have taken place at Walford Mill in Dorset; and an exhibition in Plymouth. Despite this breadth, the Committee remains focused towards the north of the region:

> It's definitely top heavy. … I think we've only got one [Committee member] in Taunton and the rest are Bath upwards; Bath and Bristol which it wasn't before, because we're still trying to pull somebody back in from Falmouth as well … we do want to include further down.
>
> (Amy Houghton, interviewed 13 October 2008)

Efforts to engage across the region and incorporate all membership into the Forum's activities have resulted in TFSW extending its mapping exercise in a creative project, engaging across the regional territorial space, binding representations of the region and practices of the region together:

> The next exhibition will be a *members only* open [that is, non-competitive] exhibition around the theme of mapping, with the aim of attracting a contribution from the whole of the TFSW membership. This is something that we are very passionate about in relation to the mapping and networking of textiles in the region. … [E]ach TFSW member will receive a piece of a map of the south west to make into or incorporate into a new piece of work, which will all then be brought back together to be exhibited.
>
> (Amy Houghton, personal communication 10 February 2010; original emphasis)

Engaging with the members' practices to create a 'regional' exhibition for TFSW work brings into creative tension the challenges of the region as a geographical space and the challenges of bringing a dispersed membership together in a meaningful way. Stepping inside the networks of TFSW reminds one that the practices of networks constitute regional space: TFSW simultaneously practices the region's territorial boundaries, but also works beyond them in relational terms: the region is constituted through the connections with other regionally orientated groups. TFSW emerged during a period of growth in terms of a UK regional governance agenda, and it can be seen how this regional agenda has become entangled within its practices. However, in examining TFSW one is also shown the importance of attending to the multiple territorial practices that regional organizations are negotiating within their remits. These multiplicities become even more apparent when one considers how other craft organizations, such as guilds, which predate regional devolution, are now having to negotiate their own practices within this new regional governance terrain.

CRAFT GUILDS: HISTORICIZING REGIONAL PRACTICES

Craft guilds have an enduring presence in the UK, emerging as powerful and ubiquitous institutions in the Early Modern period and experiencing a revival in connection with the Arts and Crafts movement in the late nineteenth century (PRAK *et al.*, 2006; HASSARD, 2008, pp. 287–288). The Guild of Handicraft (1888–1909) and guild-like associations, such as the Society of Designer Craftsmen (1887–present), were inspired by medieval guild principles, fused with the socialist and aesthetic ideals of the Arts and Crafts movement (for example, ASHBEE, 1909). The legacy of this Arts and Crafts context can be seen in the formation of territorially defined guilds at critical moments through the twentieth century, supported initially by the Rural Industries Bureau (RIB) (BAILEY, 1996, 2006) and later emerging as artist-led networks during periods of craft revival. Guilds have emerged as resilient organizations that govern 'standards' in crafts practice; offer members an institutional mark of respect; provide mutual support; provide training and marketing; alongside allowing access to retail and exhibition spaces.

The South West has a number of county-based craft guild organizations, including The Gloucestershire Guild of Craftsmen (established 1933), Somerset Guild of Craftsmen (established 1933), Devon Guild of Craftsmen (established 1955), and Cornwall Crafts Association (established 1973).[7] The establishment of craft guilds delineated through county boundaries requires interrogation, since it represents a departure from previous Arts and Craft movement-inspired practices, where a guild might establish itself at a specific location around a workshop. An example pertinent to the South West is the influential Guild of Handicrafts under C. R. Ashbee, which moved from its London location in 1902 to the Gloucestershire market town of Chipping Campden. Ashbee moved the Guild of Handicraft to a disused silk mill and established workshops for metalwork, furniture, jewellery, silversmithing, wrought-iron work and printing (RUSSELL, 2008, p. 12; also MACCARTHY, 1981). Although this venture failed, the legacy of this historical guild narrative continued to mobilize craft workers in the area, with the formation of, for example, the Campden Guild of Craftsmen and the Cotswold Handicraft Guild (1921–1936), which came together for exhibitions of their work (ROBINSON, 1983, pp. 4, 7). The rise of the county-based guilds in the inter-war period draws heavily from this legacy, but needs to be set in the context of the work of what BAILEY (1996, p. 35) has termed 'rural development agencies' operating in this period.

The rural development agencies operating in the inter-war period were concerned with the decline of what were identified as 'rural industries', a catch-all term to take into account crafts that were associated with the agricultural and building industry, such as blacksmithing, wheelwrighting, carpentry, brick-making and thatching; alongside hand-craft practices such as handloom textile weaving, basket-making and pottery (WILLIAMS, 1958, p. 7). Such industries were considered to be under threat as a result of economic decline in the agricultural economy and increasing industrial production. The RIB, funded by the government's Development Commission, was established in 1921 to plan and deliver 'a national policy designed to maintain and develop rural industries' (WILLIAMS, 1958, p. 2). The RIB was a national organization whose activities were delivered through 'county' organized bodies such as the Rural Community Councils. These councils usually had a separate Rural Industries Committee and employed Rural Industries Organisers as agents for the organization, whose role was meeting and advising craftspeople in the county area.[8] An official history of the Gloucestershire Guild of Craftsmen shows that the Guild's founding members were involved with the Rural Industries Committee of the Gloucestershire Rural Community Council (formed in 1923), including George Hart (one of Ashbee's original craftsmen), who reformed a Guild of Handicraft in Chipping Campden following Ashbee's departure (ROBINSON, 1983, pp. 4, 8–9).[9]

The relationship of 'county'-scale craft guilds to the Rural Industries Committee and Gloucestershire Rural Community Council under the aegis of the RIB became more strongly articulated in the years running up to the formal establishment of the Gloucestershire Guild of Craftsmen in 1933. The Gloucestershire Rural Industries Committee sponsored public exhibitions of craft from 1926, and in 1927 the Gloucestershire Rural Community Council offered a room in its new headquarters to the 'Gloucestershire Guilds of Rural Craftsmen' alongside a showroom and selling area for the rural industries (ROBINSON, 1983, p. 7). The many guilds, arts and crafts societies, and individual craftsmen circulating in Gloucestershire offered something of a problem to the Rural Community Council and following consultation in 1932 the decision was taken by the Rural Industries Committee to

> merge all the Guilds and Societies existing under the aegis of the Gloucestershire Community Council into one body: the Gloucestershire Guild of Craftsmen.
>
> (ROBINSON, 1983, p. 9)

The Council continued the work linked to training, advising businesses and providing loans, while the newly formed Guild took over the marketing of craft-makers' work and established a regular pattern of exhibitions in order to make connections to markets. In the Guild's official history, the rupture with the Rural Industries Committee occurred in April 1969, when the

> Rural Industries Committee was taken over by the Council for Small Industries in Rural Areas, and so the last official link between the Guild and its parent body was severed.
>
> (ROBINSON, 1983, p. 20)

In 2008 the Gloucestershire Guild of Craftsmen celebrated its seventy-fifth anniversary and maintained its tradition as a creative-maker-led network that provided mutual support, a mentoring system, and opportunities for exhibition and sale each year from its permanent headquarters in Painswick and also through temporary exhibitions across Gloucestershire.

It is fruitful to note the governance-led agenda that steered the foundation of the county-based guild organization. Understanding the history of the Guild deepens one's appreciation of the histories of the creative industries, together with the connections to territory and the spatial organization that the Guild has operated through over time. As seen within TFSW, the Guild of Gloucestershire Craftsmen has always made connections within and beyond the region. Although much more archival research is needed on the past practices of guild activities, one can glean indications of this from official histories of the Gloucestershire Guild of Craftsmen. The 'traditional' craft-based institutions were continuously negotiating different markets, within and beyond

Gloucestershire. In the 1950s Lady Cripps, Chair of the British Handicrafts Export Ltd, asked the Gloucestershire Guild of Craftsmen

> to arrange for her to make personal visits to craftsmen who are prepared to divert some of their work to the export market.
>
> (Robinson, 1983, p. 15)

In addition, members supplied influential galleries in London such as The Little Gallery and the Three Shields Gallery, alongside noted design-led stores such as Liberty, Heal's, and outlets in Birmingham, Liverpool and Manchester. The account books of Hart's Gold and Silversmiths (Chipping Campden, Gloucestershire), which date back over a century, demonstrates the international market place that the workshop was serving. As David Hart noted (interviewed 3 December 2009), looking back at the order books that his father had filled in during the first decades of the twentieth century, customers from countries from the British colonies, alongside America and Japan, are frequently recorded.

The contemporary Gloucestershire Guild of Craftsmen has sixty members (Mary Greensted, personal communication, 19 February 2010). The attraction for these members of belonging to the Guild includes a connection to a community of practice within their local area. For makers moving to an area, the establishment of a ready-made community is vital:

> Because of course makers are very, very isolated and it if wasn't for guilds and associations none of us would have a community. ... So being part of a guild is fantastic because all those people, no matter how different their work is from mine, they have an understanding of what my life is like. ... I don't actually think I would still be in Gloucestershire or in the countryside if I hadn't had that grounding from a community of other makers.
>
> (Sarah Cant, interviewed 12 May 2009)

For others, the imaginary of the Guild and its links to the Arts and Crafts history is important in creating the connection to the county:

> I do now feel very attached to the county and I feel very attached to the Guild of Gloucestershire Craftsman because of its history and because of this Chipping Campden movement, where people came out of London [such as] Ashby.
>
> (Sarah Beadsmore, interviewed 21 July 2009)

Not all craft-makers interviewed by the authors were so positive about the Guild; for some, the volunteer stewarding at the Annual Exhibitions was a burden, while for others the perception of the Guild being old fashioned was a drawback. For those who embraced the Guild, however, and 'have taken onboard about the community feel of it and that it is a self-help group and they have to do this duty' (Sarah Beadsmore, interviewed 21 July 2009), the benefits in terms of community and opportunities to access peer support, mentoring and marketing (such as selling exhibitions) are valued. The Gloucestershire Guild continues to demonstrate its sub-regional, national and international connections. For instance, one member talked of an exchange visit to Swedish craft guilds and an opportunity presented by the Cornwall Craft Association to join a retreat to discuss the conceptual development of their practice.

Given the strong county base to the crafts guilds in the South West, the authors have been interested to see how these guilds negotiate the new creative governance discourse that is practised at this regional level. In exploring this angle, attention now turns to the Devon Guild of Craftsmen, established in 1955 and running for its first thirty years as an artist-led, volunteer network, with an established summer exhibition. In the mid-1980s the Guild developed a permanent gallery space for its work at Bovey Tracy, on the edge of Dartmoor National Park, employing paid staff led by a director and with a new charitable status. The shifts in the Guild through the 1990s have included a development of its site to include an enlarged shop; an exhibition space with an attached programme showing the work of guild members alongside national and international practitioners; education and community events; and a continuing professional development programme for practitioners. Regular funding from the Arts Council for 'showing really rather more innovative, exciting and different work' (Erica Steer, interviewed 28 July 2009) has led to the Guild being associated with cutting-edge contemporary practice that members seeking to position themselves in this area appreciate. As Sarah Cant (a member of both the Devon and the Gloucestershire Guilds) noted: 'I think about them like a gallery that represents me and I love it, it's working really, really well for me' (interviewed 12 May 2009).[10] Through the activities of the professional team running the Guild, it has 'become an organisation with not just a regional but a national profile' (Erica Steer, interviewed 28 July 2009).

It is important to draw attention to the way in which the close connection with arts governance organizations has enabled the Devon Guild to develop. As Director of the Devon Guild of Craftsmen since 2008, Erica Steer has developed the links with arts agencies at a regional and national scale. Working closely with ACE-SW and the UK Crafts Council, the Devon Guild of Craftsmen has become an exemplar. In doing this, the Guild has developed a regional, national and international agenda, sharing this regional agenda with allied creative governance organizations. This does not mean that the Guild has lost sight of its past:

> Our heritage is very important and we've got to retain that, and that is our unique selling point in many ways in that we can work in a national and international arena, we know what our members want and need. It does give you that sort of credibility having that so we can't ignore it and we don't want to lose it.
>
> (Erica Steer, interviewed 28 July 2009)

The Guild has over 250 members, drawn not only from the county of Devon, but also from across the South

West region, indicating the Guild's accommodation of the official regional boundaries for its membership criteria. With members located across the region, enabling them to take part in the business of the Guild is a management concern and similar challenges to connect with members articulated by TFSW were expressed. For example, in 2009 the Devon Guild started a consultation process around the Guild's memorandum and articles:

> at the moment there are all sorts of anomalies in it. ... It means that any time there are certain decisions that have to be made which require me to get all the membership to vote it's a huge administrative task.
>
> (Erica Steer, interviewed 28 July 2009)

No doubt when the Guild was county-based, with fewer members and a less ambitious programme of activity, getting a 10% quorum of members to expedite decisions was more achievable. In the context of the Guild's expanded membership, the problems of practising regional space and managing the broader base of activities have become acute. Recognizing that 'to expect someone from Gloucestershire to drive two, two and a half hours down here and back is too much', Erica Steer visited members in their own homes (interviewed 28 July 2009) to discuss such items. These regular meetings are held in sites across the region and enable convivial spaces for members to network and perform the function of the guild as a space for mutuality whilst enabling the governance of the guild to progress:

> it's hosted in a member's house [and] everybody brings a bit of food. We have small numbers there, sometimes as few as four or five people, but it's actually been incredibly valuable.
>
> (Erica Steer, interviewed 28 July 2009)

The role of key personnel in responding to regional policy agendas and shaping the trajectory of organizations such as the Devon Guild of Craftsmen is critical to this paper's analysis of regional space. Just as Jones (2007, p. 6) argued that 'state personnel have been key producers of state apparatus', the present authors should also pay attention to the role of intermediaries in producing the region (for example, Harvey *et al.*, 2011). The biography of Steer, Director of the Devon Guild of Craftsmen, is illuminating in this regard. Steer's previous role as Crafts Officer of ACE-SW saw her help develop TFSW before joining the Devon Guild of Craftsmen. Steer has firmly allied the Guild to the agendas of the regional creative sector, drawing on her own networks to cement the Guild's activity base. As Crafts Officer of ACE-SW, Steer was able to work across the region, talking to the regional creative-makers and organizations, championing their practice, leveraging opportunities, and networking at a national level with organizations such as the Craft Council. In addition, working with the previous Director of the Devon Guild, Steer established a regional network of crafts organizations. This emerged as the Director of the Devon Guild of Craftsmen was 'constantly being asked for advice and information by other guilds and societies'. As Steer, reflected:

> there must be a better way of doing that; why don't we try and set up a network of guilds, societies and associations?
>
> (interviewed 28 July 2009)

The South West Crafts Guilds, Societies and Associations Network (SW-CGSA) was thus formed with the aim to 'join the common goals and issues of the numerous contemporary craft membership groups in the South West of England'.[11] Although the group has met over three years on a regional basis (facilitated by the regional cultural agency ALIAS, the Artist-led Initiatives Advisory Service), the plan to develop a regional marketing and online sales presence has not evolved.[12] The aim of a regional alliance of organizations appears to have been too ambitious, given the constraints of under-funded organizations, which were often heavily dependent on volunteer time. This points to the fragile nature of the accomplishment of regional territory and the difficulties of aligning bodies with different organizational structures within a regional agenda.

CONCLUSION

In thinking about the territorial practices of these creative organizations and their governance, the authors see a need, following Jones (2009), to reconcile thinking about the region territorially with thinking the region topologically. Whilst the territorial naming of TFSW and craft guilds suggests a spatial fixity, the present empirical work has demonstrated these creative governance organizations and their practices of regional space can only be understood by grasping their investment beyond the territorial region. Both inter-war and contemporary creative industries policies point to the importance of providing opportunities for makers to develop national and international connections. This need for such relational practices therefore challenges conceptions of territorial fixity.

It is not only narratives of flow and connectivity that disturb one's understandings of the region as a '"manageable" geographical space ... [and] definable regional territory to rule over' (Amin, 2004, p. 36). As the present study has shown, there is a need to appreciate the multiplicities of territorial practices with which the governmentally determined region is entangled. The importance of looking at the micro-relations of governance, often conducted through individual personalities, as well as creative practices and networks, is demonstrated in this paper. Only by interrogating the networks of TFSW together with the Gloucestershire and Devon Guilds of Craftsmen, does one see how regional space is practised through individual membership, key personnel and policy rhetoric. Following methodological calls to step inside networks (CASTREE, 2002), therefore, it is interesting to note the reoccurring presence of these individuals throughout the analysis of these organizations, interweaving the case studies. What becomes clear is the key role of individual actors and their changing engagement with regional organizations during their own life courses, as well as throughout the development of the organizations in question.

The reorganization of regional policy and imposition of the 'South West' regional territory has had a differential impact on the activities of the case study organizations, with both the county guilds and TFSW coping with a perceived spatial fixity in diverse and sometimes innovative ways. TFSW's and the guilds' coping mechanisms would seem to correspond to the institutionalization process of the region as an imminent 'becoming' entity, where agency is fragmented and complex, and bound up with a multitude of actors and often mundane practices (PAASI, 2010). This clearly has policy implications. Whilst some organizations have embraced the opportunities afforded, others have simply accommodated the change within a pre-existing organizational structure, resulting in the interaction and overlay of contemporary boundaries with past practices of territory. As a result, the region as a territorially discreet thing that is available for governance is challenged by both the multiplicities of territorial practices that sometimes predate, and co-exist alongside, the 'regional' organizations, and the instances of more fluid organization based upon relations and (often personal) networks.

The UK's devolved regional governance agenda has created a raft of new regional organizations. Such governance organizations, however, are by no means a new thing. It is important to acknowledge that the need to negotiate the complexities of territorial practices that were witnessed through the RIB activities in the inter-war period are similar in kind (if different in scale) to those that confront the contemporary regionally based organizations today. As this paper makes clear, these new regional bodies have not supplanted previous territorial incarnations of creative governance. One must appreciate the value of legacies of both governance and practice, whilst considering how these past and present articulations are mutually entwined. This is increasingly important in the context of wider regional policies which frequently co-opt historical creative legacies into contemporary place-making strategies.[13]

The empirical research demonstrates different scales of practice, social action and multiple geographies of affiliation, linkage and flow (AGNEW, 1994). Thus, alongside thinking about the region topologically in terms of networks and connections that happen beyond the territorial region, this research illustrates the importance of attending to the multiplicities of territorial practices entangled within governmentally determined 'regions'. In particular, this research underlines the need to situate the contemporary articulations of regional space in their historical context. In so doing, therefore, this paper reinforces work by PAASI (2002, 2003; also JONES, 2007), as well as a group of historical geographers who point towards historical articulations of relational practices (LAMBERT and LESTER, 2006), by making clear that such perspectives should not be restricted to one's contemporary understandings of territory. Research on the understanding of regional space requires further empirical engagement that will ground the sometimes-abstract debates of relational ontologies where they concern regional territories. Further, the binding together of historical and contemporary practices of territory is especially valuable for the perspective it gives to these relational ontologies. Such an approach allows an exploration of the multiplicities and continual processes of the making and remaking of regional space.

Acknowledgements – The authors' thanks are due to the research participants for their generosity in sharing their experiences with them. The authors were fortunate in that the participants felt able to spend time with them and were happy for repeat engagements. The authors would also like to thank the Editors of this special issue and the anonymous referees for their advice and for enabling them to participate in this collection of papers.

NOTES

1. In the South West, for example, the creative industries are worth £5.4 billion annually and in 2006 they employed over 144 000 people (HARDWICK, 2010, p. 103).
2. These interviews were carried out as part of a larger body of empirical work undertaken between 2007 and 2010 with creative practitioners and arts organizations across the South West of Britain. Amounting to over one hundred interviews in total, as well as six periods of ethnographic work, this research forms the core of an Arts and Humanities Research Council (AHRC)-funded project entitled 'Negotiating the Poetics and Politics of Cultural Identity within the Creative Industries in South West Britain' (Grant Reference AHRC AH/E/008887/1).
3. Originally a group of textile artists who trained together in Bristol, the Brunel Broderers formed a network of support, which also enabled opportunities for innovation and exhibition (Amy Houghton, interviewed 13 October 2008). The group still operates as an arts collective (see http://www.brunelbroderers.co.uk) (accessed on 21 April 2011 for details).
4. This agenda is set out in policy documents such as SOUTH WEST ARTS (2002) and CRAFTS COUNCIL (2004, 2009).
5. This need to network beyond the region was reinforced by comments made during the authors' interview with Amy Houghton (13 October 2008) and by the reporting

of links made between TFSW and Eastern Region Textiles Forum (ERTF) via the TFSW email circulation list (circular received 9 October 2008) and in ERTF's (2008) newsletter.

6. An example of an online community tool serving the digital media industries of the South West community is the Digital Peninsular Network (see http://www.digitalpeninsula.com) (accessed on 19 September 2011). For further discussion of the online craft communities, see GAUNTLETT (2011).
7. For the web presence of these guilds, see: http://www.guildcrafts.org.uk/; http://www.somersetguild.co.uk/; http://www.crafts.org.uk/; and http://www.cornwallcrafts.co.uk/home (all accessed on 15 March 2011).
8. For further discussion of the organization and structure of the RIB, see WILLIAMS (1958) and BAILEY (1996, 2006).
9. As BAILEY (1996) noted, there remains a need for a history of the RIB and its associated county-based organizations.
10. It is worth noting here that Sarah Cant also has links with TFSW and that it was Erica Steer who was the ACE-SW Crafts Officer involved in helping to set up TFSW; on leaving that post she joined Devon Guild as its Director in 2008.
11. See http://www.a-n.co.uk:81/artist/nan/organisation/62391 (accessed on 22 February 2010).
12. Set up in 1999, ALIAS is an artist-led organization that provides an advisory service to 130 artist-led groups across the South West. ALIAS organizes seminars, workshops and conferences, providing practical and conceptual advice for artist-run groups and projects across the region (see http://www.aliasarts.org) (accessed on 15 March 2011).
13. See, for example, the UK's 'Living Places' strategy, which aims to build 'stronger communities through culture' (see http://www.living-places.org.uk) (accessed on 15 March 2011). See also the CULTURE SOUTH WEST (CSW) (2008a, 2008b) regional cultural strategies and delivery framework.

REFERENCES

AGNEW J. (1994) The territorial trap: the geographical assumptions of international relations theory, *Review of International Political Economy* **1**, 53–80.

AGNEW J. (2000) From the political economy of regions to regional political economy, *Progress in Human Geography* **24**, 101–110.

ALLEN J. and COCHRANE A. (2007) Beyond the territorial fix: regional assemblages, politics and power, *Regional Studies* **41**, 1161–1175.

ALLEN J., MASSEY D. and COCHRANE A. (1998) *Re-thinking the Region*. Routledge, London.

AMIN A. (2002) Spatialities of globalisation, *Environment and Planning A* **34**, 385–399.

AMIN A. (2004) Regions unbound: towards a new politics of place, *Geografiska Annaler: Series B, Human Geography* **86**, 33–44.

AMIN A., MASSEY D. and THRIFT N. (2003) *Decentering the Nation: A Radical Approach to Regional Inequality*. Catalyst, London.

AMIN A. and THRIFT N. J. (2002) *Cities: Re-Imagining Urban Theory*. Polity, Cambridge.

ANDREW S. (Ed.) (2006) *At the Edge: Extending Textile Boundaries*. Textiles Forum South West (TFSW), Bristol.

ASHBEE C. R. (1909) *The Guild of Handicraft, its Deed of Trust and Rules for the Guidance of its Guildsmen, together with a Note on its Work*. Broad Campden.

BAILEY A. (1996) Progress and preservation: the role of rural industries in the making of the modern image of countryside, *Journal of Design History* **9**, 35–53.

BAILEY C. (2006) Rural industries and the image of the countryside, in BRASSLEY P., BURCHARDT J. and THOMPSON L. (Eds) *The English Countryside between the Wars: Regeneration or Decline?*, pp. 132–149. Boydell, Woodbridge.

BASSETT K., GRIFFITHS R. and SMITH I. (2002) Cultural industries, cultural clusters and the city: the example of natural history film-making in Bristol, *Geoforum* **33**, 165–177.

BROWN A., O'CONNOR J. and COHEN S. (2000) Local music policies within a global music industry: cultural quarters in Manchester and Sheffield, *Geoforum* **31**, 437–451.

CASTREE N. (2002) False antithesis? Marxism, nature and actor-networks, *Antipode* **34**, 111–146.

CHAPAIN C. and COMUNIAN R. (2010) Enabling and inhibiting the creative economy: the role of the local and regional dimensions in England, *Regional Studies* **44**, 717–734.

COE N. M. (2000) The view from out West: embeddedness, inter-personal relations and the development of an indigenous film industry in Vancouver, *Geoforum* **31**, 391–407.

COE N. M. and JOHNS J. (2004) Beyond production clusters: towards a critical political economy of networks in the film and television industries, in POWER D. and SCOTT A. J. (Eds) *Cultural Industries and the Production of Culture*, pp. 188–204. Routledge, London.

CRAFTS COUNCIL (2004) *An Independent Report for the Crafts Council: Making it in the 21st Century*. Crafts Council, London.

CRAFTS COUNCIL (2009) *The Craft Blueprint: A Workforce Development Plan for Craft in the UK*. Crafts Council, London.

CULTURE SOUTH WEST (CSW) (2008a) *A Better Place To Be: Framework for Action*. CSW, Bristol.

CULTURE SOUTH WEST (CSW) (2008b) *People, Places and Spaces. A Cultural Infrastructure Development Strategy for the South West of England*. CSW, Bristol.

CURRID E. and WILLIAMS S. (2009) The geography of buzz: art, culture and the social milieu in Los Angeles and New York, *Journal of Economic Geography* **10**, 423–451.

DANIELS S. (1993) *Fields of Vision: Landscape and National Identity in England and the United States*. Princeton University Press, Princeton, NJ.

DEAS I. and GIORDANO B. (2003) Regions, city regions, identity and institution building: contemporary experiences of the scalar turn in Italy and England, *Journal of Urban Affairs* **25**, 225–246.

Department of Culture, Media and Sport (DCMS) (2000) *Creative Industries: The Regional Dimension. A Report of the Regional Issues Working Group*. The Stationery Office (TSO) for DCMS, London.

Eastern Region Textiles Forum (ERTF) (2008) *ERTF: Taking Textiles Forward* (available at: http://www.ertf.org.uk/) (accessed on 24 August 2012).

Gauntlett D. (2011) *Making is Connecting: The Social Meaning of Creativity, from DIY and Knitting to YouTube and Web 2.0*. Polity, London.

Goodwin M., Jones M. and Jones R. (2005) Devolution, constitutional change and economic development: explaining and understanding the new institutional geographies of the British State, *Regional Studies* **39**, 342–343.

Hardwick S. (2010) *State of the South West*. South West Observatory, Bristol.

Harvey D., Hawkins H. and Thomas N. (2011) Regional imaginaries of governance agencies: practising the region of South West Britain, *Environment and Planning A* **43**, 470–486.

Hassard F. (2008) Intangible heritage in the UK: the dark side of the enlightenment, in Smith L. J. and Akagawa N. (Eds) *Intangible Heritage*, pp. 270–288. Routledge, London.

Jackson P., Thomas N. and Dwyer C. (2007) Consuming transnational fashion in London and Mumbai, *Geoforum* **38**, 908–924.

Jayne M. (2005) Creative industries: the regional dimension?, *Environment and Planning C: Government and Policy* **23**, 537–556.

Jazeel T. (2005) The word is sound? Geography, musicology and British Asian soundscapes, *Area* **37**, 233–241.

Jessop B., Brenner B. and Jones M. (2008) Theorising socio-spatial relations, *Environment and Planning D – Society and Space* **26**, 389–401.

Jones M. (2009) Phase space: geography, relational thinking, and beyond, *Progress in Human Geography* **33**, 487–506.

Jones M. and MacLeod G. (2004) Regional spaces, spaces of regionalism: territory, insurgent politics and the English question, *Transactions of the Institute of British Geographers* **29**, 433–452.

Jones R. (2007) *People/States/Territories*. Blackwell, London.

Jones R., Goodwin M., Jones M. and Simpson G. (2004) Devolution, state personnel, and the production of new territories of governance in the United Kingdom, *Environment and Planning A* **36**, 89–109.

Knell J. and Oakley K. (2007) *London's Creative Economy: An Accidental Success?* Provocation Series. The Work Foundation, London.

Kong L. (2005) The sociality of cultural industries: Hong Kong's cultural policy and film industry, *International Journal of Cultural Policy* **11**, 63–75.

Lambert D. and Lester A. (Eds) (2006) *Colonial Lives across the British Empire: Imperial Careering in the Long Nineteenth Century*. Cambridge University Press, Cambridge.

Luckman S., Gibson C. and Lea T. (2009) Mosquitoes in the mix: how transferable is creative city thinking?, *Singapore Journal of Tropical Geography* **30**, 70–85.

MacCarthy F. (1981) *Simple Life: C. R. Ashbee in the Cotswolds*. University of California Press, Berkeley, CA.

MacLeod G. and Goodwin M. (1999) Space, scale and state strategy: towards a re-interpretation of contemporary urban and regional governance, *Progress in Human Geography* **23**, 503–527.

MacLeod G. and Jones M. (2001) Renewing the geography of regions, *Environment and Planning D: Society and Space* **19**, 669–695.

MacLeod G. and Jones M. (2007) Territorial, scalar, networked, connected: in what sense a regional world?, *Regional Studies* **41**, 1177–1191.

Matless D. (1998) *Landscape and Englishness*. Reaktion, London.

Norcliffe G. and Rendance O. (2003) New geographies of comic book production in North America: the new artisan, distancing, and the periodic social economy, *Economic Geography* **79**, 241–263.

Paasi A. (2001) Europe as a social process and discourse: considerations of place, boundaries and identity, *European Urban and Regional Studies* **8**, 7–28.

Paasi A. (2002) Place and region: regional worlds and words, *Progress in Human Geography* **26**, 802–811.

Paasi A. (2003) Region and place: regional identity in question, *Progress in Human Geography* **27**, 475–485.

Paasi A. (2010) Commentary: Regions are social constructs, but who or what 'constructs' them? Agency in question, *Environment and Planning A* **42**, 2296–2301.

Pike A. (2007) Editorial: Whither regional studies?, *Regional Studies* **41**, 1143–1148.

Power D. and Scott A. J. (Eds) (2004) *Cultural Industries and the Production of Culture*. Routledge, London.

Prak M., Lis C., Lucassen J. and Soley H. (Eds) (2006) *Craft Guilds in the Early Modern Low Countries: Work, Power and Representation*. Ashgate, Aldershot.

Pratt A. C. (1997) The cultural industries production system: a case study of employment change in Britain, 1984–91, *Environment and Planning A* **29**, 1953–1974.

Pratt A. C. (2004) Mapping the cultural industries. Regionalisation; the example of the South East of England, in Power D. and Scott A. J. (Eds) *Cultural Industries and the Production of Culture*, pp. 19–36. Routledge, London.

Pratt A. C. (2006) Advertising and creativity, a governance approach: a case study of creative agencies in London, *Environment and Planning A* **38**, 1883–1899.

Pratt A. C. (2008) Innovation and creativity, in Short J. R., Hubbard P. and Hall, T. (Eds) *The Sage Companion to the City*, pp. 226–297. Sage, London.

Pratt A. C. and Jeffcutt P. (Eds) (2009) *Creativity and Innovation in the Cultural Economy*. Routledge, London.

Rantisi N., Leslie D. and Christopherson S. (2006) Placing the creative economy: scale, politics, and the material – the rise of the new creative imperative, *Environment and Planning A* **38**, 1789–1797.

Robinson S. (1983) *A Fertile Field: An Outline History of the Guild of Gloucestershire Craftsmen and the Crafts in Gloucestershire*. The Guild of Gloucestershire Craftsmen, Cheltenham.

Russell R. (2008) *The Harts of Chipping Campden: An Insight into Four Generations Creating Fine Silver in the Arts and Crafts Tradition*. Hart Gold and Silversmiths/Loose Chippings Books.

Sassen S. (2006) *Territory, Authority, Rights. From Medieval to Global Assemblages*. Princeton University Press, Princeton, NJ.

Scott A. (2000) *The Cultural Economy of Cities*. Sage, London.

South West Arts (2002) *The Real World, a Prospectus for the Crafts in the South West*. South West Arts, Exeter.

Steer E. (2006) Conference introduction, in Andrew S. E. (Ed.) *At the Edge: Extending Textile Boundaries*. Textile Forum South West (TFSW), Bristol.

Storper M. and Christopherson S. (1987) Flexible specialisation and regional industrial agglomerations: the case of the U.S. motion picture industry, *Annals of the Association of American Geographers* **77**, 103–117.

Storper M. and Venables A. (2004) Buzz: face-to-face contact and the urban economy, *Journal of Economic Geography* **4**, 351–370.

Textile Forum South West (TFSW) (2009) *Website Homepage* (available at: http://www.tfsw.org) (accessed on 24 August 2012).

Tomaney J. (2000) End of the Empire State? New Labour and devolution in the United Kingdom, *International Journal of Urban and Regional Research* **24**, 677–690.

Tomaney J. (2007) Keeping a beat in the dark: narratives of regional identity in Basil Bunting's Briggflatts, *Environment and Planning D: Society and Space* **25**, 355–375.

Turok I. (2003) Cities, clusters and creative industries: the case of film and television in Scotland, *European Planning Studies* **11**, 549–565.

Waitt G. and Gibson C. (2009) Creative small cities: rethinking the creative economy in place, *Urban Studies* **46**, 1223–1246.

Williams W. M. (1958) *The Country Craftsman*. Routledge, London.

Unusual Regionalism in Northern Europe: The Barents Region in the Making

KAJ ZIMMERBAUER
Department of Geography, Oulu, Finland.

ZIMMERBAUER K. Unusual regionalism in Northern Europe: the Barents Region in the making, *Regional Studies*. This paper focuses on the institutionalization of the supra-national Barents Region, which is located in the extreme north of Europe and consists of the northern parts of Norway, Sweden, Finland and Russia. The aim is to scrutinize how this newly conceived region has become institutionalized as a manifestation of business-oriented regionalist aspirations and international geopolitics. The case study contributes to the ongoing discussions on the power of regionalism and the construction of 'regional competitiveness'. These discussions are set against the issues of identity within emerging regional spaces. The analysis is also linked to the advocates/activists dichotomy and the controversial 'relational turn' in regional geography.

ZIMMERBAUER K. 北欧非同寻常的区域主义：逐渐成形的巴伦支海地区，区域研究。本文重点关注超国家的巴伦支海地区的制度化，这一区域位于欧洲最北部，组成区域包括挪威、瑞典、芬兰及俄罗斯北部。文章旨在审议这一新近概念化的区域如何反映出以业务为导向的区域需求和国际地缘政治。本案例分析丰富了目前针对地区主义的权力和"区域竞争力"构建相关的讨论。此类讨论均分析了区域空间中的定位问题。本文的分析是基于区域地理学中备受争议的倡导者/活动家二分法以及"相关论转向"。

ZIMMERBAUER K. Un régionalisme original dans l'Europe du Nord: la région de Barents en marche, *Regional Studies*. Cet article porte sur l'institutionnalisation de la région supranationale de Barents qui est située à l'extrême nord de l'Europe et comprend les zones septentrionales de la Norvège, de la Suède, de la Finlande et de la Russie. On cherche à examiner comment cette région nouvellement établie s'est institutionnalisée comme manifestation des aspirations régionalistes orientées vers le commerce et de la géopolitique internationale. L'étude de cas contribue au débat en cours sur la force du régionalisme et le développement de la 'compétitivité régionale'. Ce débat se déroule à la lumière des questions de l'identité au sein des espaces régionales naissantes. L'analyse se rapporte aussi à la dichotomie défenseurs/activistes et au 'virage relationnel' controversé dans la géographie régionale.

ZIMMERBAUER K. Ungewöhnlicher Regionalismus in Nordeuropa: das Entstehen der Barentsregion, *Regional Studies*. Im Mittelpunkt dieses Beitrags steht die Institutionalisierung der supranationalen Barentsregion im hohen Norden Europas, die aus den nördlichen Teilen von Norwegen, Schweden, Finnland und Russland besteht. Untersucht werden soll, wie diese neu konzipierte Region als Ausdruck der geschäftsorientierten regionalistischen Aspirationen und internationalen Geopolitik institutionalisiert wurde. Die Fallstudie versteht sich als Beitrag zu den andauernden Diskussionen über die Macht des Regionalismus und die Konstruktion von 'regionaler Wettbewerbsfähigkeit'. Diese Diskussionen erfolgen vor dem Hintergrund von Fragen der Identität innerhalb neu entstehender regionaler Räume. Ebenso ist die Analyse mit der Dichotomie der Fürsprecher/Aktivisten und der umstrittenen 'relationalen Wende' in der regionalen Geografie verknüpft.

ZIMMERBAUER K. Regionalismo inusual en el norte de Europa: la región de Barents en ciernes, *Regional Studies*. En este artículo prestamos atención a la institucionalización de la región supranacional de Barents, que se encuentra en el extremo norte de Europa y está formada por las zonas septentrionales de Noruega, Suecia, Finlandia y Rusia. Con ello pretendemos examinar de qué modo esta nueva región se ha institucionalizado como una manifestación de las aspiraciones regionalistas con orientación comercial y de la geopolítica internacional. Este estudio de caso contribuye a los continuos debates sobre el poder del regionalismo y la construcción de la 'competitividad regional'. Estos debates se sitúan en el contexto de cuestiones de identidad dentro de los espacios regionales emergentes. El análisis también está vinculado con la dicotomía de defensores/activistas y el controvertido 'giro relacional' en la geografía regional.

INTRODUCTION

Through much of the twentieth century, regional space has been defined to a large extent territorially (or as 'spaces of places'; cf. CASTELLS, 2000), which culminated in Europe in the notion of a 'Europe of the regions'. However, the present century has witnessed a challenge to territorial perspectives by more relational approaches, which conceptualize regions as more open 'spaces of flows' and override some significance of territorial boundaries. While the Europe of the regions has witnessed the emergence of many new regional spaces and institutions (JENSEN and RICHARDSON, 2004), contemporary relational thinking has materialized particularly through the establishment of so-called unusual (or non-standard) regions. These are mostly based on supra-national collaborative initiatives, but may 'transcend and jar against established territorially bounded bodies' on sub-national scales as well (DEAS and LORD, 2006, p. 1848). As DEAS and LORD (2006, pp. 1847–1849) write, new regional territories derive basically from three different yet overlapping principles that are essential to thinking within the European Commission. The first is the idea of a single European market, which occupies a key role in rendering national boundaries more porous. Secondly, the aim is to promote competitiveness throughout the European Union, which is increasingly being done by creating new internationally significant regions. The third main principle is to improve cohesion and reduce interregional disparities, which is seen as a way of further increasing competitiveness. Although the hollowing-out thesis might be controversial (JESSOP, 2004; BRENNER, 2004; HARRISON, 2006, 2008), these three principles have also contributed to the rescaling of the nation-state. Territorial reorganization of the state has thus had a great impact on the emergence of non-standard regional spaces and vice versa.

The single European market, with its increasingly porous borders, has paved the way for transnational regions within the European Union. As inter-regional (and also intercontinental from the Union's standpoint) competition is considered more or less unavoidable, there is considerable support for the institutionalization of internationally competitive supra-national regions. The Euroregions are a good example of this; there are about seventy such units at the moment, concentrating on cross-border cooperation in culture, tourism and other economic activities. Some of the Euroregion initiatives have their roots in the 1950s, but most of them were created in the 1990s (VIRTANEN, 2004; PERKMANN, 2007; EUROPEAN PARLIAMENT, 2009). The end of the twentieth century witnessed the mushrooming of transnational regions also elsewhere, proved by the prominent examples of the Singapore–Johor–Riau growth triangle (SPARKE *et al.*, 2004) and Cascadia in North America (CLARKE, 2000).

Supra-national regionalism has also been a focus of geographical research lately, although much of this research has however been on cross-border regions within the European Union (SCOTT, 2000; KRAMSCH, 2002; KAPLAN and HÄKLI, 2002; STRÜVER, 2004; SIDAWAY, 2004; PERKMANN, 2007; HALL, 2007). Although there are some studies on supra-national regions that include both European Union and non-European Union areas, studies of regions located on both sides of the former Iron Curtain are rarer (ESKELINEN, 2000; MEINHOF, 2002; VIRTANEN, 2004; ROUGE-OIKARINEN, 2009). This study of the Barents Region – straddling the border between the North Atlantic Treaty Organization (NATO) and Russia – aims to bring further understanding to region building across borders that are considered both high and hard. Barents is also a distinctively peripheral cross-border region, making it more atypical of the current research agenda, where regionalism is often synonymous with (metropolitan) city regions (STORPER, 1995; SCOTT, 2001; WHEELER, 2002; HALL and PAIN, 2006; HERRSCHEL, 2012).

The aim of this paper is to study how and why the supra-national Barents Region, located in the extreme north of Europe, has become institutionalized as a manifestation of both business-oriented regionalist aspirations and international geopolitics. Its institutionalization will be studied through the 'identity talk' that the advocates have produced for it, with the objective of examining especially how its region-building narratives can be understood in the light of contemporary theories of the institutionalization of regions, in which region building occurs as a process with several distinguishable stages. At a more general level, the paper also aims to add a further note to current discussions of regionalism and regional competitiveness. The Barents Region makes a highly interesting case in this respect, since in spite of its long historical roots, it can be seen as having been established relatively recently. It is also both politically and economically complex due to its strict East–West division. While cross-border region building has presumably been mediated largely through top-down national, state-bound processes, this paper also aims to study the role of supra- and sub-national structures and institutions (such as regional councils and the European Union) in institutionalization.

The three main research questions are as follows:

- Which actors and constellations have played a key role in the institutionalization of the Barents Region?
- What elements has its institutionalization been built upon?
- How has the territory of the Barents Region been conceptualized and contested?

Each question will be analysed in its respective part under the headings of networks of cooperation, elements of institutionalization and vagueness of the territorial setting. While the first of these parts reviews the dynamics and abundance of actor constellations and networks, the latter two stem from – and become more closely tied to – the theory of the institutionalization of regions and regional identity. Through this structure the case study region comes to be treated as a space for political aspirations, economic governance and, above all, spatial planning. The paper will begin with a conceptualization of regions on the lines of the theory of institutionalization. Emphasis will also be placed on the special character of cross-border regionalism. After that the Barents Euro-Arctic Region (BEAR) will be presented by means of a short history and certain key distinctive features. After analysing the research questions through empirical data[1] in the next three sections, some concluding remarks and discussion will be presented in which the outcomes will be considered in the light of the theoretical basis. Finally, the future of the Barents Region will also be discussed.

THE INSTITUTIONALIZATION OF A REGION: THEORETICAL BACKGROUND

Regions can be conceptualized and categorized in many ways (for example, GILBERT, 1988). It is possible, for example, to distinguish administrative, functional and identity regions (VEGGELAND, 1994), and also old and new regions. Administrative regions are typically those that have been imposed in a top-down manner in order to take responsibility for the implementation and administration of laws, for instance, whereas functional regions have evolved around interaction and integration, sometimes across traditional administrative borders. Identity regions are frequently formed on the basis of cultural and historical homogeneity and are usually created by a bottom-up process, although a sense of identity can obviously evolve in administrative regions as well, as PAASI (1986a) pointed out in his theory of the institutionalization of regions. New regions bear some resemblance to administrative regions, as they are often created ad hoc to increase the competitiveness of the spatial unit in question. They thus serve as units of competitiveness and governance, usually at a sub-national level, although they can also be supra-national ones. New regions are more independent of the nation-state and can lobby the Eurocrats in Brussels directly on their own behalf, for example. By contrast, the more traditional (old) regions are usually thought of as having some kind of 'historical depth' which makes them meaningful for their citizens and strengthens a regional identity (PAASI, 2009). Furthermore, precisely because they are the typical units of regional identity, the regions with a longer history are also often developed and defended by regional activism (SYSSNER, 2006; PAASI and ZIMMERBAUER, 2011). Old regions are thus usually synonymous with identity regions.

It has been customary lately to conceptualize regions in terms of their boundaries. In this context some academics have adopted a more relational approach rather than the 'territorialist' one (ALLEN *et al.*, 1998; ALLEN and COCHRANE, 2007, 2010; AMIN, 2002, 2004). This relational thinking emphasizes a region as an open, fuzzy and internally diverse 'kaleidoscopic web of networks', whereas the territorialist approach stresses the concept of a more spatially defined and articulated entity that has certain distinguishable characteristics (PAASI, 2009; cf. PAINTER, 2010). Some scholars have suggested that the boundedness of regions is ultimately an empirical rather than a theoretical matter (JONES and MACLEOD, 2004; MACLEOD and JONES, 2007; HUDSON, 2007). It is also historically contingent. LAGENDIJK (2005), for example, reminds us that boundaries in the European Union area used to be mere administrative lines that were of interest only to a few bureaucrats and statisticians, whereas more recently they have become core themes in both public and academic debates. This emphasizes borders as multi-contextual constructions with different layers (GIAOUTZI *et al.*, 1993; SCHACK, 2000).

While the different conceptualizations indicate something about the character of regions, it is evident that only a few bounded regions fall neatly into such categorizations. Yet they help one recognize that region-building processes are not always alike, and that both their starting points and their outcomes can vary. By distinguishing the various paths of institutionalization and the characteristics of regions, one can come to understand the processes, and even the power struggles, behind region building and regionalization. Institutionalization of a region demands inputs from various actors, and the region gains its justification and character depending on the actors themselves and their motives.

Supra-national region building, which is the focus of this article, can be described as a process in which sub-national regions from two or more states are brought together, either voluntarily or sometimes even compulsorily, to form new territorial configurations (ZIMMERBAUER, 2010). According to PERKMANN (2007), such configurations entail 'more or less institutionalized collaboration between contiguous sub-national authorities across national borders' (p. 156).

The process of region building contains elements 'from below' as well as 'from above'. 'From below' means simply that the sub-national authorities do not wait for formal procedures from above, but use new types of interaction without formal administrative justification. 'From above' refers to what some scholars call 'centrally orchestrated regionalism' (HARRISON, 2008; also MACLEOD, 2001; RODRIGUEZ-POSE and GILL, 2003), a development process in which regions are established and given power and a certain freedom of action by the formal authorities and central governments (SVENSSON, 1998). It is crucial to emphasize that many supra-national region-building processes are managed from below, but perhaps more often from above (RODRIGUEZ-POSE and GILL, 2002; PERKMANN, 2003; BOMAN and BERG, 2007; HARRISON, 2008). In fact, supra-national region building can take quite different shapes and paths and aim at quite different things. Sometimes it can be quite explicit, as in cases of new competitive regions or 'growth corridors', but on occasions it can be more vague, veiled and contested.

Although region-building processes are in many ways fuzzy and occur differently in different territorial settings, Paasi's acknowledged model of institutionalization, originally developed in the mid-1980s when studying the Finnish provinces (PAASI, 1986a, 1986b, 2009), is also useful when examining supra-national and/or non-standard regions such as the Barents Region. According to this model, the institutionalization of a region has four overlapping stages. First, its existence draws on a certain territorial shape, making the region distinctive and usually also bordered in some way. This phase is often contested, as the process may be crucial for the political cohesion of the region and its even economic performance (cf. gerrymandering and mergers to alter the rank order of cities). Borders vary from hard to soft, making them in some cases highly permeable and in others relatively closed. In the second phase of institutionalization, naming and the creation of regional symbols are essential. Here the purpose is to strengthen the idea of the existence of a region and to boost regional consciousness. This phase is also contested, as symbolization is about representation, which is about choices that involve power relations and political intentions. Place names and symbols (such as flags, songs or coats of arms) distinguish the region (and the inhabitants of one region) from others and serve as elements of collective regional identity by arousing divisions of the 'us and them' type (PAASI, 1986a, 1986b). Symbolization is achieved nowadays to a large extent through place-marketing processes, that is, promotional actions taken in order to stand out in inter-regional competition (ZIMMERBAUER, 2009).

Institutional shaping is substantial in the third phase (PAASI, 1986b). Here various informal and formal institutions emerge to produce and reproduce regionalist thinking. Regional policy and development institutions are established, for example, and also various social organizations emerge. Common to all these is that they might not exist without the region but are in some ways regionally based, or else their activities are defined by the region. In any case, their actions are such that they strengthen the 'cognitive map' of the region. The fourth and arguably the last phase is the establishment of the region so that it is accepted as part of the regional structure and exists in the broader social consciousness. At the state level this means that its sovereignty is recognized and at the sub-state level it implies that the region has an unquestioned administrative status in the accepted regional system. At this stage the region is fully established and it has a role equal to that of other similar regions. In practical terms, the region is ready to be mobilized for purposes such as place marketing, or alternatively in ideological struggles over resources (PAASI, 1986b; MACLEOD and JONES, 2001).

The phases do not follow each other neatly, but they can occur simultaneously and their order can even vary (PAASI, 1986b; MACLEOD and JONES, 2001). The model nevertheless gives a well-thought-out background against which to contemplate the emergence of regions. It emphasizes the regions are not separate, bounded units or 'scales' but *processes* of institutionalization that simultaneously bring together local, national and global practices, interactions and power relations. Regions are thus not understood as fixed or everlasting but as being subject to continuous renewal and restructuring processes in which they are socially constructed and deconstructed. The institutionalization of a region is thereby linked not only with various processes of regional transformation and renewal, but also with de-institutionalization, in which the region ceases to exist officially as a result of integration or dispersion, making this largely a reverse process to that of institutionalization (PAASI, 1991; RAAGMAA, 2002; RIIKONEN, 1995). A de-institutionalized region, although lacking administrative status, can nevertheless still be symbolized and identified with (ZIMMERBAUER and KAHILA, 2006).

There has been some debate as to whether cross-border regionalism occurs in the same way as sub-national regionalism. It is clear that cross-border cooperation and region-building processes are bound to each other and cooperation and strong interaction across borders can result in the emergence of a functional region (PROKKOLA, 2008; PERKMANN and SUM, 2002). Institutional practices and social relations alike thus serve to maintain cross-border regions. However, many supra-national regions are overtly constructed by administrators on a regional level, and often on a nation-state or even a supra-national level. On the other hand, supra-national regionalization also evolves through culture and the tourist industry. In fact, the facilitation of border crossing has turned many peripheral border regions into valuable tourist settings and the borders themselves into tourist destinations

(PROKKOLA, 2008). This is tantamount to saying that although there are no predestined mechanisms of institutionalization for supra-national or sub-national regions, an administrative emphasis and top-down region building – sometimes implemented by a relatively closed network of public agencies (HALL, 2007) – is in many cases more relevant in a supra-national context. Other aims that are conspicuously present in supra-national region building are those of promoting security and reducing political tensions (SVENSSON, 1998; MANSFIELD and MILNER, 1999).

Although the sub-national, state and (especially in the case of European Union member states) supra-national levels are usually deeply encompassed in the institutionalization of cross-border regions, supra-national region building is not only a matter of authorities and governments. It should, at least ideally, also involve various actors from supra-national businesses and non-governmental organizations, as besides decentralization from above, mobilization from below is also vital. This means that, on the one hand, moves by the central authorities to establish regions and increase their freedom of action and resources are desirable, but on the other hand, interaction between non-governmental organizations, regional activists and individuals across the border is required alongside the formal procedures managed by the advocates in order to achieve full progress (SVENSSON, 1998, pp. 65–70). Activists refer here to persons (or social groups) who participate in the politics of the region and struggle over specific meanings either which they represent as 'regional' or which are generated in a specific regional context, whereas advocates are actors operating in certain institutionalized subject positions that entail continuity, so that even if the actors as such change, their advocacy will continue (PAASI and ZIMMERBAUER, 2011). Advocates can be activists at the same time (for example, journalists), but much of their power in the production of identity narratives and regional ideologies emerges from their institutional position.

THE BARENTS EURO-ARCTIC REGION (BEAR)

The official establishment of the Barents Euro-Arctic Region (BEAR) took place in Kirkenes, Norway, on 11 January 1993, in the form of a declaration that the region should serve as a forum for considering bilateral and multilateral cooperation in the fields of economics, trade, science and technology, tourism, the environment, infrastructure, educational and cultural exchange, and projects particularly aimed at improving the situation of the indigenous peoples of the North (BAEV, 1994, p. 177). The initiative to establish the region (also known as Barents Region cooperation) actually originated with the Norwegians, as the proposal was put forward by the Norwegian Ministry of Foreign Affairs. According to SVENSSON (1998), the Barents Regionalization project was an example of using a political strategy to handle both the opportunities and the problems arising out of the post-Cold War reality of East–West relationships. The initiative has thus often been described as an attempt to widen and restructure ongoing activities in order to promote security (SVENSSON, 1998), even though military cooperation as such was left out of the framework (BAEV, 1994). The political statements also treat the region as a terrestrial phenomenon, with the exception of certain environmental matters (HOEL, 1994, p. 115). The Kirkenes Declaration lays down that

> Co-operation in the Barents Euro-Arctic Region will contribute substantially to stability and progress in the area and in Europe as a whole, where partnership is now replacing the confrontation and division of the past. The Participants felt that such co-operation will contribute to international peace and security.

Norway was also pursuing other motives as well as security when advocating the Barents Region initiative. A geographically interesting one is that Norway wanted to be the leader of a truly European project, one in which the target was to emphasize Norwegian intentions and create links not only between Russia and the Nordic countries, but also between the Barents Region and the Continent of Europe. In a way, Norway was seen as an unlikely key player in the Baltic Sea Region, which is why the country strove for the Barents initiative (SVENSSON, 1998).

The history of cross-border cooperation in the region is naturally longer than the sixteen years for which official collaboration has existed. When the Barents Region was being established, the Norwegian negotiators often mentioned the Pomor trade, which took place over a period of more than two centuries and was particularly vigorous between 1814 and 1917. This was based on bartering and took place every spring and summer, when inhabitants from Northwest Russia came to Northern Norway to exchange wood products and grain for fish (NIELSEN, 1994; SVENSSON, 1998). Another example of earlier East–West commercial activities in the region is the activity of the Nordic forest companies in the Murmansk and Archangel areas of Russia, attracted by the huge reserves of raw materials. They were not particularly successful, however, as some went bankrupt and others were nationalized after the Russian Revolution in 1917. The forest sector has traditionally been important in Finland and in the Republic of Karelia (SVENSSON, 1998).

When the Barents Region was established in 1993, it comprised the province of Lapland in Finland, the counties of Finnmark, Troms and Nordland in Norway, the counties of Murmansk and Archangelsk in Russia, and the county of Norrbotten in Sweden. It was already written into the Kirkenes Declaration, however, that the region could be extended to include other provinces or similar regional units in the future. This has indeed been the case, as at the moment the Barents Region includes thirteen sub-national territories that are also members of the Barents Regional Council (BRC). The total population is about 5.54 million (slightly more than the population of Denmark) and the size of the region is 1 755 800 km^2 (over two-and-a-half times the size of France), so that the average population density is 3.15 inhabitants per km^2 (BARENTSINFO, 2009).

According to ELENIUS (2006) and VEGGELAND (1994), the various parts of the region have many developmental features in common, such as:

- A peripheral location.
- A sparse population over a large area.
- A harsh climate.
- Many ethnic minorities (for example, the Saami).
- A delayed onset of industrialization followed by a rapid catch-up phase.
- The immigration of large groups of the nation's majority population.
- The radicalization of the workforce and polarization between radical and traditional groups.
- A certain 'polar romanticism'.
- Strong efforts to strengthen higher education.
- A process of revitalization of many of the national minorities during the last part of the twentieth century.

As CASTBERG (1994, p. 101) puts it, however, the most marked characteristic of the Barents Region is the vast contrast between its Western and Eastern parts. The differences between the Nordic countries and the Northwest Russia part apply to practically all areas of life: standards of living, language and culture, religion, history, and political and economic traditions, and they are differences that extend back to the pre-Soviet period.

The Barents Region is also unique in at least two more ways. First, it is located in an area that was once perhaps the most sensitive locus of military confrontation between East and West, and it still encompasses the boundary between Russia and NATO and thus has strategic nuclear forces stationed within it. This aspect cannot be understated, as it means that the Barents Region encompasses multiple borders, both 'hard and soft' or 'high and low', making it distinct from many other region-building projects in Europe. Second, although Barents cooperation is often regarded as region or province led, it has a two-layered structure that also ties the national governments in with the cooperation processes, ensuring that they maintain much of the power of decision (STOKKE and TUNANDER, 1994). The aim of this two-layered organizational structure was to create a framework for regional cooperation through interaction between the governments.

> The participants recognized the features characteristic of this Arctic region, especially its harsh climate, sparse population and vast territory. They agreed, therefore, to examine how they can improve the conditions for local co-operation between local authorities, institutions, industry and commerce across the borders of the regions.
>
> (Kirkenes Declaration)

The indigenous peoples (the Saami in Finland, Sweden, Norway and Russia; and the Nenets and Veps in Russia) with their distinctive cultures also make the Barents Region unique. These people have traditionally had closer contacts across national borders than other Swedish, Finnish, Norwegian or Russian nationals, and such contacts are currently maintained through frequent cultural cooperation, so that Saami artists, for example, have their own organizations that cover the Nordic countries and the Northwestern parts of Russia (HOLST, 1994). It can thus be said that the Saami constitute an element of homogeneity in the Barents Region. One reason for this is that they have remained aloof from the state-building processes there (CASTBERG *et al.*, 1994). In fact, the area was culturally quite uniform before the current nation-states emerged. The Saami *siidas* (small local communities) and their extensive economy represented a regional force that hindered and delayed the establishment of state borders, thus effectively counteracting the state-bound structuring of the far North of Europe. The *siidas* were eventually largely ignored in the state-building processes, however (NIELSEN, 1994, p. 89).

The formal organization of the Barents Region is based on the intergovernmental Barents Euro-Arctic Council (BEAC) and the interregional BRC (BARENTS EURO-ARCTIC REGION, 2010). Although the two pillars of local/regional and governmental authority are currently present, it is the counties and provinces that are the main actors in the everyday practices of regional development (KJØLBERG, 1994). The formal organization of the Barents Region is centred around the regional councils and county administrative boards (BRC), as they organize much of the activity and serve as places where leading representatives of the sub-national regions and the indigenous peoples meet. A number of other bodies have also been established at various levels, however, including sixteen working groups created to discuss more specific issues. The working groups have an advisory role in relation to both the BEAC and the BRC.

It is difficult to specify the volume and content of Barents cooperation exhaustively for two reasons. First, it is funded by numerous instruments (for example, the European Neighbourhood and Partnership Instrument (ENPI) and Interreg 4c programmes), none of which covers the region totally or exclusively. Thus, the projects either cover only part of the region or may exceed its borders. Second, there are many rather small-scale bilateral and locally funded initiatives that are not classified as Barents cooperation despite taking place in the region. As some of them nonetheless are classified in this way (depending largely on the managing organization), the overall picture is blurred.[2] In any case, Finland alone allocated about €293 million to projects carried out jointly with Russia between 1990 and 2009 (MINISTRY OF FOREIGN AFFAIRS, 2010).

ECONOMIC AND POLITICAL INSTITUTIONALIZATION OF THE BARENTS REGION

Networks of cooperation

Before turning to the elements of institutionalization and the vagueness of territorial shaping, it is important to contemplate the dynamics of network constellations over the course of time. Here the twofold basis of modern Barents cooperation must be stressed. On the one hand, the purpose is still to some extent political, as the aim is to ensure stability and security in the region. On the other hand, another target is to improve economic networking and business opportunities in the Northernmost part of Europe. As SVENSSON (1998) put it, the Barents Region is about politics and business. According to the interviews, however, the business aspect has become more significant of late:

> It has changed since, of course, to become more economically oriented, or at least economics has gained more emphasis now as the region has expanded, two more provinces in Finland and Sweden have acceded, as has the Komi region in Russia. ... So now the co-operation as a whole is motivated by the economic aspect. But on the other hand, if one thinks of Russian politics, there is in some way also a political background involved, in that we could make the borders lower and by doing that we could build regional foreign and development policies. ... This has also been the clear aim of the European Union, and therefore the pieces have matched. But as a whole this is a very long-term undertaking.
>
> (Regional Council Chairman, male)

This change indicates not only that some of the key political obstacles, related, for example, to different legislation and administrative systems, have managed to be overcome (cf. MATTSSON and PETTERSSON, 2005), but also a more general 'economization' of (regional) politics (MOISIO, 2011). Thus, the interplay between politics and business has been based on both securing smooth conditions for small and medium-sized enterprises and promoting overall competitiveness. Accordingly, the shift has brought large numbers of new actors into Barents cooperation, as besides the sub-national government bodies and the regional administration the business side is deeply involved. This means, for example, that chambers of commerce, consulting enterprises, various business clusters, and individual companies claim to be working for Barents development. If the networks are studied in more detail, though, it becomes evident that there are currently many bilateral processes going on, mostly including actor(s) from Russia and a partner from one of the Nordic countries. It is not uncommon for businesses in Sweden, Norway and Finland to treat each other as competitors in the race to gain profits from Russia. At the same time, however, Russia has become less independent of foreign investments and know-how. Furthermore, business networks can just as easily be formed with enterprises located outside the region. The balance between bilateral and multilateral collaboration from the institutionalization and identity perspective was one theme that was discussed with the interviewees. Some mentioned that multilateral collaboration should not be a purpose in itself and that the current trend for bilateral cooperation is acceptable. The participation of enterprises and other organizations is based on the added value they gain by networking with other actors in the Barents Region, and in many cases the highest added value comes through excluding similar actors.

> If we think about the Nordic countries in Barents co-operation, it is certainly the case that Russia interests us a lot, with all its natural resources and business opportunities. ... You cannot deny that that is the fact. But it can surely be said that the Norwegians, for example, are similarly interested in bilateral co-operation. So even though we are all working in the Barents context, we aspire to bilateral co-operation.
>
> (Project Manager, female)

According to SVENSSON (1998, p. 261), the inter-regional cooperation, which started in a manner reminiscent of policy communities, has later turned into constellations of the network type. From the beginning it was the advocates of sub-national governmental bodies – with legitimation from the central authorities – who were at the core of the action, whereas the number of actors has increased drastically with time, leaving the concept of cooperation more blurred and vague. Svensson also states that transnational region building in the Barents Region has come to depend on external resources and actors and the internal dynamics have been lost or were never released. As for sub-national governments, it seems that they had not been fully empowered by the central authority to play operative roles, nor had they been able to assume key roles in policy networks. The dependence of the regional authorities on central government resourcing has been too strong, making them unable to serve as the engines of supra-national region building (BOMAN and BERG, 2007; SVENSSON, 1998). Although this centrally orchestrated regionalism (HARRISON, 2008) has not occurred similarly in all countries, but is instead nationally specific, it has had an effect on cooperation at the sub-national level. This was also clearly presented by the interviewees.

> It is quite obvious that the interests of the regions and the central administration do not necessarily ... sometimes they are parallel but there are problems related to resources and different ways of operation – in Finland and

> everywhere else as well. The problem in Russia is that the link between Moscow and the regions is so obscure. You know, what the [Russian] regions can decide for themselves and which decisions are made in Moscow.
>
> (Journalist, male)

There is also some discrepancy over the role of the indigenous peoples. While the working group for indigenous peoples has a particular status with respect to the BRC and the BEAC, there is still a need for strengthened representation of indigenous peoples within the formal structures of the networks of cooperation. This is important as there are examples of activities that are remarkable sources of income and employment but at the same time have negative impacts on the original population of their areas. The *Action Plan for Indigenous Peoples in the Barents Euro-Arctic Region 2009–2012* points out that

> the present increased selection of resources will not necessarily lead to development of the local communities and communities of indigenous peoples, but rather to problems of industrial, environmental and social kinds. National and international corporations establish activities in the areas belonging to indigenous peoples without involving the local inhabitants and users of the areas in their overall strategy.
>
> (WORKING GROUP OF INDIGENOUS PEOPLES IN THE BARENTS EURO-ARCTIC REGION (WGIP), 2009)

It is thus important for the indigenous peoples that their rights to land, water, and natural resources are clarified and secured also through Barents collaboration.

Although the region-building process in this case is regarded as a top-down one, the role of the European Union was, somewhat unexpectedly, not considered fundamental to it. In fact, the interviewees stated that much of the Barents cooperation would have happened regardless of the European Union. While the European Union has played a certain role by providing resources and suitable conditions for certain processes in the region, the lack of a distinct funding instrument, for instance, has left its meaning secondary to that of other regions and the nation-states. The European Union was regarded more as a possible supporter of regional initiatives than as an active collaboration partner.

> I think that the role of the EU [European Union] is limited to what officials thinking about funding instruments are doing in their offices. So if you look at the overall picture, the role of the EU is quite marginal. The main actors are nation-states and the regions, not so much the EU, although it was involved as a founding member. Looking through the EU-publications, I noticed that the word Barents is very rarely mentioned. I suspect that the Union does not even properly perceive that it is involved.
>
> (Journalist, male)

Elements of institutionalization

The top-down and advocacy-led nature of the Barents Region process can be explained largely by its introduction at the level of the central authorities (foreign ministers). Along with the formal organizational structures of collaboration, this has made the region building distinctively institution led. It is thereby necessary to ponder over whether institutions can manage the region-building process and increase regional identity, and if so, how. According to CASTBERG *et al.* (1994) four means exist. First, institutions can help politicians and regional developers to come together and recognize subjects and areas that are particularly suitable for collaboration. Second, they may facilitate and coordinate the vital process of gathering information, which is essential for bottom-up cooperation among business and other organizations. Third, institutions can create and develop regional symbols and try to stimulate regional discourses of a certain kind. And fourth, it is possible in some circumstances for institutions to 'insulate' cooperation, which means that parties can allow it to continue even though relations have deteriorated at a general level.

The powerful role of institutions and the top-down character of region building were brought out by the interviewees when discussing the process of institutionalization. It was adduced, for example, that regional symbols are somewhat scarce and even shaping of the territory is still in progress, although various institutions have evolved or been there right from the start.

> Institutions do exist, but I think that the other phases are absent. So it [institutionalization] has taken a different path. Maybe it's because it was originally explicitly founded by establishing certain institutions that have duplicated themselves slightly since.
>
> (County Administrative Board Officer, male)

While the institutions have been relatively successful in coordinating collaboration and in forming policy-business networks, they have contributed little to the creation of regional symbols, for example. Some organizations have adopted the Barents logo, but as a whole the symbolization is currently very much work that is still in progress. More attention has been paid to this aspect recently, however. One good example is the plan to build the world's highest wooden building for the Barents Secretariat in Kirkenes. The *Kaleva* newspaper reported recently on the possible construction of a sixteen- to seventeen-storey building named Sky High Barents House (Fig. 2), which would serve as a symbol of both Barents cooperation and its prime institution.

Another approach to the elements of institutionalization can be made through newspaper analysis. The present analysis was performed by picking out all the news related to the Barents Region during the given three periods (Fig. 3)[3] and classifying their content thematically. In all, there were thirty-eight such news items in the papers examined in 1993–1994, twenty-eight in 2000–2001, and forty-two in 2007–2008. *Helsingin Sanomat* published altogether only sixteen items, most of which were related to the environment, natural

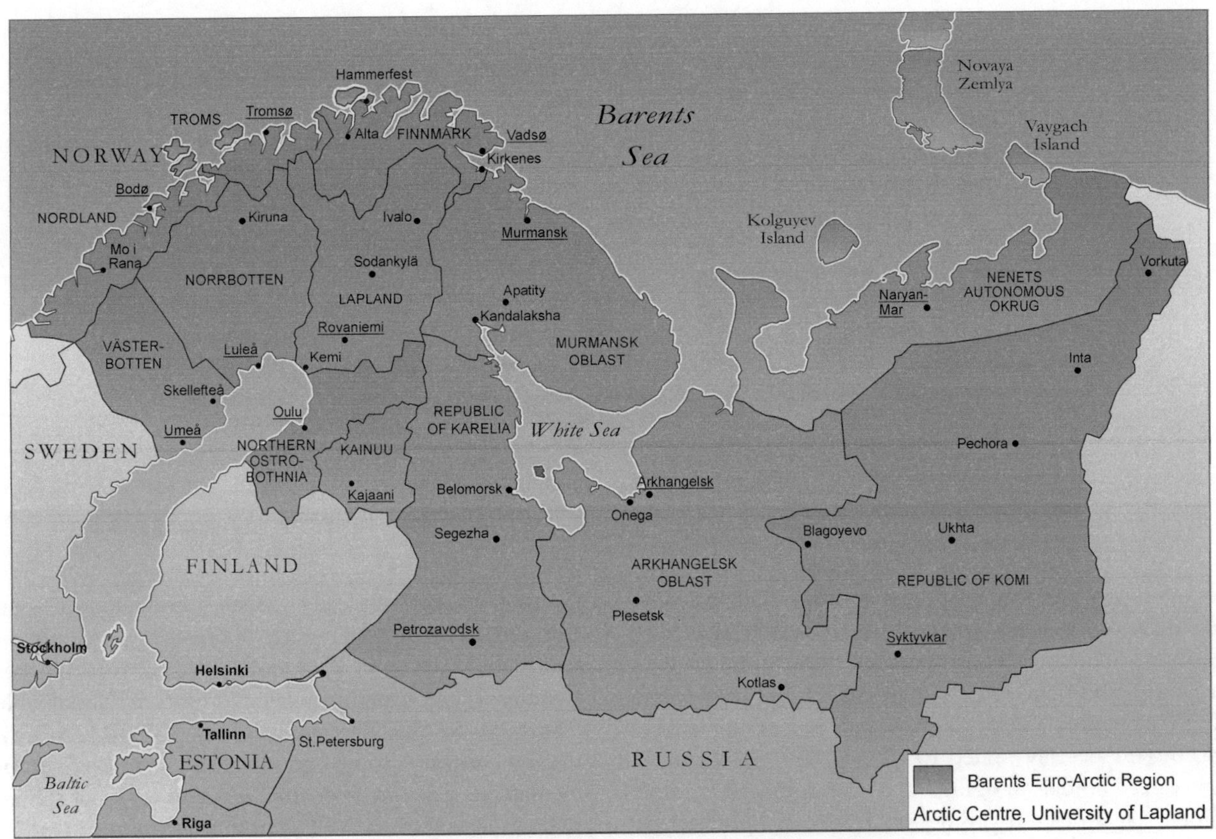

Fig. 1. The Barents Euro-Arctic Region (BEAR)
Source: Barentsinfo.org, courtesy of the Arctic Centre, University of Lapland, Rovaniemi

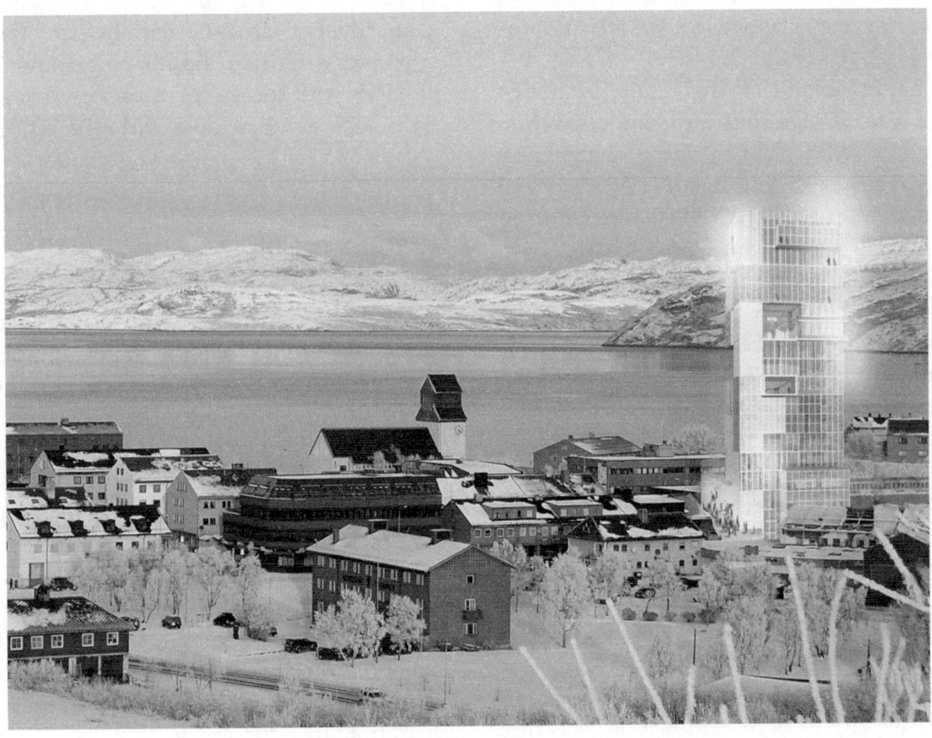

Fig. 2. Projected Sky High Barents House, planned to be the highest wooden building in the world
Source: Kaleva newspaper (19 October 2009). Photograph courtesy: Reiulf Ramstad Arkitekter AS

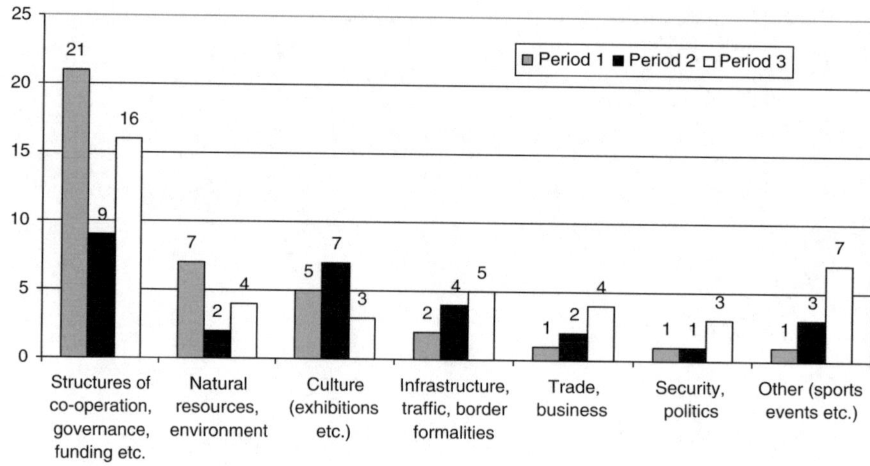

Fig. 3. Frequency and themes of news items that had Barents mentioned in the heading or in the opening paragraph

resources and business. In short, the first period analysed highlighted the establishment of BEAR and most of the news was about its institutions and structures. In the second period there was less news of this kind, whereas there were more articles about various processes, including those especially related to cross-border traffic infrastructure, border crossing and international trade. Moreover, articles regarding environmental protection were also typical of the second period, although they were also related to the maritime area in addition to the territorial regional configuration. News about cooperation structures has increased again more recently, although now couched in more critical tones. About fifteen years after reporting how the structures and institutions were established, it was time to ask whether the results had come up to expectations, as it was felt that progress could have been faster.

The region has become increasingly more institutionalized lately as a result of various experiments such as Barents exhibitions and a planned skiing competition (the Tour de Barents), with four stages in Norway and Finland (TOUR DE BARENTS, 2009). Cooperation in the field of culture has also been quite well reported, especially during its earlier years. There are relatively few examples of bottom-up symbolization of the region, however, as much of the news was about structures of cooperation and funding, which emphasized the role of public agencies and 'partnerships constructed by and for public actors' (cf. HALL, 2007, p. 433). News concerning trade and business was also scarce, although it must be stated that items were occasionally mingled with writings on natural resources and infrastructure, due to the fact that many instances of business collaboration were dealing with energy, forestry, greener technology and improved accessibility as well as with flows of goods and people within the region.

Generally speaking, the Barents Region has become institutionalized by various supra-national projects that were reported particularly during the second period. One good example is the Barents 2010 project, which focused – rather typically for such cooperation – on the environment, transport, industrial development and higher education (BARENTS 2010, 2010). Another significant infrastructure-related project is 'Sustainable Transport in the Barents Regions' (STBR), which, despite gaining some good results, suffered from inadequate support from the local and regional sphere within the region as well as from confusion caused by double work and the sheer number of parallel East–West transport initiatives (NORTHERN AXIS DEVELOPMENT IN THE BARENTS REGION, 2007). However, as HØNNELAND (2009) states, there are signs that from the late 1990s onwards increasing emphasis has been placed on people-to-people cooperation, including student exchanges, cultural projects and other projects that involve cross-border human interaction. For example, a separate health programme was published in 1999 with special focus on new communicable diseases such as tuberculosis and HIV/AIDS.

Vagueness of territorial shaping

Related to questions of territorial shaping is the overall character of the region and the ways in which it is conceptualized. According to the relational approach, questions concerning borders might appear irrelevant, as regions are seen as open spaces for movements and webs of fluid networks (ALLEN *et al.*, 1998; AMIN, 2004; also MACLEOD and JONES, 2007). This approach can easily be supported in the case of the Barents Region, as the outer borders are highly porous, simply due to the fact that they are the borders of provinces or counties within nation-states. On the other hand, the borders between Russia and Finland and between Russia and Norway are solid, dividing the space and hindering everyday actions inside the Barents Region. There are thus soft borders uniting the region but hard border(s) dividing it.

The territorial shaping of the Barents Euro-Arctic Region (BEAR) has been and still is a contested process. The province of North Karelia in Finland is currently aspiring to be included in the region, despite opposition coming mostly from Norway. The debate has so far only led to a compromise in which North Karelia has joined as an observer member. The North Karelia question was frequently brought up and the arguments for and against were related to both identity and the economics and functionality of the region.

> We as Finns very much emphasized that it is no one's loss if we have new [regions as] members. On the other hand, I also pointed out that we already have such a vast region. There are 13 sub-regions and indigenous peoples. … It no longer matters how big the region is; the essential thing is what kinds of clusters of know-how we can build up inside it. In a way, the geographical aspect vanishes. But the Norwegians were strictly against the idea. They feared that Finland would gain too strong a role in collaboration. And in the end, apart from the Republic of Karelia, the Russians did not like it, either. Sweden was supporting us with the same arguments as ours.
>
> (Regional Council Chairman, male)

> They [the Norwegians] thought that in a way the northern identity which was relevant then would to some extent be pushed aside when economic interests became dominant … rather than the fact that we live in the north, beyond or close by the Arctic Circle. So in a way the identity of the region has changed, so that now it is more of an economic and geographical identity than an identity based on culture or nature.
>
> (Regional Council Officer, male)

There have been some debates as to how big the region can eventually be and whether there should be equal numbers of regions from all the countries involved. One commonly held view is that the Barents Region might be enlarged with a province or two, but then its territorial shaping would be complete. In some people's opinion the Arctic character of the region should be emphasized, and enlargement is thus opposed, whereas some bring out the negative effects that the exclusion of some regions would cause for business and the economy. It is in any case thought that the Barents Region is too vast to be genuinely uniform. As VEGGELAND (1994, p. 210) puts is, due to its huge area it is likely that smaller core-regions will emerge inside the broader Barents Region. This likely development was mentioned in the interviews and gets further support from projects such as Bothnian Arc, although according to MATTSSON and PETTERSSON (2005) long distances were a major obstacle even between the Swedish and Finnish municipalities around the Gulf of Bothnia. The development of such regions has much to do with infrastructures, as East–West connections and networks are in many cases inferior to North–South connections.

As mentioned above, there has been a strong shared image of one part of the Barents Region being poor (in the East) and another rich (in the West). This image may still have a strong influence on interaction patterns, no matter what official statistics currently show. In practice it can influence expectations, and thereby affect the outcomes of cooperation. This image also calls the role of regional identity into question. As HANSEN (1994) asks,

> will the inhabitants of the Barents Region really come to identify sufficiently with each other in the foreseeable future – instead of identifying most decisively with their compatriots further south, who are much more similar in their language, culture and ways of life?
>
> (p. 63)

At this point it seems clearly that due to the steep East–West contrast and vagueness of the territorial setting, the Barents Region itself is not the primary context of identification for its inhabitants. The interviewees nevertheless agreed that a regional identity should be fostered, although the benefits were somewhat unclear.

> We have often pondered and talked over the problem of this Barents Region being unfamiliar for many people who are not directly involved with these subjects and do not necessarily think that they are from the Barents Region or have not even considered the matter. So it would be good to do something, but what would it be, information or marketing? This is a difficult question, and I don't know what … what would be the benefits in everyday life of knowing that you belong to the Barents Region.
>
> (Regional Council Officer, male)

> I think that building an identity throughout the Barents Region will be quite a job. But I don't see it as a bad thing if someone living in the north does recognize that he belongs to the Barents Region, as do people in neighbouring countries. So there are no alternatives but to build it, by means of road signs or something, to build an identity better than has been done up to now. It is difficult to say what the benefits would be, but it would probably bind people together better.
>
> (Development Agency Manager, female)

DISCUSSION

Direct cooperation between East and West, as is the case currently in the Barents Region, was practically nonexistent only about twenty years ago. The removal of the Iron Curtain, followed by the emergence of new economic conditions, has led to a situation of new network constellations and accordingly restructured economic cooperation, with some good results. Whereas the political and security aspects were significant at the beginning, current collaboration, as the newspaper analysis showed, is also based on culture and business cooperation, especially in the fields of tourism, energy and trade.

Although there is a certain amount of uncertainty about its prospective institutionalization, the interviewees did not see any major threats facing the region in the foreseeable future. However, it was considered that the guidelines for development might again alter. Moreover, it was felt that in order to improve regional consciousness and create a regional identity, more genuinely multilateral networks and bottom-up initiatives should be increasingly supported and funded. The strengthened identity would then boost regional activism to support advocate-led development. The significance of identity is also underlined by HALL (2008), who argues that in order to survive without external (European Union) funding, cross-border regions must gain legitimacy through their own populations. A shift in cooperation from security issues to economics and business issues has been seen, but a stronger shift towards cultural and social issues would further consolidate this legitimacy by making the Barents Region more meaningful to its inhabitants. However, this alone would not guarantee stronger identification with the region, as its sheer size, differences between the East and West, as well as the institutionalization of smaller regions within it hinder the emergence of a genuinely region-wide identity.

So far no economic or other miracles have been experienced as a consequence of the new relations, nor can such be expected. One of the most crucial reasons for this is linked to the different perceptions held by regional authorities. Since their dependence on central government approval and resourcing is too strong, the sub-national regions have not been able to act as driving forces in the institutionalization process. This has evidently had much to do with the foreign policies of the nation-states as well, as it is still controlled by the state, and regionalization can only be achieved if the regions are seen to be fully implementing the policies of the central government. In Russia, the questions of suitable authorities in the counties have to some extent been linked to very sensitive issues of regional separatism and integrity, and although the Barents Region is not a periphery when viewed from Moscow, the initiative has not been the first priority for Russia (BAEV, 1994). For Norway, on the other hand, the Barents initiative has offered the closest formal cooperation with Russia it has ever had (KJØLBERG, 1994, p. 197). Thus, besides different perceptions, region formation is also impeded by mismatching aspirations, legislation and operation cultures between the states.

The case of the Barents Region does not prove that the model of institutionalization is no longer valid, but what should be emphasized even more is that region building is not a straightforward process in which one phase follows another, but a contested one where some phases might be absent altogether. The present case study shows, for example, that established and stable region-based institutions may still be struggling to define or reach a consensus on an appropriate territorial shape for their region. It also proves that contemporary region building is not necessarily so much a matter of producing regional symbols but more of institutionalizing new network-type business constellations and reasserting formal institutions of regional development to increase cross-border cooperation. In fact, the process of institutionalizing the Barents Region reflects the broader national and supra-national policies, at the core of which lie the principles of competitiveness and economic performance. The emphasis on business aspects in the current development agenda has nevertheless reduced the concept of the Barents Region quite often to an empty word in processes which really are ad-hoc bilateral business partnerships. It was also felt that the concept of the Barents Region is of most relevance when negotiating with the European Union for financial support, that is, it is a 'brand' created largely in order to improve familiarity with the region in Brussels. This may, however, lead to the odd situation where the idea of a region as an imagined community (cf. ANDERSON, 1991) is stronger elsewhere than *in situ* (ZIMMERBAUER, 2011). A scarcity of regional symbols and their poor utilization within the region underline this event further.

Due to the top-down character, the region-building process has been carried out almost completely by advocates, while regional activism seems to be more attached to the old regions, such as the constituent provinces. It can therefore also be concluded that the Barents Region (as an administratively bred region) has to some extent an institutional identity (BOMAN and BERG, 2007), that is, a vague identity created by existing cross-border institutions. This kind of identity is more often typical of new rather than old regions, as it is by nature a top-down, institution-based feature. A 'historical–cultural identity', involving some measure of cultural, historical or ethnic affinity, is somewhat lacking at the moment, however, which is why Barents activists are practically non-existent. Thus, the Barents Region can be classified as an administrative, but not truly a functional or an identity-based, region. It is also a hybrid region, as the cooperation takes place on multiple and mixed scales. This situation (along with tensions regarding sustainable development) partly explains why the indigenous peoples, for example, are inclined to seek their contexts for cooperation elsewhere.

Regional entities such as the Barents Region may be understood as products of symbolic practices and performances (FELGENHAUER *et al.*, 2005) in which the rhetoric of relational spaces with globalization, networks and permeable boundaries is increasingly being conveyed. However, as FELGENHAUER *et al.* (2005, pp. 47–48) suggest, a rather conservative sense of bounded territories, localized places and spatial scales is often represented at the same time, especially by the mass media. This dualism means that in the practices of institutionalization as processes of significative regionalization, both the relational and the territorial aspects are imminent. Yet, and very clearly in the case of the Barents Region, the external borders are becoming increasingly represented at the same time as the hard border(s) dividing the region are blurred or softened. The soft, permeable borders are thus becoming represented as more solid and the hard borders as more porous. This may eventually have a real-life impact as well, as a funding instrument for a newly conceived supra-national region may serve as an element in region building, for example, but at the same time it can also handicap the longer-established inter-regional networks inside the nation-states.

It should be emphasized that although it encompasses distinctive administrative borders that might in some cases be hard, supra-national region building is, like all other region-building processes, about making abstractions and representations in complex social networks and processes. In other words, entities such as the Barents Region are constituted in networks and their boundedness may exist in certain social practices and may be absent in others. As seen in the case of the Barents Region, boundaries still serve as one fundamental element in the institutionalization processes, but in other contexts, such as the developing of new supra-national business clusters, the fuzziness of borders and the relational character of space will be emphasized. The boundedness of regions is thus neither an exclusively theoretical question nor an exclusively empirical one, but above all a contextual matter requiring both a theoretical and an empirical approach.

Acknowledgements – The author is grateful to the anonymous reviewers and Editors of *Regional Studies* for their comments; and to Anssi Paasi for feedback on earlier versions of this paper. The author would also like to acknowledge the Academy of Finland for research funding (Grant Number #121992).

NOTES

1. The empirical data consist of fourteen thematic interviews (each lasting about one hour), which were recorded and fully transcribed. The interviewees are key actors in Barents cooperation who were selected using the snowball sampling method and with the assistance of the head of the Barents Regional Committee. They are thus representatives of various organizations deeply involved in Barents cooperation, such as regional councils, development agencies, county administrative boards, the Barents Secretariat, and the BRC. In addition, an analysis was made of two Finnish newspapers, *Lapin Kansa* and *Helsingin Sanomat*, over three periods: 1 July 1993–30 June 1994; 1 July 2000–30 June 2001; and 1 July 2007–30 June 2008. *Helsingin Sanomat* is the largest newspaper in Finland; whereas *Lapin Kansa* is the most important in northern Finland. Furthermore, the speeches given in the International Forum for the Future of the Barents Region in Finland served as data for the analysis. Delegations from all the subregions, together with a delegation of indigenous peoples, attended this forum, which was held in Oulu, Finland, 25–26 November 2008. All data were gathered between September 2008 and September 2009.
2. It has nevertheless been estimated that the Barents Secretariat alone supported around 3000 small and middle-sized, mainly bilateral, projects implemented by Russian and Norwegian partners between 1994 and 2009 (ALNES, 2010).
3. See note 1.

REFERENCES

ALLEN J. and COCHRANE A. (2007) Beyond the territorial fix: regional assemblages, politics and power, *Regional Studies* **41(9)**, 1161–1175.

ALLEN J. and COCHRANE A. (2010) Assemblages of state power: topological shifts in the organization of government and politics, *Antipode* **42(5)**, 1071–1089.

ALLEN J., MASSEY D. and COCHRANE A. (1998) *Rethinking the Region*. Routledge, London.

ALNES M. (2010) Connecting Barents people. The Barents Secretariat's grant programme in steady change, in STAALESEN A. (Ed.) *Talking Barents. People, Borders and Regional Cooperation*, pp. 35–46. The Norwegian Barents Secretariat, Kirkenes.

AMIN A. (2002) Spatialities of globalisation, *Environment and Planning A* **34(3)**, 385–399.

AMIN A. (2004) Regions unbound: towards a new politics of place, *Geografiska Annaler* **86(1) B**, 33–44.

ANDERSON B. (1991) *Imagined Communities. Reflections on the Origin and Spread of Nationalism*. Verso, London.

BAEV P. K. (1994) Russian perspectives on the Barents Region, in STOKKE O. and TUNANDER O. (Eds) *The Barents Region. Cooperation in Arctic Europe*, pp. 175–186. Sage, London.

BARENTS 2010 (2010) *Barents 2010 Sector programmes (SP)* (accessed on http://www.barents2010.net/default.aspML=2724) (accessed on 25 November 2010).

BARENTS EURO-ARCTIC REGION (2010) Introduction (available at: http://www.beac.st/Deptid=25866) (accessed on 7 January 2010).

BARENTSINFO (2009) *Your Window to the Barents Region* (available at: http://www.barentsinfo.org) (accessed on 12 November 2009).

BOMAN J. and BERG E. (2007) Identity and institutions shaping cross-border co-operation at the margins of the European Union, *Regional and Federal Studies* **17(2)**, 195–215.

BRENNER N. (2004) *New State Spaces. Urban Governance and the Rescaling of Statehood*. Oxford University Press, New York, NY.

CASTBERG R. (1994) Economic cooperation in the Barents Region: potentials and problems in northwest Russia, in STOKKE O. and TUNANDER O. (Eds) *The Barents Region. Cooperation in Arctic Europe*, pp. 101–113. Sage, London.

CASTBERG R., STOKKE O. and ØSTRENG W. (1994) The dynamics of the Barents Region, in STOKKE O. and TUNANDER O. (Eds) *The Barents Region. Cooperation in Arctic Europe*, pp. 71–83. Sage, London.

CASTELLS M. (2000) *The Rise of the Network Society*. Blackwell, Oxford.

CLARKE S. (2000) Regional and transnational discourse: the politics of ideas and economic development in Cascadia, *International Journal of Economic Development* **2(3)**, 360–378.

DEAS I. and LORD A. (2006) From new regionalism to an unusual regionalism? The emergence of non-standard regional spaces and lessons for the territorial reorganization of the state, *Urban Studies* **43(10)**, 1847–1877.

ELENIUS L. (2006) The modernisation process in the Barents Region, in ELENIUS L. (Ed.) *Migration–Industrialisation–Regionalisation. The Use and Abuse of History in the Barents Region II*, pp. 7–17. Luleå University of Technology, Luleå.

ESKELINEN H. (2000) Cooperation across the line of exclusion: the 1990s experience at the Finnish–Russian border, in VAN DER VELDE M. and VAN HOUTUM H. (Eds) *Borders, Regions and People*, pp. 137–150. Pion, London.

EUROPEAN PARLIAMENT (2009) *Mietintöluonnos Euroregions-alueiden merkityksestä aluepolitiikan kehittämisessä* (available at: http://www.europarl.europa.eu/meetdocs/2004_2009/documents/pr/571/571582/571582fi.pdf) (accessed on 5 March 2009).

FELGENHAUER T., MIHM M. and SCHLOTTMANN A. (2005) The making of Mitteldeutschland on the function of implicit and explicit symbolic features for implementing regions and regional identity, *Geografiska Annaler* **87(1) B**, 45–60.

GIAOUTZI M., SUAREZ-VILLA L. and STRATIGEA A. (1993) Spatial information aspects and communication barriers in border areas, in RATTI R. and REICHMAN S. (Eds) *Theory and Practise of Transborder Cooperation*, pp. 103–122. Helbing & Lichtenhahn, Basel.

GILBERT A. (1988) The new regional geography in English and French-speaking countries, *Progress in Human Geography* **12(2)**, 208–228.

HALL P. (2008) Opportunities for democracy in cross-border regions? Lessons from the Øresund region, *Regional Studies* **42(3)**, 423–435.

HALL P. and PAIN K. (2006) *The Polycentric Metropolis: Learning from Mega-City Regions in Europe*. Earthscan, London.

HANSEN E. (1994) Living conditions in the north: the new divide, in STOKKE O. and TUNANDER O. (Eds) *The Barents Region. Cooperation in Arctic Europe*, pp. 57–70. Sage, London.

HARRISON J. (2006) Re-reading the new regionalism: a sympathetic critique, *Space and Polity* **10(1)**, 21–46.

HARRISON J. (2008) Stating the production of scales: centrally orchestrated regionalism, regionally orchestrated centralism, *International Journal of Urban and Regional Research* **32(4)**, 922–941.

HERRSCHEL T. (Forthcoming 2012) *Cities, State and Globalization. City-Regional Governance in Europe and North America*. Routledge, London.

HOEL A. H. (1994) The Barents Sea: fisheries resources for Europe and Russia, in STOKKE O. and TUNANDER O. (Eds) *The Barents Region. Cooperation in Arctic Europe*, pp. 115–130. Sage, London.

HOLST J. J. (1994) The Barents Region: institutions, cooperation and prospects, in STOKKE O. and TUNANDER O. (Eds) *The Barents Region. Cooperation in Arctic Europe*, pp. 11–24. Sage, London.

HØNNELAND G. (2009) Cross-border cooperation in the North: the case of Northwest Russia, in ROWE E. (Ed.) *Russia and the North*, pp. 35–52. University of Ottawa Press, Ottawa, ON.

HUDSON R. (2007) Regions and regional uneven development forever? Some reflective comments upon theory and practice, *Regional Studies* **41(9)**, 1149–1160.

JENSEN O. B. and RICHARDSON T. (2004) *Making European Space. Mobility, Power and Territorial Identity*. Routledge, London.

JESSOP B. (2004) Hollowing out the nation-state and multilevel governance, in KENNETT P. (Ed.) *Handbook of Comparative Social Policy*, pp. 11–25. Edward Elgar, Cheltenham.

JONES M. and MACLEOD G. (2004) Regional spaces, spaces of regionalism: territory, insurgent politics and the English question, *Transactions of the Institute of British Geographers* **29**, 433–452.

KAPLAN D. and HÄKLI J. (Eds) (2002) *Boundaries and Place. European Borderlands in Geographical Context*. Rowman & Littlefield, Boston, MA.

KJØLBERG A. (1994) The Barents Region as a European security-building concept, in STOKKE O. and TUNANDER O. (Eds) *The Barents Region. Cooperation in Arctic Europe*, pp. 187–199. Sage, London.

KRAMSCH O. (2002) Reimagining the scalar topologies of cross-border governance: Eu(ro)regions in the post-colonial present, *Space and Polity* **6(2)**, 169–196.

LAGENDIJK A. (2005) Regions and regional boundaries in the minds and practices of policy-makers in a unifying Europe, in VAN VILSTEREN G. and WEVER E. (Eds) *Changing Economic Behaviour in a Unifying Europe*, pp. 116–137. Van Gorgum, Assen.

MACLEOD G. (2001) New regionalism reconsidered: globalization and the remaking of political economic space, *International Journal of Urban and Regional Research*, pp. 804–829.

MACLEOD G. and JONES M. (2001) Renewing the geography of regions, *Environment and Planning D: Society and Space* **19**, 669–695.

MACLEOD G. and JONES M. (2007) Territorial, scalar, networked, connected: in what sense a 'regional world'?, *Regional Studies* **41(9)**, 1177–1191.

MANSFIELD E. and MILNER H. (1999) The new wave of regionalism, *International Organization* **53**, 589–627.

MATTSSON M. and PETTERSSON Ö. (2005) Cross-border collaboration in the North. Viewpoints of municipal representatives and firm managers on the Bothnian Arc project, *Fennia* **183(2)**, 97–107.

MEINHOF U. (2002) *Living (with) Borders. Identity Discourses on East–West Borders in Europe*. Ashgate, Aldershot.

MINISTRY OF FOREIGN AFFAIRS (2010) *Finland's Cooperation with Neighbouring Areas* (available at: http://www.formin.fi/public/default.aspxnodeid=34823&contentlan=2&culture=en-US) (accessed on 18 November 2010).

MOISIO S. (Forthcoming 2012) The state, in DODDS K., KUUS M. and SHARP J. (Eds) *The Ashgate Research Companion to Critical Geopolitics*. Ashgate, Farnham.

NIELSEN J. P. (1994) The Barents Region in historical perspective. Russian–Norwegian relations 1814–1917 and the Russian commitment in the north, in STOKKE O. and TUNANDER O. (Eds) *The Barents Region. Cooperation in Arctic Europe*, pp. 87–100. Sage, London.

Northern Axis Development in the Barents Region (2007) *Status Report*. STBR II Publications 10/2007. STBR II Management Group, Luleå.

Paasi A. (1986a) *Neljä maakuntaa*. Joensuu, Joensuun yliopiston yhteiskuntatieteellisiä tutkimuksia 8.

Paasi A. (1986b) The institutionalization of regions: a theoretical framework for understanding the emergence of regions and the constitution of regional identity, *Fennia* **164(1)**, 105–146.

Paasi A. (1991) Deconstructing regions: notes on the scales of human life, *Environment and Planning A* **23**, 239–256.

Paasi A. (2009) The resurgence of the region and regional identity: theoretical perspectives and empirical observations on regional dynamics in Europe, *Review of International Studies* **35(2)**, 121–146.

Paasi A. and Zimmerbauer K. (Forthcoming 2012) *Theory and Practice of the Region: A Contextual Analysis of the Transformation of Finnish Regions*. Treballs de la Societat Catalana de Geografia Number 69. Filial de l'Institut d'Estudis Catalans, Barcelona.

Painter J. (2010) Rethinking territory, *Antipode* **42(5)**, 1090–1118.

Perkmann M. (2003) Cross-border regions in Europe. Significance and drivers of regional cross-border co-operation, *European Urban and Regional Studies* **10(2)**, 153–171.

Perkmann M. (2007) Construction of new territorial scales: a framework and case study of the Euregio cross-border region, *Regional Studies* **41(2)**, 253–266.

Perkmann M. and Sum N. (2002) Globalization, regionalization and cross-border regions: scales, discourses and governance, in Perkmann M. and Sum N. (Eds) *Globalization, Regionalization and Cross-Border Regions*, pp. 3–21. Palgrave Macmillan, Basingstoke.

Prokkola E.-K. (2008) *Making Bridges, Removing Barriers. Cross-Border Cooperation, Regionalization and Identity at the Finnish–Swedish Border*. Nordia Geographical Publications Volume 37:3. University of Oulu, Oulu.

Raagmaa G. (2002) Regional identity in regional development and planning, *European Planning Studies* **10(1)**, 55–76.

Riikonen H. (1995) Sukupolvet ja alueellinen muutos, *Terra* **107(2)**, 88–100.

Rodriguez-Pose A. and Gill N. (2003) The global trend towards devolution and its implications, *Environment and Planning C: Government and Policy* **21**, 333–351.

Rouge-Oikarinen R. (2009) *Rajan ylittävä yhteistyö muuttuvassa Euroopassa: Euroopan unionin Tacis-ohjelma (1996–2004) Suomen lähialueyhteistyön toteuttamisvälineenä* [Cross-Border Cooperation in a Changing Europe: The Case of the European Union Tacis Programme (1996–2004) as a Tool for Cross-Border Cooperation in Neighbouring Areas of Finland]. Nordia Geographical Publications Volume 38:2. University of Oulu, Oulu.

Schack M. (2000) On the multicontextual character of border regions, in van der Velde M. and van Houtum H. (Eds) *Borders, Regions and People*, pp. 202–219. Pion, London.

Scott A. J. (2001) Globalization and the rise of the city-regions, *European Planning Studies* **9**, 813–826.

Scott J. W. (2000) Euroregions, governance and transborder cooperation within the EU, in van der Velde M. and van Houtum H. (Eds) *Borders, Regions and People*, pp. 104–115. Pion, London.

Sidaway J. (2004) The choreographies of European integration. Negotiating trans-frontier cooperation in Iberia, in Kramsch O. and Hooper B. (Eds) *Cross-Border Governance in the European Union*, pp. 173–190. Routledge, London.

Sparke M., Sidaway J., Bunnell T. and Grundy-Warr C. (2004) Triangulating the borderless world: geographies of power in the Indonesia–Malaysia–Singapore Growth Triangle, *Transactions of the Institute of British Geographers* **29(4)**, 485–498.

Stokke O. and Tunander O. (Eds) (1994) Introduction, in *The Barents Region. Cooperation in Arctic Europe*, pp. 1–8. Sage, London.

Storper M. (1995) The resurgence of regional economies, ten years later: the region as a nexus of untraded interdependencies, *European Urban and Regional Studies* **2**, 191–221.

Strüver A. (2004) 'We are only allowed to re-act, not to act'. Eurocrats' strategies and borderlanders' tactics in a Dutch–German cross-border region, in Kramsch O. and Hooper B. (Eds) *Cross-Border Governance in the European Union*, pp. 25–40. Routledge, London.

Svensson B. (1998) *Politics and Business in the Barents Region*. Fritzes, Stockholm.

Syssner J. (2006) *What Kind of Regionalism? Regionalism and Region Building in the Northern European Peripheries*. Peter Lang, Frankfurt am Main.

Tour de Barents (2009) *Tour de Barents* (available at: http://www.tour-de-barents.com/Tour_de_barents/In_English.iw3) (accessed on 2 November 2009).

Veggeland N. (1994) The Barents Region as a European frontier region: a comparative study, in Stokke O. and Tunander O. (Eds) *The Barents Region. Cooperation in Arctic Europe*, pp. 201–212. Sage, London.

Virtanen P. (2004) Euregios in changing Europe. Euregio Karelia and Euroregion Pomerania as examples, in Kramsch O. and Hooper B. (Eds) *Cross-Border Governance in the European Union*, pp. 121–134. Routledge, London.

Wheeler S. (2002) The new regionalism. Key characteristics of the emerging movement, *Journal of the American Planning Association* **68(3)**, 267–278.

Working Group of Indigenous Peoples in the Barents Euro-Arctic Region (WGIP) (2009) *Action Plan for Indigenous Peoples in the Barents Euro-Arctic Region 2009–2012*. 21 January. WGIP, Tromsø (available at: http://www.barentsinfo.fi/beac/docs/WGIP_Action_Plan_2009-2012_ENG.pdf) (accessed on 3 November 2009).

Zimmerbauer K. (2009) Regional identity and image in re-scaling of the regions, in Luukkonen J. and Äikäs T. A. (Eds) *Geographical Reflections from the North*. NGP Yearbook 2008. Nordia Geographical Publications Volume 37:6. University of Oulu, Oulu.

Zimmerbauer K. (2010) Supranational integration, in Warf B. (Ed.) *Encyclopedia of Geography*, pp. 2726–2729. Sage, London.

Zimmerbauer K. (2011) From image to identity: building regions by place promotion, *European Planning Studies* **19(2)**, 243–260.

Zimmerbauer K. and Kahila P. (2006) *Seinäjoki-Peräseinäjoki kuntayhdistymisprosessin seurantatutkimus*. Seinäjoki, Helsingin yliopiston Ruralia-instituutti, julkaisuja 8.

Between Regional Spaces and Spaces of Regionalism: Cross-border Region Building in the Spanish 'State of the Autonomies'

JACOBO GARCÍA-ÁLVAREZ and JUAN-MANUEL TRILLO-SANTAMARÍA
Department of Humanities: History, Geography and Art, Carlos III University of Madrid, Spain.

GARCÍA-ÁLVAREZ J. and TRILLO-SANTAMARÍA J.-M. Between regional spaces and spaces of regionalism: cross-border region building in the Spanish 'State of the Autonomies', *Regional Studies*. The intense development of cross-border cooperation in the European Union in the last two decades offers a privileged laboratory to reflect upon the changing nature of regions and processes of regional construction in the context of globalization. Focusing on Euroregions, this paper aims to establish some bridges between Regional World(s) and Cross-border Regional Worlds. In the first part, this kind of connection is considered under the light of the recent theoretical debates developed within the framework of regional and border studies. The second part focuses on the analysis of cross-border cooperation in the Spanish 'State of the Autonomies', and particularly on the cases of the Basque Country, Catalonia and Galicia.

GARCÍA-ÁLVAREZ J. and TRILLO-SANTAMARÍA J.-M. 区域空间与区域主义的空间：西班牙自治区内跨边界区域的建立，区域研究。在过去二十年间，欧盟内部密集的跨区域合作发展充分反映了区域变迁以及区域在全球化背景下建构的过程。着眼于欧盟区域，本文试图在区域世界以及跨边界区域世界间建立一些关联。第一类关联是基于区域以及边界研究的概念框架。第二部分基于对西班牙跨边界合作的分析，尤其关注巴斯克、加泰罗尼亚和加利西亚地区。

GARCÍA-ÁLVAREZ J. et TRILLO-SANTAMARÍA J.-M. Entre des espaces régionaux et des espaces de régionalisme: la construction des régions transfrontalières dans 'l'Etat des autonomies' espagnol, *Regional Studies*. Le développement intense de la coopération transfrontalière au sein de l'Union européenne pendant les deux dernières décennies fournit un laboratoire privilégié de la mutation des régions et des processus de la construction régionale dans le cadre de la mondialisation. Focalisant les Eurorégions, cet article cherche à établir des relations entre des espaces régionaux et des espaces régionaux transfrontaliers. Dans une première partie, on considère ce genre de connexion à la lumière des débats théoriques récents qui se sont développés dans le contexte des études régionales et frontalières. Une deuxième partie porte sur l'analyse de la coopération transfrontalière dans 'l'Etat des autonomies' espagnol et, particulièrement, sur le pays Basque, la Catalogne et la Galice.

GARCÍA-ÁLVAREZ J. und TRILLO-SANTAMARÍA J.-M. Zwischen regionalen Räumen und Räumen des Regionalismus: Aufbau von grenzüberschreitenden Regionen im spanischen 'Staat der autonomen Gemeinschaften', *Regional Studies*. Die intensive Entwicklung einer grenzüberschreitenden Zusammenarbeit innerhalb der Europäischen Union in den letzten 20 Jahren bietet ein privilegiertes Labor zur Untersuchung der wechselnden Merkmale von Regionen und Prozessen der regionalen Konstruktion im Kontext der Globalisierung. In diesem Beitrag werden unter besonderer Berücksichtigung der Euroregionen einige Verbindungen zwischen Regionalwelt(en) und grenzüberschreitenden Regionalwelten geknüpft. Im ersten Teil wird diese Art von Verbindung unter Berücksichtigung der aktuellen theoretischen Debatten im Rahmen der regionalen und Grenzstudien erörtert. Im zweiten Teil konzentriert sich die Analyse auf die grenzüberschreitende Zusammenarbeit im spanischen 'Staat der autonomen Gemeinschaften' und insbesondere auf die Fälle des Baskenlandes, Kataloniens und Galiciens.

GARCÍA-ÁLVAREZ J. y TRILLO-SANTAMARÍA J.-M. Entre espacios regionales y espacios de regionalismo: la construcción de regiones trasfronterizas en la España de las Autonomías, *Regional Studies*. El intenso desarrollo de la cooperación transfronteriza en la Unión Europea en los últimos veinte años ofrece un laboratorio privilegiado para reflexionar sobre la naturaleza cambiante de las regiones y los procesos de construcción regional en el contexto de la globalización. Centrándonos en las eurorregiones, este artículo trata de establecer algunos puentes entre la esfera regional y la transfronteriza. En la primera parte, se examinan este tipo de conexiones sobre la base de los debates teóricos desarrollados recientemente en el marco de los estudios regionales y fronterizos. En la segunda parte, se aborda el análisis de la cooperación transfronteriza en el Estado español de las Autonomías, y de modo particular, en los casos del País Vasco, Cataluña y Galicia.

INTRODUCTION

If one wishes to reflect upon new 'regional grammars' in a global world, it seems pertinent to turn one's attention to a new type of region that has emerged in Europe as of the 1990s: the cross-border region. Furthermore, some of today's debates on the regional world can be approached from a perspective that focuses on the active processes of regional institutionalization being carried out all along European borders.

First of all, this contribution aims to reflect in theoretical terms on some of these processes that have resulted in a great deal of literature from divergent fields, particularly in the last fifteen years. The Euroregions were conceived of institutionally as authentic micro-laboratories for European integration, but they have also functioned as a privileged laboratory for theoretical and conceptual debate regarding borders, territorial identities and the dynamics of regional construction within the context of globalization (KAPLAN and HÄKLI, 2002; GARCÍA-ÁLVAREZ, 2006a; PAASI, 2009a, 2009b; TRILLO-SANTAMARÍA, 2009). In the context of the new regional geographies and border studies, the development and recent growth of cross-border regions leads one to pose important theoretical questions in the field (PERKMANN and SUM, 2002; KRAMSCH and HOOPER, 2004; GEOPOLITICS, various years).

This article is structured as follows. The first part will deal with some of these questions in the light of theoretical contributions of recent years in the area of border studies, with the objective of bridging the gap between Regional World(s) and Cross-border Regional World (s). The second part will focus on the analysis of a specific case: that of cross-border cooperation in the Spanish State of the Autonomies. More precisely, this work will focus on the discourses and processes that have led to the creation of Euroregions in three Autonomous Communities (ACs) that are located on borders and that have distinct historical and cultural personalities: the Basque Country, Catalonia and Galicia. This strong character, which is expressed in the fact that they possess their 'own' language (a co-official language alongside Spanish or Castilian) politically translating into the presence of nationalist parties with varying degrees of success, has also been projected into the discourses and policies of cross-border cooperation involving these ACs (MORATA, 2006; GARCÍA-ÁLVAREZ, 2006b; AJA, 2007).

As this article will show, the Euroregions created or projected in these territories are good examples of two principal elements, which in the authors' opinion are key to understanding the genesis, success and limitations of certain cross-border cooperation processes in Europe. First, on an external level, the ACs' relations with the French and Portuguese regions bring to light the significant difference that exists between the Spanish political–territorial model, which is semi-federal, and that of its main neighbouring states, which is much more centralized. Furthermore, and at the domestic level, the initiatives to establish organizations for cross-border cooperation by ACs' regional governments that include regionalist or nationalist parties often contain a politico-cultural ingredient which, in some occasions, aims at institutionalizing an ethnic Euroregion (MARKUSSE, 2004). This not only clashes with the much more functional and autocratic approach given to cross-border cooperation policies by the European Commission, but also frequently gives rise to suspicion and even opposition in the adjacent ACs' governments of other political leanings. In this regard, this article will briefly review the content of some of these initiatives in the cases of the Basque Country and Catalonia, later to focus on the institutionalization process of the Euroregion of Galicia–North Portugal. The analysis of these cases will incorporate some of the theoretical and conceptual instruments presented in the first section, placing special emphasis on the dialectic between (cross-border) regional spaces and (cross-border) spaces of regionalism (MACLEOD and JONES, 2007).

CROSS-BORDER REGIONAL WORLD(S) WITHIN THE EUROPEAN UNION: SOME THEORETICAL REFLECTIONS

Over the past three decades, so-called border studies have grown into a rich area of study in which terms such as 'de-bordering', 're-bordering', 'de-territorialization' or 're-territorialization' have been established as instruments of analysis for border scholars (for example, NEWMAN, 2006; PAASI, 2009b). The multidisciplinary approach that prevails in this field has led some authors to propose that a new shift in social sciences should be discussed, the B/ordering turn (VAN HOUTUM *et al.*, 2005). The ways in which regions can be considered at present should include these contributions. The aim here is to review certain debates that directly link the Regional World to the Cross-border Regional World, in order to postulate that whatever happens to the region nowadays it seems appropriate to analyse it taking into account the particular cases of regions that straddle international borders.

Although the phenomenon of cross-border cooperation does not exclusively pertain to the European Union, it is undoubtedly in this space where its development has been the greatest, to the point that its cross-border regions have been defined as authentic micro-laboratories for European integration (VAN DER VELDE and VAN HOUTUM, 2003). In fact, the very act of naming this area of cooperation 'Euroregions' implies acceptance of this idea. Community policy has promoted their establishment, preferentially through the Interreg Community Initiative, which began in the 1990s. The success of this initiative has led to the creation of a specific objective within the new regional policy (2007–2013). This is known as territorial cooperation, which assumes, to a large extent, the main goals of the former Interreg. To this objective, the creation of a specific legal instrument has been added – the European Grouping of Territorial Cooperation (EGTC) – instituted in 2006 by the European Union to strengthen the Euroregions' capacity to act (LEVRAT, 2007). Currently, there are more than 120 Euroregions in Europe that promote putting a common agenda into practice (ASSOCIATION OF EUROPEAN BORDER REGIONS, 2001; PERKMANN, 2003; DEAS and LORD, 2006; OLIVERAS *et al.*, 2010).

In the framework of cross-border regions, one is witness to a continuous process of overlapping, not only of local, regional and state governments and administrations, but also of different cultures, discourses and objectives of the territorial agents. Cross-border regions can be defined as new structures that, in interaction with the dimension of the agency, emerge from the encounter between two or more areas which were separated in the past by a border and which seek to cooperate due to the border's existence (BRUNET-JAILLY, 2005). The ideas of the elite regarding cooperation, the tensions between different levels of government within a state, as well as the tensions between the diverse territorial authorities of two or more neighbouring states make this type of region a novel phenomenon in many ways.

Cross-border regions, scales, networks, new regionalism and multilevel governance

Adding the notion of the cross-border region to the debate about whether the world in which man lives is best defined in terms of scale or in terms of network can offer an interesting channel for the analysis of the processes in which scales and networks are produced and reproduced in social space (PAASI, 2004). MACLEOD and JONES (2007) speculated as to whether the Regional World is territorial, scalar, networked or connected. The answer cannot be offered in one-sided terms since the world today is at the same time scalar and networked, territorial and connected (JESSOP *et al.*, 2007; VARRO and LAGENDIJK in this issue). A one-dimensional explanation of the real world cannot be given; nor should a dilemma be posed between the so-called 'spaces of flows' and 'spaces of places' because they both coexist (CASTELLS, 1999).

Dealing with cross-border regions, KRAMSCH (2007), within a more 'radical' perspective, stated that if one wishes to think about what a cross-border region is, one must set aside ideas about scales and rescaling. For KRAMSCH and MAMADOUH (2003):

> borders and border regions would not be merely the passive objects of forces operating at higher spatial scales, but would themselves become active sites for the re-theorization of fundamental aspects of political life, bearing value in turn across a range of geographical spaces. (p. 42)

This critical vision of scalar analysis centred on regulation theory leads KRAMSCH (2007) to see an opportunity to define 'politics transcending the borders of its member states' (p. 1592) in the cross-border region. However, the notion of cross-border regions serving as the basis for a new democracy seems quite distant, since the majority of them are ruled by functionalist interests and have a technocratic profile (PERKMANN, 2003).

Nonetheless, specialists have widely linked the theories of new regionalism to the institutionalization processes of cross-border regions that aim to establish new political communities (PAINTER, 2008). The term 'cross-border regionalism' was thus coined (SCOTT, 2002; PERKMANN and SUM, 2002; PROKKOLA, 2008). Cross-border cooperation is conceived of as a response to the challenges posed by globalization, and especially by the crisis of the nation state, which loses competences from both above and below. The existence of this type of cooperation is placed, in this sense, within the global processes of multilevel governance (HOOGHE and MARKS, 2001), which has led some authors to use the term 'cross-border governance' (KRAMSCH and HOOPER, 2004; LISSANDRELLO, 2006).

Cross-border regions and regional institutionalization processes

Cross-border regions offer a fertile laboratory for testing contemporary processes of regional institutionalization. Furthermore, the cross-border region represents a truly singular case within the framework of these processes, as this type of region must overcome not only the political–administrative effects typical of a state border, but also the psychological borders linked to a nation-state, which in many cases seem to be equally or more difficult to overcome than the former. In this regard, it is useful to complement general analysis models of regional construction processes, such as PAASI's (1986) well-known model or LAGENDIJK's (2007) proposal, with other theoretical contributions specifically focused on the study of cross-border regions, such as those of BRUNET-JAILLY (2005) and PERKMANN (2007). In all of them one finds common elements of analysis that must be taken into account when studying the degrees of realization of the cross-border regions: cultural, symbolic, economic, political, institutional, discursive, functional, strategic, etc. The political, social and economic elite behind these processes wish to offer a new space in which to produce and reproduce social relations, projects that different specialists name 'imaginary spaces' (CHURCH and REID, 1999), 'cognitive regions' (SCOTT, 2000) or 'anticipatory geographies' (SPARKE, 2000). The space projects linked to cross-border cooperation clearly illustrate the emergence of 'unbounded regionalism' (DEAS and LORD, 2006).

For the time being, the research carried out demonstrates the existence of a distance between the projects led by the elite and the knowledge of the population regarding the existence and functioning of cross-border regions (STRÜVER, 2005; HÄKLI, 2008). To express it in PAASI's (1986) terms, it is possible that, as far as the elite are concerned, an identity of the cross-border region has been produced (that is, the region has been given an identity by means of the elite's actions and discourses), but it has not yet been transformed into a cross-border regional identity (in other words, people have not yet interiorized this discourse).

Cross-border regional spaces and cross-border spaces of regionalism

Cross-border regions can offer regional and local agents a favourable political arena from which to project actions of paradiplomacy (ALDECOA and KEATING, 1999). This perspective is particularly clear in states that are strongly decentralized and where the sub-state regions possess ample political competences, for example, with the Spanish ACs. In this sense, it may be useful to make use of the dichotomy proposed by JONES and MACLEOD (2004) between (cross-border) regional spaces and (cross-border) spaces of regionalism. For these authors, a regional space

> relates primarily to the work of economic geographers and scholars of regional development who – in deriving theoretical inspiration from institutional economics, evolutionary political economy and economic sociology – have uncovered successful systems of production in 'sunbelt' industrial districts and regional economies [...].
>
> (p. 435)

A space of regionalism, on the other hand,

> features the (re-)assertion of national and regional claims to citizenship, insurgent forms of political mobilization and cultural expression and the formation of new contours of territorial government.
>
> (p. 435)

However, and as will be seen below when the case of Spain is analysed, a gradient should be devised regarding the extent of the claim of the regions' political leaders in terms of politics and identity, in relation to their vision of the cross-border region. These could range from irredentist discourse, as can be seen in the Basque situation, to an eminently pragmatic and functionalist vision of external action, accompanied by a discourse of differentiated identity, as will be seen in the case of Galicia. In fact, at least in the Spanish context, it is difficult to establish a clear distinction between cross-border regional spaces and cross-border spaces of regionalism, as the political capacity of the ACs unites elements of economy, politics and identity.

In addition, to emphasize the network connections which sustain cross-border cooperation, it seems useful to integrate the dichotomies proposed by COX (1998) between space of dependence and space of engagement, and LIPIETZ (2003) between space-in-itself and space-for-itself (the latter understood in relation to the concepts of social hegemonic bloc and regional armature), as has already been done by MACLEOD (1999). Taking into account these ideas that emphasize the need for regional politicians to establish networks in various levels of government, and directing attention to the largest possible quotas of political recognition in relation to cross-border regions, this paper suggests to think either of cross-border spaces of regionalist engagement (if using Cox's terms) or of cross-border spaces of regionalism-for-itself (if drawing on Lipietz).

CROSS-BORDER COOPERATION IN THE SPAIN OF THE AUTONOMIES: BETWEEN REGIONAL SPACES AND SPACES OF REGIONALISM

The activities carried out by the ACs regarding cross-border cooperation cannot be fully understood without taking into account the Spanish political–territorial model, which differs greatly from the much more centralized ones of Portugal or of France. In effect, the pillars of the territorial model of state in Spain were established in the Spanish Constitution of 1978, at the beginning of the transition to democracy after forty years of military dictatorship (GRANJA *et al.*, 2001; GARCÍA-ÁLVAREZ, 2002; AJA, 2007). It is an extremely decentralized model that, without being federal, is similar in many aspects to federal systems, and is based on the recognition of broad executive and legislative competences at the sub-state levels (the ACs). The originality of these regional powers created in the Spanish Constitution, but based in many cases on remote geographical and historical precedents, frequently leads experts to call the Spanish territorial model the

Autonomous State or the State of the Autonomies. The strong geographical and cultural diversity within the country, together with other historical and political factors, have translated into the existence of numerous sub-state parties of a regionalist or nationalist nature. This section will focus on the case of Catalonia, the Basque Country and Galicia, outlying ACs on the border which have co-official languages other than Spanish. In these regions the weight of the nationalist parties has certainly been relevant, although also uneven.

In the case of the Basque Country, the nationalist and conservative Basque Nationalist Party (PNV) stayed in power from 1980 governing alone or in coalition until recently. In the March 2009 regional elections, the Socialist Party of Euskadi (PSE-PSOE), a regional branch of the Socialist Workers' Party of Spain (PSOE), took power through a pact with the Basque Country People's Party (PP). Regarding Catalonia, Convergence and Union (CiU), also a nationalist and conservative party, governed the AC from 1980 to 2003, when the Socialist Party of Catalonia (PSC), a federalist formation associated with (although independent from) the PSOE, entered the regional government in coalition with the Republican Left of Catalonia (ERC), a left-wing pro-independence party. Finally, the People's Party of Galicia (PPdeG), representative of a conservative ideology with regionalism leanings, has governed the AC from 1990 to the present day, except for the period 2005–2009 when a coalition of the Galician Socialist Party (PSdeG) and the Galician Nationalist Bloc (BNG) governed.

Cross-border spaces of regionalist engagement in conflict with other ACs: Basque Country and Catalonia

The first example of cross-border cooperation body on the Iberian Peninsula is in 1983, the year in which the Work Community of the Pyrenees was established by the ACs of Aragon, Catalonia, Navarre and Basque Country, the French regions of Aquitaine, Languedoc-Rousillon and Midi-Pyrenees, and the Principality of Andorra. It is the only agreement prior to the launching of the Interreg Community Initiative, which was quickly revealed to be a true 'window of change' (LAGENDIJK, 2007) for the starting up of various cooperation bodies. Regionally speaking, all ACs currently participate in some institutional framework in common with Portuguese or French regions, respectively (MINISTERIO DE POLÍTICA TERRITORIAL (MPT), 2010). These cooperation bodies are legally grounded in agreements signed by the Spanish government with both the French government (Treaty of Bayonne, 1995) and the Portuguese government (Treaty of Valencia, 2003), which regulate the specific conditions for the application of the 1981 European Outline on Transfrontier Cooperation between Territorial Communities or Authorities (MARTÍNEZ, 2006).

The importance given to cross-border cooperation by the Spanish ACs has been increasing since the 1990s. The first decade of 2000 has been very significant in this regard, as proven by the reforms approved over the last few years in the Statutes of Autonomy of several Spanish ACs. Regarding external action, and specifically cross-border cooperation, all the new Statutes approved to date explicitly include the regional governments' right to carry out policies of cross-border cooperation (GARCÍA, 2009). In addition, the ACs' growing interest in cross-border cooperation can be seen clearly in their respective spatial planning plans, as well as in the actions of those in charge of community and foreign policy for the respective autonomous governments. But although external action and cross-border cooperation in most ACs are fundamentally viewed in terms of strengthening economic and territorial development, in others, such as those governed by nationalist parties, these actions are mixed with other types of political and territorial discourses and projects, such as those geared towards national construction itself (DOMÍNGUEZ, 2005; GARCÍA-ÁLVAREZ, 2006b; MORATA, 2006).

The case of the AC of the Basque Country (or Euskadi) is perhaps the most significant in this regard, although it is not the only one. In October 2003, the government of this community, then presided over by the PNV, publicly presented a new Statute of the Community of Euskadi known popularly by the name of its key proponent, Juan José Ibarretxe, President of the regional government between 1999 and 2009. The 'Ibarretxe Plan', which was approved in the Basque Parliament with the support of the autonomous nationalist parties, was later rejected by the Spanish Parliament in February 2005 by a large majority. Without entering into the reasons why the Spanish Parliament voted against the plan, the Ibarretxe Plan illustrates in exemplary fashion the projection of a cross-border space of regionalist engagement. Moreover, the plan conceives of cross-border cooperation as an instrument for legitimizing the territorial objectives pursued by the Basque nationalist parties, which focus on the political unification of the territorial area they call Euskal Herria or Greater Basque Country (BECK, 2006) (Fig. 1). According to Basque Nationalism, the territory of Euskal Herria (which literally means 'land of the Basque language') would include the AC of the Basque Country and the Foral Community of Navarre in Spain and the eastern part of the French *Département* of Atlantic Pyrenees (the historic provinces of Labourd, Lower Navarre and Soule), which belong to the Aquitaine Region.

The preamble of the latest version of the Ibarretxe Plan explicitly states that the Basque people or Euskal Herria is divided into seven territories, and that the AC of Euskadi is simply an integral part of it. Likewise, article 2 of the Plan aims at the possibility of establishing 'some common territorial framework for relations'

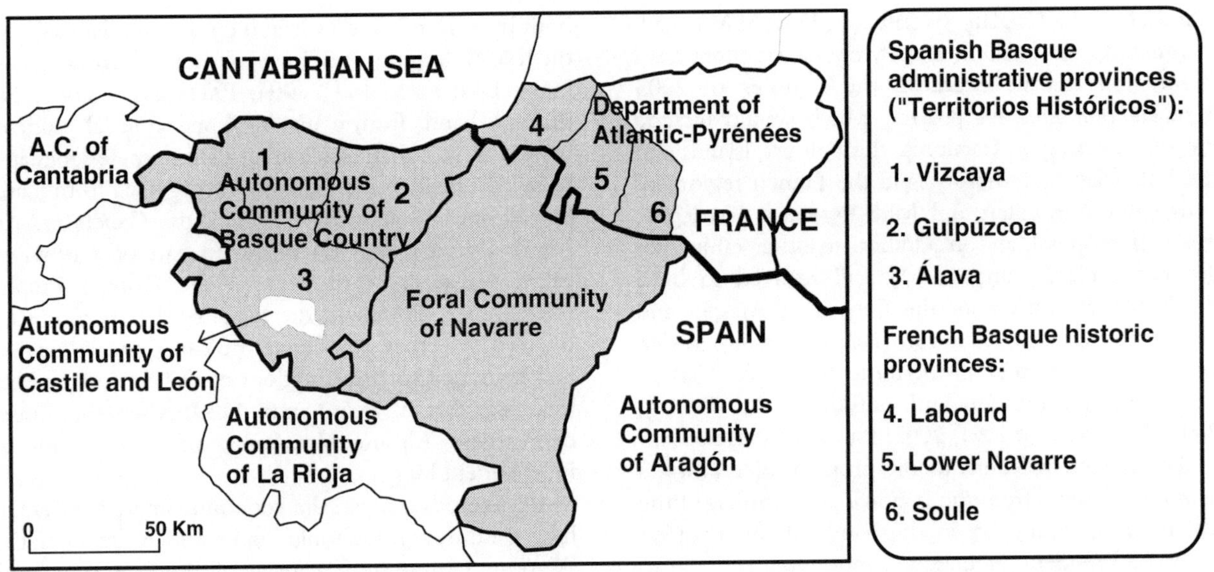

Fig. 1. Territorial components of Euskal Herria, according to the imagination of Basque nationalism

among the Basque territories and article 66.2, which forms part of Title VI (dedicated to the political relations of Euskadi with the European and international sectors), indicates what it considers the most adequate institutional framework for it within the European context: the establishment of a Euroregion.

> The Community of Euskadi will promote the creation of a Euroregion within the European Union that includes the historic territories that make up Euskal Herria and, if appropriate, other nearby regions with which it maintains historic, economic and cultural links of singular importance.
>
> (Propuesta de Reforma de Estatuto Político de la Comunidad de Euskadi (PREPCE), 2005)

After the Plan was rejected in the Spanish Parliament, the PNV did not give up the idea of creating a Basque Euroregion as a useful administrative framework to advance in the nation building of Euskal Herria, an idea extensively defended by certain academic experts in favour of nationalism (Letamendía, 1997; Ahedo *et al.*, 2004). Thus, for example, at what are known as the Loyola Negotiations (September and October 2006), in which the Spanish government together with representatives from the Basque political parties (PSE-PSOE, PNV) and Batasuna (a political organization that was made illegal due to its ties to the terrorist group ETA) held conversations with ETA in an attempt to make an end to terrorist activity, the PNV proposed the possible formation of a Basque Euroregion as a solution to the conflict (Oyarzábal, 2008).

As Markusse (2004) indicated, the establishment of an 'ethnic' Euroregion on the basis of Euskal Herria does not seem viable today, among other reasons, because the territories of French Basque Country do not have any sort of territorial power, and cooperation agreements of this type must be established regionally, that is, between Euskadi and Aquitaine. In addition to this, the aims of the former Basque government to establish some sort of framework of joint cooperation in what is called Euskal Herria clash head-on with the opinion of the government of the AC of Navarre, led by the Union of the People of Navarre (UPN) and presided over by Miguel Sanz, who have traditionally defended Navarre's singularity against the Basque Country. Due precisely to the irredentist discourse that emanates from the possibility of actually establishing Euskal Herria, the Navarre government has shown itself to be reluctant to participate in cross-border cooperation initiatives led by the Basque Country. Actually, whereas between 1991 and 2000 Navarre participated in a collaboration pact with Euskadi and Aquitaine, it stopped doing so in 2000 because, following an ETA terrorist attack the PNV government did not break its ties with its partner at that time, Euskal Herritarrok, a political party linked to ETA and in favour, as is ETA, of the creation of an independent state in the area of Euskal Herria.

President Sanz's reticence to collaborate in any cross-border cooperation organization that includes the Basque AC has continued, even with the recent change of government of this Community, now led by the PSE-PSOE which has substituted PNV's nationalist discourse for one that is regionalist or at least constitutionalist, and which does not enter into conflict with the state. Thus, on 30 November 2009, while regional Presidents Alain Rousset (Aquitaine) and Francisco Javier López (Basque Country) signed an agreement to establish a new Aquitaine–Euskadi Euroregion through the EGTC legal classification, in which the Navarre government was also invited to participate, Sanz was quick to decline the invitation the very next day.

Similarly, the reactions of certain Spanish regional politicians when faced with the proposal of the former president of the Catalan government, Pasqual Maragall, of the PSC, to establish the Pyrenees–Mediterranean Euroregion can be cited. In the summer of 2003 Maragall presented his project, which would include the ACs of Aragon, Catalonia, the Balearic Islands and the Valencian Community, and the French regions of Languedoc-Roussillon and Midi-Pyrénées. To legitimize his proposal, and in addition to other eminently geo-economic arguments, Maragall referred to both the historical concept of the Crown of Aragon and that of the Catalan Countries (*Països Catalans*), which would be made up of all the territories where Catalan is spoken, both inside and outside Spain (BOIRA, 2002; DÍEZ and PINAZO, 2005; PRYTHERCH, 2009).

The fiercest reactions to the proposal of creating a Euroregion came from the regional government of the Valencian Community, in the hands of the People's Party. Its President, Francisco Camps, went so far as to brand the initiative as unconstitutional because 'it attempts to usurp the dialogue and the capacity for decision of the ACs', as well as representing a 'real danger for the institutional and territorial stability of Spain'. The Euroregion proposal, added Camps, 'would take on competences of our Community, taking away autonomy from the Community, and rob us of part of our own autonomy' (*ABC*, 30 August 2003; SUÁREZ and RODRÍGUEZ, 2008).

These words demonstrate the strong reactions that the politics of cross-border cooperation provoke when they are mixed with certain nationalist projects or, more broadly, with arguments regarding identity, which may make one forget that on the Iberian Peninsula there already existed numerous cases of cooperation institutions that in no case went against the Constitution nor endangered the territorial model in effect. The Pyrenees–Mediterranean Euroregion got off the ground in 2004 without the presence of the Valencian Community. In May 2006, the government of the AC of Aragon also decided to abandon the Euroregion, in this case due to a conflict with the Catalan government over the ownership of certain pieces of sacred art.

The Galicia–Northern Portugal Euroregion: conceptions at stake and processes of institutionalization

Political contacts between the government of the AC of Galicia (Xunta de Galicia) and the representatives of the Portugal North Region began in the 1980s, although it was in the 1990s when they intensified. The determined commitment of two principal political leaders at that time, Manuel Fraga on behalf of Galicia and Luis Braga da Cruz on behalf of Portugal, led to the constitution of the Galicia–Northern Portugal Working Community in 1991, the first cross-border cooperation institution on the Spain–Portugal border (CORDAL, 2009). Since then the Galician governments have decisively committed to external action focused on Portugal, and especially on the Portugal North Region. This can be explained both by cultural, linguistic and custom similarities with the North region and by economic interests (LOIS, 2004; LABRAÑA *et al.*, 2004; PALMEIRO, 2009). On the one hand, from a historical and cultural point of view, the fact that Galician and Portuguese languages have the same root, Gallego-Portuguese, from Latin should not be overlooked. Present-day Galicia and the North Portugal Region made up part of a province called Gallaecia in the age of the Roman Empire (NOGUEIRA, 2002). In the times of the Reconquista, the territories that gave rise to the Kingdom of Portugal also belonged to the Kingdom of Galicia (and, within this area, that of León) until 1139, when the Count of Portugal, Alfonso Henriques, officially became an independent king.

On the other hand, the economic interests of establishing a Euroregion should not be underestimated. The Working Community manages all the European funds corresponding to the Operational Program of Cross-border cooperation Spain–Portugal. The last joint document made by regional politicians to establish the master lines of action dates from 2007 (Strategic Plan of Cross-border Cooperation Galicia/North Portugal), and refers to the 2007–2013 European regional policy programming period, within the framework of the Territorial Cooperation Objective. In the first call for projects (2007–2009), the aforementioned Operational Program received nearly €42 million, of which €31.5 million were from the European Regional Development Fund. The Eurorregion covers an area of 50 862 km^2 and has a population of 6 529 608 inhabitants (as of 1 January 2008).

As has been pointed out, the Galician government was presided over for the greater part of the last twenty years by the PPdeG, which held power in the region continuously from 1990 to June 2005, when the PSdeG-BNG coalition came to power. In April 2009 the regional elections were won by the present Xunta President, Alberto Nuñez Feijoo (PPG). Over the past years on various occasions these three parties have expressed their visions of cross-border cooperation, in which there are more similarities than differences. In order to illustrate the main similarities, it is only necessary to recall two documents that were written close in time regarding the strategic lines of external action of the last two Galician governments, one from 2004 (*Libro Blanco de la Acción Exterior*) and the other from 2007 (*Estrategias de la Acción Exterior*). Both indicate the necessity of guiding Galician external action toward the Lusophone world, and very particularly toward Portugal. In addition, they confirm the importance that the Euroregion has for Galicia to be able to project itself outwards in an area where it must be an engine of economic, political and cultural development.

But at the same time cross-border cooperation has been fully integrated into the political debate, and is even a cause for partisan disputes. The electoral programmes of the three parties (PPdeG, PSdeG and

BNG) for the March 2009 regional elections illustrate some of the differences in the way these matters are viewed. The one that places least emphasis on cross-border cooperation is the BNG, because its discourse revolves around a more general project of relations with the Lusophone world, in which 'cultural reintegration in the Galician–Portuguese world as a normalizing factor' is especially developed. For the PSdeG, the intensification of relations with North Portugal through the impetus of the EGTC is accentuated. Finally, the PPdeG dedicates a specific section to cross-border cooperation, in which it criticizes the previous government's policy, and proposes a model of greater integration and development.

In summary, cross-border cooperation with the North Region is viewed as a line of action of Galician external policy, and it does not provoke great differences of opinion among the three parties. In no case is there (at least from an official point of view) the irredentist approach, as it has been shown, in the institutional discourse of Basque nationalism.

However, in order to understand properly the meaning of cross-border cooperation both for Galicia and the North Region, it must not be forgotten that one is in the presence of a phenomenon of the overlapping of two very different political–territorial models. Compared with the deeply decentralized model of the Spanish State, the Portuguese model is characterized by its centralism. Thus, while the ACs possess their own power at the legislative, executive and judicial levels, the Portuguese Regions, with the exception of Madeira and the Azores, lack any sort of political autonomy. Apart from the two exceptions mentioned, which have the category of Autonomous Regions, the regional territorial and administrative structure in Portugal comes from the Regional Commissions of Coordination and Development (in total five, of which the North region is one), deconcentrated entities that are dependent on the central government, created by Decree-Law of 23 May 2003 on the basis of the earlier regions of planning. This essential difference between Spanish ACs and what are known as the Portuguese Regions means that cross-border cooperation between them is a tremendously complex phenomenon in political and administrative terms. In fact, on occasion, representatives of the Galician government, by virtue of their competences, must sit down to negotiate directly with representatives of the Portuguese government.

Furthermore, this overlapped territorial system translates into important differences in the way cross-border cooperation is conceived. Thus, while in Galicia cross-border cooperation with Northern Portugal is considered to be a fundamental part of the AC's external action, in Portugal this cooperation is best understood linked to the development of the northern area of the country. In other words, what is called the Galicia–Northern Portugal Euroregion is projected as a cross-border space of regionalist engagement (or a cross-border space of regionalism for itself), but for the Portuguese agents it means instead a cross-border regional space of engagement.

The principal documents of spatial planning recently prepared on either side of the border clearly illustrate these differences. On one hand, the Directives of Territorial Management of Galicia, the draft of which was initially approved by the autonomous government in 2008 (*Diario Oficial de Galicia*, 17 September 2008), deals with the Galicia–Northern Portugal Euroregion as a space around which all the external connections of the AC revolve. The very presence of the term 'Euroregion' in the document is significant, as it appears twenty times, while the term 'Portugal' is mentioned thirty-three times and the term 'Spain' ten times. The Portuguese vision, however, as is expressed in the Regional Plan of Territorial Management of the North Region, the draft of which was presented in December 2009 (http://www.ccr-norte.pt), deals with the external connectivity of the North Region, not only with Galicia, but also with the AC of Castile and León, with which it also borders and participates in a Working Community. The term 'Galicia–Northern Portugal Euroregion' is only cited seven times, although its ultimate meaning is linked to specific projects more than to a global strategy for external action.

Nonetheless, certain Portuguese politicians (especially those belonging to the Socialist Party) may see in the broad competences of their Galician neighbour a path to claims in favour of the political or administrative regionalization of the Portuguese State, a matter which has led to important debates and initiatives over the last fifteen years (FERNANDES, 2008). Therefore, the Euroregion could even be considered from the Portuguese side as a cross-border space of regionalist engagement.

In short, what this contribution tries to show is that in order to analyse the role that a cross-border cooperation body can play in internal and external politics of the states and regions, the integral parts must be considered separately. Of course, this kind of cross-border institutions must be considered as a whole as well. In this regard, the Galicia–Northern Portugal Euroregion is conceived of as a cross-border space of engagement in the European context connected to different networks. Thus, both the AC of Galicia and the North of Portugal Regional Commission of Coordination and Development belong to the Conference of Peripheral Maritime Regional and the Atlantic Arc Commission, while the 'Eixo Atlántico do Noroeste Peninsular' municipal Association (one of the members of the Working Community) participates in several networks at the state and European level.

To conclude this section, it is interesting to consider, if briefly, the institutionalization processes of the cross-border region. Among the joint institutional bodies, first of all, the aforementioned Working Community should be mentioned. In addition to forming part of the Xunta de Galicia and the North Regional

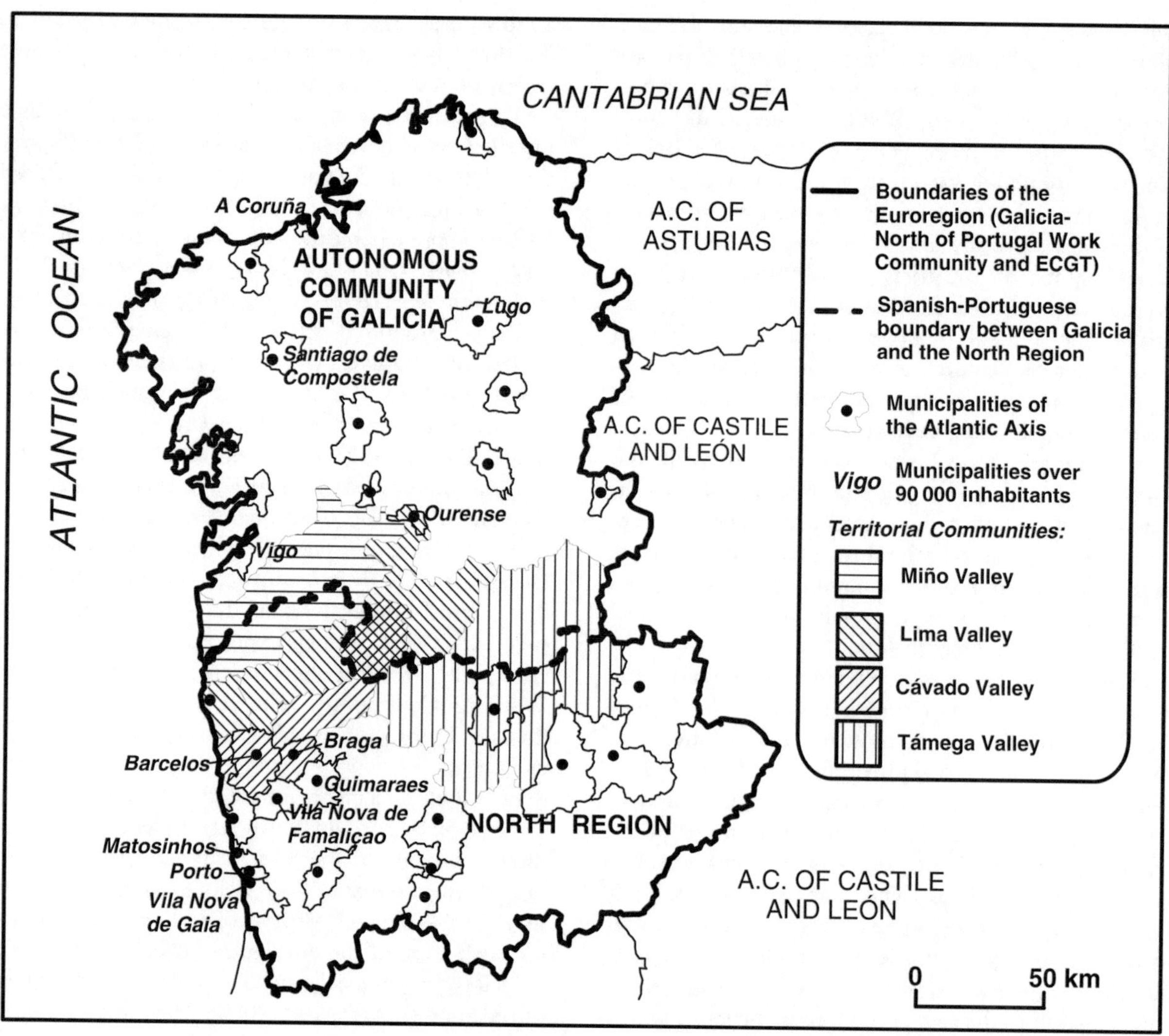

Fig. 2. Cross-border cooperation spatial structures in the Galicia–North of Portugal Euroregion

Commission of Coordination and Development, it is made up of five local organizations: four Territorial Communities and the aforementioned association of cities called 'Eixo Atlántico' (Fig. 2). One must add to this the recent creation of an EGTC called Galicia/ North Portugal EGTC (GNP-EGTC), which does not replace the Working Community, and is only made up of regional powers. The universities of Galicia and of North Portugal have also initiated a cooperation project within the foundation called FCEER (Galicia–North Portugal Center of Euroregional Studies Foundation), which began to function in 2004. This foundation aims to create itself as a forum in which teachers and students can exchange experiences and knowledge about the Euroregion.

Regarding the production of discourse legitimizing the existence of the Euroregion, the activity carried out by the Eixo Atlántico association, made up of thirty-four Galician and Portuguese cities, stands out. Its work is not limited to the analysis of member cities, but rather extends to the Euroregion area (http://www.eixoatlantico.com). Its work reinforces the production of an 'institutional thickness' (AMIN and THRIFT, 1994) or 'cross-border regional armature' (LIPIETZ, 2003), also corresponding to the territorial and symbolic shapes of PAASI's (1986) model, or to the building of an identity for the Euroregion that is not only functional or strategic, but also cultural (VAN HOUTUM and LAGENDIJK, 2001).

The Association promotes studies in diverse areas such as social development, transport, sustainable development, culture and tourism, and publishing extensively. Furthermore, the publication of two detailed studies on the political, economic, cultural and social situation of the Euroregion, published in 1995 and 2005, respectively, called *Estudios Estratéxicos* must be emphasized. Added to that is the publication, since May 2001, of the *Revista da Eurorrexión Galicia-Norte de Portugal*, with sixteen issues published by the end of 2009.

The Euroregion institutions have also driven certain actions aimed at building regional imagery, identity and awareness that can be shared by Euroregion inhabitants. In this regard, academic works such as *A Historia no Eixo Atlántico* (1999), *Xeografía do Eixo Atlántico* (1999) and *Atlas do Eixo Atlántico e Eurorrexión Galiza e Norte de Portugal* (2007) or the twelve-part series entitled *Eurorrexión século XXI. Galicia-Norte de Portugal* (2006) stand out. In all these, the underlying intention is to establish – in SCOTT's (2000) terms – a new 'cross-border cognitive region', even making use of the Gallaecia reference point to appeal to a foundational and common historic space between the Spanish and Portuguese States that had been artificially divided (GARCÍA-ÁLVAREZ, 2003). The organization of numerous cultural and sporting events in which the inhabitants from both sides of the border participate also attempts to foster the idea of a shared territory (TRILLO-SANTAMARÍA, 2010). However, the success of such initiatives seems to be, at present, relatively limited, and it is not possible to talk about a cross-border regional identity at the heart of the Euroregion (SOUTO, 2005; RODRÍGUEZ *et al.*, 2006). Despite political discourse that openly promotes 'second-generation' cross-border cooperation truly to reach the citizens, these projects are still far removed from daily life.

CONCLUSIONS

Cross-border regions seem to offer suitable contexts for putting into practice the analytical instruments for regional studies, to bridge the gap between Regional World(s) and Cross-border Regional World(s).

The political context within which the various initiatives of cross-border cooperation are framed should be taken into account in order to understand their complexity. The examination of three regional cases that are representative of the Spanish State of the Autonomies (three border regions which have a strong cultural and linguistic identity) enables one to see some key problems associated with the building of cross-border spaces within the European Union, as well as the usefulness, but also the limitations, of certain recently posed conceptualizations of the region.

In Spain, cross-border cooperation cannot be separated from the debates about the political and territorial model of the state and the dialectic between national and regional identities. As this article has tried to show, in some Autonomous Communities (ACs) with strong sub-state nationalist parties, cross-border cooperation policies can also be used as ideological instruments to put into question the state's territory and national sovereignty and, furthermore, the 'Europe of the States'. In any case, the three examples that have been commented on present similarities but also considerable differences when it comes to understanding the complex dialectic between the regional spaces and spaces of regionalism that characterize the origin of the State of the Autonomies.

The Basque case, where recent plans to create a Basque Euroregion have been closely linked to territorial projects of nationalism, can be analysed as a clear example of cross-border space of regionalist engagement of irredentist shades. Compared with the more economic and technocratic perspective of the Europe of Regions, the proposals of Basque Nationalism openly place themselves, as this type of project proves, in defence of the Europe of Peoples, which has an ethno-territorial outlook. The construction of the Euroregion is in fact viewed as a path towards the construction of a Basque nation. Regarding the other two cases that have been analysed, while one cannot speak of irredentism, the demand for a cultural space that transcends both internal borders between ACs and external ones between states can be observed. That is, what occurs, above all, with the idea of 'Països Catalans' closely present in certain Euroregional imagery connected with Catalan Nationalism and, although to a lesser degree, with the geographical and historical references used in relation to the Galicia/North Portugal Euroregion.

The connection between internal and external Spanish politics, focused on cross-border cooperation, has been made manifest in the adverse reaction of the Foral Region of Navarre regarding the projects led by the governments of the Basque Country and that of the Valencian Community in the case of the Pyrenees–Mediterranean Euroregion project led by the former Catalan President Maragall.

Finally, the analysis of the Galicia–North Portugal Euroregion, the subject of the last section of this article, has served, first of all, to illustrate the difficulties of building cross-border cooperation institutions between two states that possess different models of territorial organization. Being endowed with many more political competences than their Portuguese counterparts, Galician regional politicians view the Euroregion as an instrument of paradiplomacy, whereas North Portuguese authorities mainly think of cross-border cooperation in functional terms. Secondly, the study of the Galicia–North Portugal case has shown some of the main aspects of the institutionalization processes of cross-border regions in the Iberian Peninsula, whose discourses and initiatives are still far removed from the daily lives of its inhabitants.

Acknowledgement – The authors wish to thank A. Paasi for his comments on earlier versions of this paper, and also the are grateful for the comments provided by the anonymous referees. The usual disclaimers apply.

REFERENCES

ABC (2003) *ABC*, **30 August**.

AHEDO I., ETXEBARRÍA N. and LETAMENDÍA F. (2004) *Redes transfronterizas intervascas*. Universidad del País Vasco, Bilbao.

AJA E. (2007) *El Estado autonómico. Federalismo y hechos diferenciales*. Alianza, Madrid.

ALDECOA F. and KEATING M. (Eds) (1999) *Paradiplomacy in Action: The Foreign Relations of Subnational Governments*. Frank Cass, London.

AMIN A. and THRIFT N. (1994) Living in the global, in AMIN A. and THRIFT N. (Eds) *Globalization, Institutions, and Regional Development in Europe*, pp. 1–22. Oxford University Press, Oxford.

ASSOCIATION OF EUROPEAN BORDER REGIONS (AEBR) (2001) *Transeuropean Cooperation between Territorial Authorities*. AEBR, Gronau.

BECK J. M. (2006) Geopolitical imaginations of the Basque homeland, *Geopolitics* **11**, 507–528.

BOIRA J. V. (2002) *Euram 2010. La via europea*. Eliseu Climent, Valencia.

BRUNET-JAILLY E. (2005) Theorizing borders: an interdisciplinary perspective, *Geopolitics* **10(4)**, 633–649.

CASTELLS M. (1999) Grassrooting the space of flows, *Urban Geography* **4**, 294–302.

CHURCH A. and REID P. (1999) Cross-border co-operation, institutionalization and political space across the English Channel, *Regional Studies* **33(7)**, 643–655.

CORDAL C. (2009) A acción exterior galega e as relacións con Portugal, *Tempo Exterior* **18**, 153–162.

COX K. (1998) Spaces of dependence, spaces of engagement and the politics of scale, or: looking for local politics, *Political Geography* **17(1)**, 1–23.

DEAS I. and LORD A. (2006) From a new regionalism to an unusual regionalism?, *Urban Studies* **43(10)**, 1847–1877.

DÍEZ J. and PINAZO J. (2005) La Eurorregión Pirineos-Mediterráneo: una evaluación estratégica, *Cuadernos Constitucionales de la Cátedra Fadrique Furió Cerol* **52/53**, 119–140.

DOMÍNGUEZ F. (2005) *Las regiones con competencias legislativas: un estudio comparado de su posición constitucional en sus respectivos Estados y en la Unión Europea*. Tirant lo Blanch, Valencia.

FERNANDES J. L. (2008) El model de desenvolupament i l'organització territorial a Portugal. Inèrcies, desafiaments y oportunitats, in TORT J., PAÜL V. and MALUQUER J. (Eds) *L'organització del territori*, pp. 353–402. Universitat Catalana d'Estiu-Galerada, Barcelona.

GARCÍA R. (Ed.) (2009) *La acción exterior de las Comunidades Autónomas en las reformas estatutarias*. Tecnos, Madrid.

GARCÍA-ÁLVAREZ J. (2002) *Provincias, regiones y comunidades autónomas: la formación del mapa político de España*. Secretaría General del Senado, Madrid.

GARCÍA-ÁLVAREZ J. (2003) *Territorio y nacionalismo: la construcción geográfica de la identidad gallega (1860–1936)*. Xunta de Galicia, Santiago de Compostela.

GARCÍA-ÁLVAREZ J. (2006a) Geografía regional, in HIERNAUX D. and LINDON A. (Eds) *Tratado de Geografía Humana*, pp. 25–70. Anthropos-Universidad Autónoma Metropolitana, Barcelona.

GARCÍA-ÁLVAREZ J. (2006b) Territoire, questions régionales et dimension européenne dans l'Espagne des Autonomies: réalisations et défis, *Rives nord-méditerranéennes* **25**, 31–42.

GEOPOLITICS (various years) *Geopolitics* Special Issues **10(4)** (2005); **12(2)** (2007); and **14(4)** (2010).

GRANJA J. L., BERAMENDI J. and ANGUERA P. (2001) *La España de los nacionalismos y las Autonomías*. Síntesis, Madrid.

HÄKLI J. (2008) Re-bordering spaces, in COX K., LOW M. and ROBINSON J. (Eds) *The Sage Handbook of Political Geography*, pp. 471–482. Sage, London.

HOOGHE L. and MARKS G. (2001) *Multi-level Governance and European Integration*. Rowman & Littlefield, Lanham, MD.

JESSOP B., BRENNER N. and JONES M. (2007) Theorizing socio-spatial relations, *Environment and Planning D: Society and Space* **26(3)**, 389–401.

JONES M. and MACLEOD G. (2004) Regional spaces, spaces of regionalism: territory, insurgent politics and the English question, *Transactions of the Institute of British Geographers* **29**, 433–452.

KAPLAN D.H. and HÄKLI J. (Eds) (2002) *Boundaries and Place: European Borderlands in Geographical Context*. Rowman & Littlefield, Lanham, MD.

KRAMSCH O. (2007) Querying cosmopolis at the border of Europe, *Environment and Planning A* **39**, 1582–1600.

KRAMSCH O. and HOOPER B. (Eds) (2004) *Cross-Border Governance in the European Union*. Routledge, Oxford.

KRAMSCH O. and MAMADOUH V. (2003) Crossing borders of political governance and democracy, *Journal of Borderland Studies* **18(1)**, 39–50.

LABRAÑA S., PAÍS E. and PAÜL V. (2004) A raia galego-portuguesa em debate, in MARQUEZ J. A. and GORDO M. (Eds) *Fronteras en movimiento*, pp. 153–176. MEC, Huelva.

LAGENDIJK A. (2007) The accident of the region: a strategic relational perspective on the construction of the region's significance, *Regional Studies* **41**, 1193–1207.

LETAMENDÍA F. (1997) Basque nationalism and cross border cooperation between the Southern and the Northern Basque Countries, *Regional and Federal Studies* **7(2)**, 25–41.

LEVRAT N. (2007) *The European Grouping of Territorial Cooperation*. CdR (117/2007, Study). Committee of the Regions, Brussels.

LIPIETZ A. (2003) The national and the regional: their autonomy vis-à-vis the capitalist world crisis, in BRENNER N., JESSOP B., JONES M. and MACLEOD G. (Eds) *State-Space: A Reader*, pp. 239–255. Oxford, Blackwell.

LISSANDRELLO E. (2006) The utopia of cross-border regions. Territorial transformation and cross-border governance on Espace Mont-Blanc. PhD thesis, Radboud University, Nijmegen.

LOIS R. (2004) Galice-Portugal: des rélations transnationales privilegiées dans la Peninsule Iberique, *Sud-Ouest Européen: révue géographique des Pyrénées et du Sud-Ouest* **18**, 31–40.

MACLEOD G. (1999) Place, politics and 'scale dependence': exploring the structuration of Euro-regionalism, *European Urban and Regional Studies* **6(3)**, 231–253.

MacLeod G. and Jones M. (2007) Territorial, scalar, networked, connected: in what sense a 'Regional World'?, *Regional Studies* **41(9)**, 1177–1191.

Markusse J. (2004) Transborder regional alliances in Europe: chances for ethnic Euroregions?, *Geopolitics* **9(3)**, 649–673.

Martínez E. (Ed.) (2006) *La adaptación de los organismos de cooperación transfronteriza por las Comunidades Autónomas*. GIT, Valladolid.

Ministerio de Política Territorial (MPT) (2010) *La cooperación transfronteriza realizada por las entidades territoriales españolas*. MPT, Madrid.

Morata F. (2006) European Integration and the Spanish 'State of the Autonomies', *ZSE* **4**, 507–528.

Newman D. (2006) Borders and bordering: towards an interdisciplinary dialogue, *European Journal of Social Theory* **9(2)**, 171–186.

Nogueira C. (2002) *A memoria da nación: o reino de Gallaecia*. Xerais, Vigo.

Oliveras X., Durà A. and Perkmann M. (2010) Las regiones transfronterizas: balance de la regionalización de la cooperación transfronteriza en Europa (1958–2007), *Documents d'Anàlisi Geogràfica* **56(1)**, 21–40.

Oyarzábal J. (2008) Las verdaderas intenciones del PNV: negociación, Loyola y referéndum, *GEES* **No. 2278**.

Paasi A. (1986) The institutionalization of regions: a theoretical framework for understanding the emergence of regions and the constitution of regional identity, *Fennia* **164(1)**, 105–146.

Paasi A. (2004) Place and region: looking through the prism of scale, *Progress in Human Geography* **28(4)**, 536–546.

Paasi A. (2009a) The resurgence of the region and regional identity: theoretical perspectives and empirical observations on regional dynamics in Europe, *Review of International Studies* **35**, 121–146.

Paasi A. (2009b) Bounded spaces in a 'borderless world': border studies, power and the anatomy of territory, *Journal of Power* **2(2)**, 213–234.

Painter J. (2008) Cartographic anxiety and the search for regionality, *Environment and Planning A* **40(2)**, 342–361.

Palmeiro J. L. (2009) Transborder cooperation and identities in Galicia and Northern Portugal, *Geopolitics* **14**, 79–107.

Perkmann M. (2003) Cross-border regions in Europe – significance and drivers of regional cross-border co-operation, *European Urban and Regional Studies* **10**, 153–171.

Perkmann M. (2007) Construction of new territorial scales: a framework and case study if the EUREGIO cross-border region, *Regional Studies* **41(2)**, 252–253.

Perkmann M. and Sum N.L. (Eds) (2002) *Globalization, Regionalization and Cross-Border Regions*. Palgrave Macmillan, Basingstoke.

Prokkola E. V. (2008) Making bridges, removing barriers. Cross-border cooperation, regionalization and identity at the Finish–Swedish border, *Nordia Geographical Publications* **37(3)**.

Propuesta de Reforma de Estatuto Político de la Comunidad de Euskadi (PREPCE) (2005) Propuesta de Reforma de Estatuto Político de la Comunidad de Euskadi, *Boletín Oficial de las Cortes Generales* **21-I-2005**.

Prytherch D. L. (2009) New Eurorregional territories, old Catalanists dreams?: articulating culture, economy and territory in the Mediterranean Arc, *European Urban and Regional Studies* **16(2)**, 131–145.

Rodríguez R., Lois R., Miramontes A., Pineiro M. and Suárez A. (2006) El Eixo Atlántico del Noroeste Peninsular, in Farinós J. and Romero J. (Eds) *Gobernanza territorial en España*, pp. 123–136. Valencia, Universitat de València.

Scott J. (2000) Euroregions, governance, and transborder cooperation within the EU, in van der Velde M. and van Houtum H. (Eds) *Borders, Regions and People*, pp. 104–115. Pion, London.

Scott J. (2002) A networked space of meaning? Spatial politics as geostrategies of European integration, *Space and Polity* **6(2)**, 147–167.

Souto X. M. (2005) Euro-rexións e cidadanía no Noroeste Peninsular, *Biblio 3W* **10(No. 605)**.

Sparke M. (2000) 'Chunnel visions': unpacking the anticipatory geographies of an Anglo-European borderland, *Journal of Borderlands Studies* **15**, 187–219.

Strüver A. (2005) *Stories of the 'Boring Border': The Dutch–German Borderscape in People's Minds*. LIT, Münster.

Suárez C. and Rodríguez P. (2008) *L'Euroregió Pirineus-Mediterrània*. Working Papers on Line (WPOL) Number 18. Institut Universitari d'Estudis Europeos, Barcelona.

Trillo-Santamaría J. M. (2009) De la frontera a Europa: una visión desde la cooperación transfronteriza, in Feria J. M., García A. and Ojeda F. (Eds) *Territorios, Sociedades y Políticas*, pp. 495–510. AGE, Seville.

Trillo-Santamaría J. M. (2010) La région transfrontalière: des idées de Rougemont aux processus actuels d'institutionnalisation, *Revue Mosella* **23(1/4)**, 241–264.

van der Velde M. and van Houtum H (2003) Communicating borders, *Journal of Borderland Studies* **18(1)**, 1–11.

van Houtum H., Kramsch O. and Zierhofer W. (Eds) (2005) *B/Ordering Space*. Ashgate, Aldershot.

van Houtum H. and Lagendijk A. (2001) Contextualising regional identity and imagination in the construction of polycentric urban regions: the cases of the Ruhr Area and the Basque country, *Urban Studies* **38(4)**, 747–767.

(Small) Differences that (Still) Matter? Cross-Border Regions and Work Place Governance in the Southern Ontario and US Great Lakes Automotive Industry

TOD D. RUTHERFORD* and JOHN HOLMES†

*Department of Geography, Maxwell School of Citizenship and Public Affairs, Syracuse University, Syracuse, USA.
†Department of Geography, Queen's University, Kingston, ON, Canada.

RUTHERFORD T. D. and HOLMES J. (Small) differences that (still) matter? Cross-border regions and work place governance in the Southern Ontario and US Great Lakes automotive industry, *Regional Studies*. Workplace governance is a critical element in determining regional competitiveness. While contemporary rescaling of economic and social relations has produced new territorial configurations, including cross-border regions (CBRs), there is little research on the reshaping of workplace governance within such regions. It is argued that changes in CBR workplace governance are contingent upon (1) firms' ability to transfer corporate employment practices across national borders; (2) labour law and other employment regulatory institutions; and (3) the response of labour organizations. Using this framework, workplace governance change in the automotive industry in the Southern Ontario and US Great Lakes States CBR is examined.

RUTHERFORD T. D. and HOLMES J. 小差异（还）起作用吗？南安大略及美国大湖区汽车工业的跨境区域与工作场所管治. *区域研究.* 工作场所管治是决定区域竞争力的关键因素。尽管当今经济与社会关系的尺度变化已经产生了新的地域结构，如跨境区域，但有关这些区域内工作场所管治重构的研究几乎还没有。本文认为跨境区域工作场所管治具有不确定性，它取决于：（1）企业跨越边境复制公司雇员习惯的能力；（2）劳动法及其他就业管制机构；（3）劳工组织的响应。利用这个研究框架，本文探究了南安大略及美国大湖区汽车工业工作场所管治的变化。

RUTHERFORD T. D. et HOLMES J. De (légères) différences qui comptent (toujours)? Les régions transfrontalières et la gouvernance du lieu de travail dans l'industrie automobile située dans le Sud de l'Ontario et dans la région des Grands Lacs au E-U, *Regional Studies*. La gouvernance du lieu de travavil constitue un facteur déterminant primordial de la compétitivité régionale. Alors que la reterritorialisation des rapports économiques et sociaux a produit de nouvelles configurations territoriales, y compris les régions transfrontalières, rares sont les recherches sur la transformation de la gouvernance du lieu de travail au sein de telles régions. On affirme que des transformations de la gouvernance du lieu de travail dans les régions transfrontalières sont subordonnées (1) à la capacité des entreprises de transférer leurs pratiques en matière d'emploi au-delà des frontières nationales; (2) au droit du travail et à d'autres institutions de régulation en matière d'emploi; et (3) à la réponse des organisations ouvrières. Ce cadre permet d'examiner la transformation de la gouvernance du lieu de travail dans l'industrie automobile située dans les régions transfrontalières du Sud de l'Ontario et de la région des Grands Lacs au E-U.

RUTHERFORD T. D. und HOLMES J. (Kleine) Unterschiede, auf die es (immer noch) ankommt? Grenzübergreifende Regionen und Unternehmensführung am Arbeitsplatz in der Automobilindustrie von Südontario (Kanada) und Great Lakes (USA), *Regional Studies*. Die Unternehmensführung am Arbeitsplatz ist ein wesentliches Element zur Bestimmung der regionalen Wettbewerbsfähigkeit. Die aktuelle Neuskalierung der Wirtschafts- und Sozialbeziehungen hat zu neuen territorialen Konfigurationen wie z. B. grenzübergreifenden Regionen geführt, doch die Umgestaltung der Unternehmensführung am Arbeitsplatz innerhalb solcher Regionen wurde bisher nur wenig untersucht. Wir argumentieren, dass die Veränderungen bei der Unternehmensführung am Arbeitsplatz in grenzübergreifenden Regionen abhängig sind von (1) der Fähigkeit der Firmen, Unternehmenspraktiken bei der Beschäftigung von Arbeitnehmern über nationale Grenzen hinweg zu übertragen, (2) dem Arbeitsrecht und weiteren

Institutionen zur Regelung der Arbeitsbeziehungen und (3) der Reaktion der Arbeitnehmerorganisationen. Anhand dieses Rahmens werden die Veränderungen bei der Unternehmensführung am Arbeitsplatz in der Automobilindustrie der grenzübergreifenden Region von Südontario (Kanada) und Great Lakes (USA) untersucht.

RUTHERFORD T. D. y HOLMES J. ¿(Pequeñas) diferencias que (todavía) importan? Regiones transfronterizas y dirección en el lugar de trabajo en la industria de automoción del sur de Ontario (Canadá) y los Estados de los Grandes Lagos (Estados Unidos), *Regional Studies*. La dirección en el lugar de trabajo es un elemento esencial a la hora de determinar la competitividad regional. Aunque el reescalamiento contemporáneo de las relaciones económicas y sociales ha producido nuevas configuraciones territoriales, como por ejemplo las regiones transfronterizas, existen pocos estudios sobre la reorganización de la dirección en el lugar de trabajo en tales regiones. Sostenemos que los cambios de la dirección en el lugar de trabajo de las regiones transfronterizas dependen de (1) la capacidad de las empresas de transferir las prácticas corporativas de empleo a través de las fronteras nacionales; (2) la legislación laboral y otras instituciones de reglamentación laboral; y (3) la respuesta de los sindicatos. Con ayuda de este marco de trabajo, analizamos el cambio de dirección en el lugar de trabajo en la industria de automoción en la región transfronteriza del sur de Ontario (Canadá) y los Estados de los Grandes Lagos (Estados Unidos).

INTRODUCTION

Over the last decade, human geography and other social sciences have focused on the rescaling of economic and social relations linked to globalization (JESSOP, 2002a, 2002b; BRENNER, 2004). The primacy of the national scale of political–economic organization and regulation has been destabilized and qualitatively new supranational, regional and local state institutional forms have been forged. In particular, the role of sub-national governance has become decisive 'to position urban and regional economies optimally within global and supranational circuits of capital' (BRENNER, 2004, p. 3). The 'new scalar hierarchies' associated with this rescaling include cross-border regions (CBRs) – territorial units comprised of contiguous sub-national units from two or more nation-states (PERKMANN and SUM, 2002; JESSOP, 2002b; PERKMANN, 2007; BRUNET-JAILLY, 2008). Although CBRs are not an entirely new phenomenon,

> [w]hat is new in recent developments is that the construction of cross-border regions has become a more or less explicit strategic objective pursued by various social forces within and beyond border regions.
>
> (PERKMANN and SUM, 2002, p. 3).

The development of CBRs between Canada and the United States has been well-documented in government policy documents (PRI FEDERAL GOVERNMENT OF CANADA, 2006) and academic research (COURCHENE and TELMER, 1998; BLATTER, 2001; SPARKE, 2005; BRUNET-JAILLY, 2008). A key theoretical and policy question is the impact of increased economic integration on policies and institutions viewed as crucial in determining competitive economic advantage within CBRs. A critical element in determining regional competitiveness is workplace (WP) governance – which includes work organization, firm-level and worksite industrial relations/human resource (IR/HR) practices, local labour market regulation, and state labour regulations and employment law.

Despite recognizing the role played by transnational corporations (TNCs) and global production networks (GPNs) in CBR formation, relatively little research has focused on WP governance within such regions. The debates concerning the impact of TNCs on WP governance are often framed in terms of whether convergence of IR/HR practices is occurring (RUTHERFORD, 2004). The focus in this paper, however, is to develop a better understanding of the factors shaping changes in WP governance within CBRs. The goals are two-fold. First, to develop an analytical framework for examining changes in WP governance in CBRs, the paper reviews the relevant literature in both economic geography and IR/HR management. It is conjectured that such changes are contingent upon (1) the ability of TNCs to transfer corporate HR and employment practices across national borders; (2) the degree to which labour law and other employment regulatory institutions actually change due to pressures generated by economic integration and CBR formation; and (3) the response of labour unions and employee representatives in the WP to such processes. The second objective is to use this framework to provide an initial assessment of how WP governance is changing in the automotive industry in the CBR that encompasses Southern Ontario and the Great Lakes States of the United States (primarily Michigan, Ohio and Indiana). Nation-state labour laws and unions remain influential, but their relative powers have become less determining of TNC WP governance practices within CBRs. Continued production-system integration, coupled with the emergence in the Southern United States of a rapidly expanding non-union automotive cluster, mean that differences in such practices have narrowed significantly within the CBR. the paper concludes by assessing the theoretical implications of these findings.

PRODUCTION GLOBALIZATION AND THE EMERGENCE OF CROSS-BORDER REGIONS

The last decade has witnessed a growing interest in CBRs by policy-makers and researchers (PRI FEDERAL GOVERNMENT OF CANADA, 2006; BLATTER, 2001; PERKMANN and SUM, 2002; JESSOP, 2002a, 2002b; PERKMANN, 2007; BRUNET-JAILLY, 2008). While not a new phenomena (PERKMANN and SUM, 2002, p. 7), the current interest in CBRs reflects increased transborder flows of goods, services and people as a result of trade and investment liberalization. CBR formation is also related to what JESSOP (2002a) terms the 'relativization of scale' in which national-scale primacy is increasingly challenged as formerly national-state regulatory activities are transferred upward to the supranational level, such as the European Union and the North American Free Trade Agreement (NAFTA), downwards to sub-national regions and localities, or sideways to private sector and civil society organizations.

CBRs are not the product of a singular logic and have differing characteristics (JESSOP, 2002a, pp. 32–33). Thus, PERKMANN (2007) observes that in contrast to the European Union where CBRs are often comprised of local or regional authorities integrated into multilevel implementation networks under European Union regional policy, North American CBRs are linked more closely to a free-trade logic and feature 'particularist and issue-driven interests [which] appear more loosely organized with a variety of private and public actors involved' (p. 253).

The formation of CBRs has important implications for institutional governance. Economic geographers have examined GPNs and the role of national and regional state policies in capturing key network segments within the value chain (COE *et al.*, 2004), but relatively little attention has been paid to WP regulation. Yet the WP occupies a critical intersection where the vertical processes of GPNs cut across horizontally constructed territories and is a site of regulation, social formation and struggle (PERKMANN, 2007, pp. 255–256). Given the geographic contiguity and often institutional similarities between the national territories integrated into specific CBRs, the latter represent a useful 'test case' for investigating the impact of deepening economic integration on WP governance. The present paper adopts a political economy framework developed by EDWARDS *et al.* (2007, p. 213) for analysing WP governance which views institutions as objects of contestation subject to change by TNC restructuring and with local outcomes shaped by the relative power of actors, including employees and unions. The extant literature suggests that the following are of prime importance in shaping WP change: (1) the ability of TNCs to transfer employment practices across borders and between production facilities; (2) the degree to which labour law and other employment regulatory institutions may change due to restructuring and CBR formation; and (3) the role of unions and employee representatives, especially at the WP level.

The ability of transnational corporations to transfer human resource 'best practice'

Research, especially in economic geography, has challenged claims of a declining relevance of national institutions in the face of globalization (DICKEN, 2007). Thus, GERTLER and VINODRAI (2005, p. 34) found that German-owned plants in North America did not display many of the distinctive attributes of German manufacturing practices such as close collaboration between suppliers and customers, advanced training, strong internal labour markets, and mechanisms for formal worker representation. Similarly, EDWARDS *et al.* (2005, p. 1283) emphasized the importance of national 'administrative heritage' in constraining a TNC's ability to introduce innovative HR practices developed in their overseas subsidiaries in their home-country operations).

Yet, the formation of GPNs and TNC-integrated production systems has led some authors to argue that TNC HR strategies are becoming less distinctively national and more ethnocentric or firm based (LOOISE and DRUCKER, 2002). This is uneven, however, and while pay determination, union recognition and consultative structures are likely to be reflective of national legislation (CALIGUIRI *et al.*, 2010), practices such as direct employee involvement, WP organization and managerial development are more likely to be company specific and similar across a company's WPs in different countries (LOOISE and DRUCKER, 2002). Finally, institutional similarities between the TNC's home nation and the host nations of its subsidiaries may make it more likely firms will transfer core employment practices (ROCHA, 2009, p. 487).

National institutions, labour and employment law

Many argue that national institutions still have a significant impact on the WP strategies of global firms. CHRISTOPHERSON (2002) argues that differences in national financial governance explain why national labour market regimes have not converged. Similarly, CHRISTOPHERSON and VAN JAARSVELD's (2005) study of new media industries in Sweden and Germany illustrates the continued significance of national institutions in shaping the development of those industries.

However, the role played by national institutions in shaping WP governance is changing due to rescaling. JONAS (1996) and COE *et al.* (2004) point to greater regulation of IR and WP governance at the local labour market level (see also HEROD *et al.*, 2005). A more 'disorganized' pattern of governance among local labour markets is developing as formal state regulation is replaced by an uneven and complex web of mostly private institutions and labour market intermediaries (BENNER, 2003).

Clearly, an important factor shaping WP governance is the legal regulation of WPs through labour law and legislation governing such things as employment standards and health and safety. Researchers argue that there is little evidence of a strong direct effect of economic globalization on labour and employment law (GUNDERSON, 1998). But as ARTHURS (2006) suggests, while the impact on domestic labour law may not be normative it can nevertheless be formative. Thus,

> instead of intervening directly, [TNC] head office tends to shape local labour practices through its global business strategies ... which either permit local managers to treat workers decently or force them to do the opposite: and to adopt a worldwide policy of obeying, ignoring or rewriting local labour law.
>
> (pp. 55–56)

Similarly, the embracing by governments of free trade, balanced budgets, privatization and anti-inflationary policies has 'very predictable' negative consequences for worker solidarity and unionization. Even where significant institutional differences exist between a TNC's home nation and the jurisdictions of its subsidiaries, TNCs can effectively 'hollow-out' legislated IR institutional practices (ROCHA, 2009).

Employees and their representatives

A critical and often overlooked factor shaping WP governance is the role played by employees and their representatives, especially at the individual WP scale (KUMAR and HOLMES, 1997; KRISTENSEN and ZEITLIN, 2005). Labour movement lobbying can shape wider national legal institutional frameworks and collective bargaining can force firms to develop labour and employment standards that exceed the legislated minimum standards (RUTHERFORD and GERTLER, 2002).

Unions develop cross-border networks in support of particular industrial actions (HEROD, 2001; CROUCHER and COTTON, 2009; MUNCK, 2010) and work with civil society organizations to foster improved labour standards in newly industrializing nations (WATERMAN and WILLS, 2001; BRONFENBRENNER, 2007). The formation of European Works Councils has fostered greater cross-border labour links within Europe (WILLS, 2001; ROCHA, 2009). Yet overall, restructuring and GPN development have significantly weakened many national IR institutions without adequately developing equivalent transnational institutions (CASTREE *et al.*, 2004).

Some TNCs have instituted sophisticated non-union 'employee voice' practices across their North American production facilities (BELANGER *et al.*, 2006; LEWCHUK and WELLS, 2007). Even in non-union firms, individual and collective employee response to company WP initiatives remain important (VERMA, 2006). The significance of WP-specific 'micro-politics' may also increase (ETTLINGER, 2003) and gender, race and other identities may play an important role in shaping such response.

In summary, WP governance is complex and multiscalar and a simple convergence in WP governance stemming from increased cross-border economic integration should not be assumed. KATZ and DARBISHIRE (2000) argue for 'converging divergencies'; namely, greater industry- or sector-level commonalities across countries producing more variation within countries as different manufacturing and service sectors integrate into the global economy at different rates. The result as envisaged by SMITH *et al.* (2008), is

> a more complex world for management and workers (especially within the internationalizing firm) than that suggested by the discourses of convergence and divergence. In this world, national and local routines, international competition and universal 'best practice' concepts elide and interact and outcomes never favour one force over another in a straightforward manner.
>
> (p. 2)

SMITH *et al.* (2008) raise critical questions regarding how to frame TNC WP governance. Clearly rescaling is weakening national differences as production systems become more integrated. However, while some predict WP governance hybridization (ABO, 1996), even changes at the margin can erode national distinctiveness (EDWARDS *et al.*, 1996) especially if the managerial logics between TNC and host nation practices are completely opposed and the ability of the TNC to transfer practices is strong (ROCHA, 2009, p. 505). Yet while TNCs may seek to implement standardized corporate HR strategies there remain important variations in these strategies and in the national and sub-national institutional contexts in which they must be embedded (CALIGUIRI *et al.*, 2010). In particular sub-national institutions are emerging as increasingly critical as regions reposition themselves to attract key value-segments of TNC-led GPNs (BRENNER, 2004; COE *et al.*, 2004; KRISTENSEN and ZEITLIN, 2005).

The purpose of this paper is to move beyond binary convergence/divergence debates by seeking to understand better how WP governance is changing within a CBR by focusing on different key actors such as TNCs and unions. While scholars such as BRENNER (2004) stress how contemporary rescaling is an outcome of the interplay between different political projects, the actual agents and institutions involved in CBR WP governance projects remain relatively unexplored (although see PERKMANN, 2007). The principal focus of previous research has been on the global (for example, between the European Union and North America or between Japan and North America) transfer of WP governance practices where geographic and institutional distances are large. In US–Canadian CBRs where

> the creation of the liberalized level playing field for business has … profoundly changed the meaning and force of links between the nations and states
>
> (SPARKE, 2005, p. 115)

the trajectories of change may be very different due to institutional and geographic proximity.

THE EMERGENCE OF US–CANADIAN CROSS-BORDER REGIONS

United States–Canada integration is both a discursive project (GILBERT, 2005; SPARKE, 2005) and one based on increasing levels of economic interdependence. United States–Canada CBRs are not a new phenomenon (PRI FEDERAL GOVERNMENT OF CANADA, 2006). Since the mid-1960s, however, and especially since the signing of the US–Canada Free Trade Agreement (FTA) in 1988 and NAFTA in 1994 there has been an increased impetus towards economic integration and CBR formation. In the automotive industry, integration accelerated after the signing in 1965 of the US–Canada Auto Pact, a conditional FTA in parts and assembled vehicles (HOLMES, 2004). The implementation of the FTA and NAFTA served to rationalize and reorient many Canadian branch plants towards North American and global markets. The subsequent foreign acquisition of many Canadian-owned firms has led to fears of a 'hollowing out' of ownership and higher managerial functions (ARTHURS, 2006).

Although when corrected for population size and distance, internal Canadian trade remains roughly twenty times that of cross-border trade, this ratio is falling (COURCHENE and TELMER, 1998, p. 278). The north–south realignment of trade has facilitated CBR formation, such as between Southern Ontario and the Great Lakes States, for

> as globalization causes firms and cross-border activities to become more integrated, border provinces and states become more interdependent, and firms and communities become more specialized in cross-border supply chains.
>
> (PRI FEDERAL GOVERNMENT OF CANADA, 2006, p. 25)

Intra-industry trade is higher within CBRs than in other jurisdictions, and an increasing amount of trade is in intermediate goods within the cross-border integrated production networks of TNCs. Economic integration has significant implications for governance. BRUNET-JAILLY (2008) stresses that the post-FTA and NAFTA period has witnessed a significant increase in Canadian and US private and public-sector linkages leading to a distinctive 'policy parallelism' stemming from

> shared policy goals which are not necessarily implemented similarly [and] from a multitude of low-level politics and high-level administrative linkages.
>
> (p. 114)

The restructuring and reorienting of the Canadian economy has had important implications for Ontario. Not only has Ontario seen an increasing share of its exports, especially in intermediate products, destined for the United States, but also some argue that Ontario has become less the Canadian Heartland and more a North American region state (WOLFE, 1997; COURCHENE and TELMER, 1998). Indeed, Ontario is now a party to a large number of bi-national institutional relationships, including the Economic Council of Great Lakes Industries (economic), the Great Lakes Commission (environmental), and the Council of Great Lakes Governors (governmental).

However, CBR formation is being led principally by the private sector and since 1990 the cross-border integration of the key automotive industry which began with the 1965 Auto Pact has intensified. By 2004, there were approximately 90 000 employed in the Ontario automotive parts sector and another 45 000 in vehicle assembly, representing 90% of the total employment in the Canadian automotive industry. Close to 90% of the vehicles assembled in Ontario are exported to the United States along with a significant proportion of automotive parts production. In 2004 the key automotive states with which Ontario trades (Michigan, Ohio and Indiana) each had more than 100 000 employed in the automobile industry for a total of 465 000 workers in the region. The D(etroit)-3 original equipment manufacturers (OEMs) (Ford, Chrysler and General Motors (GM)), Toyota, Honda and many key tier-one component suppliers operate plants both in Southern Ontario and neighbouring Great Lakes States; plants that are tied together in complex supply chains and production networks. During the 1990s, and spurred on by the low value of the Canadian dollar and lower healthcare costs, the Southern Ontario auto industry grew significantly such that in 2004 Ontario surpassed Michigan as the largest automotive producing jurisdiction in North America.

AUTO INDUSTRY RESTRUCTURING AND CHANGES IN WORKPLACE GOVERNANCE

In both Southern Ontario and the US Great Lakes States, Fordist WP governance in the automotive industry shared several distinctive features. The labour force consisted mostly of skilled and unskilled men working in large OEM assembly and captive parts plants (YATES and VRANKULJI, 2006). There was strong occupational segmentation by gender with most women employed in indirect operations. Union density was high throughout the industry and production workers in both countries belonged to the same US-based international unions, most notably the United Auto Workers (UAW). The Canadian Region of the UAW, however, enjoyed significant autonomy and developed its own organizational dynamic (YATES, 1993). Internal labour markets based on seniority were regulated through collective agreements. In the OEM sector, annual real wage increases were explicitly linked to productivity growth. While labour contracts were negotiated at the individual WP level, pattern and connective bargaining led to uniformity in wages and working conditions across OEM companies and plants (HOLMES, 1991). The timing of wage bargaining was coordinated between the United States and Canada and by the early 1970s the UAW had successfully bargained nominal wage parity between the two countries (HOLMES, 1983). By the late 1970s the auto industry WP regime exhibited a significant degree of uniformity across the CBR.

This system of WP governance also rested on broader nation-state Keynesian 'full employment' policies. Periodic lay-offs in the auto industry were mitigated by union-negotiated supplementary unemployment benefits (SUBs) and (in the United States) job-banks that enabled auto workers to maintain income and employment security. Although both countries had similar adversarial based labour relations systems, there was considerable state and provincial autonomy in the development and administration of labour law and employment standards (CLARK, 1989; DRACHE and GLASBEEK, 1992; O'GRADY, 1994).

Despite continued deepening of production integration, differences in WP governance between Canada and the United States began to emerge during the 1980s. These changes stemmed from challenges faced by the D-3 as a result of higher fuel prices and competition from more fuel-efficient imported vehicles. The deep 1981–1982 North American recession triggered a period of major restructuring by the D-3. The companies pressed the UAW to grant concessions on compensation and work practices and to transform traditional Fordist work and labour relations practices into a 'new industrial relations system' emulating Japanese production methods (WOMACK *et al.*, 1990). The outcomes of the restructuring were markedly uneven between the United States and Canada.

In the United States the UAW, faced with plant closings and layoffs and a declining union membership, made employment security its priority during the 1980s by making concessions on wages and work practices and promoting a more 'cooperative partnership' with management. The significant production cost advantage enjoyed by Canada (due to the dollar exchange rate and lower health insurance benefit costs) resulted in a much stronger industry performance. The Canadian UAW experienced fewer layoffs and plant closings and actually saw its membership grow significantly. From a position of strength, it adopted a 'no concessions' stance and continued to pursue an income security strategy and the maintenance of traditional wage-setting rules. It also stoutly resisted management's efforts to forge less adversarial shop-floor relationships (GINDIN, 1989; YATES, 1990). Mounting tensions over bargaining strategy led to the secession of Canadian autoworkers in 1985 to form the independent Canadian Auto Workers (CAW) union (GINDIN, 1989; HOLMES and RUSONIK, 1991). By 1990 there were essentially two 'patterns' of labour contract in the North American auto industry: a Canadian one, which was still essentially Fordist; and a US pattern that embraced contingent compensation schemes and 'modern operating agreements' (MOAs) (HOLMES, 1991).

The D-3 experienced only limited success in introducing new standardized 'best practice' forms of work organization into their Canadian plants. Indeed, as late as the mid-1990s there had been only a very limited move away from standard Fordist work practices in the D-3's Canadian assembly plants (KUMAR and HOLMES, 1997). However, whilst the CAW National Office espoused strong resistance to MOA practices such as lean production and team working, the union was pragmatic when it came to negotiating work practice changes in individual plants (KUMAR and HOLMES, 1997). The quality and productivity ratings of Canadian plants remained consistently high and often higher than US plants that had fully embraced MOAs.

Diverging union strategies reflected what CARD and FREEMAN (1993) term 'small differences that matter' between US and Canadian labour law. During the 1980s it became apparent that labour relations institutions were more favourable to workers in Ontario than those in the United States (DRACHE and GLASBEEK, 1992; CARD and FREEMAN, 1993). Unlike the United States, Canadian federal labour law prohibits provincial right-to-work legislation and provides for greater union security, more limited use of replacement workers and labour relations board-imposed first collective contracts. Moreover, in Canada, labour boards composed of labour and business representatives are more likely to rule against employers charged with unfair labour practices (JENSON and MAHON, 1993, p. 10). Canadian unions enjoy greater success in certification/recognition votes, and even though unionization rates are similar, overall labour standards are higher in Canada and Ontario than in the US Great Lakes States (BLOCK and ROBERTS, 2000). Finally, for much of the 1980s and 1990s unemployment and welfare policies provided greater income security for Canadian workers (CARD and FREEMAN, 1993).

These persistent institutional differences contradicted expectations that cross-border economic integration should lead to closer similarities in WP governance

(TROY, 2000). Yet, after the year 2000 the picture began to change. In the 1980s, Japanese OEMs built new greenfield assembly plants in the Great Lakes region (including Ontario), Kentucky and Tennessee. Japanese, Korean and European OEMs subsequently have added more assembly plants, but mostly in southern US right-to-work states. In the wake of economic liberalization by the Mexican government and NAFTA, the D-3, overseas OEMs and TNC component producers also rapidly expanded production in Mexico. The overall result was significant excess capacity in the integrated North American auto industry and a steady loss of market share by the unionized D-3 to the non-union 'new entrant' OEMs and a renewed round of industry restructuring.

As in previous rounds of restructuring, the D-3 pressed their workforces hard to renegotiate critical elements of WP governance. In the United States this began in 2005–2006 with major suppliers such as Delphi demanding dramatic wage rollbacks and creating permanent two-tier employment contracts for new as compared with existing employees. Delphi served as a model for the negotiation of new contracts between the D-3 and the UAW in 2007. The creation of two-tier wages and the offloading of healthcare and retiree benefit costs, which for GM were estimated to be US$1400 per vehicle (STANFORD, 2005), from the companies to a trust to be managed by the UAW, eroded some of the all-in labour cost difference (up to US$30 000/year per worker) between union and non-union plants in the United States (COONEY, 2007).

The buoyant production and employment conditions that prevailed in Canada during the 1980s and 1990s changed significantly after the year 2000. The Auto Pact was struck down by the World Trade Organization (WTO) in 2001 (ANASTAKIS, 2005) and the value of the Canadian dollar rose from US$0.65 in 2002 to parity in 2007. The result, when coupled with the 2007 UAW contract settlement, was a dramatic reduction in the Canadian labour cost advantage.

The global financial crisis that began in 2007 led to a sharp decline in new vehicle sales and as the financial situation of automakers deteriorated rapidly; many national governments were forced to intervene. In North America,

> the overall rescue effort was larger and more complex [than in Europe], by virtue of the fact that two of the three North American OEMs (GM and Chrysler) sought bankruptcy protection.
>
> (STANFORD, 2010, p. 397)

The US and Canadian governments directly contributed close to US$100 billion to enable GM and Chrysler to restructure under bankruptcy protection. As a condition for providing financial support, both governments required that labour contracts at GM and Chrysler be renegotiated in order to bring labour costs closer to those at Japanese plants in North America.

As the crisis wore on, the D-3 dramatically reduced employment and closed numerous assembly and captive parts plants across the United States and in Ontario. By the end of 2009, the hourly workforce of the D-3 in North America was half the levels of 2005 (STANFORD, 2010). Employment in the Canadian automotive industry fell from a peak of 184 000 in May 2001 to 109 000 in June 2009, with much of this loss occurring during the 'Great Recession' of 2008–2009. In Ontario, while the D-3 and their suppliers were shedding workers, production capacity continued to expand at non-union Toyota and Honda and their suppliers. Union density in the assembly sector in Canada declined from 100% in 1987 to 71% in 2007, and in the independent parts sector from about 50% in the 1990s to around 25% by 2010.

The decline in union density was also linked to the sophisticated HR practices utilized by Japanese assemblers and independent parts suppliers such as Magna. Canadian-owned Magna has grown to be the third largest global automotive parts supplier utilizing a network structure with small, often geographically clustered, plants managed by relatively autonomous divisions (ANDERSON and HOLMES, 1995; LEWCHUK and WELLS, 2007). In late 2007, Magna employed 18 000 hourly workers – 25% of all independent parts workers – at forty-five plants in Canada. Within the WP the company developed a governance system consisting of extensive communication with employees, management-directed work teams, and contingent pay and benefits (LEWCHUK and WELLS, 2007, p. 114).

This rise of non-union WP governance in Southern Ontario coincided with a wider series of changes in the Canadian labour market. During the 1990s, the working time necessary for employees to qualify for unemployment benefits was increased and benefits were reduced. Provinces such as Ontario adopted workfare policies and eligibility rules for social assistance were tightened (PECK, 2001). Globalization and restructuring contributed to the politicization and privatization of Ontario labour law during the 1990s (ARTHURS, 2006, p. 58). The Ontario Progressive Conservative's neo-liberal 'Common Sense' revolution (1995–2004) rolled back more progressive labour laws introduced in the early 1990s and made union organizing more challenging. Explicitly modelled on US reforms, the Ontario government changed employment standards to allow longer working hours and greater management flexibility in work scheduling.

Such changes eroded private sector union density in Canada, which fell from 25% in 1995 to just 17% by 2006. Arguably, these developments have made Southern Ontario labour market conditions more akin to the Great Lake states. Workers are now more likely to be employed in smaller non-union operations owned by a mix of TNCs and small, mostly newer, locally owned firms. Direct state regulation and union standard setting has been eroded as private labour market intermediaries and local supply and demand conditions become more dominant. Auto parts wages are still higher than the manufacturing average, but there is greater geographical differentiation than previously, whilst the gender, ethnic and racial composition of the workforce is now much more diverse than it was under Fordism (YATES and VRANKULJI, 2006, p. 2).

Unions such as the CAW have been put on the defensive. This is evident in the controversial 'Framework of Fairness' agreement the CAW reached with Magna in late 2007. This allows Magna employees to choose the CAW as their bargaining agent, but it commits the union and firm to settle contracts by final-offer arbitration without the option of either lock-outs or strikes (CAW UNION, 2007, p. 17). In CAW-represented plants while Magna's existing HR management system is modified to require the election of employee advocates and the Fairness Committees to be subject to employee majorities and referenda, the Magna agreement still represents a weakening of the union's traditional shop-floor representation. After years of achieving only minimal success in organizing Magna plants, the CAW viewed these compromises as the only way to secure a more significant foothold in the company which would enable it to continue to set wages and standards across the Canadian parts industry. However, critics view the CAW's giving up the right to strike as a betrayal of a fundamental labour principle and further evidence of a weakening of CAW power (GINDIN, 2007).

Faced with a scheduled round of D-3 bargaining in 2008 and a rapidly deteriorating economic environment, the CAW elected to bargain several months in advance of the normal deadline and to reach a quick agreement. The union successfully resisted management demands for two-tier wages and benefits for new hires agreed to by the UAW in 2007. However, it was forced to freeze base wage rates and grant other cost-saving concessions.

DISCUSSION AND CONCLUSIONS: DO SMALL DIFFERENCES STILL EXIST AND DO THEY MATTER TO CROSS-BORDER REGIONS?

This paper analysed CBR WP governance in an exploratory case study of the automotive industry in the Southern Ontario and the US Great Lakes States CBR. It conjectured that the principal factors shaping CBR WP governance are (1) the ability of TNCs to transfer 'best practice' work organization, (2) the role of labour law at national, provincial and state scales, and (3) the agency of unions and employee representatives. The evidence presented, albeit tentative, supports the argument for the continued importance of national differences, but nonetheless it recognizes the significant formative impact of economic globalization and restructuring. It suggests not only changes in how national institutions matter, but also heightening the significance of governance institutions and regulatory activity at other scales.

In both Canada and the United States competition for investment underscores the importance of local differences in labour markets and municipal/local coalitions in 'place marketing' (JONAS, 1996). Within Southern Ontario, and compared with the Fordist period, there is increasing differentiation in workforce composition in terms of geography, ethnicity, race and gender. There are also differences in this regard between the Southern Ontario and the US portion of the CBR. Much of this reflects both earlier and current Canadian federal and provincial government labour market policy (YATES and VRANKULJI, 2006, p. 12). In Ontario, the Liberal/NDP governments in the 1985–1995 period stressed a 'progressive competitiveness' strategy – based on high skill, high wages, and bipartite coordination of technology and training. Although Great Lake states have a stronger skill infrastructure than southern states, Ontario still enjoys a comparative advantage as a result of its more highly educated labour force. This was a key factor behind Ontario's ability to attract new automotive investments. Moreover, as Yates and Vrankulji stressed, the Canadian federal immigration policy of attracting highly educated/skilled workers has benefited Ontario localities with a high percentage of new immigrants employed in the automotive parts industry. As such, firms can recruit a higher skilled and more ethnically and racially mixed workforce in a context that is less politically charged than in the United States (RUTHERFORD *et al.*, 2001, p. 26).

Similarly, and despite the compromises in its recent framework agreement with Magna, the CAW argues that there are still different WP contexts between Canada and the US Great Lakes States. Whereas unionization in US independent parts stands at less than 15%, it is still well over 25% in Canada. The CAW maintains that it can still influence standards in this sector of the industry much more so than can the UAW (CAW UNION, 2007, p. 7). Thus, Japanese plants in Canada still tend to match D-3 assembler wages, adopt similar shift systems, seniority and other practices as part of a 'union substitution' strategy.

The fact that the Canadian automotive industry is concentrated within one sub-national jurisdiction – the province of Ontario – also strengthens CAW's influence. In contrast, the UAW must organize and represent workers across a number of Great Lake states. None is a 'right to work' state, but employment law varies between individual states and they are, at best, average in terms of overall US employment standards (HEINTZ *et al.*, 2005). The UAW's declining bargaining power means that firms such as Toyota no longer tie their wages to national standards, but now benchmark to the state in which their plants are located (SHAIKEN, 2007, p. 4).

However, differences in automotive WP governance between Canada and the United States should not be exaggerated. Unlike southern states, the UAW remains a credible force within the Great Lakes States forcing Japanese transplants to match D-3 wages (STANFORD, 2010, p. 399). Moreover, over the last twenty years restructuring and the transformation of managerial practices (LEWCHUK *et al.*, 2001) mean that WP governance differences between Southern Ontario and the US Midwest–Great Lakes States have significantly narrowed. As STANFORD (2010) emphasized,

> there is a high degree of similarity in work practices between the US and Canada. Overall there has been a global harmonization of management which has been standardized from the top to emulate Toyota.
>
> (p. 402)

For the CAW, the question is whether it can continue to influence standards if union density continues to fall. This is a major reason why the CAW is prepared to trade-off the right to strike in order to represent Magna workers. Yet the CAW's ability to represent an independent worker interest may be increasingly subordinated to sustaining firm competitiveness. MALIN (2010) argued that by giving management the right to veto changes in the union's WP representation the CAW–Magna agreement would be considered illegal under US labour law which bars company unions. He emphasizes that the UAW voluntary recognition and neutrality agreement with parts manufacturer Dana is more protective of the union's independent voice. Thus, at the scale of the individual firm and WP, the CAW's position may not be significantly stronger than the UAW in the Great Lakes States.

One of the most notable differences in UAW and CAW contract positions is the latter's rejection of two-tier wages/benefits. This is significant, even though the CAW agreed in the last round of bargaining to a 'grow-in' period of three years before new hires reach 100% wages and benefits (CAW UNION, 2008, p. 46). While the UAW aims ultimately to bargain for career paths that allow workers to achieve the top pay and benefit rate (UAW, 2011, p. 9), unlike the CAW this is not embedded within current contracts. However, in the short-run, the impact of this difference may be muted since the deep recession has meant that very few new workers have been hired in either nation (STANFORD, 2010, p. 400). The ability of the CAW to retain a more traditional contract system rests in part on the union's power and a more supportive labour law regime, but more important are the continued cost and quality advantages that CAW plants enjoy over both UAW and non-union transplants (STANFORD, 2005, 2010). Yet such advantages do not necessarily secure production in Southern Ontario with GM recently threatening to move Impala production from its Oshawa facility to the UAW Hamtramck plant in Detroit.

In short, differences derived from national institutions remain and indeed still matter in Canadian WP governance, but how they matter is changing. Although some argue that continued labour law differences are simply an institutional 'lag effect' which will be eroded as market-driven convergence advances (TROY, 2000), differences in labour law still matter to WP outcomes (GODARD, 2003; ARTHURS, 2006). Whilst Supreme Court rulings and the Canadian Charter of Rights have been ambivalent towards collective employee rights, they are more supportive than comparable US institutions.

Globalization, restructuring and neo-liberalism are having a formative impact. ARTHURS (2006, p. 60), for example, argues that shifts to more project-based employment may be transforming 'reasonable notice' requirements and definitions of bargaining units as 'a community of interest' that make current Canadian labour laws more difficult to enforce. There has also been a narrowing of strategic differences between the UAW and the CAW. Increasingly, both unions have unsuccessfully lobbied for legislative changes that would make union organizing easier. In the United States, the Employee Free Choice Act that would have assisted organizing by using a card-check system was passed by the House of Representatives but defeated in the Senate (COONEY, 2007); it is not a priority for the Barack Obama Administration. Similarly, unions in Ontario have been unable to reinstate card-check abolished by the Mike Harris Conservative government (CAW UNION, 2007). Yet despite being faced with similar challenges and common employers there remain relatively few cross-border organizational links between the UAW and the CAW.

While Southern Ontario and the Great Lakes States are increasingly integrated economically with states and unions facing common pressures, the formation of the CBR is in some ways tentative. Consistent with PERKMANN's (2007) distinction between the European Union and North American CBRs, the Southern Ontario–Great Lakes States CBR is driven more by private and especially TNC interests. Inter-governmental and non-governmental links grew in the latter decades of the twentieth century, but post-9/11 security concerns are likely to limit further institutional integration (CLARKSON, 2008). Within the automotive industry, however, there is evidence of a distinctive Southern Ontario–Great Lakes CBR based on (1) the high degree of production integration, (2) overall higher levels of unionization and labour standards, and (3) a strong skill base and training institutions. WP governance differences within this region will likely continue to narrow, but not necessarily converge given enduring institutional path dependencies.

Some significant implications for the study of cross-border region workplace governance flow from the preliminary analysis

Despite geographic contiguity and institutional similarities, small institutional differences matter. The primacy of national-scale regulation has been destabilized by the emergence of new scalar institutional architectures. In an era of neo-liberalism, the relative power of TNCs has been enhanced, whilst those of the state and unions are now less determining. As BRENNER (2004) argues,

> it is no longer capital that is being molded into the (territorially integrated) geography of state space, but it is state space that is to be molded into the (territorially differentiated) geography of capital.
>
> (p. 16)

Thus, the impacts of TNC-led production integration on WP governance go beyond a simple binary of convergence/divergence, but neither are they the result of a contingency-dependent process of hybridization. While scholars have viewed rescaling and CBR formation as a product of socio-spatial projects (BRENNER, 2004) and agents (PERKMANN, 2007), the present paper emphasizes that these are a product of the powers and struggles between different actors and institutions. Even though labour law was never uniformly produced or administered under Fordism (CLARK, 1989), the present evidence suggests that one result of the formative impact of restructuring is an intensification of unevenness with respect to labour law and unions now less able to impose uniform WP standards across space. One result is that TNC corporate practices and local and plant-level factors appear to be playing an increasingly defining role in WP governance within the Southern Ontario–Great Lakes States CBR. Thus, increasing TNC production integration and HR centralization are actually consistent with deepening territorial unevenness (see also SPARKE, 2005), not only as a product of state policies and labour's agency, but also because they facilitate institutional arbitrage by TNCs. Contestations over WP governance by actors are both a cause and a consequence of rescaling and CBR formation, but the outcomes are ultimately subject to power asymmetries that favour some actors over others.

Acknowledgements – The authors gratefully acknowledge the helpful comments of two anonymous reviewers; and the support and patience of the Editors of this special issue, Martin Jones and Anssi Paasi. Financial support for the research was provided by the Social Science and Humanities Research Council of Canada.

REFERENCES

ABO T. (1996) The Japanese production system: the process of adaptation in national settings, in BOYER R. and DRACHE D. (Eds) *States against Markets: The Limits of Globalization*, pp. 136–154. Routledge, London.

ANASTAKIS D. (2005) *Auto Pact: Creating a Borderless North American Auto Industry, 1960–1971.* University of Toronto Press, Toronto, ON.

ANDERSON M. and HOLMES J. (1995) New models of industrial organization: the case of Magna International, *Regional Studies* **29(7)**, 655–671.

ARTHURS H. (2006) Who's afraid of globalization? Reflections on the future of labour law, in CRAIG J. and LYNK S. M. (Eds) *Globalization and the Future of Labour Law*, pp. 51–74. Cambridge University Press, Cambridge.

BELANGER J., HARVEY P.-A., JALETTE K., LEVESQUE C. and MURRAY G. (2006) *Employment Practices in Multinational Companies in Canada: Building Organizational Capabilities and Institutions for Innovation.* Centre de recherché interuniversitaire sur le mondailisation et le travail (CRIMT), Interuniversity Research Centre on Globalization and Work, Université de Monteal/Université Laval, HEC Montréal, Montreal/Quebec City, QC.

BENNER C. (2003) Labour flexibility and regional development: the role of labour market intermediaries, *Regional Studies* **37**, 621–633.

BLATTER J. K. (2001) Debordering the world of states: towards a multi-level system in Europe and a multipolity system in North America: insights from border regions, *European Journal of International Relations* **7(2)**, 175–209.

BLOCK R. and ROBERTS K. (2000) A comparison of labour standards in the United States and Canada, *Industrial Relations* **55**, 273–307.

BRENNER N. (2004) *New State Spaces: Urban Governance and the Rescaling of Statehood.* Oxford University Press, Oxford.

BRONFENBRENNER K. (Ed.) (2007) *Global Unions: Challenging Transnational Capital through Cross-Border Campaigns.* ILR Press, Ithaca, NY.

BRUNET-JAILLY E. (2008) Cascadia in comparative perspectives: Canada–U.S. relations and the emergence of cross-border regions, *Canadian Political Science Review* **2(2)**, 104–124.

CALIGUIRI P., LEPAK D. and BONACHE J. (2010) *Managing the Global Workforce.* Wiley, Chichester.

CANADIAN AUTO WORKERS (CAW) UNION (2007) *CAW and Magna: A Window of Opportunity* (available at: http://caw.ca/) (accessed on 23 March 2008).

CANADIAN AUTO WORKERS (CAW) UNION (2008) *Chapter Four: Big 3 Bargaining* (available at: http://www.caw.ca/assets/pdf/08-Chapter_4.pdf) (accessed on 18 June 2011).

CARD D. and FREEMAN R. (1993) *Small Differences that Matter: Labor Markets and Income Maintenance in Canada and the United States.* University of Chicago Press, Chicago, IL.

CASTREE N., WARD K. and SAMMERS M. (2004) *Spaces of Work: Global Capitalism and the Geographies of Labour.* Sage, London.

CHRISTOPHERSON S. (2002) Why do labor market practices continue to diverge in a global economy? The 'missing link' of investment rules, *Economic Geography* **78**, 1–20.

CHRISTOPHERSON S. and VAN JAARSVELD D. (2005) New media after the dot.com bust: the persistent influence of political institutions on work in cultural industries, *International Journal of Cultural Policy* **11**, 77–93.

CLARK G. (1989) *Unions and Communities Under Siege: American Communities and the Crisis of Organized Labour.* Cambridge University Press, Cambridge.

CLARKSON S. (2008) *Does North America Exist? Governing the Continent after NAFTA and 9/11.* University of Toronto, Toronto, ON, and Woodrow Wilson Press, Washington, DC.

COE N., HESS M., CHUNG H. W., DICKEN P. and HENDERSON J. (2004) 'Globalizing' regional development: a global production networks perspective, *Transactions of the Institute of British Geographers* **29**, 468–484.

COONEY S. (2007) *Motor Vehicle Manufacturing Employment: National and State Trends and Issues.* Congressional Research Service, Washington, DC.

COURCHENE T. and TELMER C. (1998) *From Heartland to North American Region-State: The Social, Fiscal and Federal Evolution of Ontario.* Faculty of Management, University of Toronto, Toronto, ON.

CROUCHER R. and COTTON E. (2009) *Global Unions, Global Business: Global Union Federations and International Business.* Middlesex University Press, London.

DICKEN P. (2007) *Global Shift: Mapping the Changing Contours of the World Economy*, 5th Edn. Guilford, New York, NY.

DRACHE D. and GLASBEEK H. (1992) *The Changing Workplace: Reshaping Canada's Industrial Relations System.* James Lorimer & Son, Toronto, ON.

EDWARDS P., ARMSTRONG P., MARGINSON P. and PURCEL J. (1996) Toward the transnational company?, in CROMPTON R., GALLIE D. and PURCELL K. (Eds) *Changing Forms of Employment: Organisations, Skills and Gender*, pp. 40–64. Routledge, London.

EDWARDS T., ALMOND P., CLARK I., COLLING T. and FERNER A. (2005) Reverse diffusion in US multinationals: barriers from the American business system, *Journal of Management Studies* **42**, 1261–1286.

EDWARDS T., COLLING T. and FERNER A. (2007) Conceptual approaches to the transfer of employment practices in multinational companies: an integrated approach, *Human Resource Management Journal* **17(3)**, 201–217.

ETTLINGER N. (2003) Cultural economic geography and a relational and microspace approach to trusts, rationalities, networks and change in collaborative workplaces, *Journal of Economic Geography* **3**, 145–171.

GERTLER M. and VINODRAI T. (2005) Learning from America? Knowledge flows and industrial practices of German firms in North America, *Economic Geography* **81**, 31–52.

GILBERT E. (2005) The Inevitability of integration? Neoliberal discourse and the proposals for a new North American economic space after September 11th, *Annals of the Association of American Geographers* **95**, 202–222.

GINDIN S. (1989) Breaking away: the formation of the Canadian auto workers, *Studies in Political Economy* **29**, 63–89.

GINDIN S. (2007) The CAW and Magna: disorganizing the working class, *The Bullet: Socialist Project E-Bulletin* **no. 65 (19 October)**.

GODARD J. (2003) Do labor laws matter? The density decline and convergence thesis revisited, *Industrial Relations* **42**, 458–492.

GUNDERSON M. (1998) Harmonization of labour policies under trade liberalization, *Relations Industrielle, Industrial Relations* **53**, 24–53.

HEINTZ J., WICKS-LIM J. and POLLIN R. (2005) *Decent Work in America: Work Environment Index.* PERI, Amherst, MA.

HEROD A. (2001) *Labor Geographies: Workers and the Landscapes of Capitalism.* Guilford, New York, NY.

HEROD A., PECK J. and WILLS J. (2005) Geography and industrial relations, in ACKERS P. and WILKINSON F. (Eds) *Understanding Work and Employment Industrial Relations in Transition*, pp. 176–192. Oxford University Press, Oxford.

HOLMES J. (1983) Industrial re-organization, capital restructuring and locational change: an analysis of the Canadian auto industry in the 1960s, *Economic Geography* **59**, 51–71.

HOLMES J. (1991) From uniformity to diversity: changing patterns of wages and work practices in the North American automobile industry, in BLYTON P. and MORRIS J. (Eds) *A Flexible Future?: Prospects for Employment and Work Organization in the 1990s*, pp. 129–151. De Gruyter, Berlin.

HOLMES J. (2004) The Auto Pact from 1965 to the Canada–United States free trade agreement (CUSFTA), in IRISH M. (Ed.) *The Auto Pact: Investment, Labour and the WTO*, pp. 3–21. Kluwer Law International, The Hague.

HOLMES J. and RUSONICK A. (1991) The breakup of an international union: uneven development in the North American auto industry and the schism in the UAW, *Environment and Planning A* **23**, 9–35.

JENSON J. and MAHON R. (1993) *The Challenge of Restructuring: North American Labour Movements Respond.* Temple University Press, Philadelphia, PA.

JESSOP B. (2002a) The political economy of scale, in PERKMANN M. and SUM N.-L. (Eds) *Globalization, Regionalization and Cross-Border Regions*, pp. 25–49. Palgrave, Basingstoke.

JESSOP B. (2002b) *The Future of the Capitalist State.* Polity, Cambridge.

JONAS A. (1996) Local labour control regimes: uneven development and the social regulation of production, *Regional Studies* **30**, 323–338.

KATZ H. and DARBISHIRE O. (2000) *Converging Divergencies: World Wide Changes in Employment Systems.* Cornell University Press, Ithaca, NY.

KRISTENSEN P. H. and ZEITLIN J. (2005) *Local Players in Global Games: The Strategic Constitution of a Multinational Corporation.* Oxford University Press, Oxford.

KUMAR P. and HOLMES J. (1997) Canada: continuity and change, in KOCHAN T., LANSBURY R. and MACDUFFIE J. P. (Eds) *After Lean Production: Evolving Employment Practices in the World Auto Industry*, pp. 85–108. ILR Press, Ithaca, NY.

LEWCHUK W., STEWART P. and YATES C. (2001) Quality of working life in the automobile industry: a Canada–UK comparative study, *New Technology Work and Employment* **16**, 72–87.

LEWCHUK W. and WELLS D. (2007) Transforming worker representation: the Magna model in Canada and Mexico, *Labour/Le Travail* 109–137.

LOOISE J. and DRUCKER M. (2002) Employee participation in multinational enterprises: the effects of globalization on Dutch works councils, *Employee Relations* **24**, 29–52.

MALIN M. (2010) The Canadian auto workers–Magna international framework of fairness agreement: a US perspective, *Saint Louis University Law Journal* **54**, 525–564.

MUNCK R. P. (2010) Globalization and the labour movement: challenges and responses, *Global Labour Journal* **1**, 218–232.

O'GRADY J. (1994) Obstacles to progressive adjustment: labour law in Ontario, in SEGENBERGER W. and CAMPBELL D. (Eds) *Creating Economic Opportunities: Labour Standards in Industrial Restructuring*, pp. 141–153. International Labour Organization, Geneva.

PECK J. (2001) *Workfare States*. Guilford, New York, NY.

PERKMANN M. (2007) Construction of new territorial scales: a framework and case study of the EUREGIO cross-border region, *Regional Studies* **41**, 253–266.

PERKMANN M. and SUM N.-L. (Eds) (2002) *Globalization, Regionalization and Cross-Border Regions*. Palgrave Macmillan, Basingstoke.

PRI FEDERAL GOVERNMENT OF CANADA (2006) *The Emergence of Cross Border Regions between Canada and the United States*. Government of Canada Policy Research Initiative, Ottawa, ON.

ROCHA R. (2009) The impact of cross-border mergers on the co-decision-making process: the case of a Danish company, *Economic and Industrial Democracy* **30**, 484–508.

RUTHERFORD T. (2004) Convergence, the institutional turn and workplace regimes: the case of lean production, *Progress in Human Geography* **28**, 425–447.

RUTHERFORD T. and GERTLER M. (2002) Labour in lean times: geography, scale and the national trajectories of workplace change, *Transactions of the Institute of British Geographers* **27**, 195–212.

RUTHERFORD T., PARKER P. and KOSHIBA T. (2001) Global, local or hybrid? Evidence of adaptation among Japanese automobile plants in Japan, the United States and Canada, *Environments* **29**, 15–34.

SHAIKEN H. (2007) *Unions, the Economy and Employee Free Choice*. Briefing Paper Number 181. Economic Policy Institute (EPI), Washington, DC.

SMITH C., MCSWEENEY B. and FITZGERALD R. (Eds) (2008) *Remaking Management: Between Global and Local*. Cambridge University Press, Cambridge.

SPARKE M. (2005) *In the Space of Theory: Postfoundational Geographies of the Nation-State*. Borderlines Number 26. University of Minnesota Press, Minneapolis, MN.

STANFORD J. (2005) CAW–Big 3 bargaining, 2005: Economic and financial context. Presentation given to financial analysts, New York City, NY, USA, 7 September 2005 (available at: http://www.caw.ca/whatwedo/bargaining/big3automakers/auto05/pdf/CAW_Presentation_to_NYC_Analysts_Sept05.pdf) (accessed on 6 January 2008).

STANFORD J. (2010) The geography of auto globalization and the politics of auto bailouts, *Cambridge Journal of Regions, Economy and Society* **3**, 383–405.

TROY L. (2000) US and Canadian industrial relations: convergent or divergent?, *Industrial Relations* **39**, 395–713.

UNITED AUTO WORKERS (UAW) (2011) *Special Convention on Collective Bargaining 22–24 March Detroit Michigan* (available at: http://www.uaw.org/) (accessed on 18 June 2011).

VERMA A. (2006) *The Role of Employee Voice in Obtaining better Labour Standards*. Prepared for the Federal Labour Standards Review Commission, Human Resources and Social Development Canada, Ottawa, ON.

WATERMAN P. and WILLS J. (Eds) (2001) *Place, Space and the New Labour Internationalisms*. Blackwell, Oxford.

WILLS J. (2001) Uneven geographies of capital and labour: the lessons of European Works Councils, *Antipode* **33**, 484–509.

WOLFE D. (1997) The emergence of the region state, in COURCHENE T. (Ed.) *The Nation State in a Global/Information Era: Policy Challenges*, pp. 205–240. John Deutsch Institute for the Study of Economic Policy, Queen's University, Kingston, ON.

WOMACK J., JONES D. and ROOS D. (1990) *The Machine that Changed the World*. Rawson Associates, New York, NY.

YATES C. (1990) The internal dynamics of union power: explaining Canadian autoworkers' militancy in the 1980s, *Studies in Political Economy* **31**, 73–106.

YATES C. (1993) Public policy and Canadian and American autoworkers, in APPEL MOLOT M. (Ed.) *Driving Continentally: National Policies and the North American Auto Industry*, pp. 209–230. Carleton University Press, Ottawa, ON.

YATES C. and VRANKULJI S. (2006) *Labour as a Competitive Advantage in the Canadian Automotive Parts Industry: A Study of Canada and Four Local Labour Markets (Brantford, Stratford, Guelph, Windsor)*. Labour Studies Program, McMaster University, Hamilton, ON.

Index

[Note: numbers in **bold** refer to tables; numbers in *italics* refer to figures.]

For Product Safety Concerns and Information please contact our EU representative GPSR@taylorandfrancis.com Taylor & Francis Verlag GmbH, Kaufingerstraße 24, 80331 München, Germany